THE PRENTICE-HALL SERIES IN FAMILY AND CONSUMER SCIENCES

WILLIAM H. MARSHALL, editor
The University of Wisconsin, Madison

social development of the child

WILLIAM H. MARSHALL (series editor)

nutrition, behavior, and change

HELEN H. GIFFT
MARJORIE B. WASHBON
GAIL G. HARRISON

home economics teaching

RUTH HUGES

introduction to family life and sex education

ROSE M. SOMERVILLE

family literature anthology

ROSE M. SOMERVILLE

introduction
to
family life
and
sex education

introduction
to
family life
and
sex education

ROSE M. SOMERVILLE
San Diego State College

prentice-hall, inc., englewood cliffs, new jersey

To my husband, John Somerville,
and our sons, Greg and Kent,
and to Judy, Susan, and Tara

THE PRENTICE-HALL SERIES IN FAMILY AND CONSUMER SCIENCES
William H. Marshall, Editor

© 1972 by Prentice-Hall, Inc., Englewood Cliffs, New Jersey

ISBN: C 0-13-483149-7
      P 0-13-483131-4

Library of Congress Catalog Card Number: 72-1551
Printed in the United States of America

10   9 8   7   6   5   4   3   2   1

Prentice-Hall International, Inc., *London*
Prentice-Hall of Australia, Pty. Ltd., *Sydney*
Prentice-Hall of Canada, Ltd., *Toronto*
Prentice-Hall of India Private Limited, *New Delhi*
Prentice-Hall of Japan, Inc., *Tokyo*

contents

selected readings in the history, standards, and prospects of family life and sex education

278

preface

A well-known but lesser-used approach to the educational process is John Dewey's *learning by doing*. This book will adapt that principle: the reader will *learn by teaching*. The student will be operating in two frameworks. At the same time that he is acquiring knowledge, he will be testing his comprehension by thinking ahead to his ability to impart this knowledge to others. Each student already has some experience of this kind in trying to explain his ideas to a classmate, to a brother or sister, to a parent, or to a child he is tutoring. But rarely has the student approached a whole field of study in this way.

Each topic, then, will in a sense test the student's factual knowledge and understanding of a wide range of feelings, values, and alternatives by readiness to transmit knowledge and encourage understanding in others. Some readers may wish to become family life and sex educators. The experience in a course that uses this book will be a significant step toward that career objective, both in personal growth and in practice for playing the teacher role. Other readers will wish to follow other lines of work, but they too will find the role of informal teacher appropriate in many situations—discussions with less knowledgeable peers and relatives and later on as parents and as community participants.

The family is only one of the many institutions in society. It is greatly affected by decisions students make, especially with the passage of the Twenty-Sixth Amendment which extends the franchise and, thereby, the citizenship responsibilities of those still in their teens. The choice of legislators, judges, governors, and others who make and carry out policy has great significance for the present and the future of marriage and the family. Think of all the issues now before federal and state legislatures and courts, as well as local communities, in one form or another: abortion, pornography, homosexuality, divorce, remarriage, child abuse, prostitution, nudity, age of marriage. Are we able to consider these issues rationally? Do we know what sources to turn to in order to acquire relevant facts? Can we listen critically to political speeches which have family implications and know why, what, and whom we support? Lawyers do not carry all relevant materials in their heads and give immediate guidance to those who come for help. But they know where the relevant materials are and can get the answers for each particular case.

You as the student–teacher are not omniscient either. One of the gains to be derived from working with this book—note, working with, not merely reading—will surely be an appreciation for the complexity of marriage and family phenomena. It is this very complexity that makes the dialogue aspect of learning by teaching so helpful. The dialogue allows a pooling of knowledge, a cross-checking of attitudes, a recognition of a diversity of value orientations. Dialogue is facilitated by the use of many classroom devices to explore attitudes and feelings, the use of many kinds of reading materials from a variety of sources to feed into the knowledge pool, and by a stance that maximizes both empathy and critical evaluation. The latter may at times seem in contradiction. Can you disagree strongly and at the same time understand what made the other person take the position he does? Can you help your classmates, your future students bring out their thoughts and feelings about marriage and the family, and at the same time contribute constructively to the diminution of stereotypes and the exploration of unconsidered issues?

This book will hopefully add to your abilities in these regards and,

for those who wish to be family life and sex educators, other opportuni
ties for growth of a personal and of an academic kind will be part of
total preparation. The Appendix (p. 281) contains the Criteria for the
education of family life and sex educators adopted by the National Coun
cil on Family Relations.

1

what
is
family
life
and sex
education?

INTERDISCIPLINARY STUDY

You may be working with this book in a course in the social sciences or psychology or home economics or health education or still another department. That a course in family life and sex education can be taught by so many disciplines suggests an outstanding characteristic of the subject matter: it is interdisciplinary. It brings together knowledge about individuals as sexual beings and as family members and about the relationships between the family and the rest of a society's institutions. Such knowledge comes from the research and insights of many different professionals—historians, sociologists, demographers, counselors, playwrights, and novelists, to name only a few. And a correspondingly diverse group of professionals transmits this body of knowledge in the classroom. However, most teachers are more familiar with the methods and conclusions of their own particular field—sociology, psychology, anthropology—than with the other related disciplines.

In the future perhaps there will be a whole program of family life and sex education courses at the high school and then at the college level which will provide every future teacher with detailed knowledge of the many disciplines which contribute to understanding of marriage and the family. Right now, the student who is planning to teach in the area of family life and sex education must choose a discipline and then take enough courses in other disciplines to ensure that he has the multifaceted preparation required for dealing with these complex subjects. If you are not planning to teach, you will still need practice in integrating the findings of many disciplines. You will want your thinking about all the topics which pertain to marriage, sex, and the family to be enriched by the many resources available.

You can start right now along the interdisciplinary path by being alert to what the other courses you are taking or have taken contribute to understanding some question about sex role allocation or changing family forms or the child versus the adult-centered home. In a course in political science or civics, watch for what it reveals of how state power has been used to regulate matters which affect the family directly and indirectly. If you know the ideology, the political ethos of a country, you can make certain predictions about the family you are likely to find there. From a course in history, light may be shed on what marriage and the family were like in other times and places and what part religion has played in family life through the centuries.

Through a course in economics you may see what kinds of economic systems encourage what kinds of family relationships. Here is where history and economics begin to overlap.

A course in the arts reveals the part history plays. Which societies have encouraged the painter, writer, or sculptor to reflect the family life of his day? Were women always the household representative of esthetic appreciation? In which times and places was it "unmasculine" to be interested in the arts? All these are questions you may consider.

A course in biology may help you discover whether the line between innate and learned, or acquired, needs is clear, or in what ways the nature–nurture question touches family as well as individual development.

Can you think of other examples from other courses which are relevant to your attempts to understand marriage and the family? As a family life and sex educator in the future, which examples might you substitute for those offered above?

The artist tells us something about marriage among the wealthy of his time and place. The marriage proposal depicted here features not two lovers but lawyers and documents to secure the property in a family-arranged union.

William Hogarth, The Marriage Proposal. Reproduced by courtesy of the Trustees, The National Gallery, London.

A LIFELONG STUDY

As you know, there is a beginning and an ending for each individual and each family. Fortunately, our longevity rates are rising and the span of years between birth and death has grown longer. If you are in your teens or early twenties, you can probably expect to live the proverbial threescore and ten. You have gained twenty years in life expectancy over your chances had you been born in 1900. Averages do not talk about *you*, of course.

To you, forty may seem to be ancient, although you may hesitate to say this in front of your parents—they do not even like to be called middle-aged. We shall come to the significance of this fact of family life later, but you can begin to figure out the connections between a youth-oriented culture and reluctance to face up to advancing years.

Family life and sex education is pertinent to every stage of individual and family life. Informally, every infant and young child is learning whom he may trust to care for his needs, which of his actions are rewarded or discouraged, and to whom he may show affection as well as from whom he can expect to receive affection. He is also a sexual being; some parents are uncomfortable in facing this fact. Often this is rooted in the poor sex education they have had, with little chance to talk over their puzzlements and choices. There are still some subcultures in the United States where it is inappropriate for a mother to prepare her daughter for menstruation. There are also some subcultures that insist on certain attitudes toward menstruation, masturbation, and like topics, and are fearful that any discussion of them in the classroom may result in less adherence to these attitudes.

The question is, Do you as students want to hear all sides of a question? Will you as teachers (and possibly as future parents) allow boys and girls to explore a wide variety of topics that pertain to their lives and the choices they must make at various points in their lives? Your answer is likely to be yes. And indeed, an affirmative answer fits in with the belief held in the abstract that "the truth shall make you free," that you arrive at truth by testing ideas against one another. In the concrete, however, we all have individual value systems, derived in part, as we shall see, from experience as a family member. We are all more comfortable when *our* ideas are being aired and *our* side presented. Just as some males do not want to hear Women's Liberation arguments in behalf of greater opportunity for women, some Women's Liberation adherents do not want to hear about the difficulties men have occupationally, sexually, or in playing the father role.

As you work with this book, notice how your intellectual feet are dragging when you are asked to consider some facts you wish did not exist. When you read a play like *A Raisin in the Sun,* do you manage to put out of your mind what the white characters were doing to the blacks by paying them low wages, by trying to bribe them not to move into a white neighborhood, by not giving them the opportunity to develop business know-how? What will you do when your students write a review and come up with a simple explanation that the whole trouble was the bossy grandmother? Or the trouble was that her son and daughter were too ambitious and should have just accepted things the way their mother did?

A teacher in an all-white southern college, knowing his students would be extremely reluctant to air any fact about sex or family life that would redound to the credit of blacks rather than whites, introduced formal debates into his classroom before any open discussion could begin. Students were assigned by lot to sides in a debate. Some were not happy with the assignment at first, but as they began to dig into the books to get material to support the side they were arguing, they became interested. They grew more empathetic because they were standing in the emotional and intellectual shoes of people with different life experiences. Certainly it is open to question whether any of this changed their attitudes permanently, but the classroom went as far as education *can* go. As students and as teachers we recognize that while schools interpenetrate with the world outside we have to figure out the changes in economy, government, and the law that would support the truths discovered in debates and discussions.

Adult education is needed in every decade after graduation in order to ensure that those whose lives are interlocked with yours keep abreast of new developments affecting themselves and their families. There is much talk about a communication gap between generations, but perhaps this is lessened where parents and grandparents as well as their children have had continuing opportunities for family life and sex education. It is a question worth investigating. Even if it should be shown that the communication gap continued despite education, we should have to look both at the quality of the programs (maybe prejudices were deepened in classrooms that proselyted rather than educated) and at the consequences of the very different roles people play at successive periods of their lives.

For example, some studies have shown that parents in their youth held very different views about premarital sex than they hold now. As young people they were in the children role, with lesser legal and community responsibility for consequences. In the parental role they are more aware both of the physical and emotional injury risks for their children and of the blame society will lay on them as neglectful, overindulgent, contributing to the delinquency of a minor, and so forth. Perhaps this role-conflict can never be resolved as long as children are reared in the present family structures rather than in apprenticeship homes as among the Puritans or in age-segregated institutions as among the Hutterites or the Kibbutzniks.

Even if family life and sex education cannot solve the problems of intergenerational relationships, it is still a valuable experience for all ages. Parents are easier persons to live with if they understand themselves as men and women, as sexual beings, as grown children of elderly men and women who are sexual beings, as brothers and sisters of those who have their own decisions to make. An understanding of past changes can prepare us for those to come. Any reduction of "future shock," or the pain that accompanies a swift change of norms and the redefinition of roles, is a mental health benefit. To be sure, there is sometimes a sense of regret and anger or bitterness on the part of middle-aged and older men and women for whom family life and sex education courses reveal alternatives they had not considered before. Often, however, they are able even in the later decades of life to introduce changes that make them pleasanter to be with, as well as more fulfilled and understanding. Hopefully work with this book will build a better basis for decision-making, and will serve as a basis for the new learnings you will add as you make the study of yourself and of marriage and the family a lifelong pursuit, as a vocation or as an avocation. (Can you think of a more rewarding hobby?)

SEX IN A FAMILY/SOCIETAL CONTEXT

There is a long history, counted in decades to be sure, and not in centuries, concerning the terms *family life and sex education*. If you are interested in the details, you may want to turn to a long article on the subject in Appendix III entitled "Family Life and Sex Education in the Turbulent Sixties." Here let me mention briefly only that nobody is truly satisfied with the terminology.

Family life education basically includes sex, since nuclear families almost by definition are founded by the sexual union of a man and a woman. Society is very much concerned with regulating the sexual behaviors of family members, with laws embodying the incest taboo as well as the sexual rights and duties of spouses. In teaching about marriage and the family, however, some educators have lacked adequate preparation and so have shied away from including the sexual aspect of various topics. Even today some courses, particularly in junior high school but also in senior high, talk about dating and ignore the sexual dimension which for many boys and girls is the most problematical. Because of this reluctance to include sex in family life education, there has developed a movement to offer sex education separately. It soon became obvious that it was not possible to talk about sexual matters without awareness of the culture or subculture in which they take place; the changing views of churches and other influential social agencies; the modification of roles within the family, whether of women in relation to men or children in relation to parents; or the many other social and familial forces which influence sexual attitudes and behaviors. There is wide agreement that the compromise term that has been adopted—family life and sex education—does not mean that the two parts are separable. The *and* is a kind of reminder to sex educators to include the family and society in the consideration of sexuality and to family life educators to include sexuality as an important dimension of all topics.

2

---

will
there
always
be a
family?

It is rare for any of us to reach adulthood without at some point wondering discontentedly why families exist. This thought occurs most frequently when we have been frustrated by the demands of some authority figure in the home or by the interruptions of a younger sibling. However, a new level of discontent has manifested itself in recent years, taking the form on the one hand of efforts to get away from present marriage and family conventions, and on the other hand taking the form of more serious consideration in professional conferences and journals of what alternatives to the family have been tried in the past and what can be expected in the future.

THE LONG HISTORY OF THE FAMILY

Marriage and the family have been very different at various times in our national history, as well as in world history. Even the basic nuclear unit—mother, father, children—has had varying definitions of how long children should live with parents, how much attention fathers should pay to infants, what work outside the house women should perform, who should be responsible for the support of the aged, and how important the spousal role is to be in comparison with the parental role. This diversity not only marks our history, but also our present functioning. Unless yours is a unique classroom, it would be very hard to get all of you to agree on these matters.

Even though statistically a modal family pattern can be determined—meaning more families subscribe to a given way of functioning than to any other way—this is useful largely in pinpointing trends. For example, do we have more two-parent families now than at the turn of the century? We can discover the surprising fact that change has been slight in this area, the main difference now being that divorce rather than death, as in the earlier period, more frequently breaks up the nuclear family.

Have all societies always had some kind of family? Some thinkers insist that mankind evolved from some form of group marriage in which several adults had sexual access to one another, to polygamy in which either a man had several wives (polygyny) or a wife had several husbands (polyandry), to monogamy of the traditional, man-dominant kind, to a more equalitarian monogamy found in advanced industrial societies (with more equal spousal roles claimed in the socialist countries). Other thinkers consider it fruitless to attempt to generalize about the period before written history. They stress the variety of family forms that exist in any given historical period, and explain the variation in terms of the technological and property relationships characteristic of a given society.

When the ancient Hebrews ceased to be nomadic tribes and settled down to agricultural pursuits, they accepted polygynous marriage, in part because they were anxious that there should be sons to work the land with them and to inherit their holdings. The ancient Greeks could afford to despise physical labor with more slaves than citizens in their society, and sought sons through a monogamous system of marriage to inherit both lands and the citizenship rights of the elite. Roman families were large because they included not only those related by blood and marriage who were living together, but also slaves, servants, and others on whom family members depended for work, care, and services.

More societies throughout history have had polygamy (mainly polygyny, rarely polyandry) than monogamy, although in most only a minority

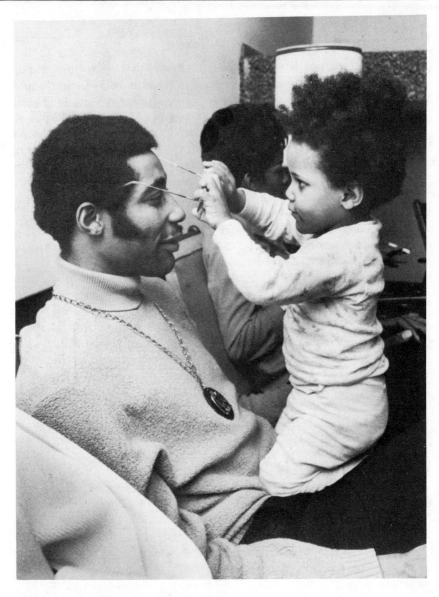

Societies have varied in the physical and emotional closeness expected between fathers and young children, with a range from isolation and avoidance to intimate play and comradeship. The relaxed interaction depicted here represents a new norm in industrialized society.

John Zimmerman, Life © 1969 Time Inc.

could afford multiple spouses, either because of the initial bride-price costs or the upkeep. In some instances, the husband who had the material resources for the initial investment was amply repaid by the economic contribution of several wives, each of whom served as traders in the marketplace (as in urban areas of Nigeria) or worked the fields. Friedrich Engels, who with Karl Marx was a critic of bourgeois family forms in the 19th century, saw similar economic exploitation of women in monogamous families, not only in rural areas where unpaid labor of wives and children allowed the patriarch to increase his wealth, but also in cities where domestic services did not entitle wives and children to share in the family property.

THE FUNCTIONS OF A FAMILY

If families are diverse, do they also have some commonalities? How can you tell whether a certain group of people is a family? Sociologists sometimes designate a "hippy" commune or a group of elderly people sharing an apartment as a parafamily, meaning something *like* a family. What is the "real thing"? If certain functions must be performed for a society to continue to exist (the functional prerequisites of societal survival), must it be the family that performs them? Are there some functions that *all* families perform? Do these questions seem simple to you? They are not simple to sociologists who try to answer them.

Some insist that the nuclear family is universal, that even where extended families are modal (mother, father, and children residing together with other kinfolk), the nuclear unit is a discernible entity and performs basic functions. According to Murdock,[1] these functions are four in number: reproduction (procreation to ensure new members of society to take the place of those who die); economic cooperation (either joint production of material goods as on a farm or in cottage industries, or joint budgeting for consumption of goods); sexual-affectional relationships (legitimate sexual resources for the spouses and emotional nurturance for all generations); and socialization (transmitting the social heritage to younger family members and preparing all family members for induction into new roles at various life stages). While other sociologists list other functions, most can fit within these four.

"Social control" can be seen as part of socialization. The family rewards and punishes behaviors of which society approves or disapproves. "Emotional maintenance or psychic security" can be seen as part of the

---

[1] George P. Murdock, *Social Structure* (New York: The Macmillan Company, Publishers, 1949).

affectional function. "Status placement," it can be argued, is not what a family does but what it perpetuates. The ethos and the economy of a society determine what qualities are valued and how they are recompensed. Families become defined by such stratifying factors, and by accepting the definition imposed by the society, shape their members accordingly. Youngsters may be taught "It's not for the likes of us," or "We have always had a reputation to maintain."

Other functions cited by sociologists either have decreased in importance in recent decades or can be fitted within Murdock's four functions. Thus the family's protective function has in one sense diminished as specialized groups, such as policeman and firemen, have taken over. In another sense, if protection means support of the aged, it has become more a community than a family responsibility. How much protection do you expect your family to give you? And how much protection do you feel you should offer? Do you phone for the police or do you tackle the intruder yourself? Do your parents expect you to support them when they are old?

Some sociologists insist that a function of the family is to maintain a sense of purpose, helping to harmonize individual and societal values and needs. This philosophical or religious function may be considered part of socialization, of the attempt to transmit a value system, and of the affectional function which assures each family member that he is worthwhile and has something to live for.

Even if we reduce the family's functions to four, we may ask, Is Murdock right in insisting that every nuclear family performs them? If we find that some perform only one or two, we shall have to say either that the nuclear family is not universal, but is at most near universal, or that there are only one or two functions performed by all families, whatever their composition. A number of sociologists have come to both of these conclusions. After looking at a number of societies and subsocieties in which relations between husband and wife or parent and child are tenuous, economically and emotionally, Reiss,[2] for example, has decided that "The family institution is a small kinship-structured group with the key function of nurturant socialization of the newborn." This allows for the distinction some societies make between biological and social fatherhood. Thus among the Nayars (on the Malabar coast of India) until quite recently, a man contributed to the economic support and socialization of his sister's children rather than his wife's; his wife could count on *her* brother.

2 Ira L. Reiss, "The Universality of the Family: A Conceptual Analysis," *Journal of Marriage and the Family*, 27 (November 1965), 443–53.

THE ONEIDA COMMUNE

However, not all sociologists would accept Reiss's definition as having universal application. For example, if you looked at the famous Oneida Commune, an experiment involving several hundred people in the 19th century in upstate New York, you would search in vain for "a small kinship-structured group," let alone one that focused on nurturant socialization of the young. That commune, based on religious-socialist principles, had no marriage, because it considered such exclusivity selfish. All men and all women could enter into sexual relationships based on consent of both individuals. The children of such unions, in a eugenics program that required the commune's consent to child-bearing, were raised in a children's wing of the huge mansion by specialized caretakers. They were supposed to be loved by and related to by all commune members, with no special privileges attached to biological parenthood.

The commune flourished and from what we can learn, adults and children were healthy and happy, perhaps more so than most 19th century families. There were some discontents with both sexual and affectional roles. Whether these problems would have seriously affected the commune in later generations, we shall never know, since vice hunters charged the Oneida group with adultery and managed to break up the experiment. Nor do we know all we should like to about the actual rather than the ideal functioning of the commune. It existed before sociology was born, before family sociology alerted us to the need for scientific study of man–woman relationships. We may ask, when the commune broke up, did the children go with their biological parents or with the nurses and educators they had learned to love in their age-graded living quarters? Were the adults not fitted for nuclear family living? Did they form extended family groups? These questions are not of remote historical interest, designed just to get the record straight. They have implications for present experiments in group living. Fortunately, some of the present communes are being studied, although this is not easy since many are small and quite diverse. It will be difficult to establish broad generalizations.

THE KIBBUTZ

By some definitions, such as Murdock's or Reiss's, the Oneida Commune had no family unless you want to stretch the concept of family to include several hundred people cooperating economically, ensuring replacement of population, sharing affection, and jointly rearing all the children. The kibbutz family too cannot fit into Murdock's definition, and there is some question as to whether the phrase in Reiss's definition, "the *key* function of nurturant socialization," accurately describes kibbutz family life.

The *kibbutzim* (plural for kibbutz) are a subsociety in Israel. While influenced to some degree by the larger setting which is theocratic and capitalist, the tiny minority of the population in the kibbutz (less than 4 percent) has a very different family form than the rest of the country. As at Oneida, there is joint ownership of the means of production, both men and women work, and the children are reared in age-graded institutions by nurses and teachers. Unlike Oneida, the kibbutz has a marriage system. Husband and wife share a room or an apartment, and jointly visit with their children a few hours a day. In a sense there is more spousal emphasis than in most nuclear families, because the parental role is mainly one of enjoyment and companionship. There is little of a practical nature the mother or father needs to do for the children. The process of raising children always requires some degree of frustration of the child's desires; in the kibbutz professional rearers are the frustrating agents of socialization while the parents are more like a combination of Father Christmas, Grandfather Frost, the good fairy, and the jolly elves.

In Reiss's view this is a part of the socialization process. Children are learning that they have a very special relationship to parents, that being a parent is fun, that parents endorse what is being taught them in the more formal learning situations. While there is some degree of difference among the various kibbutzim, and some tendency to increase the parental role, the couple typically has more time to be companions for each other and for their children than in the household where preparation of meals, supervision of homework, and attempts to budget and market consume considerable amounts of time.

I said before that there was more spousal emphasis in *one* sense. What is the other sense? It is that the commune is group living. If each couple went off by themselves and had little conversation, joint recreation, or interest in other members of the commune, there would be little but common work to cement the brotherhood and sisterhood spirit of the commune. It is part of kibbutz norms, then, that in the large dining rooms the couple do not separate themselves off for intimate twosome dining but converse with others at the tables of four, six, eight, even ten. This means built-in companionship for the widowed, the divorced, the unmarried, the aged, to be sure, but it may not meet everybody's needs for spousal closeness. Some people leave the communes and go to the cities to set up nuclear or extended families. Most remain.

There are probably several explanations for their communal preference. The kibbutzim have been in existence for over sixty years, founded by young men and women committed ideologically to economic cooperation rather than competition, to equality of men and women, and to human relationships that transcended kinship lines. These young men and women were seeking a society and a family form that had little in common with the *shtetl*, or traditional Jewish village which existed earlier in the century in Eastern Europe, and the patriarchal family they had known there. They had not liked many things about that family: the mother selecting a wife for the son and the father a husband for the daughter; the emphasis on maternal kin rather than bilateral relationships; the martyr mother always busy and always nagging, "killing herself" for her children; the lack of romance between spouses and the mother's consequent overattention to her sons; the unquestioning obedience owed parents; the sharp line between family image presented to the public and actual family interaction in privacy; the hostile mother-in-law and the consequent overdependence of the young wife on her mother.

The Eastern European Jewish immigrants who came to the United States in great numbers at the turn of the century perpetuated some of these aspects of family life in the first and sometimes in the second generations, but as years went by modified them in response to different economic, political, and social conditions here. The kibbutz, however, allowed instant change in family life. By now there is a kibbutz generation that has never known any other kind of family life. Their pioneering parents and grandparents are getting, for the most part, what they had sought. The youth are socialized from birth to kibbutz expectations and are sometimes uncomfortable in the greater competitiveness and eroticism that characterize the rest of the country.

Is the answer to the question of whether there will always be a family getting clearer for you? It should not be because there is no clear answer at present. Either you define every group performing certain functions as a family or you recognize that almost every function now performed by the family can be taken over by other social institutions. Reiss acknowledges that if public rearing becomes typical in a society, the one function he designates as inhering in the family may evaporate.

It is possible that as the socialist countries become communist, that is, move beyond their present stage of development, public childrearing will become even more widespread. Engels, writing in the 19th century, anticipated this.[3] He also saw new possibilities for the monogamous family as the relationship of a man and a woman became removed from economic considerations because both were equally involved in gainful employment, and financial burdens of rearing children were increasingly assumed by the community. He did not consider that monogamy had ever really been tried in the history of the family, and pointed to the

---

[3] Friedrich Engels, *On the Origin of the Family, Private Property, and the State* (New York: International Publishers, 1971).

existence of prostitution, extramarital relations, the double sexual standard, and other obstacles to the building of a strong commitment between a man and a woman as characteristic of traditional monogamy. He was hopeful that socialism would lay an economic basis for a new form of the monogamous family. He suggested that marriage might be a fragile institution and that a succession of marriages might characterize each life cycle since it is difficult, he believed, to predict the duration of an "attack of individual sex love." However the experience of the kibbutz suggests that the succession of marriages may be less frequent than in other societies today.

must
the
family
keep
changing?

How accurate are statements like these? The family is a mirror of society. The family is a refuge from society. The family is the fundamental unit of society. The family is society seen in miniature. As society goes, so goes the family. In other words, is the family the tail or the dog? Does society "wag" the family or the family "wag" society? Sociological research uses soberer terms. In the interactions of society and family, is the family more likely to be the dependent or the independent variable? As the dependent variable it is influenced and shaped by the society. As the independent variable it will affect the way society functions.

THE FAMILY AND THE ECONOMY

In the view of Nimkoff, widely shared by other sociologists, the economic system has greater impact on the family than the family has on the economic system, although this does not exclude the likelihood of the family's impact on other institutions of society.[1] Nimkoff, in fact, recognizes the family as an intervening variable. He points out that economic changes ordinarily come first and change the family. As the family changes it in turn alters other parts of the social system.

An example to illustrate this is the technological advances that created the factory system. The division of labor and mechanization made it possible for women to be employed at tasks for which they may have formerly lacked the muscle power. The factory system and the urbanization which accompanied it certainly changed the family. Many of the products once laboriously made in the home could be mass-produced, and the family changed from a production unit to a consumption unit. But family members retained traditional notions of what was appropriate for men and women to do. The idea that the man is the head of the family, the chief breadwinner, and that woman's place is in the home persisted for more than a century after the economy had opened up new occupational possibilities. *Institutional lag,* or the quicker change of one social institution than another in a given society, is particularly evident in a rapidly changing economy.

Another example of this lag comes close to all of us: the expansion of the system of roads and vehicles, an important technological change, has not been matched by as rapid a change in views on women's mechanical aptitudes. The view of women as incompetent drivers, not upheld by insurance data, persists. Some sociologists such as Ogburn call it *cultural lag* when political, family, religious, and educational institutions do not keep up with the potentials of the economy, while reserving the term institutional lag for the lack of fit among noneconomic institutions.[2] According to Sumner, whose ideas in *Folkways* [3] have for decades been influential among social thinkers, this lack of fit in either case does not last forever, since there is a "straining for consistency" among the institutions of any society. However, by the time there is consistency or fit among most of the institutions, the economy is likely to make another change, and the cycle of lag and the striving for consistency begins again.

Some who see change as menacing rather than fraught with positive possibilities sometimes try to hold back economic development or the

---

[1] Meyer F. Nimkoff, ed., *Comparative Family Systems* (Boston: Houghton Mifflin Company, 1965).

[2] William F. Ogburn, *Social Change* (New York: The Viking Press, 1950).

[3] William Graham Sumner, *Folkways* (Boston: Ginn and Company, 1906).

modification of other social institutions. When labor-saving machinery was first introduced, some workers sought to destroy it, attacking machines with pickaxes and hammers. They did not see that with an appropriate distribution system, everyone could benefit through shorter working hours and more abundant goods made possible through advanced technology. Similarly today, many regard automation as the enemy and attack it rather than the real sources of employment problems.

Some people see changes in church doctrine or family relationships or educational requirements as arbitrary rather than as natural outcomes of a changed economy. What is the connection between the changing positions of various religions on sexual morality, for example, and the technological advances in medicine (manufacture of contraceptives, etc.) and production (allowing women economic independence)? What is the connection between the reemergence of the nuclear family, once common in hunting and gathering societies and now increasingly typical for advanced industrial societies, and the greater reliance on educational institutions for the acquisition of work skills and on the larger community for aid in crises?

The economy will always continue to change, either because inventions never cease or because machines, skills, and ideas are diffused (sometimes borrowed, sometimes stolen) from one country to another. If the material base changes, the superstructure, or the nonmaterial aspects of society, must necessarily adapt to the changing methods of production. The folkways, mores, laws, and institutions are always in a state of flux, at some times more visibly than at others. Does this fact of social life gladden you or sadden you?

Even if you are intellectually prepared for change and recognize not only its inevitability but the improvements it often brings, you cannot be completely comfortable with every change. This perhaps goes back to the expectations we were taught in our early years about "proper" relationships—between young and old, men and women, teacher and student, doctor and patient, and so forth. We get used to things, even the frustrations and injustices, and miss them when new opportunities and choices open up. Can you think of instances in your own lives or in the lives of family members which show this nostalgic looking back? On a national level, data often reveal that the "good old days" were not that good in many respects.

THE FAMILY REFLECTS CHANGE

The foregoing must indicate that if the family is a mirror of society, or the family is society writ small, then the family at any given moment in history reflects the changing forces in society, the contradictions (lags) as well as the newly arrived-at resolutions. This makes only partly true the assertion that the family is a refuge from society and is *the* fundamental unit of society.

It is true that some families for some periods of time can resist the new folkways, mores, and laws. On the folkway level, your family may be the one in which everybody must be home for dinner, everyone including little ones must sit quietly while father reads from the Bible, father is addressed as "sir" and mother as "ma'am," and permission must be asked for use of the telephone. On the level of mores—those customs deemed of great ethical significance—your family may not permit wearing of bikinis or mini-dresses, steady dating for teenagers, or individual choice of church. Concerning laws, sometimes considered mores frozen into the legal code, distinguished from mores by the enforcement machinery provided by the state, your family may be one that insists on observance of old laws still on the statute books even though most of the community no longer takes them seriously.

Television sets, classrooms, and the mass magazines sooner or later make the younger members of society aware that most families live in other patterns; they begin to pressure the parents for change. In a larger sense, the question can be asked whether the family can ever be totally a refuge from the negative aspects of society such as polluted water and atmosphere, harmful food products, crimes such as burglary, mugging, rape, or other problems such as competition, indifference, and militarism. Moreover, if the family is the intervening variable and is so strongly affected by economic relationships in the society, can the family be said to be *the* fundamental unit? Is it possible that thinking of the family as more basic than the economy can mislead us into expecting from the family what it cannot give? We look at juvenile delinquency, for example, and blame the family, instead of searching for those forces that make it difficult for the family to perform a better guidance function.

IF THE FAMILY KEEPS CHANGING IS IT ALWAYS FOR THE BETTER?

Should the family resist some changes and insist on some modifications in economic relationships, in church and school, so that some of the former family roles can be retained? Should there be a spokesman for the family in every governmental body, ready to declare on the basis of scientific data what the implications for family functioning are in every proposed measure? What are the arguments for and against such proposals?

In a pluralistic society such as ours, can consensus be obtained on which aspects of the family should be retained, or what is good for the family? Even in countries like the Soviet Union or Communist China, with a single basic ideology which permeates all institutions, there is no unanimity on the issue of familism. In all societies there are contending emphases on individualism, familism, and communalism. Even though the United States is supposed to exemplify a philosophy of individualism, one in which ideally each man and woman fulfills his unique potentialities, there are varying shades of familial loyalties which may at times conflict with self-fulfillment. Can you think of such situations in your own life?

Consider these questions: Are Americans in agreement on nuclear familism, extended familism, affinal familism? Is each family, and each individual member of a family, willing to make the same sacrifices of individual needs and ambitions for relatives? Is there a set of priorities in which the family of procreation comes out ahead of the family of origin? Also do his in-laws command more loyalty than hers? How much agreement is there in your classroom on the questions in the checklist on familism in Appendix II. (You can see that if you and your future spouse do not agree on some of these items, there can be serious disharmony in the family. Or if some of your parents or grandparents or siblings have expectations you are not prepared to meet, there can be mutual disappointment, hostility, recrimination.)

INTERFAMILY RELATIONSHIPS

When a person's orientation is nuclear-familistic, he is inclined to say, "My wife and children come first, materially and emotionally, and I'll visit the others and help them only if I have time, money, and affection to spare from my family of procreation for my family of origin." The person whose orientation is more extended-familistic may be willing to consider his parents and his brothers and sisters just as important as his wife and children, but he may not be willing to extend his interest and obligation to his wife's family of origin. And within each of these three categories of nuclear, extended, and affinal familism, there may be shadings of loyalty which tie in with the individual's value system and make the readiness to relate conditional rather than absolute. Not my father and mother, right or wrong, but my father if he has not squandered his money on alcohol and my mother if she has not bugged me about my mate selection decision. Or my older brother was a real go-getter and I like his visiting us with his family but my younger brother gave us a lot of trouble and we don't encourage him to keep in touch with us. The strictures may grow sterner with a spouse's relatives, especially if there is not a background of pleasant interaction in the early years of the relationship.

It has been said that the American family is moving in the direction of achieved rather than ascribed relationships among its members. While older norms still operate, and many kin contacts are maintained even if strong affection is lacking, there is a discernible trend toward maintaining relationships with those we are fond of, who have earned our devotion by the way they played their role rather than by virtue of occupying a given position in the family. We may not visit all our uncles, but the one or two we perceived as affectionate are more likely to get our attention even if geographic distance would make the others more likely candidates. The friendly mother-in-law may be invited or we may attend a holiday dinner at her home, but there are many good excuses for not getting together with the less friendly one. Of course, status considerations may play a part, especially in a competitive society. Have you a crusty old aunt who is on the board of trustees of the school you may want your child to attend? Is your grandfather a noted community figure? Or, on the contrary, do your parents complain that the distant cousin, now a judge, seems to have no interest in exchanging Christmas cards?

Which present family patterns make it more possible to experience friendliness and warmth in interaction with parents, siblings, and other kin? Does the present disharmony between the generations at the time of adolescence take a later toll in reduced extended or affinal familism? In some instances the breach may be healed and in young adulthood men and women can perceive virtues in their parents and siblings they had not appreciated before—and vice versa. However, in many other instances the emotional distance generated in the teen years may persist for a lifetime. This may be more serious in lower income groups where there is a tendency to greater reliance upon kinfolk than upon friends for emotional satisfaction. Do some family forms, such as the kibbutz, avoid estrangement between generations? Does it do so at a price of more diffused relationships all through life?

IS THERE AN OPTIMAL FAMILISM?

Can we agree on which kind of familism, and in what degree, is optimal? Research on other societies as well as our own suggests that extended familism sometimes affects nuclear familism adversely. The closeness of the married daughter with her mother may exclude the spouse in each generation. Sex-segregated roles feed into and result from overvaluation of parental and filial roles at the expense of spousal ones. It was found when young couples and their children moved from a slum area in London to a suburb, the young wife and her "mum" no longer had time for daily visits and neither could afford the bus fare. The effect: the nuclear family became closer. The wife had to seek from her husband the com-

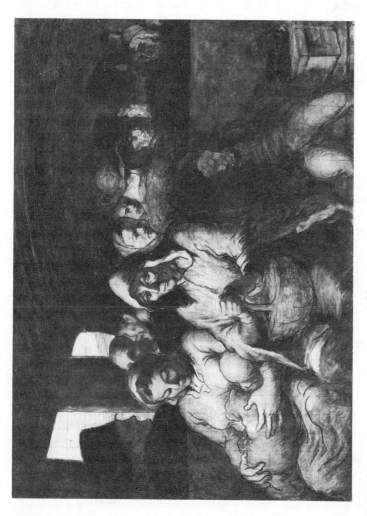

It was appropriate for women in many societies, as among the peasants depicted here, to have female kin accompany them on any journey, however brief. Nursing a baby in public was more acceptable among rural than urban folk. A class line was also drawn; the wealthy hired wet nurses for their infants.

Honore Daumier, The Third-Class Carriage. The Metropolitan Museum of Art, Bequest of Mrs. H. O. Havemeyer, 1929. The H. O. Havemeyer Collection.

panionship she had formerly obtained from her mother, and the husband responded by staying home more, relating more to the children, and sharing home chores as well as recreation. "Mum" either had some other daughters in her vicinity or she felt lonely and deprived. Further study is needed to show whether the older couple left behind also got closer, once the mother–daughter alliance ended.[4]

Was the nuclear family closeness a good thing? Your answer depends on whether you think husbands and wives should be closer than mothers and daughters, and whether the emptiness in the older women's lives should be filled by closer relations with husbands and with non-kin (neighbors and friends). The sociologists who studied this situation in England were inclined to recommend that suburbs be planned in such a way that the kin network could be moved as a body from the slum and the original relationships retained. This of course assumes those relationships were worth preserving. It could be argued that by making the move to the suburb something that only the younger couples could undertake, the housing and other community agencies were intervening in the social networks. This illustration suggests that any change in housing, zoning, bus fares, and the like affects the family one way or another. If the government or the industry or the social agency is *aware* of the impact, they can decide on what the goals should be and then create a structure that permits these goals to be realized.

This relates back to which kind of familism, and in what degree, is optimal. If there is consensus on more visiting by the older generation, extended familism, bus rides, telephones, and other aids to contact could be subsidized. There are two interrelated but different problems here: What kinds of choices are possible among family patterns within a given society considering its stage of economic development? By what kinds of actions by other social institutions (government, church, etc.) can one pattern or another or several be facilitated?

THE IMPACT OF THE ECONOMY ON THE FAMILY

It is clear that in a large country with changing employment opportunities and strong achievement values, large families of wage-earners would find it difficult to meet industry's need to shuffle skilled personnel about. When the nuclear family has a single wage-earner, it can pick up and go more easily in response to the orders of a large corporation which is

---

4 Michael Young and Peter Willmott, *Family and Kinship in East London* (London: Routledge and Kegan Paul, 1957).

setting up new branches. Does this mean that only the nuclear family is consonant with modern industry? Or does it mean that the nuclear family is likely to predominate but that alternative forms will also be found?

If the extended family in the United States (or even the nuclear one, now that over thirty million women are involved in gainful employment) has several wage-earners in the same field, it may be able to move as a unit in response to industry's call for textile workers or agriculture's call for fruit pickers. But when the extended family has members with varying skills and occupations, it may be more difficult for them to find employment for everyone if they all change their place of residence. Sometimes the extended family splits up, with the married son and his wife and children moving to a new place and the other members following when he has scouted jobs and apartments for them. Sometimes they become an extended family again, all living in the same household. More often they live close by and the nuclear families have almost as much interaction as when they lived together. The latter case we noted in the London slum example, and close geographic proximity of related nuclear families can also be found in cities in Brazil, French-Canada, and Mexico, where a high percentage of apartments in a given house may be occupied by kin. One sociologist calls this a "modified extended family," although the term is not limited to those living close by, so long as they are involved in a great many visiting, helping, and other activities together. It is not an ideal term, since an extended family by definition means joint residence.

Hopefully new terms will be invented to suggest with less confusion that the nuclear family in cities and suburbs is not as isolated as once thought. Perhaps the new terms will distinguish between related nuclear families in the same apartment house or in walking distance from one another and those more geographically separated who have to rely on telephones, cars, and other technological aids to communication. Even in advanced industrial countries with good roads, distance has been called the prime limiting condition upon interaction.

Adams found, in a study of a North Carolina city, that in his sample "all those whose parents live in Greensboro, 155 of them, stated that they see their parents at least monthly, and better than 5 out of 6 see their proximate parents weekly. Sixty-one percent of the 113 respondents whose parents live within 100 miles of Greensboro see them more than once a month. However, at the other extreme, none of the 176 whose parents live more than 100 miles away see them weekly, and less than 25 percent of them see their parents as often as once a month." [5]

---

[5] Bert N. Adams, *Kinship in an Urban Setting* (Chicago: Markham Publishing Company, 1968).

THE TEMPORARY EXTENDED FAMILY

The most common form of extended family in the United States is of a temporary kind. A young couple marries and moves in with the parents of the husband or wife until they can afford their own place; this is more apt to happen at a low income level. (In the London slum case, the housing shortage made this temporary solution necessary, until "mum" could persuade the rental agent to give her daughter the next vacancy.) An aged parent cannot continue to maintain his own home and so moves in with a married son or daughter. With the great preference for independent housekeeping in the United States, such a move is usually deferred until the parent is infirm, and the joint residence may not last very long. Even this kind of extended family may become less common when more women are gainfully employed. The aged person cannot count on a daughter or daughter-in-law to be at home.

Some counselors, clergymen, and social workers urge that we make more of an effort to learn to like extended family living. They point to the experimental communal household as evidence that people are seeking the advantages that can be found in the extended family—availability of several adults to share a given task; less trauma associated with illness, death, or desertion of one family member; built-in companionship for the young and the elderly or the unmarried, and so forth. However, quite a distinction may be made between a chosen group and a group of kin who by definition are "givens" rather than "chosen" as people we want to spend our lives with. There are conflicting values at stake, possibly expressed crudely in the two assertions: "You have only one life to live," and "You have only one mother." Since our society values both individualism and some degree of familism, there is much leeway for one emphasis or another by a given individual or family. Their degree of value congruence is an important area for a couple to explore before marriage, to make sure they both define some changes in family patterns as better than others.

4

how
we
know
about
marriage
and the
family

Scientific study of the family is largely a 20th century development. For many centuries, even as far back as Plato, various aspects of society were observed and described, and ideal societies were proposed in which the family would be changed in many ways. But a systematic examination of how the family functions in a given society in relation to other institutions and how family members relate to one another was not possible until the development of sociology and psychology in the 19th century. While Plato had urged the clarification of concepts which led to the "operative definitions" of contemporary family research, it was the Renaissance emphasis on prediction and control—knowledge is power—that was to expand the natural sciences and more recently the social sciences.

FAMILY RESEARCH PROBLEMS

Family research has increased quantitatively to a notable degree in the past two or three decades. However, it is still a very young science; the level of prediction is not as yet very high. This is in part due to the barriers which stand in the way of studying the family. Can you think of what some of these barriers are? Would you let a sociologist come into your home and watch everything all of you do in order to compare your functioning with that of other American families? And if you let him (or a team of observers) do so, how would his presence change the way you behave? If he sat taking notes, or had his tape recorder on, or even sat behind a one-way screen that had been built into your living room wall, would you talk the way you normally do, quarrel, grimace, show affection, and so on? If you did, the further question would arise, can what was observed in your family be generalized to others? Of what group is your family typical, middle-class black urban, lower-class white, third-generation Italian-American, or what?

Privacy and the many subsocieties in the United States are only two of the many problems in doing scientific research on the family. Another is the danger of harming the subjects in the study. The questions asked by the sociologist or the psychologist may stir up feelings in family members that the researcher does not stay around to resolve. Even more important is the inhibition on experimentation. The classic model of a scientific experiment is to have a control group and an experimental group, and to measure the difference between them before and after applying a given stimulus to the experimental group only. But the social scientist cannot ask people to live in settings he arranges. He must limit himself to measuring phenomena in other than laboratory conditions. Thus, he cannot ask a new housing development to take so many families with young children, so many with adolescent children, so many with widowed parents, and then calculate the different effects on these types of families that moving to the new neighborhood has, in contrast to their counterparts still living in the slum.

HOW FAMILY RESEARCH IS DONE

What can be done? What has been done? First of all, the researcher delimits a problem, a set of relationships he considers worth investigating. This differs in the various societies, not only because the family problems are different, but because what is perceived as a problem is influenced by the researcher's own society's values and assumptions. The researcher forms an hypothesis or a series of hypotheses, that certain variables will correlate positively or negatively with others. For example, stated simply, *if* families have incomes of under $3,000, *then* the proportion of female-headed families in white and black populations in the United States will be similar.

How was the hypothesis suggested? Why did the researcher decide to work on it? Clues to hypotheses are sometimes found in cases being examined for other reasons. Thus a social worker with a mixed case load of black and white families may find that in the poorest families the man seems to be gone, and ethnicity does not seem to be an indicator of what will be found in a given neighborhood. This puzzles the case worker. In the back of his mind is the thought generated by newspaper and TV statements that it is the black family that is the source of fatherless families. At a professional meeting of, say, the National Council on Family Relations, which brings together educators, psychologists, social workers, counselors, researchers, he may mention his puzzlement. One of his hearers may desire to look into the relationship of income, family form, and ethnicity; the desire itself is influenced by society's attitudes.

Is the black family worth researching? The general neglect of the black family by society was reflected in the lack of research. At the turn of the century some basic research was done by black sociologist DuBois,[1] but several decades were to elapse before some other black sociologists, such as Frazier [2] and Johnson,[3] focused on the black family. A few white sociologists also pioneered, but it was not until the 1960s when the black population made it evident that they were not going to continue to accept the hardships imposed on them by discrimination in jobs, housing, and education that research on the black family began to increase markedly.

Another source of hypotheses, more on the interpersonal level, is the clinical practice of the psychotherapist. In person after person or family after family that comes to him for therapy, he finds certain present attitudes or past experiences which suggest some regularities in relationships. Because the cases are not proof, and he may have only a selected group coming to him, the researcher will have to put the cases of many clinicians together, with due allowance for variables of income, profession, ethnicity (which includes race, religion, and nationality), age, sex, and the like. There are, in fact, so many variables—size of family of origin, size of family of procreation, ordinal position in the family, etc.

---

[1] W. E. DuBois, *The Negro American Family* (Atlanta: Atlanta University Press, 1908).

[2] E. Franklin Frazier, *The Negro Family in Chicago* (Chicago: University of Chicago Press, 1932).

[3] Charles Johnson, *Shadow of the Plantation* (Chicago: University of Chicago Press, 1934).

—that most research can select only a few, despite the likelihood that the findings can then be generalized only to specific parts of the population. There is not much research that allows us to say many things firmly about *all* American families.

Having formulated his hypothesis that certain social phenomena will have certain observable consequences in the family or that certain family phenomena will have certain observable consequences for the individual family member, the researcher defines his concepts, states his theoretical assumptions, and then proceeds to find evidence to prove or disprove the hypothesis. As a social scientist he is expected to be willing to let that evidence guide his conclusions, to gather all the relevant data even if it results in having to throw out a pet hypothesis when it cannot be substantiated. We will look at the issue of objectivity later, but at this point we will consider ways evidence can be gathered.

DATA COLLECTION

Data collection is influenced by the money and time available to the researcher. If he is doing research at the same time that he is teaching he is likely to choose a population which is both close at hand and cooperative. This is why so much family research has been done on the middle class, often with the college student as spokesman for his family. If the researcher has been funded by a private foundation or a public agency, he may have both time and money to broaden the population, to hire and train interviewers, to travel to sources of obscure documents, and to finance other methods. Family research is not well funded as a rule; some researchers think the reason is that it would make some power groups in our society uncomfortable if certain facts were brought to light. And some researchers prefer to struggle on their own in order to investigate what they want when they want, rather than to submit detailed outlines to funding organizations. It is also easier to modify an hypothesis or change the research design as preliminary investigation makes this seem necessary when no approval must be sought.

interviews

Which data-gathering techniques are used in family research? Are they all equally useful in providing firm facts? Interviews are commonly used, whether open-ended (meaning the interviewee is encouraged to talk freely and later the pertinent comments are extracted from the record) or those that focus on a particular topic and follow a particular schedule, with certain questions preceding others. The skill of the interviewer may be very important where the interviewee is reluctant to reveal certain subject matter. This makes the interview technique an expensive one. Kinsey and his two colleagues carried out 18,000 interviews, each lasting several hours, and they trusted only themselves to do the verbal probing. Kinsey was a biologist and not a sociologist, but the methods used were similar and were subjected to the same criticisms of sampling (people volunteered themselves and may not have been representative of people who do not volunteer to talk about their sex lives), and breadth of generalization— too few lower-class interviewees were included to permit the findings to apply to the whole population.

The element of expense has been one factor in overinterviewing women and relatively neglecting men in the family. Women are more apt to be home in the daytime; interviewing is more expensive and laborious when undertaken at night and weekends when men can be reached. Several studies have shown that both men and women must be questioned to get the facts. For example, a study of marital happiness found husbands reporting a happy marriage more often than their wives. If only one sex had been asked, a misleading picture could have been drawn.

the questionnaire

Interviewing has an advantage which is lacking in another widely used method, the questionnaire. If a question is not clear to the respondent, he can ask the interviewer. How many questionnaires have you filled out in which you have either left blanks or put in any old thing either because you are not interested or because you cannot recall what is being inquired about? Many questionnaires have built into them ways of finding out how seriously you are taking them. For example, a question will be repeated in a different form further down the list and then compared with how you answered when it was first asked. Recall data are often suspect. It is difficult enough to get the facts straight when they are currently happening, as when mothers of preschool children are asked about child behaviors, but when parents of adolescents are asked about those preschool years there is some confusion in their minds as to whether it was Johnny or Timmy who did this or that.

the public opinion poll

A method used to get a broad sampling of attitudes at a given time is the public opinion poll. When these attitudes are tapped at regular intervals, trends become evident as to how people feel about such topics as doing away with all abortion laws, interracial marriage, or new legislation involving divorce. One disadvantage in this form of data collection is that the individual cannot be challenged about the consistency of his views or his reasons for changing them. Sometimes the attitudes tapped are not basic but responses to some widely publicized recent event. Thus attitudes on capital punishment may fluctuate with the newspaper headlines.

observation

Observation and particularly participant observation—the latter is the classic method of anthropologists—are relatively little used by family sociologists, although there has recently been some recognition of the desirability of checking self-reports against actual behaviors as they occur. If you ask a mother how she handles certain behaviors of her child, she is likely, particularly if she is middle-class and aware of some of the literature on the subject, to give the socially accepted answer for the given time and place. Thus if asked what she would do if she saw her preschool son with his hand on his penis in public, she would have answered self-righteously earlier in the century, "I push his hand away and whisper in his ear that he'll get a good whipping when we get home." Today she is likely to say, "I just pay no attention." But is this so? If the researcher sits in a variety of public playgrounds in urban areas where mothers and small children gather daily, the behavior that can be *seen*— the mother paying no attention or offering a toy which requires the use of both hands or whispering in his ear—is indicative of her true reaction.

In a sense the observer is an eavesdropper. There are many ethical dilemmas in family research. What price data? As a private citizen, the researcher probably does not want the census, the greatest source of statistical data on the American family, to inquire into religion. As a scientist he knows how useful these data can be in correlating other family behaviors with kinds of religious adherence. As a private person, he does not want to be fooled. As a researcher he is likely to tell the mother in a "well baby" clinic that the man or woman at the next desk is part of the clerical staff who must share the interviewing room for lack of other space. The "clerk" may be recording the observed behaviors of the mother toward the baby when she thinks the interviewer is not looking at her.

Suspicion concerning assurances of confidentiality may keep family members from being completely frank. Also some sexual behaviors may make the individual vulnerable to prosecution or at least police harassment. A study showing the bisexuality of some married men has been praised for the ingenuity of the research design. The sociologist acted as a participant observer (participating as a lookout man) in homosexual gathering places and noted the license numbers of cars parked outside.

Without being recognized he was then able to go to the homes of the men he knew to be engaging in homosexual acts and to interview them on some pretext which permitted him to gain knowledge of their husband and father roles. Whether this study will be replicated in various parts of the country in an effort to broaden the sample and refine some of the variables will depend on how much condemnation continues concerning the increased legal vulnerability of those being studied.

the projective test

To overcome the barrier of reticence, some sociologists have used various forms of projective tests. These can take many forms. The *incomplete sentence test* includes a number of statements to be filled in by the respondent. (My father . . . ; Sisters are . . . ; etc.) The *picture test* consists of a number of vague groupings of people. The respondent tells what they seem to him to be. (In one picture, a husband and wife quarreling will be seen by one, a couple planning a vacation by another.) The *story test* sketches a family situation in a few sentences and asks the respondent to comment on it. Komarovsky used a story along with other data-collecting methods in research reported in *Blue Collar Marriage*.

The projective test is believed to get at what is salient in the mind of the individual, but which he might cover up if he were asked more directly. However, one problem with projective tests is that not all those examining the replies categorize them the same way. The Koell-Hoeflin test to see whether the individual has a traditional or a developmental approach to childrearing sets up a scoring system that permits wide latitude in the replies even within each category. This raises the question of degrees. Are two individuals graded traditional by their total equally traditional?

sociometry

Small group research, sociometry, has offered some methods of recording interaction which have been applied to the family. Families have been given a puzzle to solve or a question to decide and the flow of communication among them as they work on this task has been charted. Considered aspects are: who speaks most, who supports whom in his suggestions, who withdraws in subtle ways such as thinking of something else even though his eyes are on these words, who is task-oriented, who more interested in the feelings of group members, and so forth.

record linkage

Another research method, quite recently developed, is record linkage, the connecting of two bodies of information to derive a third. How can we find out whether premarital pregnancy is increasing? Even if we posted observers at each license bureau, marriage chapel, or registry office, the answer might elude us. Christensen's method seems obvious now that he has shown its usefulness, but it was not used before.[4] He took a sample of newlyweds and compared their names with the birth records in the next six months, before prematurity could be claimed, and found that one out of five brides had been pregnant. Of course, this study in a midwestern state more than a decade ago needs replication in different parts of the country at this time for any trends to be revealed.

before–after measurements

While the sociologist cannot manipulate families, he can take advantage of ongoing experiments and interventions being conducted by other groups. If he knows that a certain cluster of farm families in West Virginia is going to be persuaded by the Department of Agriculture to leave their low-yield homesteads and move to the nearest urban area, he may be able to get on the scene before the move to measure certain aspects of family relationships and then visit them again once they have been relocated.

longitudinal studies

Sociologists agree that more longitudinal research should be undertaken; that is, more families should be contacted at different stages in their development—the first year of marriage, ten years later, ten years after that, and so on. Predictions could be made in the early observations and later data would show whether they were borne out.

The marriage prediction studies of several decades ago exemplified this to some degree, with engaged couples rated as likely to achieve good adjustment in marriage and then measured after a few years of marriage to see whether the expectations were correct. The highest and the lowest scores gave a considerable amount of prediction but there was too large a fuzzy area between to permit the research instruments to serve the needs

4 Harold T. Christensen, "Studies in Child Spacing: Premarital Pregnancy as Measured by the Spacing of the First Birth from Marriage," *American Sociological Review*, 18 (February 1953), 53–59.

of individual engaged couples. Moreover, the marriages were rated at only one point in time by the original researchers. Another researcher took the same data later and examined some of the couples after two decades of marriage. The reluctance of researchers to engage in longitudinal studies because it ties up their resources for many years can be overcome by such team work in which the original researchers can turn to other subjects of interest while later researchers use the original data as a baseline.

If the gathering of data (and we have not begun to enumerate all the methods such as examination of laws, historical documents, travelers' diaries, fiction of a given period, etc.) is fraught with challenge and difficulty, the interpretation of the data is even more so. What inferences are to be drawn, how broad a generalization the data will bear, what further facts are needed, what changes in sample or methods should be introduced in further research on the subject, are all considerations. Many researchers state quite clearly the limitations of their study. Many textbook writers on marriage and the family tend to cite the research as proving more than it claims, or else they cite only that finding which fits into their own generalizations and personal convictions.

OBJECTIVITY

This brings us to problems of objectivity. Mention has already been made of the fact that even the choice of what aspects of the family are studied is itself influenced by the researcher's—and the society's—notions of what is important. This itself is a kind of value judgment. Moreover, all research takes place within a theoretical framework whether explicitly stated or not. If the researcher proceeds on Freudian assumptions, he is likely to hypothesize all sorts of dire consequences for women seeking equality with men. Since the world of evidence is very large, and some selection has to be made, he may consciously or unconsciously choose just those kinds of data that will tend to substantiate his hypothesis rather than incorporating material that brings it into question. If he is a materialist who attaches more importance to the impact of the material culture on the family, he may omit or not develop fully the impact of religious forces. If he is convinced that capitalism is the only desirable form of economy, he may ignore the family forms developing under socialism or look only for their negative features. If he is convinced that socialism—or its more developed version, communism—offers the only hope for economic problems, he may ignore some of the positive features of the bourgeois family.

Objectivity can sometimes be defined so narrowly that there is a failure to reckon with the alternatives. Thus, a recent family textbook takes pride in the referendum vote of the American Sociological Association which defeated a resolution of condemnation of the Vietnam war, which the textbook writer considers true objectivity. Could it not be argued that failure to adopt the resolution committed members of the association not to objectivity but to support of the war, i.e., the status quo? When we do not vote for a bond issue, are we neutral on the matter, or are we actually voting for the perpetuation of the condition that would have been changed by the bond issue? The textbook writer did not report to his readers that other professional associations, such as the American Psychological Association, the American Anthropological Association, and others, which value objectivity as much as the ASA, voted for a similar resolution.

And how about ourselves, you as the students working with this book and I as the writer? Surely you will have to watch me carefully to see whether I intrude my personal preferences in the guise of offering objective data, carefully selected to lead to only one conclusion. As a social scientist, I am committed to rational discussion and scientific inquiry. Through professional preparation I was supposed to transcend the particular family experiences I have had, and by awareness of the extent to which these may be influencing my presentation, to take special pains to be objective. The logicians among you will see this itself as a value position. Though I may subscribe to it in the abstract, I may slip here and there in the concrete. The student who reads critically, who seeks out weaknesses and contradictions, will gain more in working with this book than the student with a more passive, trusting attitude.

PERSONAL EXPERIENCE AND FAMILY STUDY

All readers have had family lives and looked at various marriages among family members and friends. To what extent does this handicap their study in this class? To what extent is their experience an advantage? The handicap derives from a false feeling of being an "instant expert," one who can generalize to all families what he has observed in a few. Or one who can question a finding about disenchantment in the middle years of marriage because he knows some loving couples in their forties and fifties.

The advantage derives from the other side of the same coin. There is already some degree of knowledge of the subject matter and it can form a base on which to build, to sort out the stereotypes from complex realities. Moreover, the students' own experience can bring the validity of some studies into question. For example, if the researcher is talking about dating, and class discussion reveals that nobody follows the steps he delineates or has the concerns he outlines, this is a clue to look closely at the time the data were gathered (things may have changed since), the particular research population used (a church-related college far from urban centers), or the phrasing of the interview questions which reflected the researcher's own dating experience several decades ago.

Ideally, enough time could be allocated to this course so that it would be possible for students to go back to each important research study and examine it critically rather than depend on the summaries and comments on them offered by textbook writers. Students would read book reviews which mention some of the weaknesses. The old saying that "Art is long and time is fleeting" certainly applies here. Your study admittedly cannot be as thorough as is desirable. It may be sufficient, however, to stir up your thinking on matters you have taken for granted and to clarify the choices open to you as a citizen and as a family member. If your work with this book leads you to more realistic expectations of the family and society, you will be better able to bring family life and the institutions related to it closer to defensible standards.

Family research only indirectly points the way to improvements. It shows what happens if certain factors are present. If you do not like what happens, then you may want to consider changing the causal factors. The social scientist brings these factors to your attention. The social worker tries to patch things up, to ameliorate the life conditions of a given family. But it is basically the citizen who decides what kind of family patterns should be encouraged, and how, on the broad scale of legislation and administration. Social engineering, as Sorokin has called the application of sociological know-how to the realization of social objectives,[5] must have community backing, unlike theoretical sociology which describes the culture as it is.

The student in this course will hopefully get experience in critical reading of research studies and newspaper reporting on family events, an acquaintance through literature with family patterns not within his present experience, an ability to discuss the family issues in plays and reports presented on television—in short, a whole repertoire of analytical skills that he will continue to sharpen all his life. He will need these skills in his personal, professional, and citizen roles. As a citizen, he will aid or discourage social engineering.

---

5 Pitirim A. Sorokin, *Social and Cultural Dynamics* (New York: American Book Publishers, 1937).

5

the individual and his relation to family and society

Who am I? How did I come to be the way I am? How can I change what I do not like about myself? Why am I attracted to some people and not to others? These and many similar questions are asked by all of us at various points in our lives.

By some definitions, society is the totality of interacting personalities sharing a common culture. Culture or civilization, as we have noted, can be material or nonmaterial, and includes all the folkways, mores, and laws. When these latter cluster around a particular human need or set of needs, they comprise a social institution, like the family, education, and the economy. If I am one of the personalities interacting in a society or a subsociety, how did I get the personality—values, attitudes, ways of coping—that I have? According to Cooley, whose views are still widely accepted, the personality comes from the very process of interacting. Later thinkers have emphasized that since the process of interacting does not cease, we keep changing and developing new facets to our personality all our lives. While we carry some of our previous ways of functioning into a new neighborhood or into a new circle of friends, these new influences begin to affect us. "You seem like a new person," one of your old acquaintances may exclaim, meeting you after several years.

THE INDIVIDUAL AND SOCIETY

The individual is a product of his society. This may make some of us uncomfortable. Some of us like to think of ourselves as self-made, as the people we are despite our families, despite society. To what extent is this possible? First let us consider Cooley's ideas, which the famous economist turned sociologist first expounded in 1929 in his book, *Social Organization*.[1]

Cooley emphasized what he called primary groups (the family, the neighborhood, and play groups) as the main links between the individual and society. The child becomes a social being and develops a concept of self through interaction in small, intimate groups. These "significant others" in our lives, family members and peers, transmit the cultural heritage to us and reward us by approval for acceptance of their language, ideas, attitudes. The self, Cooley concludes, is a looking-glass self, derived from the reflected appraisals of the significant others in our lives. We internalize their approval, and thereby develop values without being aware of the process.

We even learn what our sex is by accepting the word of significant others.[2] "That's a good girl," says mother. "We men must stick together," says father. Is it good to be tall or short, blonde or brunette, thin or fat? Societies transmit their notions of the ideal physical characteristics; these may change as life conditions change. Thus, in a society where survival is difficult and food is in short supply, the fat person has status; his weight proclaims him as a person who has access to the society's resources. When there is a change in the economy and affluence spreads, the ideal mate image may change to a person of slim lines.

[1] Charles Horton Cooley, *Social Organization* (New York: Charles Scribner's Sons, 1909).

[2] ". . . gender identity and role are not preordained by genetic and intrauterine events alone, but . . . psychosexual differentiation is largely a postnatal process and highly responsive to social stimulation and experience." John Money, "Sex Errors of the Body," in C. Broderick and J. Bernard, eds., *The Individual, Sex, and Society* (Baltimore: Johns Hopkins Press, 1969), p. 299.

Cooley was not alone in his emphasis on primary groups as pivotal in the creation of the individual's selfhood. George Herbert Mead spoke of the self as a social product. "The individual experiences himself as such, not directly, but only indirectly, from the particular standpoints of other individual members of the same social group." [3] Freud's concept of the superego, with conscience or ego ideal deriving from the social and psychological interaction that takes place between the child and early parent figures, differs mainly in the emphasis—some psychologists think the over-emphasis—on the importance of the first five years in personality formation.

Current terminology would see Cooley's primary group as a psyche group rather than a task-oriented group. Many secondary rather than primary groups fall into the latter category. Thus a study group may get together to prepare for an examination, a bowling club to enjoy a particular sport together, a trade union organization to achieve particular goals, and so forth. Cooley saw the primary group as characterized by caring, by responding to the individual as a whole person rather than as a brain for exam-taking or as a strong arm for bowling, and by relationships for personal satisfaction rather than for personal gain.

Not all these distinctions hold up firmly in analysis. Cooley was convinced that this caring and responding and personal interaction could take place only in small groups. Some would classify a whole kibbutz of fifty to several hundred members as possessing many of the attributes of a primary group, with daily intimate interaction, caring, a sense of belonging, and sharing. A Hutterite settlement might similarly be regarded as a primary group, or several large primary groups, since men dine together and women dine separately, as do the children from age three to fifteen who live in age-graded groups.

Moreover, it must be remembered that while Cooley's groups had the potentialities for playing primary group roles, they did not always fulfill these at the turn of the century nor do they always do so in their modern counterparts. The rejecting family or the competitive peer group may create an inadequate sense of self in the individual. The neighborhood may have been superseded in recent decades by the school as a primary socializing agency. When Cooley was writing, the public school was a relatively little developed institution and only a small percentage of boys and girls completed more than elementary grades. But again, the classroom may function in a psyche-enriching or a task-oriented manner. How many classrooms have you experienced that were significant in the development of your sense of self and personality enrichment? Some consider the two mutually excusive and hold that the teacher cannot convey

---

3 George Herbert Mead, *Mind, Self, and Society* (Chicago: University of Chicago Press, 1934), p. 133.

total acceptance of the student and at the same time grade his accomplishments. This begins to resemble the conditional love of the parent who offers affection on condition that the child complete certain tasks, get certain grades, or behave in certain ways.

WHAT THE PRIMARY GROUP
OFFERS THE INDIVIDUAL

What the primary group offers the individual is so important to his development that if one primary group, say the family, does not serve in this way, another will be sought out, perhaps the peer group. Specifically the primary group:

1. Offers the individual emotional support. By accepting him as a whole person, with contradictory and unresolved needs and often conflicting aspirations, it allows him to communicate frankly, to reduce his defenses, to develop feelings of trust and the ability to love. The individual, no matter how "independent" he feels himself to be, is sustained by group support. Even the iconoclast, the maverick, the deviant needs to feel that some people whose opinions he cares about—his reference groups—accept him. This is why banishment has been such an effective mechanism of social control. Solitary confinement is dreaded. In ancient societies where the stranger was treated with great cruelty, to banish someone was to doom him to misery and death. Medea in the play by Euripides begs to be allowed to remain when Jason urges her banishment so that he can take another wife in safety from Medea's sorcery. *Meidung* or ostracism of the individual who has offended the community is so effective in Amish and other subsocieties that recantation is not long delayed. The contemporary weapon of the middle-class parent, "Go to your room," suggests temporary withdrawal of group support.

2. Mediates between the individual and the larger environment, the nonprimary organizations. The family explains the child to the school, to his classmates, to his team. "He is very sensitive." "He has a toothache." "He did not understand the homework." Or it explains an adult to his place of work, his fraternal society, his church. "He is ill and must remain in bed." "He must attend a funeral." "He is so exhausted by the overtime work that he must spend Sunday morning in bed." The primary group may of course overmediate—overprotect, make too many excuses for him—and keep the individual from developing into an adult who is ready to assume responsibility for his own behaviors.

3. Recognizes him as a person, an individual, with particular needs and characteristics. The family may fail to perform this primary group function if it compares the siblings and expects all of them to be alike.

4. Confirms in the individual a sense of goal and purpose. Through the primary group, the individual is bound to the aims of the larger society.

This latter function of the primary group raises some questions about the family in rapidly changing times. If the aims of the society are in process of change, the family may be teaching its members loyalty to outmoded aims. Thus, black parents socialized in a period when deference to whites was life-preserving may try to inculcate such attitudes in their young who may then feel alienated from "Uncle Tom" types of parents. The white counterpart is equally likely. White parents may be teaching their children prejudice toward blacks and other groups in society who will no longer tolerate the mistreatment. As a result, these children feel alienated from parents they consider backward, or from all the older generations whom they hold accountable for the wars, ethnic hatreds, sexism, and other ills plaguing the society.

This gap between the values taught by the family and the values of a rapidly evolving society becomes even more crucial in a situation of revolution. Some families in 1776 were undoubtedly still committed to the former traditions and loyalties; some royalist families left these shores. In more recent days, the Russian and the Communist Chinese revolutions are examples of the need the changed society felt for weakening the power of the traditional family lest its influence go counter to new societal goals. After a decade or two, however, the family itself begins to change as children bring back to it new views learned in school and other socializing agencies. The family once again becomes the tie that binds the individual to the aims of the larger society.

Each person in a society has felt in unequal degree the impact of various primary groups in his life. Even brothers and sisters in the same household have been exposed to different combinations of group influences. Their parents have related differently to each of them—the first-born, the first son, the last child, the only daughter. Parents too had their selfhood formed in a variety of primary groups and carry into their childrearing practices and attitudes the values they had introjected. Is it any wonder that parents do not find it easy to agree with each other in childrearing?

MEMBERSHIP IN OTHER GROUPS

In a large complex society the individual belongs to many groups, both primary and secondary. For one person his family may be his most important reference group; he cares most what his kin think of him and he strives to incorporate their values into his own decision-making. For

another person, his peer group may provide the norms by which he lives. The norms or the definitions of what is acceptable behavior for a given group may be in conflict among primary groups. Thus some parents in the slum may not accept the neighborhood norm of stealing; their teachings go counter to the street gang norms. Which group, family or peer, is to be considered more important by their children? Where the family commands few resources—low pay and menial work make for low status of the parent not only in the achievement-minded world at large but also in the family—the children of such homes are more apt to make peers rather than kinfolk their reference group.

Must we be conformist, always adopting the norms of others as our own? From the foregoing, it must be evident that each of us accepts and incorporates into our functioning the norms of various groups in our society. While in our early years we make few choices and rely mainly on our family members for our ideas as to what is right and wrong, as soon as we are part of other groups in the school, in the neighborhood, in churches, and others, we have to begin the process of defining our own life philosophy, setting our own goals, and choosing among the value systems that come to our attention.

Each of us is a conformist—or a con-normist—to some degree. Some accept traditional norms; some seek out groups that are proposing and living by new norms. Even if our new reference group is one that deviates from conventional norms, we are in lesser or greater degree conforming to the new norms. To be devoid of all norms, all group allegiances, all sense of right and wrong, is to be in danger of anomie, the sense of alienation from society that develops from disgust for hypocrisy, contradiction, and confusion, with no countervailing ideals, goals, or plans.

The impersonality of mass society goes against each individual's needs for group cohesion, for caring about people and being cared about. We ourselves can struggle against such tendencies. Involvement in an effort to create warm human bonds and a society that fosters such human relationships may be the individual's best mental health insurance.

ROLES IN THE PRIMARY GROUP

Our personalities are shaped by the roles we play in primary groups. We are not only acted upon but actors in the lives of others in our families and peer groups. Even in the nuclear family a number of relationships are open to us, depending on age and sex: husband–wife; father–son; mother–son; father–daughter; father–son; brother–brother; sister–sister; brother–sister. Some of these will be lacking if there is an only child or siblings of only one sex, to be sure. Others will be added if there is a remarriage, and children of one marriage are brought to live together with children of the other marriage, and then the couple have their children: father–stepdaughter; mother–stepdaughter; brother–step-sister; sister–half-brother, and so on. One out of every ten children in the United States is being reared by stepparents. Even if divorces do not increase, and the rate of divorce has been more or less stable since the high-point at the end of the Second World War, the cumulative effect of remarriages is likely to make the stepchild and stepparent experience even more common in the coming decades.

The rules or norms specifying our rights and obligations in these roles keep changing. Is it the same to be a husband, a son, a wife, a daughter, a brother, a sister today as it was in previous decades of family history? Is the role quite different in various subcultures? If role definitions keep changing, can a young man and a young woman choose among them and decide to retain these traditional elements as well as incorporate newer possibilities? Is the choice completely free? Or do societal expectations influence the way the roles can be played, the amount of stretch in role definition permitted at a given time and place? An article appeared in a popular magazine in the mid-1960s, and described negative community responses to a husband's decision to run the household and take care of the children while his wife was the main breadwinner. Now, a few years later, community receptivity may have changed, in degree at least, under the impact of Women's Liberation writings and speeches.

While there are limits to role interpretation, particularly if role reversal is involved, there are many choices; the choices both reflect and further form our personalities. There are also choices in the timing. When do we add additional roles to those already being played? Thus some wives and mothers enter a gainful employment role as soon as pre-schools are available, some wait until the children are in their teens. Some roles we play simultaneously and some serially. Think of all the roles you are playing right now: student; son; brother (daughter, sister); grandchild; nephew; member of the dramatics club or the swimming team; after-school employee (sitter, bag-boy, saleslady, waiter); steady date; volunteer social worker, teacher or aide in hospitals, slums, nursing homes; maybe uncle or aunt to your older sibling's little ones. Is there a conflict among the roles? Is it hard for a man to earn a living and play the father role to everybody's satisfaction including his own? Is it hard to be a student and hold a job for twenty to forty hours a week? Can the busy mother play the glamour-girl role which middle-class-wife role expectations include? Is the student role threatened by efforts to play the role of boy friend?

An anthropologist has reminded us of the abruptness with which some societies ask for role changes. Ruth Benedict suggests that adolescent storm and stress may derive not so much from physiology but from cul-

Men in most societies have played a relatively small role in housekeeping and childrearing. Newer conceptions of shared roles have developed in some communes and are generally part of the ideology of Women's Liberation movements. This father in a Scandinavian household is not a "househusband" but is doing his share of kitchen and child care chores.

Enrico Sarsini, Life © 1969 Time Inc.

tural discontinuity in American society, the demand for responsible and independent conduct after puberty so soon after submissiveness and dependency have been rewarded as appropriate traits.[4] Neither parent nor child is prepared for the swift transition. Perhaps better education will help both to prepare for transition from one stage to the next.

Since personality develops in primary groups and these occur in a particular social setting with different stratification levels and ethnic influences, as well as varying interpretations of the potentialities of men and women, the next chapters will look briefly both at socioeconomic variables and ethnic ones in families and their individual members and at the reemergence of feminism as a significant influence on personality and role.

---

[4] Ruth Benedict, "Continuities and Discontinuities in Cultural Conditioning," *Psychiatry*, I (1938), 161–67.

the individual, the family, and the eth in "ethclass"

The primary groups in an individual's life help determine not only his concept of self, but also his life style, life chances, and the stereotypes others have of him. What does "He's a rich kid" or "She's Puerto Rican" call to mind for you? Can we forget class and ethnic differences? Should we? Can we understand ourselves without seeing our roles as members of a subculture?

DEALING WITH DIFFERENT GROUPS

Every large society that has groups with diverse heritages has several choices as to how the differences among groups shall be handled. Three major choices are assimilation, segregation, and pluralism. At various points in American history one or the other of these approaches has been emphasized. At present it could be said that all three are operating at once, with great gaps not only between theory and practice, but also among various theories.

assimilation

The assimilationists had the hope that an American family would evolve out of all the diverse racial, national, and religious strains that came to these shores. The melting pot theory held that a new individual, an American, would emerge from attempts to blend various cultures. Each person, regardless of his origins, would have equal opportunity to develop his potentialities and to influence the goals and institutions of this country. Some critics point out that in the back of the minds of some assimilationists was an assumption of the superiority of the Anglo culture and a desire to have all other groups melt into the Anglo model. Proof of this is seen in the demand that all schooling be conducted in English, as well as the emphasis on the early settlers, the English common law they brought with them, and English literature. The millions of immigrants who came here in the 19th and 20th centuries, mainly from Europe, but from other continents as well, were not encouraged to share their cultural riches with others. Indeed, the children of immigrants were rewarded as the public school system developed in earnest in the early 20th century to the degree that they blended into the Anglo model. This was harder for dark-skinned children and for those whose body types did not fit the favored northern European standards.

segregation

The slavery period of American history lasted some two hundred years. The first United States census, in the 18th century, showed almost three-quarters of a million slaves. Shortly before the Emancipation Proclamation in 1863 there were four million slaves and about a half million free Negroes. Not assimilation but segregation was American policy for all black people, slave or free. These forced immigrants were not permitted to retain their original cultures, diverse as these were in the various parts of Africa from which they were captured, nor were they encouraged to follow the Anglo model. Even marriage was denied them, let alone the establishment of families that could have transmitted the original languages and customs. It was more convenient for the slave owner to be able to sell off men and women and children separately and to reduce the affections and loyalties that might have hampered this commercial enterprise. The only exceptions could be found in the house servants who had opportunities denied the field hands to absorb the Anglo culture, the modes of speech, dress, and skills that were valued in this country.

pluralism

The third alternative, pluralism, is theoretically based in concepts of group identity and the need to retain original cultural differences in order to sharpen that identity. The firmest supporters of this approach in the past have been religionists; quite recently groups that have been rebuffed in their efforts at assimilation have also adopted a pluralistic outlook. This is in dispute among black leaders. Some consider pluralism a necessary transitional philosophy to help restore pride in black people and raise their status. Assimilation is seen as a distant goal to be accomplished when black people and white of equal education and occupational achievement join together naturally. Some consider pluralism an end goal and do not look forward to assimilation.

Critics of pluralism consider it the annihilator of the American dream. They urge that the whole concept of pluralism has a shaky foundation. It assumes that people can separate out along primary group lines and yet get together in secondary associations, particularly work groups, on an equal basis. The pluralist wants his race, his nationality, his religion to be the determinant of family and friendship interaction, with interfaith and interracial marriage discouraged as well as social intermingling of any kind. But he expects to get together with people of other races and religions at work, with no favoring in hiring and promotions of those in primary group association.

While industrial societies are basically universalistic, that is they assign work opportunities on the basis of merit, of individual skills regardless of family and other intimate group connections, some degree of particularism persists nonetheless, with opportunities and rewards distributed according to the individual's membership in particular social groups. The individual has to have the skill, to be sure, but his selection over others with equal skill is influenced by less objective factors. All of us are familiar in some degree with this, especially in trying to capture scarce summer jobs. Having an uncle in business does not hurt, especially if his business associates owe him a favor. They might as well take his nephew as office boy rather than one of the "strangers" who are applying. If some degree of nepotism has been characteristic along with the greater influence of universalism, will increased pluralism make this disappear or enlarge its operation?

Another criticism of pluralism is that it favors the traditional elements in any group and can hamper change. Thus certain aspects of a culture are retained not because they are sources of enrichment in individual or family lives but because they promote group identity, distinguish the group from others which do not have those particular cultural characteristics. Any number of examples can be suggested which could get members of a class arguing hotly.

A further questioning of pluralistic theory involves the lack of place for those who have crossed group lines. Marriage across nationality lines has increased with the rise in education. While this is rare in first-generation immigrant families, it becomes more likely with each generation. Often the nationalities are those that have a common church. Research in New Haven showed a rise in intermarriage among Polish, Italian, and Irish families for several decades after the turn of the century. Marriage across religious lines has also increased. Can the children of these cross-nationality and cross-faith marriages fit neatly into one slot on the pluralistic shelf? "I am an American" embraces all. Does the individual claim to be, and will the group let him claim to be, an Italian-American, a Mexican-American, or whatever, if he is one-fourth Italian or Mexican, or one-eighth or even half? Should he be forced to make a choice among his ancestors?

These issues will concern us for decades to come. Meanwhile there is considerable influence on our personalities and the kinds of families we can create exercised by various attitudes toward our ethnic origins on the part of employers, housing managers, medical personnel, and others who buy our talents or sell us services.

CHANGING GENERATIONS OF
IMMIGRANT FAMILIES

While there is no one American family, and statistical averages cloak significant differences in family lives, there are some norms toward which all kinds of American families converge. This is most clearly revealed in the change in successive generations of the originally immigrant family. The biggest wave of immigration was in the early 20th century, adding some 22 million to the 19 million in the previous century. Of course, except for the indigenous Indians, all Americans are "ethnics," descended from one group or another which came here from other countries, seeking, but not always willing to grant, greater freedom to work and worship. Even recently, according to the 1960 census, our families included 34 million people of "foreign white stock," that is, people with at least one foreign-born parent. The number would of course swell if we included people with at least one foreign-born grandparent.

These 34 million are second-generation Americans, the immigrant parent being first-generation. (The layman's language sometimes reveals that he thinks of the first to be born here as first generation.) Among them are 4.5 million or 13.3 percent whose foreign-born parent came from Italy, almost as many with a German-born parent, more than 2.7 million with a Polish-born parent, and about 1.7 million with an Irish-born parent.

The most numerous first-generation Americans at present are Puerto Ricans in the Northeast and Mexicans in the Southwest. Both groups are more recent "United States-ers" than they are Americans. Until Puerto Rico achieves independence, the child born on that island is already an American; he requires no visa to come to the mainland. Mexicans who cross the border into the United States are newcomers, but they join a large group who are descended from landowners and workers who were long settled on territory that only later was annexed to the United States.

The consideration of immigrant families and acculturation to new family norms may well include the many millions of blacks who moved from the rural South to the urban North, first in response to labor recruitment in the First World War, and more recently to join kinfolk and escape the more disadvantageous pay levels and the more limited citizenship opportunities of the southern states.

changes in the Italian family

What are the norms toward which second- and third-generation families move? Research on the southern Italian peasant families which dominated early 20th century migration shows a series of changes that find their counterparts in other ethnic groups. Rural migrants tended to bring patriarchal forms with them, but urban living and the nature of the economy brought modifications in relationships. Even in the first-generation family, the father began to lose his high status within the family or if it was fictitiously maintained, it was rarely evident in the third generation. The oldest son similarly began to lose both status and responsibility. The adult-centered household in which children were expected to live for the parents moved toward the child-centered one. The mother, expected to remain in the home, began to enter gainful employment. It is noteworthy that the textile and clothing industry, formerly counting on the needle skills of Jewish women from Eastern Europe, by the 1940s and 1950s had mainly Spanish- and Italian-speaking workers. As mother-in-law, too, the control over sons' wives decreased.

While the assumption of male superiority was little shaken, there was some recognition by the second generation of girls' abilities. The tradition of early marriage did not require very great modification since the

American norm was moving downward. While high birth rates were still regarded as an index of male virility, they began to lower with recognition of children as economic liabilities in the urban setting and with the secularization of society which encouraged departure from the biblical injunction to be fruitful and multiply.

Divorce began to be accepted. In Italy itself new legislation now permits this mode of handling marital unhappiness. The sharp distinction between the good girl and the bad girl weakened since slum living permitted less protection of the girl by family members and the double sexual standard came under attack in the larger society. It was less possible to perpetuate the curious dual ethical system which made the prostitute a frequent supplement to monogamy and yet forbade the open discussion of sex within the family.

Endogamous mate selection, which had originally limited choices to fellow-villagers, changed to permit at first marriage outside the nationality and then some marriage across religious lines. The formality of husband-wife relations which enjoined any demonstration of affection in public, particularly, but even in front of family members, began to give way first to a toleration of such behavior in their married children and by the third generation a new definition of spousal intimacy.

The changes did not occur equally throughout second- and third-generation populations. Socioeconomic class is a significant variable that we shall soon examine. Moreover, the change from generation to generation meant that the children growing up may have incorporated contradictory values of the grandparents by direct contact with them and of the parents who themselves may have represented an emotional kaleidoscope of new and old ways.

Young men who want to help in the care of the infant or in household chores often have to wrestle with their own ambivalences and with the disapproval of elderly male relatives. The student working with this book can often trace some of his present attitudes toward family relations to grandparents or greatgrandparents either directly or as some of their ideas about family relations were transmitted to his parents.

DISCRIMINATION AGAINST ETHNIC GROUPS

While there has been movement toward common norms, not all families and their members are equally acceptable in housing, marriage, and employment opportunities. A wall of discrimination still separates some ethnic groups from full participation. Stereotyping is still common. In an effort to be regarded as an individual and not be assumed to carry many of the traits attributed to a group, some people change their name, anglicize it to fit into the Anglo model, and some seek to change their physical characteristics by bleaching hair, snipping noses and ears, even eyelids.

Research on ethnic prejudice indicates its irrationality, often based on fear of the stranger, and its functionality, often based on material and psychic gain. But neither the irrationality nor the functionality vanishes through preachment. On an intellectual level we may concede that not all Scotsmen are stingy or all Jews greedy for money, and in any case, it is not wholly reasonable to admire the one group and condemn the other. On the same level we may also admit that pigmentation is not a reliable indicator of skills and potentials. We may be more reluctant to admit our personal gain in reducing the number of people who compete for the job or the promotion with us, or in increasing the number who are available to us at lower pay rates, not to mention the pleasant glow of knowing that even if we don't amount to much we are by cultural definition superior to people in *that* group.

Even when we are related by marriage to people of other ethnic groups and have some degree of intimate interaction on levels of equality, we may be victims of the self-fulfilling prophecy. We interpret all their behaviors in terms of our stereotypes, judging more harshly personal weaknesses of alcohol consumption, overambition, conspicuous clothing choice, and the like, than we would if they had occurred among "our own kind."

Our personalities are affected by racism and, more broadly, by ethnic prejudice, which permeates the society and is often transmitted through the family. Either as oppressors or oppressed, and we are usually both in relation to different groups, we decrease the level of trust and openness and deny ourselves, or are denied, many human interactions that can be enriching. Self-understanding may include recognition of the degree to which we are flawed and goals of self-improvement may include reduction of ethnocentrism.

In much the same way, our personalities are affected by the neighborhoods to which we have access. We may be comfortable only with our own ethnic group because of an initial bonding that derived from common language. Lack of economic alternatives may become defensively perpetuated. When our overtures are rebuffed, we may say about people of other ethnic origins that we did not like them anyway. This sour grapes philosophy may get incorporated into our functioning and prevent our reaching out again. On a mass scale, sorely oppressed groups may have to be for a time overassertive of their superiority to convince themselves they are indeed normal and not only legally but emotionally entitled to the full rights of citizenship. The positive side of "Black is beautiful" and "La Raza" is the mental health benefit of self-appreciation and unity. On the negative side is the exclusiveness and the fragmentation of human bonds, which, to be sure, did not start with these new movements.

RELIGION AND ETHNIC GROUPS

Our personalities are affected by religion and our individual and family definitions of religiosity. The stereotypes of nationality and race often intertwine with those of religious creed, although religion has more elements of choice than nationality and race. While there is some "passing" from one race to another, it is the product of several generations of decision-making (mate selection, etc.) and not open to everyone.

Nationality, too, is not easily changed in a single generation. The Russian emigré who went to France after the Revolution was not accepted as a Frenchman although by now his children or more likely his grandchildren have merged into the French culture. A change of religions, however, or a position of agnosticism or atheism, can occur at the will of the individual, perhaps several times in a lifetime. This choice both is an expression of personality and influences the further development of the personality—in large part by defining with whom the individual will interact, how much contact he will maintain with his family of origin, and new ethical standards for his behaviors.

While the major religions of the United States are usually classified as Protestant, Catholic, and Jewish, these broad categories can mask significant differences among the families that adhere to them. The Protestant family of Appalachia, where mountain preachers tell them that poverty is a holy state and that God is more pleased when people are satisfied with their lot, and where the family pew is a rarity, does not have the same values or the same personality traits as the Protestant family in middle-class suburbia. The contrast between the Oneida Community and a Shaker Community, both eschewing marriage but with very different views of sexuality, suggests the varied personalities drawn to and shaped by these religious beliefs.

Protestant families, numerically preponderant in the United States, are diversified in their folkways and mores by the more than 200 sects they adhere to and by the varying interpretations of proper behavior within each sect. There is little family research to indicate the kinds of strain in the relationship when, for example, a strict Methodist marries a more liberal one, although some sociologists have begun to question a concept of interfaith marriage limited to unions across the major religions.

Among Jewish families, adherence to one sect or another (Orthodox, Conservative, and Reform) affects the personalities and self-images. The Orthodox come closest to the traditional family of the *shtetl*, the Jewish community of Eastern Europe no longer in existence. The procreative aspect of marriage is emphasized, the oldest son has special prestige, the father is emotionally distant from the son, an avoidance technique is used to bolster respect and fear, strictly endogamous mate choices must be made, and ritual is used to reenforce conceptions of male superiority. The other sects have been more influenced by newer ideas of sex equality, father-child emotional closeness, and mate selection outside the group.

Family research has failed to make sufficient distinction among Jewish families. We do not know whether the "Jewish mama," the mother-martyr who is overinvolved in her children, is a feature of the Orthodox home more than of the others, or whether the concept is of little ethnic significance, with a "Jewish mama" present in every child-centered American home.

Another distinction among Jewish families is their adherence to an interpretation of themselves in nationality or religious terms. As mentioned above, religion can be more easily changed than nationality, a point of consideration for those leaving the Jewish family or marrying into it. While all religions have some influence on culture, folkways, and mores, nationality implies not only a cultural entity but a peoplehood, a belonging that is less open to choice. Jews who think of themselves as not merely belonging to a religion, but to a nationality, continue to count as Jews those who have long since ceased to practice the religion. Moreover, they do not consider the issue a matter of individual choice.

The effect of the threat to existence introduced by Hitler's annihilation of millions of Jews, among the many millions of people of all ethnic backgrounds who lost their lives, has tended to create a defensive unity among many Jewish families. Many think of themselves as a nationality as well as a religion, and a large proportion of these are Zionists, committed to building up Israel as a Jewish homeland. There is much dissension with other Jewish families who define their loyalties differently. Within a given Jewish family, the generational split is not always in the predicted direction; sometimes the younger generation takes up the Zionist or traditional position with parental disapproval.

Catholic families, too, are not monolithic in allegiances or in interpretations of responsibilities. Priests and nuns reflect a new ferment, a split between traditional and modern emphases. The large Catholic family is no longer ubiquitous, as the use of family planning by Catholics is only slightly less than among Protestants.

Family research, including study of delinquency, often ignores these complexities and takes "religion" as an independent variable, usually defined in frequency of church attendance. The research often does not acknowledge the diversity of the religious variable as it affects family functioning and personality development.

In assessing the effects of his ethnic background on his own development, the student may be inclined to ascribe to himself the characteristics he finds in cross-cultural studies that discuss some of his ancestors. It cannot be too strongly emphasized that the American crucible, even if it is not a melting pot, vitally affects the personality traits which develop here. Mechanical applications of what is known of family and individual functioning in another country cannot be made. Perhaps one illustration can suffice here. The rate of suicide in Japan has long been high. Does that mean that the Japanese-American is prone to suicide? Statistics show this is not so. Similarly, schizophrenia, high in Japan, is a rarity among mainland Japanese-Americans.

The personality constellation typical within a given society is further affected by other than ethnic factors, such as socioeconomic class, with its variations of occupation, income, education, and sex identity, which we will examine in the next two chapters.

7

the individual, the family, and the class in "ethclass"

The individual and his family exist and function not only in ethnic groups but in strata differentiated by income, education, and occupation. The two variables of ethnicity and class create different life chances and family patterns, and are so intertwined in their impact that one sociologist has coined a single word to suggest this duality, *ethclass*. There are not just Protestants but upper-, middle-, and lower-class Protestants, with the sects themselves distinguishable along class lines. There are not just Jews, however they define themselves in terms of nationality or religion, but upper-, middle-, and lower-class Jews. There are not just Catholics, but upper-, middle-, and lower-class Catholics. There are not just agnostics and atheists, but upper-, middle-, and lower-class people who do not affiliate themselves with any church. Are these just abstractions in the minds of social scientists or are they everyday realities in the lives in over 200 million Americans?

SOCIAL STRATIFICATION

Social scientists were late in coming to terms with the existence of stratification in this country. It was and continues to be an uncomfortable topic, difficult to reconcile with ideal images of democracy, equal opportunity, and upward mobility. The facts are just as hard to pin down as are the theoretical issues in stratification.

How many social classes are there? The original typology developed by Warner included six classes: upper-upper, lower-upper, upper-middle, lower-middle, upper-lower, and lower-lower.[1] Hollingshead developed a five-class typology because in the Midwest where he did his studies, there were too few long-established rich families to constitute an upper-upper class.[2] The rich families there were newly rich as of the last generation or the generation before.

Warner found that in small towns where people knew one another, they distinguished one family from another in terms of class; they thought of this family as middle class and that one as lower class. This *subjective* classification was found to correlate highly with *objective* indicators such as occupation, income, and education levels. The objective indicators were found to correlate highly with one another. Thus, although Warner developed an Index of Status Characteristics, devised by weighting occupation heavily in the total but allowing for source of income, house type, and place of residence, and although Hollingshead developed an Index of Social Position, consisting of occupation of head of the household, education, and place of residence, many family studies have tended to economize in selecting a research sample by taking only occupation or income.

Can you think of the few exceptions in our society where there is notable lack of correlation among occupation, income, and education? For example, high education or high occupational prestige and low income: ministers. High income and low education: racketeers. The college student can be temporarily poor, but his status is not low. He can occupy menial positions, but he is rarely classified by the odd jobs he holds.

Because the phrase "lower class" seems to connote to many some moral

---

1 W. Lloyd Warner and Paul S. Lunt, *Social Life of a Modern Community* (New Haven: Yale University Press, 1941).

2 August B. Hollingshead, *Elmtown's Youth: The Impact of Social Classes on Adolescents* (New York: John Wiley & Sons, Inc., 1949).

The father-absent family is an ethclass phenomenon in American society. It is found most often among the poor, but varies among ethnic groups. There are regional differences, too, with poor Appalachian white families and southern black farm families more apt to emphasize patriarchal patterns than poor families in urban areas.

Reproduced by permission of **The New York Times.**

failing or inadequacy, few of us are willing to designate ourselves or our families of origin as lower class. Sociologists have tried to pretty up the nomenclature by the use of "blue-collar" or "the common man" or "working-class" or some other euphemism, but this has often introduced confusion in comparing the findings of one study with another. Some studies do not distinguish between two levels of lower or middle class, with the result that their findings seem in contradiction. Actually in some instances they are talking about the lower-lower and in others the upper-lower, but simply calling either "lower class."

DETERMINING CUTOFF POINTS

One of the biggest difficulties in stratification studies is the determination of cutoff points. Above what income should a family be classified as rich, below which as poor? Are we a middle-class society? Or a lower-class society? What educational levels do we associate with one or the other? Which occupations are middle-class, which lower? Are poor white families more like poor black families or more like middle-class white families? How influential is the class factor when matched with the ethnic? How upwardly mobile are we as a society? What is the rate at which lower-class families move into the middle class? How much downward mobility is there? At what rate do families in the middle class move into the lower?

There are no easy answers to these questions. For one thing, family income must be related to living costs in one year as opposed to another, and these living costs vary for different regions of the country. Reformers tend to exaggerate the amount of poverty, while government officials tend to underestimate it. For example, there is little agreement on amount of income which falls below providing an adequate budget for an urban family of four members. Have living conditions of American families bettered since the Depression of the 1930s when Franklin Roosevelt referred to one-third of the nation as ill-fed, ill-clothed, and ill-housed? Does the popular concept of "the affluent society" do a disservice to realistic thinking about standards of living for millions of American families?

education

The table of family income in the Appendix may come as a surprise to many middle-class students who think of "most" people as having money to spend. Similarly, the student who is working with this book is an exceptional person in education level, even today when completion of high school and attendance at college are markedly higher than a decade ago. Going to college is still not a majority phenomenon for youths of college age. For every young man or woman in an institution of higher education, there is more than one at work or looking for a job or in the military. Graduation from college is an even more decidedly minority phenomenon. As recently as the 1960 census, less than 8 percent of adults twenty-five years of age and over had had four or more years of college. Even if the 1970s double this, which some consider an over-optimistic prediction, the college graduate will still be untypical of American educational levels.

Educational level affects not only family income, but also the kinds of family life, including degree of communication between husband and wife and level of satisfaction in the marriage. One research study did not start with the hypothesis that high school graduation is an important variable in family patterns, but the data on blue collar marriages began to point up a significant split between families of high school dropouts and those of high school graduates. Further studies are needed to see whether it is what is learned in school that facilitates self-understanding and abilty to understand other family members or whether it is the same qualities in the individual that allow him to cope with the frustrations of school life that allow him to cope with the frustrations of domestic responsibilities. Or does the satisfaction that comes with meeting societal expectations of academic performance enhance the self-image and permit more satisfaction in other relationships?

Certainly there are other ways of learning than in an academic setting. In past centuries, an apprenticeship system was more common than formal schools. Abraham Lincoln, like so many lawyers of the 19th century, read law and studied on his own, rather than going to school. And many of us know very interesting and able people who had little formal education but kept learning through reading, travel, conversation, and activity in community concerns. There are many proposals under way at the present time to give the student more initiative and more flexibility in determining his educational path.

Can you think of ways in which one proposal or the other would affect the family? Age at marriage? Number and timing of children? Parental and spousal responsibility? Self-image will undoubtedly be greatly affected by educational reform. "Dropout" may become less of a pejorative when possibilities of "dropin" increase. There is little question but that the complexity of society requires a more educated public and higher marriage and family standards also require more education. The issue for the next decade will be how education is to be acquired and the differential impact on family roles if some methods are favored over others.

CLASS DIFFERENCES AND FAMILY LIFE

Despite the lack of congruence in the definitions of lower-, middle-, and upper-class families among family researchers, few dispute the importance of income, education, and occupation levels in family functioning. How much illness and bereavement a family will experience; how much anxiety connected with job uncertainty; how much danger of crime and attack; how many of its members will spend time in jails and mental institutions; how children will be reared; how much reliance upon kinfolk rather than upon friends; timing, kinds, and frequency of sexual behaviors; when middle-age and old age are reached—all these and many more have been found to correlate with class.

Since class correlates with status and power, some families are more prestigious than others and are more powerful in decison-making for the community on local and national levels. Self-images are affected by our perceptions of our family's ranking in class, status, and power. The Protestant Ethic, the notion that rewards accrue to hard work in proportion to the individual's standing with his Maker, has allowed the rich to be smug and the poor to be self-blaming. The supernatural or religious element was a barrier to rational examination of the doctrine. When Marxist analysis saw contending classes and the instruments of reward and punishment in the hands of one class rather than another in different periods of history, it was often dismissed as "godless." However, other criticisms have begun to be heard of the notion that the poor must get poorer and the rich richer. In the late 1950s and all through the 1960s it became evident that lower-class families needed opportunities to exercise power, to develop confidence in their own abilities and the justice of their new demands, and that these opportunities would come only if they organized themselves into pressure groups to counter the pressures exercised by the middle and upper classes. This often appears menacing to the other classes, but leadership for lower-class movements has often been supplied by middle-class men and women, convinced that in the long run all Americans would gain by broader sharing of income and power.

must there always be classes?

The question arises for class differentiations among families as it has arisen for ethnic differentiations. Will there always be a class structure and different life chances for boys and girls determined at birth?

There is no classless society in existence anywhere as yet. There have been small classless enclaves or subsocieties such as the kibbutzim and the Oneida commune, but never one in which a whole society lived without class advantages or disadvantages. The socialist countries, China, the

Soviet Union, Cuba, Poland, and half a dozen other countries of Eastern Europe, believe that when they enter their communist phase they will achieve this; when automation permits such abundance that each person has access to all material goods he needs and when people have learned such cooperative attitudes that no instruments of force are needed, "the state will wither away." Some consider this an impossible dream and point out that even if antagonism among classes has decreased and a sense of all working for common goals exists since no individuals or families own the means of production, nonetheless there is nothing to ensure that socialism will move into the communist phase—not only because this phase presupposes all countries have joined in the socialist movement, but also because present advantages for some groups motivate them to keep those advantages for themselves and their families.

reducing class differences
in socialist countries

The headstart that children of lower-income families gain in the existence of a wide preschool network is already enjoyed by children in middle- and upper-income families. Similarly the leveling efforts of after school centers where homework can be supervised by professionals and creative work be undertaken in art and technology clubs still leave the advantaged groups somewhat more advantaged. There are, to be sure, many devices to reduce the sharpness of class distinctions in daily functioning, such as rents based on income to permit people of varied occupations and educational levels to live in the same neighborhoods and in the same multiple dwellings, rest homes and sanitoriums in resorts once restricted only to the wealthy, and prices for goods graduated to favor meeting basic needs for all.

There are many devices to create a sense of pride in any work, however menial, through pictures in the paper of manual workers with exceptional records, and through naming typists, street-cleaners, farmers to consultative and legislative bodies. (The lack of contested elections permits the Communist party to make these deliberate selections.)

There are also many devices to ensure that children from working-class families get some of the admissions to higher educational institutions. Free tuition and the ubiquitous scholarships or stipendia make the boy or girl less dependent on family income. However, the children of intellectuals still have some advantages in some universities deriving from habits of study observed at home, language skills, and familiarity with academic procedures and relationships. The mass media in the socialist countries keep alive the expectation of a classless society and this undoubtedly affects self-image by offering assurance of equality "some day."

CLASS DIFFERENCES IN THE UNITED STATES

In the United States most families at the low-income level tend to be fatalistic, to perceive their lack of achievement as their own fault or the fault of some vaguely defined group of oppressors, to accept the blows of poor health, low pay, layoffs, more children than they want, as part of life. Even at the height of the Depression in the 1930s, when millions lost their jobs, there was little understanding of the larger social forces at play. An unemployed husband was compared unfavorably with a cousin who managed to get a job. In family quarrels, the unemployed son or father was upbraided as lazy, inferior, dumb. Many children ran away and fathers deserted to escape the reproaches.

Similarly at the present time, especially among ethnic minorities, there is a tendency for family life to become the arena for battle that belongs in the work world. Increased understanding of the social factors in the lack of individual achievement has been a positive mental health factor in some homes.

the family and class differences

Among social scientists there is some dispute as to which causal factors are more easily amenable to intervention strategies in improving family life. Some see the family as standing on its own shoelaces and not able to take a step forward. Others see the family as responding to the stresses in the environment. In the first case, the conclusion is to work with the families, to get husbands and wives and parents and children to appreciate each other more, to use their resources more effectively, to put aside alcohol, extramarital sex, gambling, and other escape devices. In the other, the conclusion is that employment, housing, education must improve for the lower class, and particularly for the millions of poor families. With better pay for their work, with homes to live in that are not rat- and roach-infested, without depressing disrepair, and with schools which compensate for inadequate sleeping and studying conditions, families will be able to function more effectively, contributing to individual happiness, and developing role models that enhance self-image.

Not only social scientists but social workers differ among themselves in their emphases. Among those who feel the "social" has been too long omitted from social work, that individual and family guidance has not sufficiently been accompanied by efforts to change the social environment, to reduce the stress factors, to increase job opportunities, there is recognition that habits of a lifetime are not quickly changed and that supportive casework, as well as neighborhood organization, must accompany initial changes in material living conditions.

Middle-class and upper-class family members are inclined to see themselves as having different values than the lower class, and to use this as a rationalization for maintaining the status quo. Some social scientists feed into these stereotypical conceptions of value differences. Thus one study mentions as typical values of the various classes "graceful living" for the upper class and "getting kicks" for the lower class. Is it more likely that both share the same values, both want material comfort and the niceties on the one hand, and excitement and release on the other? Both are possibilities for the upper class but the lower class must forego graceful living in light of the realities. Does this mean lower-class families do not value graceful living or does this mean that there is a wider gap between what they want and what they get than among better off families?

If values are the criteria for choosing among alternatives, the way we judge the relative worth or importance of ideas, events, things, can two groups have the same values but make different choices because the consequences of the choices would differ for each group? The upper class and the lower class may both love having fresh flowers in the home. If the upper class chooses to spend part of their income on flowers, this will not threaten survival, but will contribute to gracious living. If the lower class buys fresh flowers this may threaten other values including survival. Can we conclude that the lower class does not value gracious living because it buys a can of beans and forgoes the flowers?

To what extent is the lower-class rationalization, "He doesn't need to go to school," when the son's earnings are needed for a family with a sick member or an unemployed father, an expression of a value (anti-intellectuality) and to what extent an accommodation to the realities (immediate payoffs toward family survival versus deferred gains)?

value stretch

One sociologist has suggested the concept of "value stretch," the idea that lower-class families share the same values as middle- and upper-class families but must stretch their interpretation of them to fit the grim realities of daily existence. This concept is congruent with situational ethics, which see right and wrong relative to time, place, and circumstance.

Middle- and upper-class families have different resources at their disposal in making choices. There are fewer premarital pregnancies among middle-class girls. Is this because they are more conversant with contraceptive methods or have different sexual behaviors than lower-class girls? Fewer middle-class homes rear an illegitimate child. Is this because fewer babies are brought to full term, with abortions more available to the wealthier, or because adoptions are less possible for minority groups within the lower class? The lesser bargaining power of the girl in the poor

family may lead her to settle for consensual union; the girl in the middle-
or upper-class family can afford to wait until legal marriage is offered, both
because she has more skills and can pursue career goals until her marriage
conditions are met, and because her affectional needs are more likely to
be met by parents who are less overwhelmed by material deprivation and
more aware of child development as a result of better education.

Some see this kind of reasoning as offering a copout for destructive
decision-making. Each individual, they would say, must be held fully
accountable for his own choices. The girl in the poor family is under
pressure in slum neighborhoods for early sexual involvements, but she
knows the consequences and can choose peer disapproval instead of going
along with the norm. Similarly, the boy in the poor family can refuse to
engage in the illegal acts with a neighborhood gang. Indeed, there are
some individuals in all settings that resist the norms and find an isolated
path through the fields of expected behavior, but if one kind of reasoning is a copout, the other may also be in a different way. It allows maintenance of the status quo and does not try to change the conditions that
lead to one kind of decision-making rather than another.

In any case, knowing that members of lower-income families already
suffer from impaired self-images, it may be conducive to good mental
health to help them appreciate their own strengths and take pride in
survival against odds rather than keep criticizing them for value stretches
that middle- and upper-class people would also make if faced by the same
stresses and handicaps in daily life. One scene in the film version of
"Grapes of Wrath" is revealing in this regard. Two garage attendants
watch the weary Joad family pull away in their decrepit truck, determined to reach job opportunities in California and to keep the family
together, and shake their heads disapprovingly at "people who are more
like animals than anything."

Some educators have been reluctant to teach about social class differences, holding that such knowledge will not cause classes to "melt away."
"After all, the majority of children will live out their lives in the lower
sections of the status hierarchy. . . . It may be 'better' for people to
believe that failure is the result of bad luck and lack of ambition rather
than the result of the system," they say. Such perpetuators of myths,
writing in teacher journals, have little faith in the possibilities of improvement. In study of the family, it is essential to be aware of all the
variables that affect family functioning. Ethclass is a major variable. Related to ethclass but part of the whole society's ethos are attitudes toward
women which greatly influence the kinds of families that develop. We
will explore this in the next chapter.

8

sex and role: who's who in the family

SEXUAL IDENTITY

From infancy on, the individual learns to identify himself as a member of one sex or the other. Not only his parents but other family members and even the casual passerby remind the child that "boy" or "girl" classifications are important. In some cultures the casual encounter is guided by clues to gender, with pink or blue blankets or ribbons, allowing the appropriate comment, "What a lovely little girl" or "What a fine big boy." The child learns early that mother or father is the predetermined model. What that model is, and how pronounced the distance between male and female models is, depends on the culture or subculture at different times in history.

It can be said that physiology proposes and culture disposes. Gender identity has an anatomical–hormonal base but the implications for functioning as a man or woman are written by folkways, mores, and laws. In all societies, to be sure, the sex of a baby is normally determined by fertilization of the X chromosome from the mother by either an X- or a Y-bearing chromosome from the father. A girl results when two Xs meet, and a boy results when the combination is XY. But few generalizations can be made for all societies concerning the questions raised by the anthropologist: "How do male babies and female babies learn their social roles in different societies? What types of behavior have some societies classified as male, what as female? How like have some societies felt males and females to be—and how unlike?" [1]

Differences can be far-reaching even in geographically contiguous areas. "As we . . . halt our carriers . . . in some strange and unexplored village, we do not know which sex will be adorned and which unadorned, whether the shaved head peeping over a bush is that of a man or a woman, whether the distant figure inching its way to the top of a forty-foot coconut-palm is a man, because women should not do such dangerous and difficult things as climb palm-trees, or a woman because climbing palm-trees is a job for children and women." [2]

What is called role reversal because it goes so completely counter to the sex-role allocations of most societies can be encountered among the Tchambuli people in New Guinea: "Here the . . . women, brisk, unadorned, managing and industrious, fish and go to market; the men, decorative and adorned, carve and paint and practice dance-steps." [3] Lest the reader revert to stereotypes of the artist-dancer which embody connotations of physical inadequacy, the anthropologist adds that the men are "bold and fierce head-hunters . . . often six feet tall, well set-up . . ." [4]

factors in sexual identity

While it is generally accepted among social scientists that in most societies which come within written history there has been a tendency to assign the instrumental role to the man and the expressive role to the woman, there is more disagreement as to the implications to be drawn for the future. Is anatomy destiny, as Freudians insist, or does modern technology lead the way to new definitions of masculinity and femininity that encourage convergence of sex role and equal sharing of status positions?

---

1 Margaret Mead, *Male and Female* (New York: William Morrow & Company, Inc., 1949), p. 32.
2 Mead, *Male and Female*, p. 48.
3 Mead, *Male and Female*, p. 74.
4 Mead, *Male and Female*, p. 48.

In the 19th and early 20th centuries, American women marched for the right to vote. More recently the goals have been broadened to include equality of economic opportunity as well as restructuring basic social institutions such as the family. The group shown here could be found in almost any American city in the early 1970s.

John Olson, Life © 1970 Time Inc.

These are not remote questions that have little importance in the student's present life. Each person's self-concept embodies notions of the proper way to be a man or a woman, the expectations we have of the mate we select, the children we rear, the kind of job we hold, and the way we relate to others in our sexual behaviors. Gender identity and every facet of our functioning intertwine even as ethnicity and social class were found to do. And to complicate a complex personal and social history, ethclass intertwines with sex-role allocation. In the United States, the question is not only what it is to be a woman or a man, but what the culture permits and expects of the black woman on various class levels, of the white woman on various class levels, the Mexican-American woman, the Japanese-American, the Catholic woman, and so on for men too in all the various ethclass categories.

the origins of sexual identity

On the one hand, inquiry is pertinent to how things came to be the way they are, why no matter what role men play in most cultures, those roles are defined as more honorific than the roles played by women. On the other hand, inquiry must be made both as to how present concepts of sex role are perpetuated and, if changes are desired, how the socialization process must be altered.

There is little agreement on why men have been defined as superior over the centuries. Some hypothesize that physical advantage in musculature, and hence in group survival which depended on battle with nature, gave men an early edge for throwing their weight about in the domestic group. Others stress the short tether with which the woman was tied to childbearing and childrearing needs at a time of high infant mortality and demands for sons to aid in hunting and food gathering. Some may question whether either is sufficient explanation, given (1) the notable contribution women made to group survival by sharing the instrumental role at a time when the family was a production unit; and (2) the possibility of utilizing mechanisms common in later centuries for lengthening the tether through wet-nurses and child-care surrogates in the form of older siblings, grandparents, and joint dwellings for very young male children.

THE NEW FEMINISM MOVEMENT

There is more interest at the present time, both in historical factors and contemporary practices in sex role allocation than for several decades. The issue of who does what and who should do what was a lively one in the 19th century when industrialization began to make evident that traditional definitions of age and sex hierarchies in the family could not be maintained. In previous centuries, stretching back for more than 2,000 years, women had not played a prominent part in discussing alternative roles. A handful of outstanding women intellectuals in each century had existed and had forged individual life styles for themselves—the hetirae of ancient Greece, medieval court ladies who encouraged the development of chivalry, and a few female rulers in England and Russia.

These women were not the leaders in any movement for female equality, however. On the contrary, they tended to have great contempt for members of their own sex, such as Queen Victoria who opposed female suffrage. Most of the utopias depicting expanded roles for women were dreamed up by men, beginning with Plato who in his *Republic* would do away with the inferiority attributed to women in ancient Greece and allow women to be selected along with men for the ruling class according to individual merit. It is noteworthy that men and women in that class were to be freed from family obligations; rearing of children was considered a lowly calling, fit only for the lowest ranks of the class-stratified population.

By the 19th century, however, women themselves took the lead in the U.S. and in several European countries and organized to demand new rights, notably the right to vote. The women's liberation movements of the late 1960s appear to be a continuation of the unfinished work of the previous century.

HOW HAVE SEX ROLES BEEN DEFINED AND PERPETUATED?

The student who examines his own definitions of masculinity–femininity and his own conceptions of the lines he would draw between male and female roles is likely to find some ambivalence in his feelings and some ambiguity in his thinking. He is also likely to find some lack of congruence between his thinking on these matters and that of his classmates. There is even more of a gap between his thinking and that of the older generations. A research study of college students, their parents, and their grandparents showed increasing acceptance at the present time of equal roles of husbands and wives in decision-making and sharing domestic chores.

the Parsons and Zelditch theory

For some decades American family study has been influenced by a theory advanced by sociologists Parsons and Zelditch which came out of small-group research by Bales in laboratory settings.[5] Bales had found that small groups were more cohesive when the instrumental and the expressive roles were not played by the same individual in the group. The instrumental leader kept his eye on the task to be performed, and did not allow considerations of feelings in the group to keep him from con-

---

[5] Talcott Parsons and Robert Bales, *Family, Socialization, and Interaction Process* (New York: The Free Press, 1955).

centration on productivity. The expressive role was performed by another group member who helped the group to feel comfortable with one another and increased motivation to stay together.

Parsons and Zelditch assumed that the family, like the laboratory small group, had to have husbands and wives play different roles, "complementary" roles, for the family to remain an effective, integrated group. However, this theory has not been borne out by several recent research studies in the United States as well as in Belgium and France. These studies show families to be more cohesive, better able to communicate, more satisfied, and better able to solve their problems when the spouses are less specialized in their roles and less traditional in their definitions of masculine and feminine tasks. One study found that those given maximum opportunity to play the instrumental role were better able to play the expressive role (encouraging, approving, etc.), while those denied the opportunity for instrumental leadership were more limited in their ability to offer emotional support.

Parsons and Zelditch had assumed that complementarity or specialization would enhance role effectiveness. Their assumption is, despite empirical research to the contrary, widely shared by many American families who believe that the family, and indeed the nation, would fall apart if traditional sex role definitions were not maintained. Even when modifications are introduced into a family, they may suggest the old lines of thinking: She is working outside the home to help her husband, he is bathing the baby to help his wife, and so on.

DIFFICULTY IN CHANGING
SEX ROLE DEFINITIONS

Although many demands of women's liberation movements are recognized as just or worth trying, they are not easily introduced in a society permeated in its academic and mass culture with assumptions of male superiority. Many individuals and institutions are not consciously "sexist." They have been socialized to stereotypical role definitions in so many ways that they have internalized patriarchal notions of dominance and subordination. Women themselves are often resistant to new role definitions and prefer familiar limitations to the unfamiliar, and therefore often threatening, broader horizons of activity.

Women's liberation movements have forced sociologists and psychologists, guidance counselors and physicians, and many other professionals to take a look at their own sex role assumptions. As part of this ideological house-cleaning there have been a number of critical examinations of courses of study, of advertising, of textbooks, of stories for preschoolers, and above all of the way families teach their children the relationship of gender to personality traits, educational and job opportunities, and roles in marriage and the family.

Several studies have shown that the helping professions produce clinicians, teachers, counselors who reflect the sex role stereotypes of their culture and, in their relationship with students, patients, and clients of the two sexes, perpetuate traditional notions of sex-appropriate behaviors. The sex role stereotypes, or consensual norms and beliefs about the differing characteristics of men and women, result in a double standard of mental health.

One study of seventy-nine clinically-trained psychologists, psychiatrists, and social workers, all actively functioning in clinical settings, the majority with graduate degrees, found they had different concepts of mental health for men and women and these differences paralleled the sex-role stereotypes of American society. In the view of the clinicians, healthy women differed from healthy men by being more submissive; less independent; less adventurous; more easily influenced; less aggressive; less competitive; more excitable in minor crises; having their feelings more easily hurt; being more emotional; more conceited about their appearance; less objective; and disliking math and science. Women whose behaviors went counter to these stereotypes were adjudged by both men and women clinicians to be less healthy.

As for social grounds, they reject the "adjustment" notion of health and urge their fellow clinicians to consider the following: "The cause of mental health may be better served if both men and women are encouraged toward maximum realization of individual potential, rather than to an adjustment to existing restrictive sex roles." [6]

How did the clinicians come to hold these sex-role stereotypes which differ little from those held by the layman? Clinicians were raised in the same family structures, went to the same schools, read the same newspapers, listened to the same radio, heard the same jokes, and, in short, responded to the same stimuli which influence the thinking and the self-concepts of all Americans. It is significant that the women clinicians in the above study agreed with their male colleagues as to what typical men and women are like. This is congruent with other studies that have found women valuing men above themselves. One writer calls this "group self-hate," and likens it to the self-devaluation of many minority groups.

A recent study found that when college girls were given identical articles with the author's name changed to indicate male or female, the girls rated the "male" authors higher on style, competence, profundity, and so forth. A checklist used in any classroom today can tap similar feelings about willingness to use a woman doctor in case of illness, a

---

[6] Inge K. Broverman et al., "Sex-Role Stereotypes and Clinical Judgments of Mental Health," *Journal of Consulting and Clinical Psychology*, 34, No. 2 (1970), 1–7.

woman lawyer for a court case. The reluctance may lessen when the issue is discussed. Under present admission policies, women's abilities have to be higher than men's. However, the initial hesitation is a clue to the pervasiveness of our assumptions about male superiority.

THE FAMILY'S INFLUENCE ON
SEX ROLE DEFINITION

The family's influence on the individual's self-concept, as a male or as a female, may start with the color of infant clothes, but soon encompasses all aspects of functioning. Sex role learning in the home has some social class correlations, the middle class tending less than the lower class to create in the children awareness of sharply segregated sex role patterns. Nonetheless, all children learn sex-role behaviors deemed appropriate by their parents. In a heavily masculine-oriented culture these behaviors and attitudes are likely to reflect higher esteem for the masculine over the feminine.

The toys bought by the parents or as gifts by kinfolk and parents of friends invited to children's birthday parties, the stories read to children, and television for preschoolers teach children at an early age the behavioral patterns associated with one sex in contrast to the other. Boys learn earlier than girls that certain behaviors deemed effeminate are to be avoided, especially if adults are present to offer negative feedback. Since behaviors traditionally defined as masculine are regarded as superior, there is less pressure on girls to avoid "tomboy" activities than for boys to avoid "sissy" ones.

Tests indicate that by age three boys and girls choose different toys and games when offered a choice. They have already learned before the school years what parents expect of them. Teachers reenforce these learnings as do siblings. Children with older like-sex siblings acquire sex role ideas more rapidly than the only child; boys with older sisters and no older brothers are slower to make sharp differentiations. Teachers respond differently to the questions asked by boys and by girls even in nursery school, and teacher expectations play an even greater part in later school years.

OUTSIDE INFLUENCES ON
SEX ROLE DEFINITION

Picture books for very young children and textbooks for elementary classrooms continued into the 1970s to depict girls as passive, mere onlookers to boys' venturesomeness, more interested in appearance and clothing and less ideas and achievements. Content analysis in several recent studies in the United States and in Scandinavia indicate boys are not only quantitatively predominant in pictures and text, but their range of activity is much greater.

In Sweden it was found that picture books in the 1960s continued to show cars, trains, fire engines for boys, and dolls, furniture, and cooking utensils for girls. The situation was similar in other Scandinavian countries. A Swedish report [7] tells of research in Norway and Finland which shows textbooks for seven- to nine-year-olds in all three countries characterize boys and girls differently. "Girls are invariably described as conscientious, dutiful, tidy, and helpful, but at the same time passive and timorous. Boys are sometimes described as aggressive towards each other, disdainful to girls, untidy and forgetful, but without any suggestion of reproach being made for these failings. Boyish pranks are acceptable but one never comes across girls blithely contravening the rules laid down for them."

The same Swedish report indicates that textbooks for older boys and girls ten to eighteen also perpetuate traditional attitudes despite lofty equalitarian ideals enunciated in the syllabuses adopted in the early 1960s. Whether the subject matter was mathematics, languages, literature, history, or civics, the textbooks lagged behind the actual social scene. Mothers were usually shown doing housework "though the fact of the matter is that 46 percent of the mothers of the children who use these books go out to work." [8] In arithmetic books in both Sweden and Denmark men are mentioned in relation to activities outside the home while calculations involving female subjects tend to be limited to consumer purchasing. Literature anthologies underrepresent women writers and focus mainly on male characters. In civics textbooks, contradictory messages are provided in text and pictures. Thus a textbook widely used in 1968 stated, "There is no reason to suppose that women cannot cope with, say, the following jobs just as well as men: typographer, electrician, plumber, architect, engineer, welder, goldsmith, construction engineer." But the book not only offered twice as many illustrations of men at work as of women, but women were mainly pictured in nursing, secretarial, textile, and other traditional fields.

The Swedish report hailed some developments of the late 1960s, such as a new family science textbook that gave the older student a more democratic view of the relation between the sexes and a history textbook which contained a special chapter on women in society. It seems likely that pressures for changes in textbooks will be effective sooner than in the mass media. A Swedish study in 1968 analyzed the cartoon strips of five daily newspapers. Some of the series are of American origin—"Dennis the Menace," "Blondie," "Bringing Up Father." The researcher con-

---

[7] Karin Westman Berg, "Schoolbooks and Roles of the Sexes," *Hertha* (1969), pp. 48–53.

[8] Berg, "Schoolbooks and Roles of the Sexes," p. 49.

cluded, "The strip cartoons have little to tell us, for they are almost entirely dominated by the roles of yesterday. The boy characters were marked by 'stereotyped virility,' the girls by 'drabness.' " It was felt that for the millions of readers of popular cartoon strips, "they have a viciously conservative influence." [9]

In the United States, content analysis studies reveal similar problems. Traditional views of sex roles permeate storybooks for the younger children and textbooks from elementary through high school. Some efforts are being made to change this. A bill was proposed in the California legislature in 1970 to ensure that textbooks reflect more equalitarian sex role allocations. Book reviews are beginning to call the attention of authors and publishers to the slanted material they provide.

A group of distinguished feminists who are psychologists and educators met with the woman producer of "Sesame Street" and brought to the latter's attention how this popular television show for preschool children was reenforcing sex role stereotypes. Among the unintended learnings were those about male activity and female passivity, as a consequence of which "boys learn to disparage girls, and at even greater psychological cost, girls learn to disparage themselves." [10]

Concrete recommendations were made for eliminating sex role stereotyping in future planned episodes both quantitatively and qualitatively. Increased female model presentation was suggested to change the 2 to 1 ratio of male characters to female. Episodes that show girls as considerate and concerned to please others should "avoid the implication that it is in any way sex-linked. The emphasis upon pleasing others throughout the socialization of girls may well be a major reason that women seldom become critical, imaginative thinkers, capable of asserting and defending their ideas." [11] Also recommended was the introduction of counterstereotypic characters such as the woman architect, research scientist, musician in a symphony orchestra. Portrayal of the working mother was suggested to reflect the realities in children's lives. In 1970 two out of five of the thirty million women who go to work have children under eighteen and among the children under six who are the target population of the TV show, more than a quarter of the white mothers, and even more black mothers, are engaged in gainful employment.

FACTS AND REALITIES ABOUT WOMEN

Despite the negative messages about their characters and their capabilities that American girls get throughout childhood from parents, siblings, and

---

9 Margareta Ekstrom, "Hi Blondie: Read Betty Friedan!" *Hertha* (1969), pp. 18–23.

10 Jo Ann Gardner, "Sesame Street and Sex-Role Stereotypes," *Women: A Journal of Liberation*, 1, No. 3 (Spring 1970).

11 Gardner, "Sesame Street and Sex-Role Stereotypes," p. 42.

the mass media, the effects on motivation and achievement do not show up with full clarity until adolescence. Their school grades which have compared favorably with those of boys through elementary school and into high school begin to drop. Girls develop anxiety about intellectual and occupational achievement as possible barriers to popularity and marriage. The girl who is motivated to achieve may feel she is defying conventions concerning women's proper roles, and worries about the possibility that what she has heard directly and indirectly may be true, that intellectual achievement signifies loss of "femininity."

The Freudian emphasis on "the intellectual defense" of women against their own sexuality has penetrated many writings, both professional and popular. The higher test-anxiety scores of women compared to men may be the result, one psychologist suggests, of the fact that the woman student worries not only about failure, but also about success as a result of this conditioning to put negative interpretations on achievement. One recent study of undergraduates at the University of Michigan asked the men students to tell about John and the female students about Anne in response to the following: "After first-term finals, John (Anne) finds himself (herself) at the top of his (her) medical-school class." The psychologist found among her students that "the most frequent Anne story reflected strong fears of social rejection as a result of success. The girls in this group showed anxiety about becoming unpopular, unmarriageable, and lonely." In contrast, the men projected "a grand and glorious future" for John. "There was none of the hostility, bitterness, and ambivalence that the girls felt for Anne." [12]

the effect of the female
sex role on men

This "psychological oppression" of women, as the new feminists term it, has its negative effects on men too. While the social gains may be great, because men can count on making more money even in the same job, encountering less competition for promotions with women considered less eligible, obtaining more geographical mobility when it is their job alone that is the determinant of family location, or gaining more prestige offices in professional associations, there is a psychological reverse side of the coin too.

Sex-role stereotypy, according to a 1970 statement of the Association for Women Psychologists to the American Psychological Association,

---

[12] Matina Horner, "Sex Differences in Achievement Motivation and Performance in Competitive and Non-Competitive Situations" (Doctoral dissertation, University of Michigan, 1968). Summary report in *Psychology Today,* 3, No. 6 (November 1969), 36–38, 62.

causes for men "crippling pressure to compete, achieve, produce, to stifle emotion, sensitivity, and gentleness." This statement urged "a society which allows equal opportunity for the realization of full human potential in all persons . . . in which there are no sex roles, but only roles determined by one's abilities and interest; in which problems of sexual identity will disappear because society will no longer demand that one's identity be founded on one's sex."

ARE THERE INHERENT DIFFERENCES BETWEEN MEN AND WOMEN?

Such statements may call forth either uneasy jocularity, with the inevitable invocation of the hackneyed "vive le différence," or equally uneasy questioning as to whether biology makes any difference at all. In the latter camp are psychologists who view with alarm the blurring of men's and women's roles and who maintain that gender identity will be threatened by interchangeability of social roles for men and women. They do not insist on particular occupations being allocated to one sex or the other, but they maintain that the family roles should be different. This generally brings the analysis back to the traditional assumptions of men as aggressive, firm, stolid, etc., and women as passive, hesitant, emotional, etc. Inevitably the matter gets back to a nature–nurture dispute, with several refinements.

First of all, there are the facts of biology and anatomy. Erikson considers the difference in sex organs of men and women basic to personality difference. The male organ is one of intrusion, the female of receptivity. He generalizes to all male–female relationships from this one fact. However, recent research by Masters and Johnson calls into question the sexual passivity of women, and suggests that aggressiveness sexually and otherwise has been culturally encouraged in men and suppressed in women.

A biological fact is the "premenstrual syndrome," the headache, nausea, fatigue, depression, and consequent mood variability that distinguishes the functioning of women from that of men during the monthly cycle. Research has indicated that girl monitors in school settings are more punitive toward those breaking the rules in the first few days of menstruation and the few days preceding it. Also a majority of crimes of violence among women prisoners at one state farm occurred during the premenstrual week. Again, the problem of nature and nurture. To what extent do favorable environmental conditions, equal opportunity and status with men, mitigate the negative feelings that accompany changes in glandular functioning? To what extent can the regularity of whatever change does occur be regarded as a positive factor, making for predictability? Just as wedding dates are chosen with some consideration of the menstrual cycle, so too, it is suggested, the schedule for hazardous undertakings involving women can allow for temperamental deviation if this persists under favorable environmental conditions.

the mother role

The facts of pregnancy and childbearing are sometimes generalized to the woman's whole life. This may have been appropriate in centuries of incessant childbearing to ensure a labor supply at a time of high infant mortality. At present overpopulation is more a danger than society's failure to reproduce itself. The motherhood mystique, the high valuation of the mother role as opposed to spousal, work, and other roles for women, may represent cultural and institutional lag. While the existence of a "maternal instinct" is recognized for many of the lower forms of life, it is not equally acknowledged to exist on the human level.

Desire for motherhood has seen marked quantitative changes in this century. At present the average American woman is still in her 20s when she has borne her last child, ending her pregnancies more than a decade before her 19th century counterpart. Her longevity probabilities are far more favorable than ever before—on the average she is likely to live more than forty years after she has borne her last child. As the discussion of familism has indicated, she may not be given any extensive opportunity to persist in an active mothering role once her children are in their late teens. Traditional thinking which sees her primarily as a bearer and rearer of children seems to lack congruence with social realities.

the male's biological facts

The anatomical and physiological facts of the externality of the male organ, constant production of seminal fluid, the need for male orgasm as part of the reproductive act, these and others contrast with female biology. These facts are adduced to explain the male's greater sexual activity, sexual content of male conversation and dreams, and frequency of homosexuality, exhibitionism, voyeurism, fetishism, bestiality, and consumption of pornography. Yet it has already been suggested that nurture may be in part responsible for the suppression of female sexuality. Also, social expectations of male achievement may make sexual exploits substitutes for unreachable occupational and status goals. A society that lowered these expectations for men and raised them for women might find more congruence in their sexual drives.

An assumption of greater male sex drive as an innate characteristic might make prostitution an inevitable accompaniment of monogamy. Indeed, those who oppose the elimination of prostitution rest their case mainly on such assumption. Males in the United States are reared in a way that values sexual release over affection and companionship; women value the latter over the former. Again, it may be possible with the anatomical and physiological givens to create cultural expectations that lessen the emotional and sexual gaps between men and women.

THE SOCIALIZATION OF SEX ROLES

It is fruitless to weigh competitively men's and women's physical advantages and disadvantages, to match the chemical advantage of the Y-bearing sperm which ensures that more boys will be born than girls (in the United States about 106 boys born for every 100 girls) against female survival superiority (one female fetus is miscarried in the first trimester of pregnancy to every three male fetuses; 130 boy babies die immediately after birth as compared to 100 girl fatalities). It is just as useless to match inherited male defects such as hemophilia, color blindness of the red-green type, night blindness, and defective hair follicles against the female disadvantage in throwing and running because of angle difference at the joints or smaller lungs which handicaps them in fast or long-distance running.

The question is, What does a given society make of these differences? What cultural interpretation is attached to the differences and passed on to generation after generation through the socialization process? How far are those biological differences stretched to cover preferences and vested interests?

woman's place in history

For all of written history men have occupied the positions of power in each society in secular affairs and in religions. In ancient Greece, worship was led by males in the household even though goddesses shared destiny–determination along with the gods. The history of each epoch was written or sung by men. Essays, poetry, plays, and later novels reflected mainly male viewpoints. Misogyny crept into pronouncements and writings in all centuries. Women's rights were not uniformly limited in each society, however. Nor were writers uniformly misogynists.[13] Space will not permit detailing here the variation in woman's rights under the code of Hammurabi in Babylon, under Roman law, in Sparta, Egypt, and in Asia. What is most relevant to current thinking, the attitudes of students in today's classrooms, are those historical influences that are present today even if in vestigial form.

---

13 Katherine Rogers, *The Troublesome Helpmate: A History of Misogyny in Literature* (Seattle: University of Washington Press, 1966).

The Judaeo-Christian tradition is one which bred feelings of superiority in men and inferiority in women. One historian refers to the "furious misogyny" of the early church which saw woman as the Devil's Gateway, more prone to folly and vice than man and leading him into paths of evil. St. Paul blamed woman for the world's woes and marked a path of subjection for her to follow. "But I suffer not a woman to teach, nor to usurp authority over the man, but to be in silence." The espousal of celibacy as a virtue reenforced the view of woman as temptress. The same historian sees the Mosaic law as incorporating the superstition of primitive man concerning woman's uncleanness in menstruation and in childbirth. Women were impaled on men's fears of their own sexuality, in one interpretation of the early church position.

Modern psychology offers the interpretation that envy of woman's ability to bear a child (womb envy), which in preliterate peoples sometimes took the form of the couvade with the pretense that the father had born the baby, brought on the defense mechanism of reaction formation. Later modifications of doctrine brought acceptance of sexuality but only if put to procreative use. The relational function of sexual intercourse, the physical intimacy and companionship reenforcing each other in the marital bonds, was a conception that has emerged in relatively recent times.

On the secular level, writers perpetuated stereotypes, the printing press offering a wider arena for the battle of the sexes. Fear of women, as shown in the witch trials, alternated with contempt. The fear was not only fear of woman as a temptress, seductress, the unknown one with magical powers, but fear that she might slip out of her subordinate role. The learned ladies of Tudor times became the butt of the caricaturist. Ben Jonson equated female intellectual aspirations with lack of chastity. This view was to persist for centuries. It finds faint echoes today in mass media concentration on college girls' sexual behaviors—despite statistics indicating promiscuity tends to vary inversely with educational level. The fear that he might lose his position of dominance over women made the playgoer welcome any scene in which the "shrew" was tamed or the henpecking wife got her comeuppance.

Women were denied the right to intellectual development and at the same time criticized for their triviality, coquetry, and vanity. In Roman times, Lucius Valerius saw the logical connection. "Since women cannot hold public offices or priesthoods, what can they do but devote their time to adornment and dress?" For the masses of women in each century, the choices were hardly these. Endless toil, childbearing, and revilement were their lot, with no choice between public offices and intellectual development on the one hand or adornment and self-indulgence on the other. If history has largely ignored women in the upper classes, its pages are completely blank for the majority of women: slaves, farmers, factory women.

WOMEN'S LIBERATION

If women's position today is a great improvement over past centuries, why do the women's liberation movements attract so much attention of a negative and derisive kind in the mass media? The proposals made stir up the emotions of men and women. While there are many different women's liberation groups, with different emphases in their demands, all agree on the rights of women to equal pay for equal work and equal educational opportunity with equal choice among career alternatives. All recognize that thoroughgoing changes in woman's economic position and her status outside the family will change the family and the roles men and women play in family life.

The groups differ in their conceptions of short and long term goals in this regard. Some women fear that family changes will be very slow and urge bypassing the family in the transitional period. Some of them suggest doing without men, forming communes of women and investing their affectional, if not always their sexual, lives in members of their own sex. Critics point out that this solution creates two enemy camps and a new society cannot be built without communication and understanding between the sexes. Moreover, it encourages women to use men sexually in the same shallow relationships for which men have been criticized.

Other women's liberation groups urge the creation of a network of auxiliary institutions which would reduce the mother's involvement in childrearing and, by the employment of men as well as women in nurseries, kindergartens, after-school study and recreation centers, and the like, would create greater involvement of men. In the home a minimum of services would have to be provided the child, allowing maximizing of affectional relationships both between spouses and between parents and the children. The kibbutz pattern comes to mind. Tradition dies hard, however, and it must be noted that in the kibbutzim few men are involved in infant and child care, as is the case in Soviet preschool and after-school institutions, too.

Still other women's liberation groups are convinced that neither jobs in sufficient quantity and quality nor mass educational influences freed from sexism are possible in this society and seek a new economic base and a new set of values, such as decreased competitiveness, less emphasis on material possessions, elimination of sex as advertising bait, and more involvement with community goals than with the family.

As a result of women's joining together in caucuses and organizations, marching, protesting, picketing on the one hand, filing briefs and testifying before legislative bodies on the other, they have already effected many changes, particularly in matters where there is consensus. There is no agreement as to whether all special protection for women should be thrown out of the statute books, although recent court decisions indicate this is likely.

Middle-class women and those of the working class have different life conditions and different needs. In the professions there is less need for protection against hours and kinds of work that are a threat to health. When the woman in manual labor is asked to work overtime because it is more economical for the employer than taking on another worker for a few hours, she may not be able to refuse if her job is at stake. However, some working women, fearful that they cannot survive on present low salaries, are eager for the overtime and have joined with middle-class women in demands for relief from protection. Little consideration has been given to the effects on family life. It was these negative effects in the early history of industrialization that gave rise to the child labor laws and women's protective legislation of the 20th century.

minorities and women's liberation

Black women and Chicanas have not been as active in the women's liberation movements as their disadvantaged position in employment might have led us to assume. The women in these minorities see their menfolk as exploited too, and some of them consider the struggle for women's rights secondary to the achievement of equality for their whole ethnic group. In addition, there are some women who have internalized such a strong feeling of inferiority, to white people among the female counterparts of Uncle Tom and to males among traditional Mexican-American women, that they disapprove of women's participation in current protest movements. "Chicana" has an activist connotation and is not a designation uniformly accepted among Mexican-American women.

men and women's liberation

While some men share the goals of the various groups of women's liberationists and are convinced men will gain by new work and home arrangements, many men are angered, puzzled, resentful, vindicative. Either they see their girl friends or wives becoming discontented with traditional roles and ceasing to minister to men's convenience and sense of superiority, or they see no way in which the new demands of women can be met without major changes in the society—including the family as an institution.

There is uncertainty attached to any mass movement. Men in the forefront of change are less threatened than the masses of men who are fearful as familiar relationships begin to change. A married student recently said bitterly to his classmates in an undergraduate course, "My wife was doing fine until she heard all this nonsense about psychological oppression. Now she looks critically at our relationship. The women's lib hags are destroying my marriage." One male defense against this discomfort is to dub all women seeking equality as "hags," "dikes," "failures." The implication is that girls with plenty of dates and men wanting to marry them would be content, and it is sexual deprivation that drives them to hatred of the male.

While this kind of charge is understood by more experienced women, and indeed a degree of compassion may be felt for the pain it expresses, the longing to preserve the status quo, it is often frightening to the younger girl going through the self-questioning typical of adolescence. She may not find much parental support from a mother who views the women's liberation movements as a reproach to the roles she is playing or a father who sees his comfort vanishing as wife and daughter expect him to share household chores.

Women's consciousness-raising groups have sprung up all throughout the country to meet the need for exploration of their feelings in face of this opposition and to offer one another the emotional support needed to cope with criticisms of parents, husbands, and boy friends. Women's studies courses and programs in high schools and colleges, now increasing in number as educational institutions begin to recognize how limited curricula have been in providing opportunity for study of the history, literature, economics, and psychology of relationships between the sexes, will also provide intellectual and emotional underpinnings for new concepts of the self among women.[14] Perhaps more will have to be done to help men explore the pluses and minuses of changing roles, to see how they arrive at their conceptions of appropriate roles, and how fair solutions can be achieved.

---

14 Rose M. Somerville, "Women's Studies," *Today's Education* (November 1971).

9

who communicates in the family and how?

Families, it may be obvious to students, develop distinctive modes of communication. Students may be less aware that these modes are influenced by ethnic and class considerations. For the culture as a whole there may also be changing styles of communication as rights and status of family members are redefined with shifts in the economy. The Anglo tradition of self-control and reticence, the frontier tradition of substituting the fist or the gun for lengthy discourse, the immigrant's fearfulness of seeming an outsider—all these and other broad influences set limits to openness of communication. Expressive hand gestures, loud and emphatic speech, diverse body postures, meaningful nods, winks, pouts, and grimaces have been permitted on the modern theatrical stage but are generally frowned upon in ordinary discourse although there is no objective reason why this should be so.

THE ETHCLASS AND COMMUNICATION

Undoubtedly an ethclass explanation can be found in the ability of upper-class folk to be able to speak softly and yet carry a big stick. When plantation overseers and factory foremen can do your shouting for you, you may be able to afford the luxury of a gentlemanly tone of voice, just as the gentleman's "C" at Princeton bespoke assurance of a favorable economic destiny regardless of individual achievement. For women the fishmonger was the loud-mouthed lower-class model. An upper-class woman could speak softly to her servants and know she would be listened to attentively since economic survival depended on hearing employer demands. Parents could speak softly in a patriarchal setting, knowing that governesses and tutors were ready enforcement agents or, if less propertied, that the children had no rights the community would enforce and young people could therefore not afford the luxury of revealing even nonverbally their disagreement with a parental demand. *The Way of All Flesh* is a powerful story of the soft-spoken dominance of parents over children in the 19th century propertied class.

While there are ethclass differences in ways of communicating, together with a status hierarchy of desirable communication patterns that probably will not withstand logical examination, there are also national patterns that differ from one country to another. The bluff heartiness and easygoing familiarity that is said to characterize the American contrasts with the careful formality of Japanese interaction, as well as with the markedly changed but still less open British style since the Second World War. The proletarian Soviet society comes closest to the modern American pattern and contrasts with modes of address that prevailed in the formerly highly stratified Tsarist society.

COMMUNICATION IN THE FAMILY

In each society there are distinctions made in what can be said in public and what in "the bosom of the family." Communication among family members may not be as free as among peer groups, but by Cooley's definition,[1] all primary groups permit "letting your hair down" and expressing feelings more openly and on more matters than in secondary associations. This is relative to the given historical period, to be sure. The formality

---

[1] Charles Horton Cooley, *Human Nature and the Social Order* (New York: Charles Scribner's Sons, 1902).

that marked family interaction among the Chinese gentry in the 19th century was less than that found in communication outside the *tsu* (clan). Similarly the 19th century American child was taught to address adults, including his own parents, as sir or ma'am, but was given more leeway within the home than outside it.

A recent study of modes of address in four different situations, ranging from the parent entering the house after working or shopping, to the parent discussing something personal with the son or daughter, to the parent in conflict with the offspring, to casual parent–child encounters, found a sample of American college students using twenty-three names for father and nineteen for mother. While "Dad" predominated in all situations for over half the male students, the other half used "old man," "sport," and a variety of nicknames which would not have been possible in the 19th century when, in the same social class, more emotional distance between father and son was expected.

It is noteworthy that in this study the first names of parents were rarely used in any of the four situations by sons or by daughters. Avoidance of such status-equalizing terminology may not continue into the next generation, however, if present tendencies for first name use by very young children broaden. That parents have been addressed by a role name (mother, mom, father, dad, etc.) and children by individualized names may have reflected sharper generational distinctions in previous decades. The individualization of parents, children's perception of them in diverse roles rather than the parental role alone, and increasing informality in the adult world among colleagues and acquaintances may result in general acceptance of the first name mode of address among family members in the near future.

The role designation of grandmother and grandfather has already been found inadequate when the nuclear family relates bilaterally to the kin of both parents in contrast to unilateral patriarchal interaction. Some need has been found to distinguish maternal and paternal grandparents in direct address and in discussion about them. Grandma Jones of earlier decades bagan a trend that now takes diverse forms, from Grandma Mary and Grandma Betty to granddad and grandpa, to distinguish the two maternal and two paternal grandparents now that longevity rates make it increasingly likely for a child to know all four, as well as additional ones. Remarriage brings both new parents and new grandparents.

THE IMPORTANCE OF COMMUNICATION

Communication is a bridge but not a magic carpet in family interaction. This is noted here as a caution against a recent tendency to regard each family problem as basically rooted in poor communication. People can communicate openly and still have large value gaps of an alienating kind between them. The son explains why he wants to leave college; he is open about his feelings of disappointment in the educational experience, of impatience with economic dependency, of eagerness to try new ways of learning not to be found in the classroom. The parents (or one of them, as there may be a value gap between father and mother also which communication will not lessen) explain why they fear his leaving, that he may not return to obtain formal academic credentials, that this will make downward mobility likely, that he may have to lean on parents for partial support later when they face reduced income in retirement or in illnesses that accompany aging, and that they are embarrassed among middle-class friends and relatives as failures because their children did not achieve the expected diplomas, scholarships, and honors.

Each reveals feelings and needs. By openness of discussion they have laid on the table the variety of thoughts each has and have clarified their respective positions. Assumptions and interpretations are examined and proved, or discarded. "Dad, you don't want to see me leave because you never went to college and you want to get a degree through me." If this is true, the father may learn something about himself, although he may not at first admit it even to himself. Or, "Jim, we are to blame for sheltering you from work experience. We thought studying was hard enough and we wanted to give you every chance. As a result, we see now, you have little understanding of the work world and see it as more glamorous and allowing more independence than student life."

Many variations of the foregoing are possible. Frankness and respect for viewpoints imparted allow decision-making in light of a full range of feelings. Openness allows cross-questioning so that incorrect inference as to feelings and motivations can be put straight. Hypocritical covering up of one's own needs can be reduced. Thus, the mother who cannot sleep until her young teenager is home from a date can say, not "Come home by ten, so that you'll be fresh for that exam tomorrow" but "I have a heavy day tomorrow and need my sleep so do try to get home early tonight." This may still leave room for argument, but it will more likely proceed on open recognition of conflicting needs, and an accommodation or compromise among family members may be more reachable.

empathy

Empathy, or the ability of one person to see the situation as the other sees it ("to take the role of the other," in the language of George Herbert Mead), is facilitated by the communication process. This process is, of course, verbal and nonverbal. In the latter are included all the clues we give others as to how we are responding to their current behaviors. The student who yawns conspicuously, the teacher who turns his attention from the student who is reporting to the class, the class that looks at the floor or the clock instead of at the resource person—all these express feelings.

However, sometimes incorrect inferences may be drawn from the behaviors. The student may yawn despite interest in the class; his father was hurt at work and the whole family spent the night at his bedside. The teacher may not admit to himself that he listens more carefully to students of a particular cultural level, those with good speech, or higher social standing. The class may be looking at the floor not because of interest but because they feel the subject matter so intensely or because they do not feel free to confront the speaker with feelings they have been taught in the home not to express.

Empathy facilitates the communication process as much as it is facilitated by it. We talk to those we think will understand. Generational gaps may be widened by external conditions—how often they have a chance to be together, for example—but perhaps more influential is the feeling, "It's just no good talking; they just won't understand." Sometimes the defeating circularity can be broken into only by a professional counselor if the rigidity and sense of hopelessness of both sides make communication difficult and reduce empathy.

KEEPING THE LINES OF COMMUNICATION OPEN—HOW AND WHEN

Granting the desirability of maintaining open lines of communication, of continuing to learn more about oneself as perceived by others and about others as observed by oneself, there is still a question of how open such lines can be for maximal usefulness to reciprocal pairs in the family —husband and wife, parent and child, siblings. One school of thought, exemplified in encounter groups, calls for total revelation. "This is the way I feel about you, period." Another school of thought suggests that circumstances do alter cases, that we are more capable at one time or another of bearing up under different loads of truth and revelation.

This fact is evident in studies that find the hour before dinner a fertile time for dissension which may be carried on during the meal as well. While the opportunity for dissension may itself be viewed as progress, compared to the patriarchal household in which either silence was enforced during meals or the oldest male was given priority in expression, a pattern can be built up that maximizes bickering at a low morale moment for all family members. Given commuting and working conditions, those members in gainful employment are likely to return home in a fretful state in need of quiet, rest, and release from responsibility. Those members who were at home for most of the day may similarly have accumulated tensions in handling relationships with neighbors, the children, shopkeeper, and repairmen.

Preparation of the dinner may conflict with needs of younger children for homework help, peer contact by telephone, and the fatigue and bath needs of youngest family members. Where environmental conditions are favorable, spatially and climate-wise, recovery may be rapid and the challenge of coordinating diverse needs of family members may be met with a minimum of friction. However, even in middle-class homes, picking up toys, the unfinished sibling quarrel, the frustration of men and women trying to balance their spousal and parental roles may give off sparks which at a less loaded hour might not prove so dangerous to the family's stability.

Some psychologists urge families to think through their schedules so that the overload of tension at certain times of day and days of the week may be lightened. Some stress learning to quarrel constructively. Some sociologists point to restructuring the work day and the school day as one way of diminishing stress pile-ups.

Recently some firms in one country have been trying self-determination in choice of working hours, any eight within a longer time period. Thus the family that finds simultaneous departure of working and school members most convenient would choose different hours than the family which finds shifts of departure more conducive to harmonious relationships. Similarly, the return home, with travel eased by less concentration within a narrow range of hours, would give each family some degree of choice as to what works best for them. Watching young children eat may not be a joy to all fathers; some might prefer to have them fed beforehand so as to ensure a quiet meal alone with their spouse.

Open communication would allow patterns to be set that are most satisfactory for all. The communication may at first bring into the open all sorts of suspicions and hostilities, but many of these may be resolved either by more accurate perception after explanation or by an effort to change attitudes and behaviors.

The husband may say, "I don't like the children being in bed before I get home. I feel as though you shut me off from them deliberately and I become the feared stranger." The wife may weigh her own motivations, admit she is overinvolved with them and regards them as her recompense for lack of the excitement a job brings to life. Or she may justify her action on the ground that her husband had seemed so much more relaxed and uncritical when he had no obligations toward the children before dinner. He may recognize that he is ambivalent, and wants both the intimacy of interaction and the peace of their absence. The discussion may bring into question their present life styles and, while this may seem threatening to either of them, it may result in clearer recognition of the need to alter more basic relationships than dinner schedules suggest.

PROBLEMS IN COMMUNICATION

However, communication will not always bring clarification. Defense mechanisms may operate to reduce self-confrontation and deny motivation. A wife may not recognize that she needs her husband's company after a day with the children and her needs conflict with his and theirs. He may not consider it socially acceptable to acknowledge that children are sometimes a burden. Or they may have had such different backgrounds, academically or in families of origin, that one may take offense at the other's attempt to discuss certain points of disharmony between them.

This is particularly true in the sexual realm. Despite the urging of counselors that the couple discuss their contraceptive methods to see if either wishes a change, their positioning and frequency of sexual intercourse, their foreplay to ensure joint satisfaction, and perhaps above all the nonsexual family matters that may affect their sexual feelings about each other, there may be some reluctance on the part of one or the other to discuss such things. This may depend on the kind of sex education they have experienced, especially the explicit or the nonverbal messages transmitted in the families of origin that sex is dirty and only to be joked about in male peer groups or to be gossiped and hinted about in mixed groups.

factors in communication

Communication is affected by different expectations of the various reciprocal pairs. Sex stereotypes play a role here. A recent analysis of speech patterns and tolerance of voice level and tone indicates that childhood conditioning may influence the feelings reactivated upon hearing a certain volume or intonation. Shakespeare said of one of the women characters in *Hamlet,* "Her voice was ever soft, gentle, and low, an excellent thing in woman." The notion that strong, passionate speech, loud disagreement, and harsh complaint are the prerogatives of one sex can only create communication barriers. Similarly, the sharpness of distinction among public, home, and street language and assumptions concerning how much of the latter may be introduced into the home by either sex are in process of change. Communication can be hampered by a failure to agree on the language standards to be used, between husband and wife, parent and child, and same-sex and other-sex siblings.

LANGUAGE

Often it is not the language but the tone that is most offensive in family interaction. We are all empathic with the student who reported, "When my mother asks me to pass the milk at the breakfast table, she says it in such a manner that I feel like throwing the milk at her." We have all been the recipients of remarks that communicate to us that we are unpardonably forgetful of others' needs, that we take more than we give, that we are childishly self-concerned, and so on.

CRITICISM

While criticism is never easy to take and any obvious sugar coating of the bitter pill is more resented than straightforward negative evaluation, the family, because it is more likely to permit open expression among its members, must work out ways of communicating disapproval of individual acts while at the same time communicating love to the offending individual.

Some psychologists consider that awareness of elementary facts about human functioning is helpful. Anger creates a supply of adrenalin that activates the outer muscles. The clenched fist, gritted teeth, and blood-suffused face are symptoms of a body geared for an aggressive act. At least a few minutes are required for the return to physiological balance before any rational discussion can occur between husband and wife, parent and child, or between siblings.

A high level of feeling is a natural response in the many conflicts that can be expected in the intimate family group, but it is not an ideal atmosphere for decision-making and some reduction of intensity must be sought. There is communication, to be sure, when an angry husband hovers menacingly over his wife or the parent with upraised hand demands the child's explanation, but in an atmosphere of physical threat there is little possibility of useful discussion. It may be only a matter of minutes before the body relaxes somewhat and, with one or the other or both still angry, indignant, fearful, but to a lesser degree, the argument can proceed.

KEEPING THE ARGUMENT SPECIFIC

If there is a basic bond of affection among family members, restricting the discussion to the point at issue and not generalizing it to the level of character assassination allows the criticized member to preserve his self-respect even though he may eventually agree that a given act was irresponsible, foolhardy, lazy, etc. In the heat of anger much broader accusations may be leveled than the facts will warrant. To demolish the other person may be easy, but it is likely to be a pyrrhic victory.

Even if it is the final quarrel in a family about to break up, there is more to be gained by allowing the other person to keep his ability to function with some degree of self-confidence. Moreover, the winner in a family battle may be overly self-righteous, and prevented by a seeming victory from self-examination to see what both people had contributed to the disharmony. Since the nonverbal tells as much as the verbal sometimes, self-restraint must not only apply to choice of words but to gestures and facial expressions that may communicate contempt for the person rather than merely the act in question.

Psychologists have found that the person most open to the reality of his own feelings and able to achieve self-acceptance with a minimum of shame, guilt, and regret is more likely to communicate well with others. He has had practice in honest confrontation of himself without undue condemnation, and can extend these habits of analysis and sensitive observation to others. One counselor suggests that a useful device in any argument is the requirement that before an individual speaks, he must restate the views of the other person to that other's satisfaction. The need to articulate carefully without exaggeration reduces emotionality and encourages careful listening.

COMMUNICATION BETWEEN
MEN AND WOMEN

Changing styles in dating offer the possibility of more honest communication between males and females. The use of a "line" to cover up the real self may be less common today even in random dating. Steady dating, when it is of more than a few weeks duration, whatever its disadvantages for the very young pair, does promote greater informality of interaction. This is regarded by marriage counselors as a desirable development, one that offers practice for marital communication.

However, to the extent that traditional values are retained, openness of communication will be hampered. If initiative is left to boys alone or if girls value popularity or marriage above personality enrichment, there may be the attempt to make a "good impression" to ensure being asked out again. The good impression may be based on stereotypes of male expectations. To be sure, there is often a kernel of truth in the stereotype. A large proportion of male students in recent classrooms have shown, in response to checklist questions, that they are ambivalent about surrendering the traditional privilege of male initiative. Some indicate they regard a girl as aggressive if she responds honestly to the question, "Where shall we go?" instead of demurely murmuring, "Whatever you prefer."

However, several studies show that girls tend to assume that boys have more traditional attitudes than the boys' checklist responses would indicate. It is possible, of course, that several factors are at work. The girl may, under her mother's influence, and her mother was socialized in a different era to different expectations, attribute to her own aggressiveness his failure to ask her for another date, whereas the reasons may have been quite different. Boys may mark the checklist in a way that reflects more equalitarian attitudes than their actual behaviors with the girls reflect. Thus girls may be misreading the degree of traditional behavior expected by boys or the latter may be deceiving themselves as to what their feelings are. The problematic aspects of these studies suggest the desirability of seeking verification with the particular individual as to whether the clues to expectations are being correctly perceived.

COMMUNICATION AND THE PERSONALITY

While it is true that "we cannot *not* communicate," there is much room for mistaking the meaning of what is being communicated. Role-playing in the classroom is often a helpful device for gaining experience in making inferences, in increasing empathic competencies, and in clarifying one's own values and expectations. (See "Role-playing" in Appendix II.)

Communication is important in all stages of the family cycle. The discussion of it in a separate chapter should not suggest that it can be considered apart from personality development, dating, marriage, parent–child and sibling interaction, and various family crises, large and small. Communication, the symbols by which people try to convey meaning to each other, can be supportive or destructive. It mirrors the value system, the state of knowledge, the motivations and needs of the individual. The way the parent holds the infant or "speaks" to it may impart affection and caring or tension and revulsion. The parent may fool himself but the child gets the message.

The babbling stage is an important human launching point into verbal communication. The young child who is overcorrected in his use of language may develop stammering that bespeaks an anxiety response to rejection. In all life's difficulties, the communication of support, if only through a glance or a nod of the head, can build bonds between family members. Learning to read a newspaper is another important step in communication, since changing societal expectations of family behaviors are communicated in all the mass media.

The problem of monotony in communication can only partly be solved by awareness of the limited vocabulary or the narrow repertoire of tones, postures, and gestures used. The personality that is growing and becoming more interesting tends to break out of routine responses. The family member who can predict each response of the other, the precise phrase, intonation, grimace, may look for variety outside the home. This is not to say there are not tones and words that are beloved because they are familiar and have positive connotations to the family. In general, however, the person who is growing is not so predictable; his responses differ with his added perceptions. Others in the family enjoy the excitement of sharing this growth.

RESEARCH ON COMMUNICATION

What is known about the psychology of communication can be applied in daily interactions. You are not likely to retain more than about half of what you are reading now, but this is perhaps twice what a lecture is likely to leave with you. However, if we both read and hear the same information, we may retain about three-fifths. Can you think of ways in which the phenomenon of reinforcement may be applied in the home?

Psychological research also indicates that modes of communication may bring about results desired or feared. The parent who does not trust the adolescent may speak to him in a way that reflects that distrust and evokes negative responses. The spouse who has warm, reality-based, positive expectations of good performance on the part of the other will communicate this feeling and contribute to the realization of the self-fulfilling prophecy.

HOW COMMUNICATION IN THE FAMILY
AFFECTS FAMILY MEMBERS

The family provides a training ground for the development of communication skills that can be used outside the home. There is often a high correlation between the openness of communication in the family and the student's ability to join in school discussion. However, this ability can grow beyond the limits set by family experience if small group discussion opportunities are provided in the classroom.

The family that has a broad network of friendships can help overcome the communication barriers that exist among people of different races, religions, or classes. Age and sex barriers are similarly more easily penetrated by individuals whose families encouraged communication between male and female members and between the various generations. Several studies have found that those who have had a grandparent living in the home or who have had a visiting relationship with elderly kin have a more positive attitude toward, and hence easier communication with, older people.

The family that punishes honesty of expression or blankets negative feelings does not offer a learning climate in which the personality becomes enriched. The individual is frustrated in efforts to communicate with himself, the basis of all broader communication. If the mother has said constantly, "You *can't* hate your brother. We always love our family," the child learns early not only to deny to himself his feelings of anger, hostility, and vindictiveness, but to feel unworthy because he cannot fully suppress these feelings. The family that encourages communication only of the positive—don't talk unless you have something good to say—may deprive family members of the opportunity for ventilation of negative feelings and their resolution through expression.

The youngster who can anticipate a slap, a frown, or a scolding when he attempts to tell about any unpleasant development in his life is not likely to increase communication with parents as he reaches adolescence, the critical period in life when many negative as well as positive events are likely to occur. As a young man said of his father, "When I was little, he didn't want to listen. When I got older, I didn't want to talk." A distinction must be made among silences, however; silence is not always a sign of estrangement. A happy silence may communicate parental acceptance of the independence and privacy needs of the adolescent.

"keeping in touch"

Since we are not likely to be the only ones growing and changing in the family, we need to "keep in touch" with the constantly changing needs and expectations of other family members. This is facilitated by a home atmosphere that promotes a willingness to ask what the other means and feels, the search for feedback to correct inferences, since words can disguise as well as reveal emotions. It is often helpful to recognize that given times and places ease communication. Awareness of the other's mood and the opportunity for uninterrupted interaction are general prerequisites. In any given family, sensitivity to one's own and others' functioning may have revealed that communication is eased in a walk along the shore, in one room of the house rather than another, at a time when phone interruptions are likely to be minimal, and so on.

Discussions beyond the superficial are not considered advisable in the family car, not only because of the safety factor but also because nonverbal communication is limited. Difficulty of communication in slum areas may derive less from lack of verbal skills and poor listening habits and more from negative environmental conditions: noise and lack of privacy as well as the traditional barriers of age and sex as to who may say what to whom. These latter barriers take a particularly high toll; psychological studies indicate that two-way communication is more accurate than one-way.

handling spontaneity

The line between self-awareness and self-consciousness may sometimes be a fine one. Spontaneity is a value that can sometimes be lost in over-careful choice of language and gestures, or overpsychologizing another's body stance. Moreover, it is the view of some counselors that selective communication is more conducive to harmonious family relationships than efforts at unsolicited probing or the expectation of shared confidences at all times. Momentary or temporary dislike of another family member may pass, feelings at a given moment may be ambivalent and may require time to be resolved, or the pain of a disappointment or grief may be too intense to be shared immediately.

Some sociologists see the family, by its very nature, composed of individuals with different histories and needs, as permanently in a conflict state, with only occasional relief as needs temporarily mesh. Some psychologists accept this theory and consider that awareness of it would encourage family efforts at conflict-resolution as well as tolerance of disagreement more than a conception of the family as basically in a harmonious state interrupted only occasionally by conflict.

One of the most controversial areas of communication involves sexuality. How much a parent or the teacher should tell a child, how much a couple planning to marry should tell each other about past sexual experiences or about their expectations in the marital relationship, how much husbands and wives should tell each other about the sexual attraction felt for another person or sexual behaviors with other persons are all communication problems. The word "should" implies moral issues but it also implies that the behavioral sciences have something to say about the consequences of a decision one way or another. These matters will be examined to some extent in the following chapters.

10

the first spin of the family wheel: dating and mate selection

Since the nuclear family can be said to begin with two people choosing each other as mates, dating may not be technically part of the first spin of the family wheel. But even when it begins early and has mainly a fun emphasis rather than the serious overtones of weeding out possible mates from a larger field of eligibles, dating can be viewed as a process in which understanding of the self and of others is facilitated, a process that merges right in with later mate selection.

DATING PATTERNS

Early dating is today regarded "as American as apple pie." The unsupervised pleasure relationships of boys and girls began relatively recently, however, mainly after widescale urbanization in the 20th century. The gentleman caller, committed to marriage after a few visits to the girl's home, or the farmer's son whose nocturnal visits to the neighbor's daughter were tolerated because the visits carried a marriage commitment, must be distinguished from the post-World War I pattern when the parents might not even know the names of boys their daughters were dating, let alone when or where. More recently fathers have had less opportunity to inquire into callers' marital intentions. Moreover, a succession of dating relationships—playing the field—became not only a sign of popularity and success but received some endorsement by the behavioral sciences as conducive to self-understanding and informed mate choice.

HOW DATING FITS INTO DEVELOPMENT

The developmental tasks of each period in the individual life cycle, first outlined several decades ago by a group of Chicago sociologists, included the following for the adolescent period:

1. A weaning away from the family of origin
2. An acceptance of one's own gender identity and ability to relate to a peer group
3. An ability to understand and relate to the other sex
4. A beginning of a life philosophy, including clarification of educational and work goals, fitting of sexuality into a larger interpersonal framework, and a sense of purpose and direction.

Dating as an institution, defined by sociologists as uncommitted heterosexual relationships with a pleasure goal, would appear to fit in neatly with developmental tasks for American adolescents. On dates involving dances, games, parties, sports, the teenager could watch members of his own sex relate to the other sex and could by various choices of partners learn what various females are like. The teenager could learn to transfer his reliance upon affectional response from family members to those outside the family and particularly to non-kin members of the opposite sex. Mothers and sisters, fathers and brothers could be superseded by new love objects more appropriate to mate selection.

The development of a life philosophy is stimulated by awareness of one's own sexuality, by opportunities to relate to people outside the family in a variety of ways, by various self-revelations in dating situations that either provide stimulus to educational, occupational, or other achievement or that brought prior-formed values and goals into question. In short, dating, while for fun, performs a significant educational and personality development function.

The effects of coed dormitories, as shown here at Oberlin College, have not been carefully studied as yet. Some sociologists see them as reducing the necessity for dating and thereby delaying the one-to-one relationships which precede serious commitment. Others see them as hastening intimacy and speeding the spin of the family wheel.

Bill Ray, Life © 1970 Time Inc.

Dating could also be dysfunctional. Competition for dates could force spending of a disproportionate amount of time and/or money on superficial considerations of appearance and adornment, often leading to conflict with authority figures such as parents and teachers.

Moreover, the developmental tasks of adolescence could be threatened in several other ways. If the dating were superficial, and what research several decades ago called "the rating–dating complex" was at work with daters perceiving each other not as people but as rungs in a popularity or status ladder, there was little the boy or girl could learn about his or her own personality and the kinds of people who brought out the best in them. Moreover, the necessity for dating money, particularly for the male, the frequency of dating which rose from the Saturday night date of the 1920s and 1930s to several times a week in later decades, and the need for "wheels" with the move to suburban living in the 1950s and 1960s all lowered occupational and educational goals for many males and females—particularly for the former.

Middle-class parents sought to impose curfews and other limitations, community codes were devised to ensure neighborhood support for concentration of social activity on weekends, and upper-class prep schools severely limited opportunities for dating during the academic year. Working-class boys often dropped out of school to ensure money with which to date, and working-class girls similarly curtailed their education to acquire the wardrobe and afford visits to the beauty parlor that were considered necessities for dating until quite recently.

To the extent that boys depended on parents for dating money or use of the car or girls were not permitted to date without first introducing the boy at home, there was a parental veto over choice of dating partners. Racial, religious, and class considerations came more openly into the picture than when the young people were left to their own selection. For all young Americans in choosing dating partners, there is a double message transmitted by the society through primary groups, like the family and peers, the mass media, and other forces in socialization. One message is that "love conquers all" and "everybody is equal," and also that independence of decision-making is a sign of "maturity." The other message is that mother and father "know best," only "your own kind" can be trusted, and following traditional ways makes you a "solid citizen," "a worthy member of the family," "someone who respects the family name."

It is probably a correct generalization that dating is as often fraught with confusion, uncertainty, and tension as it is with delight, excitement, and opportunity for growth. Several studies that asked adults which period of their life they would most eagerly return to found a lack of enthusiasm for living through adolescence again, with its heavy dating component and its overload of decision-making in other spheres as well.

DATING, SEXUALITY, AND LOVE

Although sexuality begins at birth and love is an important component in life at all stages, it is appropriate to examine these two concepts at this point since dating brings both very much to the fore. Each society sets its rules for sexual behavior and keeps changing them along with technological advances, degree of secularization, modification of sex role definitions, and valuation of different kinds of family.

premarital sexual standards

The choices a society has among premarital sexual standards can be briefly enumerated as follows:

1. Abstinence for both men and women.
2. Double standard. Some behaviors are permitted only for males, and those women who engage in them are by definition subject to public censure.
3. Single standard. Men and women may behave in similar ways.
   a. Sex with affection.
   b. Sex without affection.

It is notable that few societies have made the first choice. There are some subsocieties, mainly religious orders or church-related communes like the Shakers, that have lived by the principle of abstinence. There is at least one subsociety of the present day, the Sarakatsani shepherd tribe of Greece, that makes abstinence a badge of honor for the young male as well as the young female and almost reverses the machismo principle found in many Latin countries. Among the Sarakatsani masculinity attaches not to sexual conquests but to the will power to abstain. Bride and groom are both expected to be virginal at marriage, with grave threat to their families' honor if this has been violated.

The majority of societies, however, allow a period of sexual experimentation for the young, often at prescribed periods involving ceremonial occasions. Sometimes this is limited to the prepubertal period; puberty may bring isolation of the sexes in separate living quarters until marriage years. These societies would be closer to 3b than to 3a in their standard.

THE UNITED STATES

The United States, as the reader hardly need be told, represents a society in flux, with wide gaps between the ideal and real, between standard and behavior, as well as among various conceptions of the ideal. Several researchers consider the double standard still predominant, but that sex with affection is gaining, particularly among the more educated. It is a matter of debate as to how many believe and act along the lines of the "Playboy philosophy" that sexual intercourse is a pleasurable release of tensions and does not require any bonds of affection between the pair. Moreover, there is some question as to whether a double standard accompanies sex without affection.

While *Playboy* maintains it is a single standard view because it encourages women in premarital sexual expression along with men, many criticisms, especially among feminists, are heard that it is really a continuation of the machismo principle of emphasizing male sexual exploits in which women are conquered objects rather than loving persons seen as equals. To be fully on the machismo beam, *Playboy* would have to make a sharp division between girls as conquests and those fit for the marriage bed. There has been little study of whom the *Playboy*-type man marries as contrasted with those he dates.

love

Love has been variously defined, mainly by poets and philosophers, but more recently by psychologists and sociologists. Some place emphasis on it as a *process* rather than a *state of being*. Perhaps the students working with this book can pool their ideas and see if any consensus results. Perhaps they will agree with students who, when asked recently what the basic components of heterosexual love are, mentioned: trust; confidence; inspiration; and shared values, interests, and activities. They agreed that these are the components of friendship too, and this brought general acceptance of the definition of heterosexual love, offered some decades ago but still useful, as a combination of sexual attraction and friendship. Love defined in this way was rarely the basis of marriage in a majority of societies. In some the couple met only at the marriage ceremony, or the parents made the mate selection and allowed no unchaperoned interaction between the future mates.

If the concept of idealization, or fantasy, is added to sex and friendship, there is a possible definition of romantic love. This had no place in mate selection even in the Middle Ages when courtly love had its beginnings among the upper classes. Marriage was a contract between families of property at that level; strategic economic and political alliances were sought rather than the personal satisfaction of the pair. Interest in an individual personality could develop only outside the connubial tie. The lady the knight sang to or wrote poems about was a married woman. At first, the relationship was kept on a nonsexual plane but later included adultery.

Among the feudal population, the consent of the lord was required for marriage among his serfs; the lord retained rights of the first night although he did not always choose to exercise it. Thus, as in the plantation South of the United States, it could be said that adultery was built into upper-class family life. Women in the lower class were given little personal choice; they were more likely to be the victims.

LOVE AND DATING

Love is said to be "institutionalized" in modern societies, that is, it is considered a necessary basis for marriage. To ensure that people fall in love with the "right" people, parents and other authority figures start early to emphasize the importance of social homogamy and to arrange daily life in a way that will maximize contact with families of like economic status and ethnic background. Sometimes laws have been passed and upheld by courts to reenforce barriers between groups. Through formal and informal devices, a pool of eligibles is formed and from the "fish" swimming in this pool, a proper catch can be made. The dating pool is likely to be somewhat larger than the mate selection pool.

International dating is more common on campuses than marriage between foreign and American students. The same appears to be true of interfaith dating in high schools and colleges. Interracial dating is least common. There was a brief increase in the mid-1960s when common involvement in social issues brought more frequent contact. Later in the decade, however, when "Black is beautiful" expressed a new appreciation for the appearance of blacks, particularly black females, there was some pressure from within the black group to show racial cohesiveness by restricting dating to themselves. Oriental-white dating occurs commonly when American troops are stationed in Asiatic countries, as well as in Hawaii, and tends more often to result in intermarriage than does dating here on the mainland where the family network comes into operation to reduce it.

It becomes evident that while dating considerably frees individuals from parental decisions in mate selection, it is itself under societal influences directed toward social homogamy. "We are free to choose our own mates in the United States" is only partly true. The ethclass consideration often lies close to the surface and can be unearthed with little digging.

However, what is new in modern mate selection is the attempt at psychic fit. If Tom, Dick, and Harry all are swimming in the pool of eligibles, they are not all, in Mary's view, equally attractive personalities. A famous writer once said that we tend to exaggerate the difference between one man and all others and one women and all others. The dating process reveals, however, that we enjoy the company of some people more than others, even within the social homogamous grouping.

DATING AND MATE SELECTION

Some sociologists consider dating a process that meshes poorly with mate selection. They point out that the qualities sought in a date are often different from those valued in a mate. One textbook offered an exercise in which students could choose a few from among almost a dozen characteristics sought in a date: good looks; popular; courteous; modest and unassuming; similar religious background; not worried about the expense of the date; etc. The writer found in offering class after class of undergraduates choices of this kind that men chose as their three top requirements that the girl have good looks, be popular, and enjoy a good time without being too prudish. The women chose courteous, modest and unassuming, and not worried about the expense of a date. They all recognized on inquiry that these might all or in part be dysfunctional qualities in a marital relationship.

Not only are dating values not always congruent with those of marriage but access to dating is relatively limited for some. If dating is an essential part of growing up, understanding oneself and others, learning independence from the family of origin, and the like, then it would seem desirable that this experience should be available to all young people. Until quite recently, girls had to be devious in communicating their desire to be asked on a date, since the initiative was by custom given to the male. This was a mixed privilege for him, as lack of confidence in his own desirability might inhibit his taking the initiative. The result was two lonely people, the boy who did not ask and the girl who was not asked.

A number of other societies have solved this problem by encouraging many group activities for boys and girls where they can learn to relate to one another in general before undertaking particularized relationships. In the United States, couple dating has been found to begin even before puberty, more often for the girl, whose physical and social development is more rapid until about the age of fifteen. Some psychologists think this early couple dating creates or intensifies male hostility for females, with the boy continuing to perceive the girl as threateningly aggressive even after he is physically larger and she has retreated into the relatively passive role still culturally indicated among many groups.

CHANGES IN DATING PATTERNS

What changes in dating are now occurring and how will they affect marriage? Research is not extensive as yet, even though student reactions to traditional textbook descriptions of dating practices suggest new folkways and mores are rapidly developing. While initiative still largely resides in the male, there are signs of change.

Students differ in their response to the question raised in classroom discussion. Should a girl be free to invite a boy on a date? The financial consideration is frequently raised. Some girls feel that if they do the asking, they will have to bear or share the financial costs. Some boys feel that if girls pay, either the total bill or their own share ("going Dutch," which current research in Holland indicates is an appropriate term), the sexual returns on the date will be reduced. Under probing, boys and girls both tend to admit that their sexual expectations relate to some degree to the matter of expense, particularly in random dating. Few students will acknowledge that this actually represents a kind of barter, the trading of his expenditure on her for her willingness to kiss, neck, or pet. "Only if I like him" does not alter the situation markedly when it is evident that degree of liking correlates to some extent with his generosity.

Girls alert to the feminist movement decry any assumptions that the male alone has sexual needs or that affectional expression should have a price tag. This, they insist, is what has been wrong with marriage, namely, that too many women, culturally repressed in their sexuality, consider sex a duty, something done for the male, rather than viewing it as a joint pleasure, an expression of mutuality and the relatedness of equals. Many young feminists, however, are not completely consistent and yield to the temptation to reap the advantages of both worlds, the traditional and the modern. As one young man recently put it, "She reminds me not to open the car door for her or pull out her chair in the restaurant, but she never offers to pay her share of the check."

One of the newer developments in dating besides the freedom of girls to telephone boys, even if perhaps only a minority as yet will ask directly for a date, is the casualness of the dating activity. If a date used to mean a sequence of events, varying with the community, of attending a movie or sports event, then getting something to eat, and then having a chance to talk or pet, dating on some campuses today is barely distinguishable from other joint activities. Studying together, attending a meeting together, eating lunch at school together, dropping by at a local coffee house and hangout, seeing a movie, or joining friends at someone's home may flow spontaneously out of the other activities.

There are still special events that may have to be noted on calendars—school dances, a folk festival, a visiting rock band, and so forth, but the calendar seems to be in process of being scrapped in favor of spontaneous and informal relationships. It used to be a sign of a girl's popularity that she could insist on invitations coming a week ahead of time, at the very least, to ensure that she was in his thoughts and not a hasty substitute for a date he thought he had. Theater tickets would have to be bought, clothes carefully coordinated, restaurant reservations made. This still occurs, to be sure, but not as a norm for all groups.

reasons for dating pattern changes

What has changed the dating patterns? Youth's greater seriousness, the social consciousness of the 1960s in contrast to the apathy of the 1950s, is well known. The increase in steady dating has undoubtedly also had some impact. It was not unexpected that young people, taking a critical look at all social institutions, found much that was phony in traditional dating patterns. The spread of encounter groups and sensitivity sessions increased awareness in college-age men and women of the shallow relationships that often characterized dating, and this undoubtedly percolated down to the younger age groups as well.

For many years marriage counselors expressed concern that the usual dating pattern did not provide sufficient opportunity for the participants to know each other's values, needs, and aspirations, and that disillusionment followed marriage in part because the couple had seen each other only in their most attractive moments. It was suggested that perhaps the couple should make no marital commitments until they had spent several days together in a crisis situation, isolated by a storm without enough food or blankets, or caring for a sick and cranky child. Comparable stresses would inevitably occur in marriage, it was urged, and such experiences would reveal value gaps, different ways of coping, and different levels of ability to tolerate disorder, haggard looks, and uncertainty.

STEADY DATING

In a sense it might be said that such a crisis test is less necessary now that dating has become more informal and since steady dating tends to increase the variety of situations in which the two can observe each other. Steady dating is not universally approved of, however. Some psychologists see it, particularly in early adolescence, as encouraging premature closure. The individual does not test himself in a variety of relationships or learn more about himself and the other sex, although he learns much about a single individual. Experience with members of the opposite sex is limited; he may be cutting himself off from the opportunity to meet those who might have proved more stimulating and helpful life partners.

Some parents and church spokesmen add their fears that the steady relationship will increase the likelihood of premarital intercourse. If steady dating is not merely a succession of brief, exclusive heterosexual relationships but is extended in duration, it is likely to create the sense of security which research indicates correlates with female acceptance of sexual intercourse.

dating and sexual intimacy

Early sex research indicates that far more sexual intimacy had occurred between couples than would have seemed likely in days before automobiles offered unchaperoned opportunities of a different magnitude than horses and buggies.

Kinsey's research in the 1940s indicated that intercourse tended to occur earlier for boys with little education than for the college-destined group born in 1890, 1900, 1910, and 1920, all of whom reached their adolescent years in this century. Today's fathers and grandfathers who were college students in the decades up to 1950 tended to use masturbation or petting to orgasm as an outlet for sexual tension more frequently than sexual intercourse. More than half the male college students of the parent and grandparent generations had, by age twenty, experienced intercourse. This was a smaller proportion than among noncollege youths of twenty. As for female college students, a minority (about a fifth) had experienced sexual intercourse by age twenty, according to Kinsey's data.[1]

What about the present generation of young people? No study as extensive as Kinsey's has been undertaken but a number of smaller research projects, mainly involving college students, find a higher coital rate among college females in the late 1960s than in the previous decade. Two facts emerge from the studies. First, despite mass media claims that virginity is rare among college females, none of the studies found a majority had had coital experience. And second, in the various colleges studied, the extent of commitment tended to correlate highly with coital rate. Thus, in one study in 1968, 23 percent of girls in a dating relationship, 28 percent of those going steady, and 39 percent of those engaged had experienced intercourse.

Research on petting in the 1950s revealed that most college girls preserved technical virginity but experienced a wide range of sexual caresses. Psychologists disagree about the outcomes of this component in dating. Some maintain that in a society that is ambivalent about the conditions under which premarital intercourse is acceptable, petting offers a substitute which encourages appreciation of one's own sexuality and prepares one for a fuller sexual relationship in the marriage. Others emphasize the frustrations, the painful congestion in the pelvic area if the petting does not proceed to orgasm, and the feeling of hypocrisy in petting so intimately but ruling out normal consummation.

---

[1] Alfred C. Kinsey, Wardell Pomeroy, and Clyde Martin, *Sexual Behavior in the Human Male* (Philadelphia: W. B. Saunders Company, 1948).

SEXUAL STANDARDS—SITUATIONAL
OR ABSOLUTE

It is evident that the sexual dimension of dating is fraught with physi-ological and moral controversy. Reliance upon situational ethics as a newer guideline than the absolute standards, which prevailed in theory, may not obviate confusion for the adolescent. A chart drawn up by a sex educator defines as good those acts that maximize trust, increase warm feelings for other human beings, and enhance the individual's self-image; bad acts are those that increase suspicion, alienation, and self-contempt.

In favor of such guidelines, it can be said that they encourage each boy and girl to examine feelings about the other, to recognize what the impact of sexual intercourse would be on each of them and on their relationship. This contrasts with any new norm that may be shaping up that takes sexual intercourse for granted on a date or any tendency to deceive the self or the other as to the meaning of sex in their total rela-tionship. However, the guidelines do assume a degree of self-understand-ing which may be difficult to attain, especially for the younger person whose identity is in the process of formation, and a higher level of sensi-tivity to others' needs and intentions than the student may acquire by teen years.

honesty

It is commonly recognized that honesty is not always present in a couple relationship. Research indicates that boys express more affection than they feel in an attempt to reduce female resistance to sexual intercourse or heavy petting. Sometimes this is deliberate deception. One book which discusses seduction techniques urges the male to dissemble; ethical qualms are blanketed under the assurance that he will be doing the girl a favor in wakening her to her own sexuality.

Sometimes there is situational self-deception, of course. The boy who has been stimulated by a movie they have just seen, and men in American culture are influenced by erotic imagery, by the beautiful setting of a tree-lined lane in which they are parked, and the perfume and the re-vealing and sexually exciting clothing worn by his date may momentarily feel himself in love and give voice to honest but inadequately-based pro-testations of love.

Nor is the male always the pursuer and the sexual agggressor. The girl may have many motives that have little to do with her sexuality. She may view the boy as the life-preserver that can float her out of her troubled home, an unpleasant job, or unrewarding school work. Or if she has no fantasies as to what matrimony can solve, she may be so much in need of the comfort provided by temporary sexual closeness that she seeks intercourse. The boy may not know her psychological background well enough to know what effect this will have on her, whether it will send her into the depression she sensed and tried to escape through promiscuity, or indeed help her to straighten out her relationships with her family. Her need to have a child, as retaliation against parents, as a shield against her feeling of emptiness, as a symbol of adulthood, may involve the boy in legal, moral, and financial difficulties they had not agreed to face together.

THE COMPLEXITY OF SEXUAL BEHAVIORS

In short, sexual behaviors have a variety of causes and a variety of out-comes. None of the research shows that intercourse has invariably posi-tive or negative effects. It is an expression of the whole personality and meshes with other needs of the individual—or else frustrates them. In a period of changing sexual norms, the individual's path is a kind of maze strewn with vestiges of the past, new, seemingly simple alternatives, as well as with the certainty that no choice will be uniformly accepted by significant others, especially parents and peers. The vast gap between ideal and real sexual behaviors in the society means that we have in-ternalized, made part of our consciences, standards by which few people actually live but which nonetheless create guilt feelings when our be-haviors match the actual conduct of others.

education

Most of us have had poor education in sexuality. Not only are we un-likely to be familiar with our own bodies, knowledgeable about our own anatomy and physiology, but perhaps more important, we have rarely had our questions about individual sexual functioning and societal at-titudes toward masturbation, homosexuality, prostitution, and the like openly answered at home or in school. The most common solution has been for a group of peers to pool their ignorances. One negative by-product is a failure to develop a public vocabulary for discussion of sexual issues; most boys and girls know only slang terms, and this may inhibit their asking questions.

attitudes toward sex

By and large, we live in a society which is highly eroticized and offers us daily stimulation by sex symbols in dress, speech, advertising, and the like. Yet at the same time we are given the feeling that sex is dirty and that it is our lesser selves that are involved in sexual thoughts and actions. Moreover, while intercourse is not always uniformly satisfying to both partners, there is a tendency to hide its pleasure-giving aspect beneath a veil of references to motherhood.

In a highly populated world the procreational dimension of sexuality must be considered of lesser importance than its recreational and relational dimensions. It is helpful for the student to understand conception, pregnancy, and childbirth, but these physiological phenomena have important emotional accompaniments also worthy of study because they have different meanings for each individual and each family. Moreover, these phenomena occur only a small fraction of the time that men and women relate to each other sexually. It is the complex majority of sexual encounters that are omitted from the usual sex education program.

ROMANTIC LOVE

There is a sexual component in most man–woman relationships. However, its importance may be exaggerated by some schools of psychological thought. Take idealization. Are the Freudians right in considering the romantic glow merely a reflection of sexual inhibition, to be necessarily dissipated by physical consummation? Or can some degree of idealization persist into the marriage? Can romantic love survive the intimacy of steady dating and engagement? Is romantic love worth saving?

Writers of marriage textbooks used to regard romantic love with suspicion, fearing it built up hopes that had to crash with the realities of day-to-day existence. Now, however, there is beginning to be some recognition that a little idealization enhances the relationship. This is not to be confused, to be sure, with gross self-deception. Confidence in the other person, the feeling that he will continue to grow, has an element of the mysterious in it in the same sense that knowing a bud will be a full-blown flower one day imparts a sense of awe and wonder.

In the human being this confidence is part of the self-fulfilling prophecy. Obviously the confidence must have some reality basis. To dream that one's girl friend will be a great ballerina when at sixteen she has never taken a dancing lesson or that one's boy friend will be a Nobel Prize winner in physics when he is failing mathematics in high school may be regarded as sheer fantasy rather than reality-based idealization. Exceptions do occur. Einstein did miserably in a German high school and recovered his academic equilibrium only when he entered a school in Switzerland. Many "late bloomers" make notable artistic and scientific contributions long after their friends and relatives have given up hope. A change of career in middle age is becoming more common.

However, a romantic love relationship does not require the belief that "love is blind." Some degree of idealization can remain even if faults and inadequacies can be perceived clearly in the other person. It has been said that mate selection is a process in which we decide which shortcomings we can reconcile ourselves to.

SEX, LOVE, AND MARRIAGE

Whatever the qualities of the mate we select, whether perceived clearly or blurrily, these can have tremendous impact on the kind of person we become. In modern marriage (or consensual union), the partner we choose is a significant other in our lives. We spend far more of our lifetime with a mate than we do with a parent. One psychologist points out that a good spousal relationship is essentially therapeutic. Recent emphasis in psychology has been on adult socialization—how much we change and grow long after adolescence. Certainly the mate is likely to contribute, for better or worse, to this process.

Since a mate is so important in our lives, it would be comfortable to think there are adequate guidelines by which to judge the wisdom of our choice. Some counselors urge that marriage be delayed so that the individual knows himself well before making a fateful decision. Others urge that couples live together without marriage to test their feelings about each other. Some suggest that sexual compatibility can be ascertained in this way and that since the sexual component in a man–woman relationship is a significant one, it is essential for sexual intercourse to take place before marriage.

On the other hand, other counselors suggest that because sexuality is so tied into total psychological functioning, there is no way to determine whether sexual satisfaction before marriage will continue into the later years—nor indeed whether sexual incompatibility before marriage might not yield to an atmosphere of security, tenderness, and patience. Just as some students freeze up in an exam, so too some psychologists hold, the individual who feels he or she is being tested and that his or her sexual performance will determine his or her marital future, may be inhibited. One study found sexual adjustment between husbands and wives to vary greatly; in some marriages decades elapsed before full sexual satisfaction was attained. This may suggest that important as sexual fulfillment is, it occurs in a whole network of marital satisfactions. Many husbands and wives are able to find happiness with each other despite recognition that they are not models of sexual competency.

Whether young people become husbands and wives or do not legalize their relationship does not basically affect the need to think through carefully their suitability for each other. While separation is legally easier, except in the very few common law states, if the pair is not married, the emotional dimensions of mate selection and mate separation seem to be remarkably similar in legal and in consensual unions. All have similar decisions to make about contraception, relationships with families of origin, sharing of household chores, money sources, who will work and at what, further education, friends, neighborhoods, housing, and so forth.

WORKING AT MAINTAINING
THE RELATIONSHIP

For each couple, regardless of the consensual or legal basis of their relationship, there is a tacit recognition that their selection of each other is at best a working hypothesis that has to be proved in the months and years ahead. No matter how thoroughly they have discussed all the issues in the abstract during the months prior to sharing a residence, actual implementation requires modification, compromise, further discussion, and argument.

While there is some comfort in knowing some matters are settled, not much can be settled for long between two dynamic, growing individuals. (The student who is working with this book will find more on this in the next chapter, which examines the marital relationship.) While mate selection influences the kind of family life the pair can create and the kind of people they can become, it is only the first step among many.

change

The popular belief that if the right mate is selected "all will go well" underestimates the changes that occur in environmental circumstances as well as in the personalities of the spouses. It has been suggested that men and women can learn about selecting a mate from studying the marital relationships of those they know and from understanding the marriage failures of various friends and relatives. Why did two people who seemed to suit each other so well initially break up the relationship after months or years? What changed in their needs, their communication patterns, their desire to keep their love alive and growing?

THE CONSENSUAL UNION

It is commonly believed that legalization of the relationship through marriage offers a degree of security and commitment that encourages constructive effort to strengthen the bonds and solve problems together. It is possible, however, that the very legalization creates in some young people a sense of finality, a fear of being trapped, forced into unwanted responsibilities, and that these feelings have negative consequences for their ability to play a spousal role. Some maintain that this feeling reflects an unreadiness to undertake a spousal role, whether married or not, a desire to have a play relationship only and to fill in the years between schooling and marriage in a carefree way. Counseling couples who have sought this "uncommitment" reveals, however, that their joint residence itself brought to the fore issues of commitment in the allocation of chores, relations with friends, relatives, division of income, expression of sexuality, and most of the matters with which young married pairs struggle.

Not enough research has been done, it is true, on the many different forms of consensual union. Perhaps some young couples have been able to work this out without resentments, disappointments, recriminations. Moreover, there is some question as to whether in any case the failure is any worse than if a legalized relationship had failed. There are some clues in counseling cases and in panel discussions in classes that for some couples it may be worse because the relationship was undertaken with an assumption that it was a way of avoiding the difficulties of compromise characteristic of marriage and the pain of separation. The surprise and chagrin may be more acute.

The high expectations in modern marriage relationships, the desire for intimacy, joint sexual satisfaction, companionship, in addition to the traditional expectations of keeping a roof over their heads, rearing children, and weathering the inevitable crises of illness and bereavement —these expectations make mate selection far more difficult than ever before. Self-understanding, empathy, and communication are new concepts in man–woman relationships and are inextricably tied to the enrichment and maintenance of love between the couple. They spell out a lifetime of effort, the skills for which students who are working with this book are now hopefully in process of acquiring.

the second spin: spousal, in-law, and parental roles

A characteristic ending for a fairy tale was "And they lived happily ever after." Realistic fiction, on the other hand, reflects life itself and reports the likelihood that even as the wedding bells are pealing, literally in a church or figuratively in a city registry office or in the home of a justice of the peace, the sounds of discord can be intermingled with the joyous notes. This is understandable from all we know about psychology and sociology, and must be accepted by the couple and their friends and kin as inevitable. There is no dramatic personality change on the wedding day or in setting up a joint household. Plenty of unfinished business in relationships with families of origin, in achievement of educational goals,

Societies ceremonialize in diverse ways the commitment of a man and a woman to each other. A wedding day mirrors the belief system of a culture, with aleatory elements coming markedly into play. In recent years the Soviets have begun to act on the hypothesis, although evidence is still scant in any country, that solemnization of the wedding with more elaborate ceremonies promotes marital stability.

Mary Leatherbee, Life © 1970 Time Inc.

in coping with difficult physical and emotional environments remains for each of the mates separately. The slate of the past is not wiped clean just because the two decided to join together in matrimony or in a para-marriage.

To be sure, something new has been added: a couple relationship. They may have acquired some experience in being treated as a pair by others and relating to each other with increasing commitment and intimacy in the preceding months. Now, however, it is not intermittent but continuous. This introduces qualitative as well as quantitative changes in the relationship. Choices among alternatives have to be made and discarded, even if initial decisions were reached in the engagement period or its equivalent. The spousal relationship has to be fitted in with in-law expectations, work roles, pregnancy and child bearing, the rearing of children, friendships, crises of ill health, loss of family members, and attraction to other men and women. None of these can be explored in detail here, but the alternatives facing the couple as the family wheel turns will be mentioned.

SEXUAL SATISFACTION

Mention has been made in previous chapters of the greater potential for sexual satisfaction in the situation of privacy, security, and intimacy derived from a committed relationship. For those who cannot afford their own living quarters and must move in temporarily with relatives, some of this potential may not be realized.

However, many factors are at play in the area of sexual satisfaction: confidence in the contraceptive methods used, agreement on when to start having children, the physical and mental well-being of the two if both are studying or working and under pressure to perform well, frankness of communication in order to know if both are deriving pleasure in foreplay and intercourse, and the degree of satisfaction in other aspects of their functioning. The sexual relationship reflects their satisfaction in the total relationship and also colors other relationships. Counselors differ as to which is cart and which is horse, but all recognize an intertwining of sexual and nonsexual grievances and joys.

male–female satisfaction

The female in the United States has suffered some suppression of her sexuality under the double standard and may not be released from her inhibitions except gradually in an atmosphere of tenderness and encouragement. The male has probably found some support in the American culture for expressing sexual interest in more than one woman, but marriage requires that he *curtail* and she *expand* previous sexual behaviors. This often gives rise, even in the early years of marriage, to disagreements concerning frequency of intercourse as well as positions. As indicated, decision-making may be tied up, not solely with enjoyment of the sex act or lack of pleasure, but in feelings about how each perceives the other to be playing nonsexual family roles. Moreover, the firm distinction that was at least theoretically made between the married and the unmarried, the sexually available versus the forbidden, is not as commonly held now.

extramarital relationships

Both spouses will be subjected to sexual temptation and solicitation to an unprecedented degree. One recent book, widely distributed, advises the single girl who finds it difficult to get dates with single men to practice on the married. Advice is given on how to use the place of work as an opportunity for date recruitment. The woman who wrote the book justified her ethical code on the ground that the girl was only a stimulus and whether the man responded would depend on the state of his relationship with his wife.

However, it can be pointed out that marital relationships are not likely to be smooth; the man who had met a sexual rebuff the night before or who was still angry after a breakfast quarrel about a mother-in-law's visit might respond to the flirtation in a way that did not reflect the total spousal relationship. Nor are the temptations all in one direction. The married woman in gainful employment, and she outnumbers her single sister, is likely to be the object of the sexual fancy of the men she meets at work. The housewife is not isolated from repairmen, shopkeepers, and other males.

Psychologists are divided on the subject of extramarital relationships. Little sociological research exists on this important question. Some maintain that neither the man nor the woman needs the variety offered by outside sexual encounters, that the normal person will be attracted to others of the opposite sex but will be able to resist pursuing this attraction further. Others maintain that extramarital encounters will not harm the spousal relationship. The latter are divided between those who say the outcome will be favorable if the spouse is told and those who say it will be favorable only if the spouse can be kept unaware of the infidelity. In any case, little research has been done to prove one contention rather than another. Unquestionably, couples will make decisions in these regards based on the norms for their socioeconomic group and their personal definitions of what they expect in a marriage.

It is evident that although adultery is enjoined in the Judaeo-Christian tradition, it has been practiced by a sizable minority in most societies, more by men than by women however. New norms may increase adultery for both sexes or may eliminate it for both.

Two opposite developments are at work in American marriage. On the one hand, there is an increase in the number of swinging couples (although they as yet comprise only a tiny minority) who jointly have sexual activities with other couples or singles. On the other hand, there are new levels of intimacy in spousal relationships based on a single marital standard of sexual exclusivity. Again, these may comprise only a tiny minority. The swinging couples tend to separate sex from affection and accept the physical promiscuity so long as friendships and deeper feelings are avoided in relationships with other pairs. The nonswingers consider sex whether before or after marriage as embedded in a total relationship and are unwilling to threaten the deepening of spousal loyalty by efforts to relate on a friendship-plus-sex level with other persons.

Along the continuum are married people who do not swing together but are adulterous on occasion, either on a sex-without-affection level or on a level of an affair which may or may not result in breaking up the marriage. Although adultery is one of the grounds for divorce in most states, it is less used than the category of "mental cruelty." This would suggest that adultery is not part of accepted sex practice; it is still regarded as somewhat of a disgrace to be termed an adulterer.

It should be noted that communal living may or may not involve adultery. In some communes in the United States there is a kind of group marriage; in others the couples tend to maintain exclusive sexual relationships while sharing in nonsexual matters—work, politics, religion, household chores, etc. In the sexual exclusivity combined with joint work and daily living these latter communes resemble the kibbutz. The group marriage communes resemble the Oneida colony somewhat, but usually lack the religious commitment present there.

From what has been said above concerning the doctrine of permanent availability and consequent sexual opportunity for men and women, the married couple has important decisions to make, not only about their own ways of achieving sexual satisfaction but also about their sexual relationships with others. Models of what they observe in their parents' behavior or that of siblings may not be all-determining for them. As indicated in the chapter on personal development, each family member has different influences on his growth and learns a somewhat different set of sexual and relational needs.

bisexuality

A little discussed, but a reality nonetheless, is the matter of bisexuality—the physical attraction which husband or wife may feel for the same sex as well as for the other sex. If the homosexual is the subject of much disagreement today between those who see him as a sick and inadequate person and those who consider his tension and anxiety derive more from cultural disapproval and sanctions and less from initial personality disorder, the bisexual is even more in dispute among psychologists.

A recent controversial research project involved a sociologist who observed men who use restrooms in public parks for quick homosexual encounters with strangers. It was found that a large proportion of these men were married and went home to wife and children afterwards, carefully hiding their bisexuality from friends and kinfolk. The revelation of bisexuality sometimes emerges, however, creating a crisis situation for the couple who have to decide whether they are able to maintain a spousal role which includes sex without affection—not with a person of the opposite sex, but with one of the same sex. Some psychologists interpret the swinging phenomenon as reflective of bisexuality, with homosexual tendencies given vicarious expression.

monotony

The possibility of monotony in the married sexual relationship looms large in the thinking of professionals and the public. However, it is recognized that couples who are growing in nonsexual ways manage to provide each other with enough sexual stimulation to make involvements with others unnecessary if not unthinkable. Maslow's exploration of the self-actualizing person, the individual who attains great satisfaction in occupation and contribution to the community, suggests that the search for sexual variety is less characteristic in this fulfilled individual. However, some psychologists do not share this view or point to the majority of people as failing to find satisfaction in their work lives and needing a sexual escape from a sense of uselessness, dullness, and inadequacy.

possible alternatives

One novelist suggests that two or three couples may create a single household and share their sex lives, their childrearing, and their incomes in a kind of corporate marriage that does not separate sex from friendship. *Proposition 31* by Robert Rimmer,[1] which has sold widely, depicts such an attempt by two couples in their thirties. Underlying it is an assumption that the corporate home can be an escape from the corporate society, that the alienation of competitive work relationships can be excluded from a private Eden.

Other solutions have been suggested in fictional depictions of alternate months of living with one spouse and then the other, so that it is time for a change when toleration of one spouse's habits is beginning to run thin. It should be noted that in most of the proposed alternatives to present marriage and family relationships, the interaction with children and families of origin is barely sketched in. Serious attempts to see all the implications in proposed alternatives have not yet been made.

the divorced and widowed

Sexual satisfaction for divorced and bereaved persons is still a little explored area. Remarriage late in life is increasing as is group living among elderly men and women. Sexual needs of men and women in their sixties and seventies are only now beginning to be recognized. The elderly man living with a group of elderly widows suggests that what is

---

1 Robert H. Rimmer, *Proposition 31* (New York: New American Library, Inc., 1968).

sought is not intercourse but more general expressions of affection, care in illness, and companionship, all of which are less often forthcoming from married children and grandchildren. This may be due to geographic distance or to age-graded activities which predominate in modern society.

Few students have given thought to the kinds of sexual standards and modes of daily living for their relatives who are divorced or bereaved or forced by unemployment or early retirement into the category of aged poor. It is estimated that half of all those sixty-five years and older are poor. Decisions being made in the next decades locally or on a federal level will affect the alternatives available to those reading this. It is not easy in late teens or early twenties to give careful consideration to nursing homes, old age institutions, housing facilities for old couples and groups, and social security payments. Yet all of these will determine their survival and their happiness in the last decades of life as it determines those of their kinfolk now.

However, the spin of the family cycle is more rapid than the imagination can encompass, and the young individual as well as the young couple will have to consider not merely personal schemes of insurance, but also some input into the broader social structure in which their lives will be fitted.

TO BE OR NOT TO BE A PARENT

Procreation as a sole or major motive in marriage is yielding for some couples to a determination to emphasize the spousal role and reduce the time and attention given to the parental role. However, it is likely that Population Zero and other organizations which concentrate on the dangers of an overpopulated world will reduce but not eliminate the desire for children. While only the fundamentalist religions still ask that couples "Be fruitful and multiply," almost all religions are aware that replacement of their parishioners is a necessary step to their own survival. Many state so openly. In addition to the push toward parenthood that religious authority figures provide, there is the encouragement by commercial interests, with manufacturers and merchants eager to provide products.

There is little doubt that the family itself acts as a stimulus to parenthood. Boys and girls are socialized from an early age to expect to be parents. Men and women see their own immortality in their grandchildren. And siblings are often rivalrous in their procreative activities.

Despite the importance attached to parenthood in the society, there is little serious effort to prepare young people for the responsibility. Only a few study child development. As a result, childrearing is little informed by an understanding of the stages of cognitive and emotional growth. In addition to ignorance of the scientific facts, there is widespread inexperience. Ask any class how many have held an infant for more than a few minutes in the past months and only a minority is likely to respond. Sitter jobs give some girls practical knowledge of the touch and smell of the infant, but the American culture rarely offers boys the same opportunity. Advertising in the mass media may be misleading concerning the unvarying charm of small babies. Many young parents are ill-prepared for the physical and psychological inroads on time, energy, finances, and relationships which the coming of children brings.

parenthood as crisis

Research indicates that "parenthood as crisis" is a legitimate concept. Many young couples report disturbances in their sexual relationships, communication patterns, and self-concepts. Feelings of inadequacy and discontentment were found to mark even those who had enjoyed the parent preparation courses now offered couples by various community agencies and those who had eagerly anticipated the experience. To be sure, the initial destructive consequences of the birth of a child were soon offset by more positive ones for most couples.

Psychologists differ in their interpretation of this crisis. Some blame the man for lack of maturity—a basic unwillingness to forego the attention and affection previously lavished on him alone by the wife. Some blame the woman for her inability to divide her time and to bring to a triadic relationship all she was able to expend before on the dyad. Some sociologists would rather emphasize cultural and structural contributions to the intensity of the problem, citing not only the inexperience in care of young children, but also the following:

1. Health care arrangements in the society which make each baby a large financial burden for the young parents. The fear that free delivery and clinics will encourage high birth rates is not borne out by the kibbutzim or Soviet and other East European countries.

2. Geographic dispersal which may leave the young couple without nearby kin to provide services that would ease the first weeks or months of child care.

3. Some tendency for youth to interpret independence as precluding help by kin. Young marriages and childbearing at an early age are likely to occur before the boy and girl have been defined as adults in their own or parental eyes, with consequent greater assertiveness on the part of parents and defensiveness on the part of the young couple.

4. Lack of hospital space which results in return to the home before strength has been fully recovered. Some suggest a half-way house

for new parents, an institution in which for several weeks various skills in caring for the baby can be developed under the watchful eyes of professionals; young fathers and mothers can enjoy their new roles without fear of irreversible error.

5. Lack of visiting nurses and other professionals who can make up for the aid once available from close kin. As more women enter gainful employment, the working grandmother becomes unable to offer assistance even if the young couple is willing to accept it.

6. Lack of child care facilities which would permit young couples to enjoy joint recreation without the cost and uncertainty of skilled sitters. One study in England in the 1960s revealed that the majority in a sample of young couples had not been out together in the entire year following the infant's birth. A separation of the sexes for moments of relaxation and enjoyment, the wife going out while the husband stays with the baby or vice versa, may be better than no recreation, but may be dysfunctional for the relationship psychologically since pleasure becomes associated with other people than the spouse.

   In some regions of the United States, favorable climatic conditions and the availability of automobiles permit more mobility for the couple but do not solve the problem of maintaining dyadic relationships, including uninterrupted conversation, expressions of affection, and the pursuit of joint interests in sports, theater, painting, and the like. Routines may become established that threaten the perpetuation of a romantic element in the relationship. A study of divorces after twenty years of marriage in England showed that it was not sexual discontent with the wife but her immersion in childrearing and household details that sent the husband looking for someone with whom to share a sunset or poetry or other activities that had once enhanced marriage relationships.

7. Limitations in housing which create stress and reduce tolerance of children's need to explore, to make noise, etc. Divorce rates are highest among low income families. Along with financial worry there are stresses tied to poor housing, inadequate diet, and so forth.

8. Lack of doctors and hospitals which permit the husband to play a satisfying role in preparation for and delivery of the baby. While a breakthrough has occurred in the past decade in some communities, most medical personnel and institutions still consider the husband more as a provider than as one who requires consideration, care, and a role as participant in the birth process.

Several research studies have found adultery rates rise in the last trimester of pregnancy and the first months after a baby is born. While the wife may contribute to this, or even the doctor who does not consider the individual case, some interpret the problem as not primarily a sexual one even if the solution sought is on a sexual level. A sense of being overwhelmed by financial responsibility, of being excluded from emotional benefits, may assail the young husband in the present social structure.

Just as couples dissatisfied with each other can channel their quarrels into religious or racial issues (and thereby create the impression that all would be well if only these differences between them did not exist), so too the coming of children can provide a focus for discontentment. As Strepsiades declares in *The Clouds* by Aristophanes,

> When this son of ours was born,
> my good wife and I
> Wrangled over the name we'd call him.

In short, children can be not only the cause of estrangement between husband and wife but also the focus of disenchantment which has its roots in other matters. In the case of Strepsiades an arranged marriage had brought together a town lady and a rural squire, and naming the child was only one of their many disagreements. Children who witness family quarrels may needlessly feel guilty because they think they have caused the disharmony when it actually reflects unresolved issues of dominance, values, and goals between husband and wife that find a convenient handle in disputes over children.

the parental role

Not only are services lacking that would ease parental burdens and allow them more pleasure in the role, but they are held accountable for many matters over which they have little control except perhaps as citizens, and then they may be outvoted in their community. Changing sexual standards, availability of drugs, increased crime rates, lack of public transportation, war, job availability, and wage rates all affect the way the parental responsibility can be discharged. Moreover, schools, mass media, and other institutions besides the family affect the outcome.

It is safe to say that the parental role in present circumstances leaves most men and women ambivalent. Love of children, enjoyment of participating in the drama of their development, satisfaction in seeing the features of beloved kin reflected in one's own progeny, the sense of fulfillment in one's sex role, all these combine with frustration, anger, disappointment, and a sense of futility. There is room for much mutual recrimination between spouses. The woman may resent the man's relative freedom from childrearing chores; the man may envy the woman the amount of time she can spend with the children and their turning to her for many small matters of decision-making. Both may labor under the burden of the folk myth that a defective child is punishment for a parental sin. The low income father may be particularly pained by signs that his children and often his wife too judge his worth as an individual by his contribution to the family budget. High correlation of father status with work status operates to the advantage of the middle-class parent.

The maternal mystique which prevailed for many centuries assumed that mothers knew instinctively what was best for their children. This sustained a feeling of omniscience still found in some slum areas such as parts of London where the advice of "mum" is heeded over the professional's in the care of a sick child.

Increasingly, however, there is recognition that traditional parental performance—keeping a child clean and fed, respectful of property, and obedient—is not enough, and developmental conceptions include emotional well-being, social and intellectual development, and guidance which encourages children to ask and to make decisions for themselves. The importance of a father who is not merely a provider but one who can contribute to the emotional development of his children is beginning to be stressed. This creates new standards of knowledge for both parents concerning child development. Understanding the physical, emotional, and cognitive needs of a child is equally desirable for both parents so that a more consistent pattern of relating to the child will be developed between the couple. Even knowledge of child development, necessary as it is, cannot obviate the need for the couple to confer constantly in order to arrive at childrearing policies that reflect joint goals. If child development is the scientific knowledge base for parenting, childrearing is the philosophy in which the goal, the kind of child desired, is spelled out in the concrete.

parents and society

The parent role brings the family within societal control and criticism to a greater degree than the spousal role. Under present conditions, it tends to conservatize the couple, making them seek more respectable neighborhoods with better schools, surer employment even if less enjoyable, impulse control, and regularization of meals, bathing, and so on. There are exceptions, to be sure, as some young parents can be found in communes or earning hazardous livings in handicrafts or theater, establishing experimental schools outside the middle-class framework, and retaining some of the freedom they had before children came.

But for most young people, children bring unprecedented financial and emotional responsibility. The community and the broader society which will tolerate a wide range of behaviors among young people tend to tighten up when children are involved. In contrast with early historical periods when parents were all-powerful and could literally determine whether their children lived or died, there has been a steady erosion of parental power to the present when parents are held accountable for how they perform their role. The concept of children's rights is relatively new. It requires that a parent limit his child's punishment, send his children to school on time and properly clothed, provide support, and curb his own activities to ensure the child does not witness certain conduct. The neglectful or brutal parent may lose custody of his child, as may the prostitute mother or the swinging couple if their activity occurs where children may witness it.

Society seems to assume that in taking on the parent role the young man and woman know they cannot behave as they did before. This is rather a large assumption, because few young people have thought through all the consequences. There is sometimes a tendency to blame each other or to blame "marriage" for the many restraints put upon them as parents. Some express their frustration and disappointment in childbeating, some in desertion, some in increased use of alcohol or sexual exploits.

Constructive efforts to ease parental responsibility through child care centers, child allowances, guaranteed jobs and incomes, new housing for lower income families, broad medical coverage, school meals, and the like have begun. Women's liberation movements, in seeking a social structure that will permit equal opportunity for women, have urged decreased personal responsibility for children and greater contribution by the community. The impact on spousal relationships will undoubtedly be great, as the kibbutz has demonstrated in freeing the couple for more involvement with each other and with the community.

However, many parents have been socialized to a view of their role that makes it an unpleasant prospect to surrender their present power over children. It must be recognized that even though the parent role carries great responsibility it also offers an outlet for dominance needs. Not all work roles permit expression of leadership. The parental role ensures that for some years (spacing of the children can extend this for several decades), there is someone who can be ordered to bed, to study, to do chores, and so forth. It is not difficult to rationalize the pleasure in making decisions for others as simply doing one's duty as a parent. The earlier emancipation of adolescents and the principle of independence training for children at an early age go counter to expression of parental power, but this is largely theoretical for the middle class. Family reputations are too important to be entrusted to the risk-taking of the young, and subtle controls are instituted which last at least into the early years of adolescence.

This mention of parental power may seem contradictory to what has been said of the number of social agencies which share in socialization of the child. Certainly the school curbs parental power as to hours, vacations, even vocational choices, but it also acts to reenforce parental commands for getting to bed, taking baths, preparing homework, and the like.

the school and parental roles

In one sense the school, as a representative of the community, is the child's protector against parents who would exploit his labor, injure him, ignore his need for intellectual stimulation, as well as inoculations, eyeglasses, and so on. The school may be so child-focused, however, as to be destructive of the relationships of parents. The tendency to burden the parents with supervision of children's homework, a burden sometimes eagerly taken on by middle-class parents anxious for their child to excel in the academic competition, may for many homes be a negative factor in parent–child interaction. Not only does it mean an additional chore for working parents and reduce the time for carefree spousal interaction or perhaps discussions of world and community issues of importance to them as citizens, but also it ensures that parent–child interaction will be task-oriented in the few hours they have to spend together.

One solution suggested has been smaller classes in which fuller instruction takes place so that supplementation in the home is not needed. Again, the parent will have to choose among several values, one of which is greater community expenditure on teachers, classrooms, after-school study centers, and the like. Some parents welcome the assignment as teacher's assistant because, again, it permits expression of dominance needs. For other parents it may be an opportunity to "correct" teachings which do not fit in with their value systems, whether in the interpretation of history or the discussion of sexual behaviors. It is not likely that consensus among parents will be easily arrived at concerning which changes to adopt in an effort to modify parent responsibilities and frustrations.

illegitimacy

Parenthood out of wedlock has been most common among disadvantaged groups. The middle class has resorted to abortion or offered children for adoption. More children have been brought to term and reared in the girl's family of origin in the lower class, particularly among the black poor. In recent years both consensual union and children born outside of a legalized marriage have become more frequent in the middle class, even though the absolute figures are still low. In some instances this choice has been made by noted figures in theater or politics and has been widely publicized, as in the cases of Bernadette Devlin in the English parliament and Birgitta Dahl in the Swedish parliament.

While the legal consequences in matters of inheritance and paternal rights over the child differ from those in legitimized births, the emotional rewards and problems of parenthood would not seem to be different in kind for out-of-wedlock births. It is largely considerations of property and support rights that induce a society to distinguish between kinds of births. The laws which seek to ensure that family property not be dispersed among all offspring, legitimate or not, may have been appropriate when dowries and financial considerations loomed large in the marriage contract. Some now question their relevancy in a time when men and women are both in gainful employment, when they are responsible for the support of all their children in any case, and when the boundaries of the family unit are in process of revision. It is possible that the next few decades will bring dramatic changes in the definitions of the parent role as played by single persons, by nonmarried couples, by groups, as well as by the traditional couple. The impact on parent or on child has not yet begun to be measured, however, possibly because of the lack of sufficient groups in each category to be studied.

population control and parenthood

It is also likely that age of parenthood will rise as a greater interval is allowed to elapse between adolescence and the assumption of the parent role. The injunction to be young with your child is in the process of modification as sports, nutrition, labor-saving machinery ensure greater vigor for more decades. As women achieve greater equality, they may wish to defer childbearing to their late twenties. Among recent proposals is one that each individual have a first marriage as spouses and only later a second marriage undertaken for parenthood. Many organizations endorse delaying the parental role. The Planned Parenthood Association, for example, distributes among high school students a sheet asking teenagers to "Put First Things First: (1) Finish school; (2) get the job you want; (3) marry and fix up your home; (4) take time to know each other and have fun together; and (5) then have your first baby."

Biological parenthood, whether in wedlock or out, has almost no restrictions. In contrast, parental character and solvency are carefully examined when a couple wants to adopt a child. Indeed, adoption has proceeded on many questionable assumptions concerning fitness for the parent role. Until 1971, for example, it was possible for a couple to be denied adoption rights if they were atheists. The New Jersey Supreme Court, however, has held that "the question of religion or lack of it should have no bearing on whether prospective parents should be judged fit to adopt children." It is likely that adoptive parenthood will be increasingly broadened to include the single person of either sex, now that divorce has created so many one-parent families without dire consequences for the offspring although it may in many instances be more difficult for the lone parent without another person to share the many responsibilities.

The changed abortion laws in many states, making abortion a backup measure for ineffective contraceptives, have already reduced the number of children available for adoption; new emphasis may be laid on treatment for infertility. At present between a fifth and a sixth of all women reach menopause without having born a child. It is undetermined what proportion were infertile and what proportion chose to forego parenthood. Further research is needed on couples who do not add the parental to the spousal role.

IN-LAWS OR "OUTLAWS"

In a study made in a London slum, outlaws was the term applied by "mum" (with a grin) to those of her sons-in-law who did not want to fit into the pattern which made her home the emotional hub of the extended kin network.

In most early cultures, neither generation had a choice concerning in-laws. The relationships of affinal families were fairly clearly defined. In patrilocal families, with the husband bringing his bride to his parents' home, the domination of his mother was expected. Not only in Asia but in many parts of Europe the bride could be bossed, persecuted, and outrivaled in bids for affection by the husband's mother and unmarried sisters. The husband typically had very little relationship with his wife's kin who usually lived in another village. The young wife's lowly position improved as she bore sons and as her mother-in-law aged; she could look forward to replacing her as the household tyrant in the life of her son's wife. Folk sayings and songs, as well as suicide rates of young wives, as in pre-Communist China, bore witness to the unhappiness that accompanied the in-law role.

american in-law relationships

A reversal of power in the relationship of the young woman to her mother-in-law characterizes the present. In the American culture, in-law relationships are not explicitly institutionalized. Neolocal residence and the nuclear family structure tend to allow much decision-making by the individual couples. The young wife is fairly free to exclude her mother-in-law from playing any role of importance in the life of her grandchild or the social activities of the young pair. However, initially a kind of sparring may determine the limits. If the husband's mother has not opposed his marriage and is pleasant in personality, she is more likely to be accepted by her daughter-in-law. This is not by virtue of any ascribed position in the family constellation, but achievement through personal liking. If the younger woman has not resolved negative feelings about her own mother or about adults generally, she may be defensive and ready to interpret offers of help as interference.

The traditional overinvolvement of women in the lives of their family members is in process of change as more women enter gainful employment and seek fulfillment of their own potentials. However, the change may not eliminate altogether problems of relationships with affinal relatives. Moreover, the majority of women are still housewives in the United States, with more time and motivation to relate to their married children. Studies show mothers and sisters generally create more in-law difficulties than fathers and brothers. While overvaluation of the males in their lives may be one contributing factor, another is undoubtedly found in the mate selection process in which, except in the upper classes, the parent may have had little opportunity to develop affection for the "stranger" suddenly brought into an intimate relationship.

There is suspicion on both sides. The mother fears being shut out of her son's life. The young wife is fearful that she may compare unfavorably with the older woman in home management and ability to offer nurturance in illness. Where the young husband assumes equal responsibility for daily chores and childrearing, he is more likely to accept with humor his mother's comments on their housekeeping and their children. The mother is also likely to reduce the comments, although her complaints may be directed against equalitarianism as unfair to her son. Where the house and children have been the specialized responsibility of his wife, he may take the mother's comments more seriously and either be angry at the mother for downgrading the wife he has chosen or angry at his wife for depriving him of the degree of comfort his mother reminds him to expect.

The critical mother-in-law who comments on the young husband's loss of weight or tired look, the soiled towels in the bathroom, the missing buttons on the children's clothes, to say nothing of voicing disapproval of the young wife's working, going to school, or political activities, may find herself shut out by the new norms which make family visits a matter for negotiation rather than taken for granted.

in-laws' effect on the
spousal relationships

This may make for wariness in the relationship. One psychiatrist reports a characteristic comment by a mother-in-law in a discussion session: "I have to walk on eggs around my son's family." On the other hand, unlike traditional in-law relationships which assumed emotional distance between the women and avoidance techniques across sex lines, there is the possibility today of greater intimacy, genuine liking and deep friendships, and strong affection between the generations with both affinal families. The historical heritage, however, expressed in cartoons and jokes which assume trouble in the relationship may sometimes make it difficult to express the actual affection felt. The audience still laughs ruefully when the comedian refers to his mother-in-law, and discussions among young wives still define "her" as the enemy even though all may not share equally in feelings of antipathy.

The mother's clinging to a son and feeling jealous of his wife is socially disapproved. The discontinuity of roles is greater for her than for the mother of a married daughter. Industrialization has made the patrilocal family rare and has increased the emphasis on mother–daughter relationships. It is a rare society now in which the daughter is expected to be wholly engrossed in her husband's family. It is more common for in-law relationships to focus strongly on the wife's family. The girl and her mother have socially approved channels for the expression of joint interests: shopping, child care, cooking, and the like. Changes under way in women's roles will undoubtedly have some impact on this relationship in future decades. The old saying, "A man is a son until he takes him a wife, the woman a daughter all of her life," which finds much support today, may not survive the growth in equalitarian relationships which pulls spouses closer together or women's involvement in activities outside the home which dissipates the extent of common interests among women.

All through their married lives, husbands and wives will be making decisions about their relationships with in-laws, especially now that longevity rates ensure the older generation is likely to be around to see their grandchildren start families of their own. These decisions will involve recreational visiting; financial help; emotional support; and aid in times of illness, bereavement, and other crises. How the spouse feels about his own parents will be an important variable in these determinations.

working out in-law relationships

How much should mate selection take in-laws into consideration? If it is difficult enough to determine whether one is in love and whether one's interests and values are sufficiently congruent to encourage a joint life, to say nothing of learning about each other's mental and physical histories, it is even more difficult to anticipate all the outcomes, emotional and financial, of interaction with the various members of each other's family of origin.

It is usually left to the marital years, despite early attempts before marriage to reach some agreements, to work out the nature of the social and help relationships with affinal families. Situations and feelings change. The couple that moved far away to ensure freedom from both pairs of in-laws may find after a few years that they miss them more than anticipated and that they can now tolerate some of their annoying habits with greater equanimity than before. The old joke about how much smarter the father seems to have grown in the years between the son's adolescence and young adulthood has some reality basis. The years can bring new perspectives to both generations.

Most difficult for the younger couple to work out between themselves are wide gaps in their feelings about certain family members. A son may maintain resentful feelings toward his parents while his wife finds in them many positive qualities. Or the wife may feel fondness for a brother which her husband does not share. Children tend to get the messages, verbalized or not, as to which grandmother is more welcomed, which grandfather leaves the parents quarreling after a visit, which relatives are tolerated, shunned, or warmly welcomed. It is not easy for a disliked mother-in-law to establish a positive relationship with a grandchild, although in adolescence there is sometimes a defensive alliance formed with the oldest generation against the one in the middle.

Just as young couples fear interference from their parents, so too in later years the parents fear a reversal of roles, with decisions made by their grown children without prior consultation of their wishes in such matters as a place to live in case of infirmity, which doctor to call, the kind of funeral, and the like.

The assertion, "I'm marrying him (her) and not his (her) family," would seem to be a debatable one. Certainly greater couple independence is possible now, but some intertwining of the lives of a couple and their families of origin is likely to occur. The outcomes vary in satisfaction and in grievance. The lack of clearcut norms offers flexibility and individual decision-making. On the other hand, lack of norms may be confusing and provide few guidelines for "what is right."

The tangle of conscious motivations in in-law relationships seems simple, however, in comparison with the unconscious motivations stressed by Freudians, as suggested in the following:

> In-law troubles involve incestuous prototypes and anaclitic elements which go deep into the life history of individuals. The wife's

mother may cause discord because she leads the daughter to demand of the husband what she herself would like to have if she could live her life over again—this time with him. . . . The husband's mother may demand of the daughter-in-law that she treat him the way he would have been treated if he had married his mother, his first love, from whom he has been stolen. The wife's father may look upon the husband as an interloper who took his love-object away. The husband's father may be jealous of his own son who is living a youth which the father would like to relive. . . .[2]

---

[2] George Simpson, *People in Families* (New York: Thomas Y. Crowell Company, 1960), p. 204.

12

the
next
time
around:
family
dissolution
and
reintegration

Societies differ in their definition of how much strain should be tolerated in the marriage relationship and the means by which such strain should be alleviated. In some countries the only relief for the woman comes in suicide, prayer, or immersion in the maternal role; for the man a wider latitude may be offered through additional wives, concubines, or a mistress system. Most societies, however, allow family dissolution through divorce. The judgment as to how much strain should be tolerated before divorce is rarely left up to the individuals themselves. Laws and judges usually set limits to the ease with which the divorce alternative may be used. In some societies divorce is not equally available to both sexes. Patriarchal societies have favored the male either by limiting grounds for divorce severely, permitting no divorce on the wife's initiative, or giving custody of children to the father and his kin.

THE DIVORCE PROCESS

In the contemporary world the marriage contract may read "for better or for worse, in sickness or in health, and until death do us part," but few couples or legal systems consider this commitment binding in any literal sense. It has not been evident that in countries like Brazil, Spain, and Portugal, and until recently Italy, the denial of divorce has kept the embers of a dying marital relationship alive. On the contrary, mistresses, prostitutes, and consensual unions have highlighted the difficulty of enforcing human regard by fiat.

Each society struggles with the problem of how easy or how hard to make the divorce process. Some argue that making it too easy may encourage impulsive separations and quick remarriages. In the Soviet Union where revolution and difficult civil war years brought many family separations and remarriage became impossible because of the uncertain whereabouts of family members, the 1918 laws requiring a court decision were modified to permit easy divorce through a simple system of registration at ZAGS, the civil statistical bureau. As of 1926, postcard notice to the other spouse permitted the spouse seeking divorce to obtain it quickly and remarry if desired. The informality, low cost, and speed of procedure encouraged a high divorce rate in the absence of positive environmental and interpersonal conditions. However, this is seen by some as a natural consequence of long years of enforced togetherness under restrictive Tsarist laws, and urge that Soviet experience under negative historical and economic conditions should not be taken as an example of the marital chaos that must necessarily follow from easy divorce.

When the Soviets abandoned the postcard procedure and reintroduced courts and judges into the process in 1936, divorce rates fell. This did not mean that husband–wife strain was diminished; it represented state intervention to slow the decision to divorce. When in 1944 the Soviets introduced further complexities into the divorce procedure and developed what many deemed a very difficult divorce process, the result was in many cases de facto bigamy, with a marked increase in consensual unions. The divorce process was eased in the 1960s in response both to this outcome and to improved living conditions. Soviet history exemplifies in a short span of time the twin dangers of too easy and too difficult divorce systems. Other countries have had similar experiences with one or the other. But the debate continues as to which has the most negative effects on the individual and his family, personal decisions with a minimum of state intervention or a series of barriers deliberately set up by the state.

Some societies have used a mistress system or consensual second marriages as substitutes for divorce.
In Italy the advocates of legalizing divorce cam-
paigned successfully in the streets, as shown in this
photograph, and by 1970 the divorce law was on
the books. However, it is in danger of abrogation as
conservative forces have rallied to force Italy back
among the no-divorce societies.

Reproduced by permission of The New York Times.

divorce in america

New York law for many years made adultery the sole ground for divorce,
although felony convictions carrying long sentences were also acceptable.
Such restrictiveness resulted in flights to Nevada, or other places with
easy divorce laws, by the well-to-do, including the state's first lady, to
take advantage of the variation in laws among the states. For the less
affluent there was recourse through perjured adultery testimony in the
courts. Until recently not only the parties to divorce but lawyers, judges,
and witnesses felt sullied by the process.

If divorce can be regarded as the burial of a dead marriage, there
were more corpses than funerals in 19th century America. It is estimated
that there were several "empty shell" marriages for every one that went
through legal dissolution ceremonies. In 1860 1.2 per 1,000 existing marriages ended in divorce. Each decade after that there was a rise, however,

with a more than threefold increase to 4.0 by the turn of the century, and more than sixfold to 7.7 shortly after the end of the First World War. The spectacular rise after the Second World War to 18.2 per 1,000 did not maintain itself, and the rate of divorce of less than 10 per 1,000 existing marriages continued with only slight variations into the 1960s.

FACTORS IN LOW 19TH CENTURY DIVORCE RATES

In the 19th century, many factors contributed to a low divorce rate. Women were a small proportion of the labor force and had to accept negative marital conditions for lack of another support base. Husbands did not always seek the divorce available to them. A double sex standard made adultery a common alternative. The expense of divorce deterred many low income families. Public censure deterred those of more means. Many husbands and wives maintained a joint home but did not speak to each other, except through the children. Some women of strong will managed to achieve physical separation despite the law's endorsement of forced cohabitation. Mrs. Pantier talks from her grave in Edgar Lee Master's *Spoon River Anthology* and tells why she drove her husband away from home "to live with his dog in a dingy room back of his office." She found him disgusting as a sex partner, smelling of whiskey and onions and failing to match her "delicate tastes" in food and poetry. The census statistics would have listed the Pantiers as an intact family.

It should be evident that divorce statistics, weak in any case on a national level with many estimates for lack of precise data, give little indication of the totality of marital unhappiness. They tell us only how many families have legalized their emotional separation. Nor are they a reliable indicator of family stability, except in a most formal sense.

The late 19th and early 20th century saw great public debate about divorce. While divorce rates were rising, they were kept lower than they might have been by a new tendency to defer marriage. In contrast to the early 19th century when teenage marriages were common, by 1890 fewer than half of women twenty to twenty-four years of age were married. Only about half of women college graduates in the 19th century married. This finds an interesting historical parallel with findings in India today where women college students fear that husbands will expect them to retreat into traditional roles and men college students are fearful of marrying "the new woman" with her equalitarian expectations and her unwillingness to be subservient to his mother.

PRESENT ATTITUDES TOWARD DIVORCE

Many of the arguments about divorce heard decades ago are still with us today. The Catholic church officially maintains the same position of opposition to divorce and especially to remarriage, despite the wide use of secular means by former parishioners. The Protestant churches were split, some in the Episcopal church going so far as to urge excommunication for any who attended remarriages of divorced friends or relatives. Some in the Presbyterian church sought to have ministers forbidden to remarry divorced persons.

Divorce was seen as resulting from character defects, especially in women who were said to expect too much from marriage. Theodore Roosevelt, president at the height of the debate, saw an international plot spearheaded by socialists seeking to destroy the moral fiber of a capitalist society by creating marital turmoil. The more serious argument advanced against divorce was that marriage was not intended to achieve happiness and that the individual's satisfaction must derive from doing his duty in maintaining a stable family unit for his society.

On the other side there were the now familiar arguments that the individual has a right to happiness, and a marriage which is destructive of this has no right to continue to exist. Also argued was that divorce was not the cause but the effect of weaknesses in the family system; these weaknesses should be overcome by institutional reform rather than by limiting divorce. It was further urged that divorce strengthened the family in the long run and was a morally positive act, for only those homes would remain intact which had a strong love base, conducive to personality enrichment of spouses and offering inspirational models to offspring.

The arguments heard among feminists today that marriage and family life are destructive of women and children's potentials, that marriage contracts should be of limited duration, that institutional aids should relieve women of bondage to domestic duties, that men themselves would benefit by new family forms, had their faint beginnings at the turn of the century. Mona Caird in 1890 proposed a marriage contract that would have to be renegotiated periodically, a kind of automatic divorce at intervals unless specific effort was made to continue the marriage. Margaret Gilman in 1903 was writing and speaking about the importance of gainful employment for women and a rational home in which domestic labor would be streamlined by communal housing and catered meals, co-operative nurseries, and the like.

Despite the pressures for more divorce, most family dissolutions in the late 19th century and early 20th came about not from divorce but through the death of a spouse. At the time of the Civil War, 31.5 of every 1,000 existing marriages terminated by death; 26 in 1,000 ended this way in the early 1900s. By the 1950s the rate had fallen to 17.5 as the country's health improved and longevity rose. Black families do not enjoy as favorable rates; black women are widowed at an earlier age than white women. Some demographers maintain that despite the rise in divorce rates, the dramatic decline in the death rate has brought more stability to the American family now than ever before; that is, in the sense of legally unbroken marriage. Increases in accident rates, however, have created a new threat to family stability.

DIVORCE AND ETHCLASS

Many unhappy or dissatisfied couples remain married today. Why do some families break up and some remain together? Research in the 1940s suggested that children of divorced parents in a middle-class sample were more likely to use legal means of ending their own marriage relationship. However, some psychiatrists report that children of divorced parents are reluctant to follow the parental example, and tend to work harder at keeping the family together. Lower-class families have the highest divorce rate. Not only are there various environmental stresses of unemployment, of low pay, poor housing, poor health, but also the lack of education is often accompanied by lesser skills of communication, more stereotypical conceptions of appropriate sex roles and hence lesser flexibility, and lesser sensitivity to needs for sympathy, companionship, and emotional closeness. Moreover, lesser knowledge of birth control results in more children, and these may add to stress in crowded homes.

In advantaged homes, too, divorce occurs, but there seems to be some tendency to tolerate lack of emotional closeness because of the other gains in the relationship. Cuber's examination of over 400 upper-middle-class men and women in the late 1950s, those with annual incomes over $20,000 at that time, married over ten years, and with considerable autonomy in the occupational sphere, revealed that even among those termed "significant Americans" because of their status achievements, few were in the top categories of marital satisfaction.[1] "Total" and "Vital" were the highest levels in a five-part typology of marital relationships devised by the researchers, which descended to "Passive-Congenial," "Devitalized," and "Conflict-Habituated." Most of the marriages investigated fell into the "Passive-Congenial" slot, in which there was little conflict, some common interests, but also lack of enthusiasm and excitement in the relationship. Extramarital affairs were commonly accepted as a supplement to a somewhat monotonous monogamy.

Some readers of the research would admire these couples for staying together. Some would consider them immoral to be living unintimately in an intimate relationship. The basis of judgment is tied to a broader societal and personal value system. If a society values keeping families

---

[1] John F. Cuber and Peggy B. Haroff, *The Significant Americans: A Study of Sexual Behavior Among the Affluent* (New York: Appleton-Century-Crofts, 1965).

intact, even though emotional satisfaction is at a low level, the maintenance of passive-congenial relationships, even if within a system of prostitution, mistresses, and periodic affairs, will be seen as desirable and will be given public approval. If a society values fulfillment of emotional potential, it will regard such marriages as inadequate, even hypocritical.

Actually, all societies seem to be conflicted, valuing both stability and personal growth. Divorcing couples do create problems for a society in which children are reared in families and supported by parents. The majority of divorced couples are parents. The father's wage that could barely support one household can rarely be stretched to two or three. In the lower class where divorce is the principal escape mechanism from marital failure, either the divorced wife must enter the job market or the community must pick up the tab for support of the children. If the job market is limited and the community reluctant to pay, there is a tendency to welcome stability at any price.

divorce in the kibbutz

In the kibbutz divorce brings no added economic burden to the individual or the collective unless a parent leaves. Husband and wife have both been working and continue to do so after the divorce. Housing assignments are shifted, to be sure, with both returning to the singles house or section until remarriage. If a divorced parent leaves, he or she must send back to the kibbutz part of the wage earned elsewhere. This can create personal or community hardships in case of remarriage. But if both remain in the kibbutz, divorce creates a minimum of financial upset. The visitation problem which looms so large in other societies is relatively easily solved when children continue to live as they did before the divorce and parents can see them in neutral settings.

divorce in the Soviet Union

In the Soviet Union the divorce rate is high and will undoubtedly continue so until marked reductions in stress connected with housing and domestic duties come about. With the majority of women in gainful employment, inadequate development of communal services makes for fatigue and irritation at home. The large and well-supported system of child care services even in urban areas is inadequate to the demand. The birth rate has fallen markedly, with the one-child family modal in large cities, but this has not wholly solved the problem of comfortable family living, although a comprehensive health care system reduces many family anxieties.

While the Soviet society considers it desirable to hold the divorce rate down and seeks sober reflection in choice of a mate, there is no admiration for unhappy or indifferent couples who remain together. The ideology stresses equality and companionship in the spousal relationship. Soviet theorists would probably claim that Cuber's passive-congenial pair relationship represents a trading of individual potential for a mess of middle-class porridge—indeed a kind of legalized prostitution with the woman entering into cohabitation not because of a great love but to gain the comforts and status that the husband's salary and status provide.

divorce in America

It might be said that many young people in the United States view their parents' marriages in somewhat the same light and are determined that their marriages will either be deferred until they can enter a relationship of great meaning or will be broken if the relationship ceases to be an intense and satisfying one. This would seem to augur more divorces and more remarriages in the future. Today a fifth of those entering marriage are doing so for the second time. The trend is not likely to be a sharp or dramatic one, however. Most couples tolerate unhappiness for some time, indeed some for decades, before filing for divorce. Research on blue collar marriage in the early 1960s in a sample of some eighty couples found that about a third were happily married, another third moderately so, and a third were unhappy. Nationwide data are lacking, but several studies of disenchantment in marriage suggest that the findings may be generalized to most marriages in the United States.

Some of the deterrents include state laws which make divorce difficult, expensive, or degrading. Several states, notably California, have recently changed their laws in a direction that eliminates adversary proceedings. Mental health specialists have long urged that pitting husband against wife and trying to affix "blame" for failure of the relationship is harmful; it prevents each spouse from doing the "homework," the effort to reach greater understanding, that is necessary if remarriage is one day to provide greater happiness. Moreover, if there are children, it is essential that the parenting proceed after the divorce in a way that maximizes cooperation between the former spouses. This is less likely if one of them has been declared the "injured party" and the other the "wrongdoer."

THE EFFECTS OF DIVORCE

Major studies of the effects of divorce or of bereavement on the lives of men, women, and children are very much needed. The few studies so far have been limited geographically, have had small samples, or have tapped feelings characteristic of a different decade. It is likely that attitudes and

behaviors have changed in recent years. While divorce rates have remained fairly stable since 1946, the cumulative effect of almost half a
million divorces a year means that it is a rare family that today is not
related to one or another divorced man or woman. Familiarity undoubtedly has tended to destroy some of the persistent myths that divorce is
usually an arbitrary and willful decision, that the divorced person will
never be able to find happiness in marriage, that it would have been
better for the children if the unhappy pair had remained together.

At the same time this familiarity with divorced family members has
tended to provide a realistic awareness of the difficulties that follow divorce. As in any surgical procedure, there are likely to be complications;
this may hardly dictate burying the scalpel. One writer refers to the alien,
bewildering, unmapped land of the Formerly Married, and describes
those in the first year or two following divorce as constituting a kind of
subculture, with common problems and few well-developed norms to
follow. Some experience relief, some grief. Some find friends who had
enjoyed relating to them as a couple reluctant to continue with an available single. Some find sexual overtures too abundant; some feel sexually
neglected. Most blame themselves, the spouse, or circumstances, but few
seem to lose confidence in marriage as an institution. The majority remarry within a few years, and the majority of first remarriages do not
end in divorce.

This latter fact suggests that either more careful mate selection occurs
the second time around, or the divorced person knows himself better, or
there is a lowering of expectations in marriage and greater reality orientation. It is possible that the couple who has lived consensually and
breaks up the relationship after several years goes through a similar
process and enters a legalized marriage with all the experience, pain, and
changed expectations of the formerly married. There are some indications
that remarriage rates will be lowered or the mate selection process slowed
down as cohabitation before marriage becomes more common for second
marriages.

children and divorce

Children of divorce have not been carefully studied, nor have stepparent–stepchild relationships in the United States. One in every ten
children now has a stepparent. Folklore provides negative images, comparable to the stereotype of the mother-in-law. But just as many instances
of warm relationships are now being found in the one, the other has
similar positive potential. However, it must be recognized that not only
is courtship more difficult with children in the picture but the marital
relationship is likely to be affected.

Custody is still given mainly to mothers. This is changing, and the change will accelerate as more women go to work. But at present the man who dates a divorced woman with children is more aware of her responsibilities and emotional ties than a woman who dates a divorced man. However, the latter situation may be deceptive as the full extent of his involvement with his former wife and with visiting and supporting the children may come to light only after the new marriage occurs. In both instances, there may be some degree of sexual jealousy of the former mate and some hostility to the children as symbols of that former intimacy. At a period when premarital abstinence or the double standard was more in evidence, this was probably more of a problem than today when each person is aware that the other may have had a sexual-affectional history of some complexity.

REMARRIAGE

Nonetheless, the remarriage, particularly when children are involved, has more problems to cope with than first marriage. Various psychologists have emphasized one or another of the following questions that must be faced by a man or a woman who is considering marriage to a divorced person. The questions seem to have pertinence for the establishment of any new, serious relationship whether in marriage or outside.

1. Was the first marriage ever happy, beyond the first few weeks? (Is the divorced person one who can be happy in a continued relationship? Is the person constructively at odds with society or continuously at odds with life and needing a partner as a butt for hostility expression?)

2. Is this new relationship a rebound phenomenon? (Has the divorced person had enough time to get perspective on what happened and to know his own needs?)

3. Do you find yourself being compared to the first spouse? (Is this a source of irritation to you and will it affect the relationship?)

4. Will you set up a new home together, live in your place, or will you enter the place left vacant by a previous relationship? (If the latter, will question 3 become even more pronounced a problem?)

5. Is there resistance on the part of his friends and relatives? (Do they perceive him as entering a new relationship too soon? Have they any axes to grind or are they solicitous for his welfare?)

6. Is this a divorce-prone individual, with several previous unfortunate relationships? (How much time had elapsed between remarriages, and was the kind of dissatisfaction similar in each of the relationships?)

7. Will the former mate be reconciled to the new relationship or constitute a disrupting factor? (What financial and visitation arrangements have been made?)

8. Are children of the former marriage to reside with you? (What ages, sexes, and are you prepared to play a parent role either continuously or for visitation periods?)

9. What is the relationship of the children of a former marriage to their various grandparents and what will be your obligations in this regard? (Are you prepared to relate to a network of kinfolk which includes affinal relatives of the divorced person?)

10. Was the first marriage interfaith, interracial, international, and are you prepared to be involved in the rearing of children being brought up in a different religion or subculture? (Do you know the kinds of bias you are likely to introduce into the relationship with the children of the divorced person?)

It will be seen that most of the questions are equally appropriate in selecting a widowed person as a mate. That person has various affinal commitments, and if there are bereaved children, many financial and emotional problems similar to the divorce situation will be part of the new relationship. The aftermath of the Vietnam War will leave many younger widows who will undoubtedly remarry. Older persons, too, are increasingly likely to seek remarriage. Their motivations, according to one study, may be more practical, a pooling of scarce resources in old age, but elements of companionship are an important consideration along with sexual satisfaction. In short, remarriage or further paramarriages would seem to be a lifelong probability for the American family.

the remarriage relationships

Relationships with the new spouse have few norms on which kin can base their behaviors. Just as the questions raised above prior to a new relationship indicated a variety of variables, there are questions, some major, some minor, which reflect problems in integrating the new relationship once it is established.

1. *Mementos?* Do scrapbooks, pictures, favorite chair, etc., all tangible reminders of the past, stand in the way of unity in the new family? These memorabilia are usually thought of in connection with bereavement, but similar records of previous spousal and parental relationships are present in divorce as well. They have emotional meaning which can be violated by the new member of the family or can rekindle feelings in others.

2. *Names?* Terms of endearment previously used by the absent spouse or parent may be resented when coming from the lips of the new family member. Stepchildren, especially older ones, may have difficulty finding a way of addressing the parent's new spouse. This may be less of a problem where the first name is used than where the role name (father, mother) is expected.

3. *Location?* A given neighborhood may have many emotional connotations. Yet a new locale may be viewed negatively by children who must adjust not only to a new parent but to a new community. This is even more complicated if both spouses bring children to the marriage. The children who remain in their old neighborhood may regard the new members of the family as invaders and resent sharing their home.

4. *Adoption?* There are important legal consequences of a support and inheritance kind. The emotional impact can be unifying or it can create feelings of disloyalty in children toward the missing biological parent.

5. *Competition and favoritism?* The tendency for the deceased to be overvalued—the halo effect—may make the new spouse uneasy in the effort to become the favorite, to compete successfully with the shadow of a former relationship. While this is not usually a problem in divorce, assuming the rejected spouse has worked through feelings of anger roused by an unexpected demand for divorce, the rearing of children assumes added complications at several generational levels. Competition for the children's affection may take place:

   a. Between the children's biological parents now divorced.

   b. Between the new parent and the biological parent of the same sex.

   c. Between the parents of the former spouse and the parents of the new one; not only these sets of grandparents but additional ones are involved. The child may be neglected by all for whom the child is a symbol of an unsuccessful relationship, or be overwhelmed by additional kin, not only grandparents, but multiple aunts, uncles, and cousins.

Competition is not limited to the adults. The children may compete with the new father for the mother's affection or with the new mother for the father's affection. The children may compete among themselves for parental affection.

Many of these same problems occur in first marriages, too, with competitive bids for attention from both sides of the family, mementos of premarital loves, location changes which are threatening to one spouse or to the children. The complexity, or the potential for it, is greater in remarriage. One sociologist claims that the heterogeneity of American cultural patterns and the wide range of personality types increase the danger of personality clashes between stepparents and stepchildren and menace the stability of remarriages. But it is also likely that an increasing tolerance of variations in behaviors and appearances that has marked the last few years, together with the frequency of the stepparent phenomenon, may tend to decrease apprehension and encourage friendships within the family. There have been no studies to show that the generation gap is any wider in the family of remarriage than in the intact family.

As self-understanding grows and people are freer to confront their own feelings, recognition by parents and by children of the sources of their hostilities and resentments, and acceptance of the right to release negative emotions, may permit a more comfortable togetherness in the relatively few years of intensive interaction between the generations. Auxiliary institutions like preschool and after-school centers may relieve both generations in original or divorced homes of some of the emotional overload of the small nuclear family. Awareness that most years of their lives will be spent with each other and not with their children may encourage spouses to reduce the intensity of their involvement with their children.

epilogue: the future of the family

In various chapters of this book mention has been made of trends and likelihoods for the future. It was stated that certain tasks must be performed if a society is to continue to exist, but it is not necessarily the family unit that must perform them. Most societies call some grouping that performs one or another of four basic functions (replacement, socialization, economic, sexual-affectional) the family. These groupings are structured in a variety of ways and divide power among their members diversely.

KEEPING THE FAMILY

The attempt to abolish the family unit altogether was tried in the Shaker subculture, but their sex-segregated communities had no way of replacing themselves except by recruitment from the host culture. In most revolutionary societies the call was not for abolition of the family but of the older family forms. Thus, the French Revolution and the American Revolution saw the aristocratic family as outdated, and the Russian and Chinese Revolutions aimed at replacing the bourgeois family with the socialist family. Projections for the future in socialist countries are not spelled out in any detail, but there seems to be an assumption that some family unit will persist into the stage of communism.

With the community services lightening domestic responsibilities, men and women will consider their own development, their relationship to each other and to the community, as important as their relationship to their children. The crystal ball seems to foretell a unit of man and woman united by ties of affection, sexual attraction, joint ideological commitments, with much of child care in community hands and economic abundance freeing the family from financial obligations. In such a setting, men and women, humanized by leisure for participation in the arts and aided in mobility and life styles by technological advances, will maintain their relationships as long as they find satisfaction in them. There is no estimate offered for how long such love and companionship based families will endure.

It is assumed that even in favorable living conditions, with people who are sensitive and growing, there will be shifts of marital partners. The mechanisms to achieve stability will be incorporated in the value system rather than in governmental control. In a stateless society there may be no divorces because there are no marriages. Consensual union may place the emphasis on personal consent. There seem to be no guarantees in the offing, even for communist society, that the readiness of one partner to move on to another relationship will mesh neatly with the readiness of the original partner to sever the bond. It would seem that absence of pain in man–woman relationships is promised in no society, present or future.

THE AMERICAN FAMILY

As for the projection of trends in the American family for the next decade or two, it has been pointed out by one sociologist that extrapolation from current developments is hazardous. Not only do we lack knowledge of what the future economy will be—and we have seen how important the economic variable is for family form and functioning—but some trends are short-term and some long. For example, among trends visible by the early 1960s were more people getting married, younger age at marriage, larger family size for the middle class, more births out of wedlock for the lower class, and so forth. Not all of these trends were still evident a decade later. It is likely that the 1970s will show some rise in age at marriage as more couples defer legalization of their relationship, smaller family size as the women's liberation movement combines with population control groups to de-emphasize the maternal role, and fewer births out of wedlock as abortion laws in more states are modified or abolished.

Demands for more flexibility in division of domestic tasks, the provision of child care services, and more equalitarian power allocations in the home will undoubtedly influence husband–wife relationships in the future. The degree of influence will undoubtedly be dependent on job

Communes of diverse types can now be found on almost every continent. There are probably more of them in the United States than elsewhere. Those in China's rural regions are production communes rather than family combines. The picture shows one attempt in Sweden to find alternatives to the nuclear family.
Enrico Sarsini, Life © 1969 Time Inc.

availability, willingness of government to underwrite child care costs, and expansion of educational opportunities for men and women to come to grips with the load of traditional beliefs that still burden their thinking about themselves and each other.

The commune movement will probably continue to grow, and will remain diverse in form. Further study of communes may indicate that they do not replace the family but are themselves a new family form. Some seem to model themselves on role allocations within equalitarian nuclear units, although patriarchal communes can be found too; but more often there is a search for the extended family pattern with its interchangeability of adult roles and the availability of a whole array of significant others in the same household.

The difference from the family would seem to be the crucial element of choice. The family, once it is founded by the marriage of non-kin, tends to expand on consanguineous lines. The commune, in contrast, erases the importance of blood relationship and substitutes friendship or joint commitment to a set of values. However, the commune has not yet met or faced fully the problem of socialization of the next generation. If the commune were to supersede present family patterns on any considerable scale, it would have to ensure economic survival for the group and create some structure to ensure childrearing when biological parents are either not easily ascertainable or are uncommitted to the responsibility. Most communes with young children in them have been in existence too few years for the effects of multiple parenting to be measured.

MODIFYING THE FAMILY

A spate of books in recent years demonstrates the great interest not only among youth but among professionals in the family field to modify the present family. Many suggestions have been made, such as the following:

1. Slow down the mate selection process and test compatibility through a prolonged relationship.

2. Offer premarital education and counseling to encourage self-understanding and help the individual determine his or her readiness for a serious yet enjoyable and enduring yet severable relationship.

3. Offer child development education and institutional aids to childrearing so that couples may understand the parental role, their readiness for it, and be aided in maintenance of a close spousal relationship all through the years of parenting.

4. Reform the divorce process to simplify it and reduce emotional and financial trauma connected with it.

5. Reduce working hours for men and women, in keeping with the greater productivity of advanced technology, and create time for more self-development, interaction among friends and relatives, and involvement in community problems.

6. Redesign housing as well as educational and medical institutions to take advantage of new psychological knowledge concerning stress, sexual needs of all groups in the population, and the dual desires for intimacy and privacy.

7. Socialize children to new concepts of male–female relatedness.

8. Encourage a variety of family forms and allocate funds to study their differential consequences.

Behavioral scientists are at odds in their predictions and their preferences. Some think greater attention should be given the spousal pair in the family of the future, with emphasis on their growth as individuals and as community members to ensure variety and excitement in their sexual and social encounters. Others think the pair bond should be only one in a complex of relationships with kin, colleagues, and friends, with sexual activities not limited to marriage. Some ask that a variety of relationships be legitimized, ranging from group or corporate marriage to polygamous and homosexual associations. Others ask the state to stay out and remove all regulation of marriage and divorce by law, permitting couples and groups to stay together only so long as they find their relationships fulfilling.

Along with these proposals are heard suggestions for alleviating strains in conventional marriage: child care institutional aids, preventive and curative medical care available to all, housing and jobs, cradle to grave family life and sex education, and innovative counseling and social work. In the latter category is the suggestion that a trained professional "third parent" be a common feature of family structure; he would add the male image to a network of homes deprived of fathers either because of hours of work or total absence in bereavement or divorce.

It is evident that many proposed changes in the family would require thoroughgoing economic and distribution changes. The student as individual, family member, citizen, and future professional will find it helpful to examine each proposal in terms of its possibility—which basic changes will the American people underwrite—and its desirability—what kinds of people would the modified family or the nonfamily tend to produce and is this the direction in which he wants to go? The vote, voice, thinking, and activity of each student will determine the kind of family structures that emerge.

suggested activities for students

I. Finding out what others think family life and sex education is.
  A. Each student may interview a few people to see what they think. Will students work in groups or alone?
    1. This will raise questions of a representative sample or deliberate choice of only a selected population.
      a. Are you mainly interested in what students in your school think?
      b. What parents think?
      c. What "the man on the street" thinks?
    2. This will raise questions of record keeping.

a. Will the student have a tape recorder and ask the interviewee to say a few sentences into the mike? Will these be subjected to content analysis or will the class listen to the tapes?

b. Will the student have index cards and write down the remarks as the interviewee speaks?

c. Will the student distribute a ditto sheet of preformulated descriptions of family life and sex education for the interviewee to check off several items? How will the answers be tallied and reported?

B. Some students may prefer to get to know whether various authorities in the field agree or disagree. A start in this direction can be made by looking at several books or professional journals. Appendix III offers a pertinent reading, "Family Life and Sex Education in the Turbulent Sixties." Another useful reading is Curtis E. Avery and Margie R. Lee, "Family Life Education: Its Philosophy and Purpose," *The Family Life Coordinator,* 13 (April 1964), 27–37. This basic article can also be found reprinted in a collection of readings, *Sex Education: Concepts and Challenges,* E. C. Brown Center for Family Studies, 1969.

II. Finding out whether selected age groups think they have had enough opportunity to discuss and learn about changes in family life and sexual behaviors. How to find this out will get students again involved in problems of data collection and interpretation. Should these opinions be matched against a level-of-information quiz given to each interviewee? Is the degree of satisfaction with past family life and sex education experiences congruent with the actual knowledge as shown in the quiz score?

III. Listing controversial topics in family life and sex education for which it may be useful to organize debates or panel discussions. Will these be listed on the blackboard as students name them or will students be asked to jot down their ideas anonymously and place them in a suggestion box? Will a student committee collect them, in the latter case, and report back to the class? How, by dittoing up the class suggestions? All? Some? Will the teacher work with this committee? Will the class be asked to indicate which of the debate topics are of most interest? Will volunteers for one side or another be asked for? What about the side that is not volunteered for: will students be chosen by lot? A helpful reading may be: Don W. Rapp and Margaret B. Baker, "Classroom Debates of Controversial Family Life Questions," *Journal of Marriage and the Family,* 28, 3 (1966), 362–64.

CHAPTER 2: WILL THERE ALWAYS BE A FAMILY?

I. Finding out what people consider the best thing about family life and the worst thing about family life.

A. Will this be undertaken by all the students in the class or will some prefer some of the other activities listed below?

B. Will people of different ages and incomes be asked? Will you go to their homes or to a shopping center or a PTA meeting in the neighborhood? Will you interview perhaps outside a church or a welfare office? Outside the family court building?

C. Will a tape recorder be used? A checklist? Will you ask the English teacher's cooperation so that an essay on this topic can be assigned to selected classes in the school? Should a code number be given each paper to ensure anonymity in case students get specific about the short-comings of their particular families?

II. Learning more about a selected family system at another point in history or in another society.

    A. Is a student particularly interested in the ancient Hebrew family, or the Greek, or Roman, or the Puritan, or the Victorian? How helpful will the history teacher be or the librarian? Sometimes one book leads to another. *The Family in Various Cultures,* a paperback by Stuart Queen, Robert Habenstein, and John Adams, 3rd ed. (Philadelphia: J. B. Lippincott Co., 1967), has chapters on the ancient Hebrews and Greeks, as well as the American colonial family. Each chapter ends with an extended list of readings, perhaps more than the student will need to meet his general interest or his class assignment or term paper. Until quite recently, the history of the American family was not widely researched. Arthur W. Calhoun, *A Social History of the American Family* (New York: Barnes and Noble, 1945), is in three volumes, but the latest takes us only through the period of the First World War. E. S. Morgan, *The Puritan Family* (Boston: Trustees of the Public Library, 1944), is worth looking at. It may change the student's ideas of what is "puritanical" and he may enjoy catching up authors who use this term when they mean Victorian. A more recent look at our colonial family history can be found in J. Demos, *A Little Commonwealth: Family Life in Plymouth Colony* (New York: Oxford University Press, 1970).

    B. Is the student more interested in contemporary family systems, such as the kibbutz, or another commune-minded culture such as Communist China? Or does he expect to travel and want to know about family life and sex education in England or the Scandinavian countries? There are dozens and dozens of books available. Only a few titles will be suggested here. If the student is writing a term paper or giving a class report, he will perhaps want to supplement some of the older books with more recent articles in professional journals.

BRONFENBRENNER, URI, *Two Worlds of Childhood: U.S. and U.S.S.R.* New York: Russell Sage Foundation, 1970.

CLARKE, E., *My Mother Who Fathered Me: A Study of the Family in Three Selected Communities of Jamaica.* New York: Humanities Press, Inc., 1966.

LEWIS, OSCAR, *Five Families.* New York: New American Library, 1959. (Mexico)

LINNER, BIRGITTA, *Society and Sex in Sweden.* New York: Pantheon Books, Inc., 1967.

MACE, DAVID, and VERA MACE, *The Soviet Family.* New York: Doubleday & Company, Inc., 1963.

ROSS, AILEEN, *The Hindu Family in its Urban Setting.* Toronto: University of Toronto Press, 1961.

SCHOFIELD, M., *The Sexual Behaviour of Young People.* Boston: Little, Brown & Co., 1965. (England)

SPIRO, MELFORD, *Children of the Kibbutz.* Cambridge, Mass.: Harvard University Press, 1958.

———, *Kibbutz: Venture in Utopia*. Cambridge, Mass.: Harvard University Press, 1956.

VOGEL, E., *Japan's New Middle Class*. Berkeley: University of California Press, 1967.

YANG, C. K., *The Chinese Family in the Communist Revolution*. Cambridge, Mass.: Massachusetts Institute of Technology Press, 1959.

YOUNG, MICHAEL, and P. WILMOTT, *Family and Kinship in East London*. New York: Humanities Press, Inc., 1957.

C. Is the student more interested in experimental family systems in the U.S.A. in the 19th and 20th centuries?

BERGER, BENNETT, "Childrearing Practices of the Communal Family," in ARLENE S. SKOLNICK and JEROME H. SKOLNICK, *Family in Transition*. Boston: Little, Brown & Company, 1971, pp. 509–23.

CARDEN, M. L., *Oneida: Utopian Community to Modern Corporation*. Baltimore: Johns Hopkins Press, 1969.

DAVIDSON, SARA, "Getting Back to the Communal Garden," *Harper's*, June 1970, pp. 92–102.

NOYES, PIERREPONT, *My Father's House*. New York: Farrar and Rinehart, 1937. (Oneida)

OTTO, HERBERT, *The Family in Search of a Future: Alternate Models for Moderns*. New York: Appleton-Century-Crofts, 1970.

RIMMER, ROBERT H., *Proposition 31*. New York: New American Library, 1968. (Fiction)

ROBERTSON, CONSTANCE NOYES, *Oneida Community: An Autobiography, 1851–1876*.

WEBBER, EVERETT, *Escape to Utopia: The Communal Movement in America*. New York: Hastings House Publishers, Inc., 1959. (Chapter 19: Oneida)

YOUNG, KIMBALL, *Isn't One Wife Enough?* New York: Holt, Rinehart & Winston, Inc., 1954. (Mormons)

III. Is the student interested in examining in greater detail discussions relevant to basic concepts such as universality, function, monogamy?

ENGELS, FRIEDRICH, *On the Origin of Family, Private Property, and State*. Significant excerpt reprinted in ARLENE S. SKOLNICK and JEROME H. SKOLNICK, *Family in Transition*. Boston: Little, Brown & Company, 1971, pp. 279–82.

REISS, IRA, "The Universality of the Family: A Conceptual Analysis," *Journal of Marriage and the Family*, 27 (November 1965), 443–53.

STEPHENS, WILLIAM, *The Family in Cross-Cultural Perspective*. New York: Holt, Rinehart & Winston, Inc., 1963.

CHAPTER 3: MUST THE FAMILY KEEP CHANGING?

I. Finding out whether family folkways seem to change more slowly than community folkways or classroom folkways.

A. Buzz groups can be asked to list different folkways, one group taking folkways reflected in advertising—magazines or on television—one listing folkways of different classrooms and schools, another citing the folkways that are alike and different in their various families.

B. The whole class on hearing the reports of the various buzz groups can see if a generalization based on these data is possible. It is a good opportunity to use the concepts mentioned in this book and see if they facilitate communication about the subject matter.

II. Finding out whether the class can agree on which mores are in more rapid change than others and whether changes in laws have accompanied the process.

III. Finding out the different kinds of familism subscribed to by members of the class, by discussing the answers given to the checklist on familism in Appendix II.

IV. Finding out how the experience of the class compares with the research that finds more visiting of wife's family of origin members than husband's as a trend in industrialized societies. A tally can be taken of all those who have a married brother and sister to see whether residential proximity follows a pattern favoring one side of the family rather than the other.

V. Finding out how common is the experience of extended family living. A tally can be taken of class members who have lived any part of their lives (a year or more?) with some kin present in the household besides the nuclear family. Perhaps a class member lived in the home of an aunt or a grandparent. Or perhaps his mother's brother stayed with them for a few years after his wife died. If the effort is to find out what kinds of family circumstances result in extended family living, the class may prefer to learn this anonymously. Students can jot their answers on slips of paper which are collected and listed on the blackboard. No record is kept of who wrote what. Thus Jim's experience is fed into the class without a spotlight on Jim if it is likely to make him uncomfortable or reveal facts which his parents would prefer they not be identified with.

VI. Finding out how pleasurable or disadvantageous the experience of extended family living was. This may require less anonymity, and may be brought out in open discussion. An alternative is to have a ditto form distributed so that the student may write in (anonymously or not) the advantages on one side of the sheet and disadvantages on the other. A student or a small committee can read them aloud to the class. A more elaborate survey can be undertaken with this as a base. The class may decide to ditto up all the advantages and disadvantages cited and thereby create a checklist to be distributed among all the students of a school or of a grade who have experienced extended family living to see whether most of them agree on them. An open-ended question at the bottom of the ditto sheet (What others do you think should have been on this list?) may elicit additional thoughts and views for the class to consider. One of the journalism-minded students may report the findings to the school newspaper.

CHAPTER 4: HOW WE KNOW
ABOUT MARRIAGE AND THE FAMILY

I. Finding out the kinds of books and journals available in the family field, both in the school library and the local public library.

A. A student committee can draw up a list of textbooks, either by looking on the library shelves, the book store racks, or consulting a bibliographical source such as *The Student's Guide to Marriage and Family Life Literature,* by Lester A. Kirkendall and Wesley J. Adams, 5th ed. (Dubuque, Iowa: William C. Brown Co., 1971), or the Minnesota Council on Family Relations annotated bibliography, *Family Life: Literature and Films,* a new edition of which appears every few years. A check could be made in *Books in Print* as to whether the book is currently available, and in *Paperbacks in Print,* to ascertain whether inexpensive editions have been issued. In each instance, the latest edition should be listed. Even the latest edition will often have statistics that are out of date, and this situation is worse in earlier editions, of course. A ditto sheet of pertinent books and journals may be distributed by the committee to all students in the class.

B. Each student may want to examine one book or journal, and report to the class orally or on a ditto sheet the content of the book or journal (which subjects are included, which omitted), the age level to which its style would appeal, and its particular weaknesses and strengths. Some teachers encourage the student to look for book reviews written by professionals in the field. Some want the student to form his judgment independently. Student attitudes vary in this regard also.

II. Finding out the research methods used in current family and sex studies.

A. Each student may take one issue of the *Journal of Marriage and the Family,* a quarterly publication of technical family research, and list all the methods of data collection used by the various researchers.

B. Some students may prefer to note in a particular issue of the journal how the researcher, in presenting his findings or conclusions or interpretations, indicates the limitations to generalization.

C. One student or a student committee may wish to read *Five Families* by Oscar Lewis and report to the class on the problems of generalizing from these cases of families in Mexico City environs.

D. Some students may prefer to list, for any issue of a family research journal, what the population consisted of in terms of size of sample, sex, age, socioeconomic status, etc. Do these lists bear out the criticisms of research populations which find too few husbands interviewed or too few lower-class families?

E. Some students may prefer to look at research reports to find out how many were done by a single researcher and how many by a team, how many were funded and how many depended on the researcher's investment of time and money.

III. Finding out how the mass media report family developments.

A. Students may wish to set up a bulletin board, either in their classroom or in a place the whole school can see, and post current clippings from newspapers and magazines. *The New York Times* is distributed nationally and is a useful source. Perhaps one of the parents subscribes and would donate it to the class when he is through with it. Other students may have access to *Life, Time, Newsweek,* and other widely distributed "glossies." How often should the clippings be changed? The two opposite problems are that not enough time is allowed for all to read them or they stay up so long that nobody looks at the bulletin board any more, expecting to see the same old material. Perhaps once a week can be tried initially.

How can reading of the clippings be facilitated? Group them under a subject matter heading: child development, communication, aging, etc.? Underline the most important sentences in the clipping so that those who must "read and run" will turn to those? Encircle a sentence that makes a questionable statement? Have those students who in turn take charge of the bulletin board call attention, in a short period allotted in class, to the stereotypes perpetuated in the article, slanted reporting, contradictory statements?

When each set of clippings is taken down, they may be filed in folders so that students may consult them at their convenience. Sometimes class discussion of a given topic encourages some to go back to clippings related to that subject matter. Or this problem of relevance may be solved by posting only those clippings that pertain to the week's discussion.

IV. Finding out how the humanities contribute to our understanding of sex, marriage, and the family. Some teachers prefer to suggest this activity late in the course, in order that the student have a good background of knowledge about family functioning against which to examine the specific instance in a novel, play, story, or poem. Some recent autobiographies are almost as effective as fiction in revealing family interaction in an emotional context. Claude Brown's *Manchild in the Promised Land* (New York: The Macmillan Company, 1965) is an example.

A. The whole class may read a play like Lorraine Hansberry's *A Raisin in the Sun,* or be asked to watch a T.V. revival of a filmed version of a play or novel—*The Dark at the Top of the Stairs* or *The Forsyte Saga,* for example—and then discuss it in class. When does the action take place and what was happening in the larger society at that time that affected family life? How did the behaviors of the various family members in the fiction differ from or illustrate those reported in research studies of the given group or subculture? How did the children in the story exemplify what has been learned in the study of child development concerning needs, stages of growth, sex-related cultural demands?

B. Some students may find it helpful to write a review of the fiction before the class discusses it. Either this can be graded or the student can retain it and use it to compare his original reactions with his level of understanding after class discussion.

There are arguments for and against the use of a guide sheet which lists several questions about the fiction. Some think it forces the student to think not about those matters in the novel or play that are of interest to him but those selected by the teacher. Others, however, think it is helpful to the student in focusing on the *family* implications, since so much of his experience in English classes has been with the esthetic dimension of the fiction.

This latter point suggests that often students can select books to review for this course they have read for English classes. This overcomes the obstacle of finding time to read many extra assignments, enjoyable as they may be, and may highlight new learnings. The student knows what he "got out of the book" before and can recognize the additional learnings and further insights.

C. Some students may wish to compile a list of the best story, play, or novel their classmates have read in the past year. This could be made a school-wide survey, if desired. Such information can add immeasurably to the teacher's own lists of good literature—good as a piece of writing, rather than as meeting conventional standards of vocabulary—and with each passing semester can become an ever richer resource for the classroom. The library (school or local) can be encouraged to arrange an exhibit of such favorite reading. Student copies can be brought to the classroom for borrowing or exchange. English teachers may want to share in these clues to student interest and preferences.

D. Paintings and sculpture of different historical periods can add to understanding of the various subcultures in which families functioned, as well as the standards of modesty, the conceptions of male and female roles, the influential institutions in the lives of family members. Cooperation with the art department of the school or a local art museum may result in a display on one or more themes. An effective series of slides focused on women came out of research at the University of Minnesota, with paintings and sculpture depicting woman as temptress, woman as mother, idealized woman, etc.

CHAPTER 5: THE INDIVIDUAL AND HIS RELATION TO FAMILY AND SOCIETY

I. Finding out different ways personality manifests itself.
  A. Students may wish to look at various dictionary definitions and compare them with the content of personality tests. Do the latter assume fixed personality traits or allow for growth all through life, including adult years?
  B. Students may wish to examine their own personalities and trace the changes in recent years to specific influences of primary groups. Is there satisfaction with present development? Which aspects of their personality would they like to change, and how would they go about doing this? Some students may want to write a log, or brief autobiography, that allows them to have a long introspective look. The writing may be brief, but even brevity may demand a good deal of self-examination and thinking about relationships with significant others in one's life. Some may prefer to describe the personality of a close friend, showing awareness of negative and positive qualities and clues to the sources of such aspects of personality. Some students may wish to write on what they like and do not like in people. Others may write about the very many different kinds of people they are in very different situations, even in different classrooms. (What kind of people bring out the best in us?)
  C. Some students may wish to try the exercise on defense mechanisms in Appendix II. Some students may wish to write on these defense mechanisms as they have observed them among friends or relatives.

II. Finding out the diverse personalities which exist within a group as contrasted with stereotypes of the group.
  A. Some students may wish to visit a home for the aged and chat with several residents, after which they can write thumbnail character sketches. Were the old men and women all alike? Did age mute their personality

differences or were the latter clearly diverse? Perhaps some of the personality traits can be recorded on tape, with the way of speaking a clue to ways of relating. How do different people take illness, bereavement, loss of job? Some students may want to interview those in a crisis situation and write down their findings as a report to the class, with problems of anonymity carefully considered.

B. Some students may wish to interview some housewives and get their reactions to role alternatives.

C. Some students may have grandparents accessible to them and may get them talking about the way the husband role was defined when they first got married and how this differs from today's expectations.

CHAPTER 6: THE INDIVIDUAL, THE FAMILY, AND THE ETH IN "ETHCLASS"

I. Finding out the feelings people have about belonging to or relating to various ethnic groups.

A. Some students may wish to devise an adaptation of the original Social Distance Scale first used decades ago. Appendix II offers one illustration of a kind of checklist which can be filled in anonymously by class members. If the teacher wishes to see whether any attitudes have been changed as a result of the reading of Chapter 6 and class discussion, a checklist devised by the teacher or by a previous class can be used early in the course and compared with replies at the end of the course. To preserve anonymity the student could put a symbol at the top of his checklist each time he fills it out, and matching of the symbols can allow comparison of the two points in time. The student can note in his textbook what the symbol was he had first used in order to use the same one later.

B. Autobiographies permit students to see how others have felt in being identified with a particular ethnic group, Piri Thomas as a Puerto Rican, Claude Brown as a black, John Griffin as a temporary black. Novels, plays, and stories also allow the student to step into the shoes of someone from another ethnic group at dramatic moments in his life: Sammy in *The Dark at the Top of the Stairs,* Serafina in *The Rose Tattoo,* David in *Call it Sleep,* Walter in *A Raisin in the Sun,* James Baldwin in the short story, "This Morning, This Evening, So Soon."

C. A guest panel can allow exploration of which aspects of ethnic culture should be retained and which are dysfunctional in the American setting. The panel could be all of one ethnic group or a mixture of several. It could include students, faculty members, resource people from outside the school, particularly those identified with current movements among various ethnic groups. Class discussion could pull together the implications for family life of what is being advocated.

D. The teacher may ask a show of hands as to how many nationalities students have in their backgrounds: all those with two, with three, with four, with five, and so forth. In most classes it will be evident that most Americans have several heritages to relate to. Discussion will reveal whether they feel closer to some than to others and whether their choices are influenced to some extent by knowledge that some subcultures are more prestigious than others in a society that does not consistently live by the assumption that "All men are created equal." Awareness may develop that choices are also influenced by parental decisions to be involved more with one side of the family than another.

E. A student debate can be organized on controversial topics such as: Resolved, that black families can develop greater strength by restricting their social life to fellow-ethnics. Or, Resolved, that white families are emotionally impoverished by failure to relate to black, brown, red, and yellow families.

II. Finding out the stereotypes that exist concerning various ethnic groups:

A. Some of these may be revealed in class discussion of the results of the social distance checklist mentioned above, and they can be listed on the blackboard as they emerge. If the checklist is not used, a student committee can garner from classmates a list of the adjectives they would use to describe given subcultures or those they have heard used by others concerning various ethnic groups.

B. Buzz groups may be formed in which students sift out how they got the ideas they have about familiar and unfamiliar ethnic groups. Problems of generalizing from specific instances can be discussed in the class as a whole when the groups report back. The lack of adequate treatment in history books of the role played by various ethnic groups may become clear if students bring their current history books to class and read aloud passages that are grudging, ambiguous, misleading, or omit relevant data.

C. Some students may wish to prepare a bulletin board of clippings from the mass media which contribute to the perpetuation of stereotypes: those that mention only the problems, not the achievements of particular groups; photographs that reveal only one aspect of functioning; etc.

D. In an election year, students may wish to add to such a bulletin board items which reveal the efforts of candidates to appeal to the various ethnic groups by overflattery, an assumption that ethnic identity is a fixed feature of American society, or by fomenting hatred of other ethnic groups.

CHAPTER 7: THE INDIVIDUAL, THE FAMILY, AND THE CLASS IN "ETHCLASS"

I. Finding out what the students consider appropriate cutting off points in family income to distinguish among low income, middle income, and high income families.

A. Buzz groups can bring their recommendations to the larger group. The reasoning behind their choices can be explored. What are the standards as they see them for middle-class family life? Do the students agree among themselves? Some of the materials the teacher can offer either before the buzz groups or after would be the data offered in Appendix II in "Family Incomes in the United States" or data shown on a projector from a sociology textbook in which cutoff points have been created by the given writers. What criticisms can the students offer of the cutoff points selected?

B. Some students may wish to report to the class the results of their efforts to distinguish various levels of low income families: the nonworking poor, the working poor, the upper-lower class. This may be part of a larger project to compare the way several family research studies have defined the class levels. See Appendix II, "Class Typologies in Several Family Research Studies." They may wish to note particularly the different status accorded various occupations, such as bus driver, policeman, fireman, or whole categories of workers, such as skilled, semiskilled, or unskilled.

C. The class may discuss a film, such as *Social Class in America, Walk in My Shoes, Superfluous People, The Tenement,* or *The Neglected,* to gain insights into the influence of income, education, occupation on the kinds of family functioning and the self-images of family members.

D. Some students may wish to report on several of the life styles of American families that relate not only to ethnicity and class, but also to geographical region and temporal elements. A useful resource is a compilation of articles, *Life Styles: Diversity in American Society,* edited by S. Feldman and G. Thielbar (Boston: Little, Brown and Company, 1971).

II. Finding out what literature and painting reveal about families of various income levels.

A. Some students may wish to read the first volume in Sean O'Casey's autobiography, *I Knock at the Door,* or John Steinbeck's *The Pearl,* for cross-cultural glimpses of low income families. Others may wish to read Lewis's *The Children of Sanchez* or *A Death in the Sanchez Family,* or Gorky's *Lower Depths.* For the American scene, *A Tree Grows in Brooklyn* or *The Grapes of Wrath* offers insights. Their reports to the class may allow exploration of the concept, culture of poverty, and its relation to "poverty of culture." What are the commonalities among deprived families in various societies? What are the differences?

B. Some students may wish to bring in reproductions of famous paintings of the family and other groups at a variety of income levels, from Van Gogh's *The Potato Eaters* and Liebermann's *At the Canning Factory* to Renoir's *Maternity* and Degas's *Count Napoleon Lepic with His Children.* The photographs in *Family of Man* or other compilations can be shown on the projector in the classroom for student comment.

III. Finding out what influences of socioeconomic class students note in their own development or in people they have known. They may wish to write a log, or autobiographical essay, or a description of a friend's functioning, seen in ethclass terms. This exercise may be postponed until discussion of dating, in which the ethclass consideration is usually highly pertinent.

CHAPTER 8: SEX AND ROLE: WHO'S WHO IN THE FAMILY?

I. Finding out what are considered appropriate sex roles in American society.

A. A committee can formulate a checklist on the basis of known checklists together with the questions or statements in which they think their own classmates would be most interested. (For examples, see Appendix II, "Some Questions About Sex Roles.") The class or the whole school can be asked to fill out the ditto or mimeograph form. It may be less important to arrive at a score for each student as to whether he is more traditional or equalitarian in his expectations than to encourage class discussion of the ideas, feelings, and learnings that lie behind the different views expressed. Class attention can be drawn to the variation among class members in answering a particular question as well as the variation within one sex or another. Is there a *right* answer, or is it more important for the student to gain a clearer picture, as the class goes down the checklist, of the consistencies and inconsistencies in his expectations? Is the student conscious of any tendency or tendencies to choose the advantages in each set of role expectations, whether the advantages of patriarchal emphases or newer equalitarian standards? How do girls think boys will answer one of the items? How do boys think girls will answer? Are they operating by stereotypes of each other?

B. What does it mean to be masculine or feminine today? Perhaps several students will go to the blackboard and list the characteristics they associate with each. A male student may be asked to list what a "truly feminine" woman is like, and a female student to do the same for a "truly masculine" man. Some students may prefer to work in teams, selecting a classmate to deliberate with them in the task. Their differences of opinion can be inquired into to see whether the pair disagreed on some traits and why. When the blackboard lists are complete, the class may be asked to volunteer additional traits before each list is discussed. Is there an overlap of traits between the two lists? Is there anything that truly distinguishes the two? Can the stereotype be separated from the reality? What conclusions can be drawn?

II. Finding out what sex role allocations were made in different societies or in different periods of American history. Students may want to write brief summaries of what they found in one or two sources. If each student examines a different society and reports to the class orally or by the distribution of a ditto sheet, the whole class will be able to see the many commonalities and differences. Some students may wish to look at depictions of utopias including Plato's *Republic,* and see how differently male and female roles were structured in these.

III. Finding out what the mass media teach about sex roles.
A. Several students may wish to create a display (bulletin board, collage, scrapbook) of how mass magazines (perhaps five of them for the past year or two) depict men and women in advertising, in stories, in news items. To what extent do these displays corroborate or go counter to any statements made in this book or other class readings?

B. Several students may wish to report on television programs of the past few weeks, analyzing the images of men and of women presented on popular series. Other students may wish to do the same for educational television to see whether stereotypes are less evident.

C. Several students may wish to report on television or live theatre performances of landmark plays of the turn of the century which brought the issues of men's and women's roles to the fore. Ibsen's play, *A Doll's House,* lends itself to this particularly. How were his plays received? What views of women's potentialities came out in George Bernard

Shaw's plays? How do these compare and contrast with women in Shakespeare's plays? What phrases did the commentator who introduced a play on television use that revealed his view of the women characters?

D. Several students may wish to analyze the content of short stories printed in current women's magazines and those in magazines of the 1950s. What changes can be found and what commonalities? Others in the class may wish to report on what Betty Friedan brought to public attention in this regard in her widely sold work *The Feminine Mystique*.

IV. Finding out what story books and textbooks are telling young children in preschool and elementary grades about male and female roles. The school librarian may be invited as a resource person to display a variety of books for young children and to answer questions about role depictions. Sometimes the parent or sibling of a class member has easy access to such materials and can serve as a speaker. An exhibit of books, with succinct student summaries of role "messages" in them, can be displayed in glass cases so that all students in the school can be alerted to this problem of early sex role socialization.

V. Finding out what older men and women perceived as the advantages and disadvantages of traditional sex role definitions.

A. Several students may want to visit an old age home and talk with the residents. They may want to share with the men and women in such an institution or in a retirement village what they have been studying in class and get their reactions. One group of students may devise a checklist, another may wish to taperecord comments, another to try a focused interview.

B. Students who have grandparents within commuting distance may want to write a brief log (confidential) or paper (for the class) on "The roles open to my grandmother (grandfather) when she (he) was my age, and those open to me" or "How the conception of mother, wife, sister, father, husband, brother, has changed in three generations." Perhaps ethnic and class variables will be seen as significant.

VI. Finding out how cartoons and the jokes of comedians reflect current views of sex roles. The cartoons can be pinned on the bulletin board or in a scrapbook, the jokes typed on ditto sheets for class distribution.

VII. Finding out what popular songs reveal about sex role expectations. Do the various music styles have a modal set of attitudes? Some students who are already familiar with records and tapes can ditto up the words of the songs for class distribution. These ditto sheets help students follow the lyrics as the record player or the tape recorder in the classroom may not allow the words to come through clearly enough.

VIII. Finding out what is said in meetings of the board of education, the state or national legislature, and other governmental bodies about women's roles. Data presented by psychologists, sociologists, and other professionals and the questions put to them by "the servants of the people" provide clues to changing attitudes. A hearing on abortion legislation may be as revealing of attitudes toward sex role allocation as one on employment or on the equal rights amendment which some women's groups, but not all, consider important for women's progress. *The Congressional Record* is a good source for this purpose.

IX. Finding out the differences and the commonalities of goals enunciated by various women's liberation groups, as well as the varying attitudes of women not associated with such groups. Some students may wish to comb through back issues of the late 1960s of major mass publications (*The New York Times, Time, Newsweek,* etc.) for comments by notable females. How often do women who have careers (writing, acting, etc.) declare that other women should be content with a domestic role? Some students may wish to prepare a larger project, perhaps comparing the items appearing on the woman's page of a major newspaper before the advent of women's movements in the mid-1960s with those published in 1970 or later. What conclusions can be drawn?

X. Finding out the views of various religions on sex role allocations.
   A. Some students may wish to comb the literature of a given denomination for clues to change.
   B. Some students may wish to interview clergymen of progressive and fundamentalist orientation, and taperecord their statements, so that the class may pinpoint the significant differences in assumptions.

XI. Finding out how differently parents treat little boys and little girls.
   A. Observations in playgrounds, zoos, picnic places, as well as other areas where less formal interaction is likely to occur.
   B. Interviews with nursery school teachers as to differential parental expectations in behaviors of boys and girls.

XII. Finding out how differently male and female students behave in classroom settings. Taperecording one session and playing it back to the class may permit frequency and kind of participation to become evident.

CHAPTER 9: WHO COMMUNICATES IN THE FAMILY AND HOW?

I. Finding out which modes of communication characterize which groups.
   A. Some students may wish to observe the ethclass variable at work in different situations.
      1. Expressiveness in word, gesture, and body stance at a variety of family affairs such as christenings, weddings, birthdays, funerals.
      2. T.V. programs in which couples are game contestants, guessing at what the other had said was his favorite food, color, etc., and how they reveal their feelings about each other, especially in reacting to the answers.
   B. Some students may wish to analyze what and how classmates communicate in the course of discussion. Does each student tend to play consistent roles? "Communication: Categories for Interaction Analysis" in Appendix II may help the class devise a typology of its own.

II. Finding out how patterns of communication in the home have influenced student functioning in dating relationships, classroom (small groups, large ones), and so forth.
   A. Some students may wish to write an analysis of their present ways of communicating with others and how these compare with their family patterns of speaking, listening, gesturing, as well as with family perspectives on male-female roles, age-youth prerogatives, etc.

B. Some students may wish to survey the class or the school as to how they address their mothers or their fathers in several selected situations —in anger, in casual relationships, etc. Some students may wish to compare the results of this survey with the findings of a series of interviews with elderly people (in their own kin network or in senior citizen clubs and other groups).

III. Finding out how words can intensify and reflect a generation gap.

A. Some students may wish to draw up a list of ten or more slang terms and see how many of these their parents or grandparents can define. Reports to the class can offer the basis for some generalizations as to whether the generations have different vocabularies.

B. Some students may wish to examine yesterday's slang as it occurs in the speech of older relatives. The list of terms can be brought to class for discussion. Does it offer perspective on the assertion that today's slang is tomorrow's "squaresville," that the children of the students will be amused at the terms the students consider very much "with it" today? (Which terms in the preceding question are already dated?)

IV. Finding out clues to feelings and motivations in the behaviors of others. (See "Role-Playing" in Appendix II.)

A. Some students may wish to write up role-playing situations involving a pair relationship (husband and wife, parent and child, siblings, boy friend and girl friend, engaged couple, etc.). These can be anonymous contributions. If students write their own, they are more apt to choose situations which are important in their lives.

B. Some students may volunteer to play the roles in a situation selected from among those proposed. After role-playing, the role players may be asked for their feelings as they played the parts, and the class can join in the discussion of what was said, why, and the emotions revealed or concealed in the spoken dialogue.

CHAPTER 10: THE FIRST SPIN OF THE FAMILY WHEEL

I. Finding out the kinds of dating that students have found most helpful in their own growth.

A. Some students may wish to write a log anonymously, or for the teacher's eyes only, reviewing their dating histories with major emphasis on what was growth-producing and what was destructive to self-concept and to feelings about the other sex.

B. A student committee may wish to prepare a checklist for distribution among classmates and to be filled in anonymously to tap feelings about key aspects of dating.
Note: The Dating Checklist provided in Appendix II may not reflect current practices or problems and is included only for its suggestive value. A student committee can undoubtedly improve it.

II. Finding out how qualities sought in a date resemble or differ from those expected in a mate.

A. Some students may wish to analyze anonymously how their expectations differ and whether they can be reconciled. If not, what conclusions can be drawn?

B. Some students may wish to interview married men or women to find out how their dating partners resembled or differed from the mate they finally selected. Permission to tape-record may allow some excerpts to be played in class.

C. Some students may wish to portray through selected clippings from magazines or through art prints the qualities sought in a date and those sought in a mate. The class can view the pictures and discuss any implications of the differences.

CHAPTER 11: THE SECOND SPIN: SPOUSAL, IN-LAW, AND PARENTAL ROLES

I. Finding out how various kinds of wedding ceremonies and honeymoons aided or had negative influence on the couple's relationship.
  A. Some students may wish to interview couples married within the past year to see if they would modify the kind of wedding or honeymoon they had had if they could make the choice now.
    1. Was it their own choice? How much did the families of origin influence the decision-making?
    2. Did they write their own service for the wedding?
    3. Did the wedding depart from the conventional? Was it in a park? Everyone invited?
    4. Were traditional schedules adhered to such as the bachelor party?
    5. Which superstitions were heeded? ("Something old, something new . . .")
  B. Some students may wish to interview remarried couples and encourage comparisons with the first wedding, such as elaborateness, presence of kin, superstitions observed, decision-making, etc.
II. Finding out attitudes toward child care institutions as an aid in family living.
  A. Some students may wish to visit day care centers for preschool children or after-school centers for older ones to interview parents when they come to pick up the children. The child care staff may also be questioned about their attitudes. ("Would you enroll a child of your own here or do you plan to stay home with your children?") Are the child care institutions perceived as equally helpful to father, mother, and child, or mainly to one or another of these? What improvements do they see are needed?
  B. Several students may wish to interview young mothers whose children are not in nurseries and kindergartens and find out their views of such institutions. How do these views compare with their husbands'?
III. Finding out how young parents view the emotional and financial aspects of pregnancy, childbirth, and child care.
  A. Several students may wish to prepare a checklist to be filled in by fathers and mothers of young children in different socioeconomic and ethnic neighborhoods.
  B. Several students may wish to interview parents of two children to ask about the differential impact of the first pregnancy and the second on their relationship.
    1. Who helped when the child came? (Husband took days off from school or work, her mother came, his mother came, etc.)

2. If they could fantasize an ideal situation for the new parent, what would they include?

C. Some students may wish to interview parents who have experienced natural childbirth to ask their reactions. What was the effect of husband's presence in the labor room?

D. Some students may wish to interview parents who have children between the ages of one and two to find out how the dyadic relationship changes with a young child. Do they go out less, find their sexual life more limited, and so on?

IV. Finding out the various definitions of the good parent offered by various socioeconomic groups.

A. Some students may wish to prepare a list of qualities for the given population (students, disadvantaged parents, middle-class parents, etc.) to rank in order of importance.

B. Some students may wish to interview young parents to find out what they think stands in the way of being good parents.

C. Some students may wish to interview school teachers (preschool, elementary, high school) to see if they agree as to the qualities of a good parent.

V. Finding out which modifications in the parent role are introduced in a commune.

A. Some students may wish to visit a rural commune to observe and discuss the attitudes toward parent roles.

B. Some students may wish to visit an urban commune for this same purpose.

VI. Finding out what your community offers in child care, such as nurseries and kindergartens, free health clinics, after-school study and recreation centers, etc.

A. Some students may wish to consult social agencies—Family Service Association, for example—to get their view of available services.

B. Some students may wish to interview a women's liberation center on a nearby campus to get their perspective.

C. Some students may wish to write the Office of Child Development in the Department of Health, Education, and Welfare to find out what the national picture is at present.

VII. Finding out attitudes toward men's involvement in infant and child care at home or as professionals in preschool institutions.

A. Some students may wish to prepare a checklist to be filled in by young mothers and fathers.

B. Some students may wish to interview child care staffs to ascertain their attitudes in having men colleagues.

C. Some students may wish to interview adoption agencies to get their attitudes toward child adoption by a single father.

VIII. Finding out newer attitudes toward in-laws.

A. Some students may want to interview those who report favorable feelings about in-laws.

B. Some students may want to create a checklist that taps feelings among their classmates or others in the school concerning the kinds of relationships with in-laws they anticipate.

C. Some students may wish to interview divorced persons who have re-married to get their comparisons of in-law relationships in the two marriages.

CHAPTER 12: THE NEXT TIME AROUND: FAMILY DISSOLUTION AND REINTEGRATION

I. Finding out student attitudes toward divorce and remarriage.
   A. Some students may wish to write a log or essay, perhaps anonymously, telling of the causes and consequences of divorce as they have seen them among family members and friends.
   B. Some students may wish to form a committee and prepare a checklist on divorce for the class to fill in and then discuss.
   C. Some students may volunteer to debate topics related to divorce and remarriage. (Several topics are suggested in Appendix II.)

II. Finding out what creative writers have revealed of the psychodynamics of divorce.
   A. Some students may wish to report on "Love and Like" by Herbert Gold in *Fiction of the Fifties* (Doubleday & Company, Inc., 1959); "A Country Weekend" by Marvin Schiller in *New World Writing* (New American Library, 1957), or "We're All Guests" by George Clay in *New World Writing* (New American Library, 1955). The whole class may wish to read and discuss these stories or additional titles suggested by students. Do stories depicting the 1950s reveal different feelings about divorce than those written today? Which aspects of the social structure have changed or remained constant, and what can explain the answer to this question?
   B. Some students may wish to report on relevant films they have seen, such as *Divorce—Italian Style*.

III. Finding out how divorced and/or remarried persons feel about the ending of a relationship, the problems they met, and how they coped with them.
   A. Some students may invite a panel of divorced or remarried friends to appear before the class and answer questions.
   B. Some students may interview a group of men and a group of women who have been legally divorced or who have ended a consensual relationship, and report to the class whether the problems differed for the two sexes or for the two categories of relationship.

IV. Finding out how the mass media treat divorce and remarriage.
   A. Some students may wish to clip from current newspapers and periodicals and create an exhibit for the class to discuss.
   B. Some students may wish to report on recent television programs on related subjects.

V. Finding out what the process of divorce is in a given state.
   A. Some students may wish to invite a lawyer as a resource person to discuss recent changes in divorce law.
   B. Some students may wish to attend divorce proceedings in local courts.

VI. Finding out the perspective of children in divorced homes.
   A. Some students may wish to visit meetings of organizations like Parents

Without Partners and discuss ways in which the one-parent home functions.

    B. Some students may wish to invite a psychiatrist as a resource person.

VII. Finding out how communes attempt to solve problems common in group living.

    A. Some students may wish to invite members of a nearby commune to serve as a panel for class discussion of family alternatives.

    B. Some students may wish to create an exhibit of newspaper and magazine accounts of communal life for the class to discuss.

II

teaching approaches, methods, and materials

TEACHING AND LEARNING IN FAMILY LIFE AND SEX EDUCATION

In recent years, efforts have been made to render the educational process more enjoyable, to give the student a larger role, and to use the teacher mainly as a resource and a stimulator to independent thinking by the student.

Modern psychology underwrites these efforts.

1. We tend to remember pleasant events and experiences better than unpleasant ones.

2. We learn more the greater our involvement in subject matter and process.

3. We take more responsibility for our own development in a democratic classroom than in one with authoritarian controls.

In family life and sex education this new emphasis has resulted in less reliance upon lecturing and greater use of a variety of teaching methods which recognize that different students respond to different stimuli. The subject matter of family and sex is intrinsically interesting and challenging, but methods of examining it may result in boredom, resentment, and contempt on the one hand, or excitement, cooperation, and respect for complexity on the other.

It is a fact that some people grow moralistic about this attempt to make the classroom an enjoyable place. "If they don't want to learn, just kick them out and save the taxpayer some money." Actually, everyone wants to learn. Curiosity is built into the human being, but some classroom procedures can stifle that curiosity. The following pages seek to help the teacher or the future teacher to learn to clarify teaching goals, offer interesting exercises and assignments, and gain satisfaction in the opportunity to participate in a classroom where students and teachers are both learning about themselves, about one another, about the subject matter.

It is doubtful that the teacher who relies mainly on lecturing is learning very much, or that the student who is passively taking notes is learning very much, or that either is enjoying the learning process. Enjoyment here must be taken to mean deep satisfaction and not surface amusement only. One can enjoy a sad play. The family life and sex class examines many unhappy events in people's personal and family lives and many instances of community neglect and destructive living conditions. The enjoyment comes in the feeling of increased sensitivity to the real world, including our real selves, and increased competency in recognizing and dealing with our own needs and those of the people around us.

The lecturer, however dynamic, can be replaced, and may indeed be by electronic devices that allow students to listen at their own convenience. The following pages deal with those aspects of the classroom that cannot be replaced, the sharing of information and questions among peers in small group interaction in response to diverse stimuli: fiction, role-playing, debates, data-gathering, and the many other teaching devices discussed in terms of their potentials and weaknesses.

Family roles are more difficult to play today, when the family is only one of a number of socializing agencies in the society (although this does not make the roles less important to individual and societal development). And the teaching role is far more difficult when students bring to the classroom a vast store of information garnered from TV and other mass media sources, some of it incorrect, and when student interest cannot be commanded by the martinet ruling from a throne at the front of the room. The classroom is more important than ever as a place to sift through information and views picked up in diverse places and to discover that the ways of one's family of origin are not necessarily those one will choose for himself. This process of sifting and discovery is sometimes painful, as all growth is, and requires a degree of sensitivity on the part of the teacher never asked for in the traditional classroom. The student who is considering various career choices may find that family life and sex education is a field that offers unending challenge and fulfillment.

COURSE DESIGN

With the limited time allotted for any course, some decision has to be made as to which topics will be included and in what sequence. This decision to a large extent depends on the age of the students, or perhaps more important, their degree of social maturity. The latter is not easy to determine before the class has already met, and even the first few sessions may not allow for precise conclusions.

the checklist and scheduling topics

Some teachers find it useful to distribute a checklist and involve the students in choice of topics. (See "Topics in Family Life and Sex Education" in Appendix II.) Other teachers follow a similar procedure but feel it necessary to interpret the results of such balloting rather than accept them without question. Did students avoid some topic, not because they lacked interest, but because they were uncertain how it would be handled? They may have had unfortunate experiences in earlier classrooms where the teacher preached at them or sought to frighten them rather than allowing them to reach their own decisions. Perhaps such students will accept introduction of this topic later in the course when they have developed confidence in the teacher and their classmates.

This suggests that the custom of outlining a course in advance and indicating in just which weeks certain topics will be covered may have some problems where flexibility is sought. On the other hand, some tentative outline is needed if only to ensure that the teacher himself has given some thought to the interrelationship of topics and has concluded that students can learn more if one sequence is followed rather than another.

By using different sequences in different classes, the teacher can find out which ones work better. This cannot be done with any exactitude, to be sure, since there are many variables such as sex ratio, academic ability, events outside the classroom which focus student interests (new abortion bill, increase in unemployment, etc.) which influence the outcomes.

No matter what the title of the course in family life and sex education, no two teachers will select exactly the same topics, with or without class balloting, or teach them in the same way, even if they all used the same exercises provided in this Appendix. Each teacher is more qualified for, interested in, and deems more important certain topics rather than others. At the high school level, some school districts provide syllabi in the hope that this will ensure some degree of uniformity in the various courses at the various schools. It is not likely that the syllabi are strictly adhered to. Perhaps it is not desirable that they be, although there are admitted difficulties in articulating a course in sophomore year with one in senior year if too much deviation from the syllabus occurs.

However, repetitiveness may be the lesser danger, especially since each student group will discuss topics differently. What is important is that omissions and inclusions should not be haphazard or based on ignorance or bias. The teacher who omits the topic of homosexuality, for example, when the class ballot shows student interest, may feel incompetent on the subject. This is more easily remedied, with many readings available, than the teacher's emotional unreadiness. It is hoped that future teacher preparation will give sufficient opportunity in small group discussions to work through such feelings which may derive from attitudes transmitted in the family. Students cannot be expected to discuss freely in a classroom with a reluctant, fearful, or unprepared teacher.

bases

Courses can be designed on several different bases. Most commonly used is the family life cycle, starting with dating and mate selection and continuing through the preparental years, followed by the period with small children in the home, then with older children, then the empty nest with children in homes of their own, aging, and bereavement. Few courses give adequate attention to the second half of the family life cycle.

Another common course design is based on the individual life cycle, starting with birth and infancy and continuing with key periods through adolescence to adulthood and old age. Again, most courses concentrate on the earlier periods. Still another design selects broad topics such as personality and individual development, communication, conflicts, family and society, and examines these topics for all periods of the individual or family life cycle. There are dozens of major topics and even more subtopics to be considered within any of these designs.

Two main problems in course design are omission and overlapping. In discussing the broken family, is only divorce or the impact of bereavement to be considered? In considering parent–child relations is only biological parenthood or adoptive and stepparenthood to be discussed? It becomes evident that there is enough subject matter for a whole sequence of courses, and that no one course will ever deal with all the complex relationships of men and women, parent and child, and family and society. Seemingly paradoxical, there is a danger of overlapping of subject matter, as some topics can be introduced in a number of places. Thus dating focuses on the young people but later discussion of spousal relations in the rearing of adolescents brings up some of the same issues from the viewpoint of the middle-aged parents who have legal and financial responsibility for those dating behaviors.

Similarly, mate selection must include the possibility of choosing someone divorced or bereaved, since about a fifth of all marriages involve someone who had been previously married. Almost half of these involve young children. The stepparent role can thus be discussed under mate selection or under child-rearing or relations with grown children in the couple's older years. The teacher, to whom the course design may be clearer than to students, has a responsibility to serve as coordinator, to remind the class of the relevance of topics already discussed, and to choose readings which minimize repetition.

EDUCATIONAL OBJECTIVES

In any classroom, there may be two kinds of objectives, those that emphasize cognitive growth and those that focus on emotional development. Family life and sex education has both goals. The teacher needs to be aware throughout the course as a whole as well as during a particular class meeting what kind and level of growth will be sought.

One noted educator offers an outline of cognitive objectives, ranked from lowest to highest, as follows:

> Knowledge
> Comprehension
> Application
> Analysis
> Synthesis
> Evaluation

How would the outline be filled in so far as family life and sex education is concerned? The following are suggestions.

1. *Knowledge.* This is mainly the ability to recall. The student may be asked to list the methods of contraceptive control or name the body parts in the male reproductive system or give the median age at marriage for females in 1890 and 1970. At this lowest, but essential, cognitive level, correct terminology, classification, and structure have been memorized, and are ready for use at the next cognitive stages.

2. *Comprehension.* Building on the knowledge base, the student can make some use of the material that shows his understanding. He may, if he knows marriage ages in 1890, 1910, 1930, and 1950, be able to suggest a trend and predict its continuance in 1970. (The new census data of 1970 will permit him to check the accuracy of his comprehension.)

3. *Application.* Building on the knowledge and comprehension bases, the student can use the ideas, generalizations, and principles in new situations. Thus, if the student knows the defense mechanisms, he may be able to examine the behavior of an engaged couple and apply his knowledge to a specific instance. The use of cases, fiction, and films allows this level of cognitive growth to be reached.

4. *Analysis.* Building on the learning experiences at the knowledge, comprehension, and application levels, the student can separate out the various elements in a complex whole and see the interrelationships of the separate parts. Thus the student can see cause–effect relationships, whether it is in the functioning of a particular family or in the relationship of family and society. Analytic skills can be fostered by classroom debates, as well as by the use of cases and fiction.

5. *Synthesis.* Building on knowledge, comprehension, application, and analysis, the student draws on many sources and puts these together in a way not

clearly evident before he unified them. Thus the student is able to tie together learnings from many experiences, inside the classroom and outside, and perhaps offer a new typology of dating relationships or an interdisciplinary interpretation of childrearing procedures.

6. *Evaluation.* Building on all the foregoing, the student is able to make judgments about the value of proposed solutions and methods. The student can, for example, offer a balanced critique of a proposed abortion law.

It is evident that the knowledge level is basic to all other cognitive objectives. However, any course that offers learning experiences and tests only at this level keeps the student at an introductory stage of learning.

As for affective growth, the range is from simple awareness of alternatives to making choices and ordering value priorities, culminating in a fully developed life philosophy, including both emotional expressiveness and social action. This progression is more difficult to measure than cognitive growth, and may require the accumulation of many course experiences. However, the teacher who is concerned for the student's emotional as well as cognitive growth will try to provide classroom experiences that promote sensitivity, empathy, value clarification, and familiarity with the world outside the classroom.

PROBLEM-SOLVING

Competency in problem-solving requires sensitivity in human relationships and rational thinking about alternatives. The two basic components, are:

1. *Empathy:* The more awareness of other people's motivations and feelings, the better the student's ability to predict whether a given decision will have the effects sought.

2. *Logic:* In making intelligent choices, the student must be able to entertain the possibility of various alternatives and anticipate correctly their probable outcomes. Debate in the classroom can introduce the student to serious consideration of alternatives, and case study, fiction, and analyses of research can permit the student to see logical consequences of decisions in many different situations.

The cognitive tools used are concepts and generalizations.

A *concept* is a mental image of the underlying structure of objects, events, and situations. Thus the concept of the family involves its definition. The census bureau concept of the family, namely, two or more persons living together who are related by blood, marriage, or adoption, may not be useful for thinking about a couple who live on the next street from the parents of the girl but take all their meals together, do their laundry in common, and share a car. They are functioning like an extended family despite the physical separation of the dwellings.

A research project may choose its "operative definitions" as those it will proceed by. Thus in the instance cited, a study may use the concept of a family that assumes all kin who, despite separate residence, perform x number of functions together daily. In the classroom concepts need to be clearly defined so that students all share a similar "mental image" of what is under discussion.

Generalizations are statements of the relationships among concepts, and underlie the application of knowledge to new situations. A work of fiction or a case study may present a new situation such as a particular family meeting particular problems. Familiarity with generalizations derived from psychology and sociology allow the student to analyze that particular instance against the broad findings of the behavioral sciences.

How do these facts about concepts, generalizations, and problem-solving relate to classroom functioning?

1. The various facts, the disparate data, need to be brought together into a generalization which uses clearly defined concepts and shows the interrelationships of these concepts. For example, as a result of examining various studies, a generalization may be arrived at that premarital sexual behaviors correlate with socioeconomic status.

2. Who arrives at the generalization, the teacher or the students? For maximum learning, the teacher arranges a series of class activities, including readings, resource persons, panels, films, checklists, and so on, which bring the students to awareness that a generalization is possible. The students are encouraged to make their own formulations of the generalization. Questions put by the teacher can contribute greatly in stimulating the student thinking process and help them arrive at valid generalizations.

3. Teachers-to-be who have been taught to make up a lesson plan for each class meeting will usually name the generalization to be sought for and the various class activities designed to lead to formulation of the generalization or its application to specific new instances. How useful is this procedure? On the plus side the lesson plan is a reminder to the teacher to offer those experiences which will allow a generalization to be formulated or illustrated. On the negative side, it may pin the teaching too rigidly to "today's lesson." The experienced teacher, imbued with a concepts-and-generalizations approach to ensure a search for regularities in a vast body of otherwise unassimilable material, will probably be able to discard the lesson plan. The beginning teacher should be encouraged to experiment to see what happens in the class when the lesson plan is left home. Several lesson plans are included in this Appendix to illustrate how different teachers have conceptualized the device.

4. Not all problems are easily solved, and neat charts of steps in problem-solving may be misleading. Without suggesting that within a single class hour, or even a semester, complex conflicts of needs within a family can be straightened out or major social reconstruction be accomplished, it may be helpful for teacher and students to be aware of the basic progression in problem-solving that brings the process close to the methods of science.

a. *Define the problem.* The effort at stating it may help establish its dimensions. It may be found to consist of several interrelated problems, each of which must first be examined by itself. In defining the problem, some key questions are: "What is the matter; just why is it a problem? What is being sought?"

b. *Form a hypothesis.* If something is done, there will be certain effects. What is a likely solution on the basis of present knowledge or with some further collection of information?

c. *Discover alternatives.* Are several lines of conduct possible? Which seems most congruent with the value system of the individual or group? Try this one first.

d. *Test the solution.* Does it have the effects sought? Does it bring other problems which outweigh the gains?

e. *Try other solutions.* If it does not have the effects sought and creates serious new difficulties, discard it and test one of the other possible solutions.

an example

The problem may be the siblings' sharing equitably in the care of an ailing bereaved parent in order to create living conditions which facilitate recovery.

possible solutions

1. All the siblings contribute to hiring a nurse. (Only the sons and not the married daughters contribute? Married daughters in gainful employment contribute?)

2. The parent is placed in a nursing home with all (some) of the siblings contributing toward the expense.

3. The unmarried daughter moves back into the parental apartment. (Was she advised by the psychiatrist to live apart from her family of origin?)

4. The mother is brought into the home of a married son. (Is the wife of this particular son ready for the responsibility? Does the mother prefer her married daughter's home?)

What generalizations derived from research underlie each solution suggested? What are the effects of each solution considered in turn?

LEARNING TO BE EMPATHIC

Empathy is the process of seeing things from another person's perspective, of understanding how he feels and why, without necessarily sharing those feelings at the same moment.

Empathy is	Empathy is not
a means to understanding feelings and behaviors	a way to change the other person
a method of reducing tensions in relationships	a way of eliminating tensions

Empathy differs from sympathy. Both have Greek word origins:

> em (Greek *in*) and pathos (Greek *feeling*), or "I know how you feel. I have been sad or angry in the past and know what you are going through now."
>
> sym (Greek *with*) and pathos (Greek *feeling*), or "I feel as you do. You are sad and I am too; you are angry and I share your feeling of anger."

Sympathy is sometimes resented: "How can you be sad? It's I who have lost a father." Empathy is more likely to be appreciated and helpful. "You are allowing me to have my emotions and not burdening me with yours at this moment. Also, your objectivity allows me to get a clearer view of my own feelings."

The empathic process includes:

1. *Motivation:* The desire to be useful, to clarify a relationship.

2. *Listening:* Concentration on cues to how the other is feeling as communicated in words, actions, and gestures.

3. *Formulating:* Testing your understanding of what the other is feeling by putting it into words.

TOPICS IN FAMILY LIFE AND SEX EDUCATION

To be numbered by each student in order of preference.

1. Self-understanding
2. Changing concepts of masculinity and femininity
3. Dating
4. Homosexuality
5. Premarital sexual standards
6. Abortion
7. Prostitution
8. Contraception
9. Pregnancy
10. Variations in family patterns: class and ethnic backgrounds
11. Mate selection
12. Interfaith and interracial marriage
13. Love
14. Marriage readiness
15. Heredity and eugenics
16. Engagement
17. Alternatives to marriage
18. New forms of the family
19. Bereavement
20. Sexuality in marriage
21. Parental roles
22. Aging
23. Sex education of children
24. Family planning
25. Divorce and separation
26. Remarriage
27. Stepparenthood
28. Adoptive parenthood
29. Unemployment
30. In-laws
31. Empty nest
32. Siblings
33. Pornography
34. Mental illness
35. Alcoholism
36. Drug addiction
37. Women's roles, past and present
38. Family experiments: 19th century
39. The family in revolutionary societies
40. Others (list):

YOU DON'T HAVE TO LECTURE

There are many ways students can acquire information, broaden their experience, and clarify values. The following list suggests some alternatives and supplements to lecturing.

1. Autobiography, log, or diary
2. Small group discussions (buzz or circle)
3. Committee work
4. Debates
5. Field trips (individual student, whole class, small group)
6. Projective devices (pictures, incomplete sentences, etc.)
7. Interviews
8. Observations
9. Panels
10. Resource persons
11. Role-playing
12. Skits (writing, playing)
13. Bulletin boards
14. Checklists
15. Exhibits
16. Films
17. Filmstrips
18. Flip charts
19. Flannel boards
20. Opaque projectors
21. Overhead projectors
22. Telelearning
23. Gisted ditto and mimeograph materials
24. Surveys
25. Textbook reading
26. Tapes
27. Records
28. TV
29. Progress reports
30. Book reviews
31. Puppets
32. Questionnaires
33. Objective tests
34. Essay tests
35. Slides
36. Creative literature
37. Suggestion boxes
38. Newspaper critiques
39. Whole class discussions
40. Brainstorming
41. Chalkboard
42. Sociodrama

THE DISCUSSION GROUP

This is regarded by most family life and sex educators as the basic method in a dialogue-centered classroom.

buzz groups

These are small groups, usually four or five students in each. How are they formed? The *count-off* is one method which allows for chance and ensures various members of the class getting to know one another even if they would not have initially chosen to be with those other individuals. Some students may be eager to sit together, but this sometimes goes counter to student growth. It puts together in a single group those who have well-defined roles already established in their interaction, on the one hand, and on the other, who have other opportunities to exchange views.

To offset this clique tendency, another method is having the teacher name several students and letting these name others in rotation, similar to choosing up sides in a ball game. If the teacher has used a sociogram, it is possible in this way to give the isolate or the near-isolate a chance to choose the students he wants to relate to. The "star" generally functions well in any group for which he is selected. Greater consideration must be given, then, for the student who has more difficulty in relating to others.

circle discussion

This group can be slightly larger than the buzz group, with four to eight members, and can be set up by the methods described above. Circle discussion is distinguished by the rule that nobody may speak until his turn around the circle comes. He is not forced to speak; he may say, "I pass." The effort is to ensure that all have an opportunity to speak, and is particularly useful where more articulate students may dominate the discussion. It compels restraint, for one's reply to a comment by another student cannot be immediate but must await the student's own turn in the circle. The main disadvantage is the feeling reported by students of being overcontrolled with a consequent loss of spontaneity.

whole group discussion

Whether buzz groups or circles are used, it is helpful at some point to terminate these groups and bring the class together for a joint discussion of what the groups have brought forth. The teacher may have set a specific time limit for the small group, rarely less than fifteen minutes, preferably at least half an hour to allow the group to proceed beyond the initial efforts, or the teacher may have preferred to leave the time indefinite in order to note when the groups are beginning to fall silent or show signs of disinterest. Sometimes a warning, "Shall we get together in two minutes?" allows the group to bring discussion to a close without too much of a feeling of being choked off. In the whole group discussion, the teacher may ask each group to report in turn or may ask a question related to the subject matter and inquire, "Which of the groups touched on that issue?"

In this connection, it should be noted that sometimes small groups are asked to choose a recorder or reporter to represent the group in the class discussion. Two cautions should be mentioned here. The student selected may be too busy making notes to take his full part in discussion. Secondly, selection of the student sometimes can take place better at the end of the buzz group discussion when the group is aware of how it has functioned and who had contributed a good deal to the group's task performance. It is helpful, after a student has reported, for the teacher to ask, "Would anyone in that group have some additional comment to make?" Neither too much status nor too much burden should attach to any one student in a small group. The emphasis is on group interaction and productivity rather than on reenforcement of a "star" system.

THE CHECKLIST

The checklist is a convenient way of listing many alternatives and shades of opinion. Several examples which allow discussion to focus on specific topics are offered in Appendix II, such as "Familism Checklist," "A Dating Checklist," and "Social Distance Checklist." It is worth emphasizing that any checklist already in existence should be modified by students and/or teacher to make it most relevant to class needs and interests. Only for research purposes are checklists used in their identical form in a number of different institutions.

The one disadvantage with checklists, other than their possible outdated quality if not revised, is the problem of wording and interpretation. It is useful for the teacher to ask, as each item is read aloud or mentioned by number, for a show of hands. Agreeing and disagreeing reveals the diversity of views. "What was your thinking as you made your decision?" This open-ended question allows students to see the different meanings each had attached to the question, and to recognize, almost as in a debate, the kinds of reasons that can be adduced for one side of the question or the other.

THE DEBATE

This device for getting the student to think through both sides of a question has important implications for problem-solving. The student is helped to transcend the limitations of his family and community settings. Some teachers prefer to have the student choose his own side of the debate. Others prefer to ensure that a student who feels strongly should be encouraged to develop the arguments for the other side, to ensure that he has given them sufficient consideration. When there is strong community feeling about a given topic, such as miscegenation in the South or extramarital sex in a small town, it may be helpful to have students assigned by chance to one side or another, by flip of a coin. One teacher reports finding a progression of debates from less emotional topics to more emotional ones as the term goes on ensures group solidarity before strong disagreements are encouraged.

To ensure that the debate is not a bull session or an off-top-of-the-head response to a serious issue, various requirements will be established by the teacher. One teacher requires an outline to be submitted a week in advance, listing several references other than the textbook, main points of argument, provocative questions to stimulate discussion, and a ditto sheet for class distribution to ensure that students who become interested by the debate can follow up on the listed readings. To involve the class in empathic consideration as well as cognitive growth, the teacher may assign half the class to be rooters for one side of the debating team and the other half for the other side. The time schedule is adhered to. One suggestion is initial presentations by each of two sides, pro four minutes, con four minutes, con four minutes and pro four minutes. A toss-up for rebuttal will allow one speaker from each side to reply to the arguments of the other side. All this has taken about twenty-four minutes. The rest of the class period can be allocated to free discussion without time limits, allowing each half of the class to resume their own individual preferences. If prejudices are revealed, untouched by the logical arguments presented, the teacher may focus class discussion on this fact.

Follow-through experiences can include student essays or logs, pertinent film showings, book review assignments, and picture exhibits or bulletin boards on the given topic.

PROJECTIVE TECHNIQUES: A PICTURE APPROACH
(VISUAL STIMULI TO DISCUSSION)

In the same way that a projective test presents a blurred stimulus (an incomplete sentence, a blob of ink, and so on) to the individual and elicits from him what is in his mind concerning personal and family relationships, so too various pictures can encourage class discussion in which the student projects his ideas and feelings and the teacher learns what the class is thinking about.

1. The teacher can find ready-made sets of pictures, but these may be dated or made up of cartoons which turn some class members off by their caricatures of human beings. Without much effort, the teacher can put together a set of pictures that is more current or artistic by clipping materials from the mass media and mounting the pictures on cardboard or showing them on an overhead projector.

2. If clippings are mounted, several can be given to each buzz group; the smaller group will ensure that more students participate in the discussion. If an overhead projector is used, while there is a possible loss in the number of discussants, it allows many students to respond to the pictures rather than a few.

3. In a sense the picture is a case study in visual form, with the students deciding the details of the case and addressing themselves to aspects that interest them. They may wish to name the characters in order to discuss them more easily. However, this is less necessary where only two people are in the picture. References to the man or the woman, or the older woman and the younger woman, would be clearly understood.

4. Appropriate questions in connection with each picture would be:

   a. What is happening in the picture as you see it?
   b. What might have happened to bring things to this pass?
   c. What are the possible outcomes?
   d. What may change these outcomes?

5. Several other activities can combine with the picture discussion. Role-playing can pursue a situation or relationship perceived in the picture by the students. A student committee may draw up a list for class distribution of community resources, with names, addresses, phone numbers for help with one or another problem. Students may bring in additional pictures. Reading assignments may be made. There is no "right" answer to what is in the picture, but discussion of the various student perceptions may make the class aware of information needed to broaden their knowledge base for decision-making. This may become particularly evident where stereotypical thinking concerning minority families, women's roles, sexual behaviors is revealed by the picture discussion.

THE CASE METHOD

The case provides a means whereby the individual student, small group, the whole class, or all three in succession analyze a specific set of relationships among family members or between a family member and others. To "analyze" means to select the important factors in a whole set of circumstances, to recognize a need for new factual material in order to arrive at cause and effect conclusions, and to see the relationship between the specific instances and generalizations derived from the behavioral sciences. The analysis separates out the interwoven strands of feelings and behaviors, makes inferences as to motive and need, and allows the student to feel with the characters (empathy) and to recognize the consequences of their choices (logic, rational thought). The analysis may stop at this point or it may also encompass suggestions of possible alternatives that are reasonable in the given circumstances, that may "solve the problem" for some of the characters if not for all.

In addition to cognitive growth stimulated by the need to get the facts of the case clear, identify the problem on the basis of previously acquired understanding of psychosocial principles, and consider alternatives, there is the possibility of affective growth in identifying with people in difficulty. The possibility of affective growth is enhanced with the skill of the case presentation. Some consider the fictional case, because told by a master of detail and involvement, superior to the more usual case taken from clinical records, counseling, student logs, and other real life situations.

advantages of the case method

1. It provides an opportunity to think carefully about a family and its problems.

2. It allows personal material to be handled impersonally. The student can express views about the character's behaviors which can be openly and critically analyzed by his classmates. If the student is identifying with the character, he can learn the perspectives of his classmates on the given behaviors without revealing more about his own functioning than he wishes. As in fiction, the character is a cloak behind which feelings and views can be expressed and tested.

3. It allows the class to see that there is more than one way to understand or solve a problem. The usefulness of different conceptual frameworks gets tested in the concrete.

4. It emphasizes interdisciplinary learning; understanding of the facts in the case may call on a knowledge of biology, sociology, psychology, and other fields.

5. It bridges the gap between theory and practice.

6. It encourages active involvement and stimulates independent thinking, especially if group and class discussions supplement the student's initial efforts at understanding a case. The teacher's role is limited to asking for relevancy or evidence in the discussion and suggesting additional readings in response to student interest in some dimension of the case.

limitations of the case method

1. It is not effective for imparting facts and presupposes student mastery of background knowledge against which to discuss the case.

2. It can be addictive in the sense that students become impatient with non-personalized material and resist efforts to become involved at higher levels of abstraction necessary for fullest understanding of cases.

The case method can be used to:

1. Initiate discussion of a unit. Interest in the case may motivate reading of assigned material on a given topic.
2. Make concrete the behavioral principles discussed in a previous meeting.
3. Test comprehension of previous course work.

writing cases

While this takes skill and students will rarely produce cases that can serve for analysis, the practice of introducing salient facts from which motives and needs can be inferred provides a useful exercise in observation, recall, and imagination. It often has a secondary effect of increasing respect for cases already written, in the same way that attempting to write a poem reenforces admiration for great poets.

length of case

Class time may not permit the use of lengthy cases. Sometimes a situation can be stated succinctly, yet the problem in the relationship is clearly inferable. In the area of fiction a short story sometimes serves this way, although a novel permits more complexities in the relationships to be introduced. The class may find it useful to use both short cases and long, to see which was more meaningful for their understanding and discussion. This Appendix offers one illustration of a one-page case and another of a lengthier write-up.

THE CASE METHOD: A BRIEF CASE

Mr. and Mrs. Miller have been married for eighteen years. They met initially at a square dance sponsored by their church. Mr. Miller had been failing in math in his senior high school year and when his father became sick, he immediately quit school.

Mr. Miller has been steadily employed as a telephone repairman since his marriage. He enjoys taking hikes and singing in the church choir. He takes his twelve-year-old son on long walks each weekend. The youngster who is an excellent student would rather play with his friends or read. However, he "grins and bears it."

Mrs. Miller was graduated from college. This week she has reminded her husband of it three times. She has enjoyed participation in a great books discussion club and is thinking of taking some courses in the local college. The seventeen-year-old daughter, Harriet, has a "B+" average; the mother has pleaded with her to complete high school. Harriet seems determined to quit. Yesterday she shouted at her mother, "Get off my back! I have my own life to lead." Across the hall her brother called out, "Will you pipe down—I have studying to do."

Mrs. Miller is certain that her daughter would change her mind if her father spoke to her. Since last year Mr. Miller has adopted a "hands off policy" about school. He insists that the academic area is his wife's "department," and "since she wants it, let her have it."

CASE STUDY: MARIAN AND DAVID

As told by Marian:

We were married when I was seventeen and he was eighteen. We are happy together, but it is amazing that we are still together at all. We are still trying to work out one problem that has faced us all the eleven years of our marriage; that is, lack of agreement on whether a wife should work or not.

Before we married we agreed that my place was at home. My mother had always worked, leaving many of her responsibilities on my shoulders, such as looking after my younger brothers and sisters and taking care of the house. My father had steady work and my mother worked only because she wanted the things she couldn't have as a child. David's mother had also worked all the time, but her income was a necessity after a divorce that took place while David was very young.

David worked hard but his net pay was $180 a month and we could not pay our bills, no matter how closely we cut our spending. With two babies to feed, something had to be done. David took a second job. I handled all the responsibilities at home, including chores a man would ordinarily take on in the yard, garage, etc. This was not a satisfactory solution. When other families were enjoying outings, David was at work, since his second job involved evenings and holidays. It was all work and no play, and both of us became tired and bitter.

Our bickering led to a decision for David to give up the second job. Again our bills piled up. I decided to make some money by offering day care for other people's children in our home in the hours David was away at work. After two weeks, David became critical. It was too much work for me, not fair to the kids, and so forth. Actually, he could not stand to see me contributing to the family's finances despite the pressing need. I gave up the child care, but in a few days I had an opportunity to take a temporary job. Against David's wishes, I went to work. Those three months were probably the longest, most miserable months we ever experienced in our marriage. David refused to care for the kids, wash a single dish, or even pick me up after work. But I refused to quit work. I wasn't making any money by the time I paid the expenses of child care, transportation, clothes, and added grocery money, and I was exhausted every night. But I was trying to prove a point, that I could hold down two jobs, outside and at home, with no worse effects than his holding two jobs. He got his second job back, but I continued working.

Our discussions became more open. He stated that it was the fact I could become independent like my mother and buy things I wanted without consulting him or like his mother who had concluded that a husband was more trouble than he was worth.

My job ended. For about half a year, David held two jobs. Again, life became intolerable. No family outings—just work, work, work. We went back to his one job and just about managed financially due to his having gotten a small pay raise, when suddenly hospital and doctor bills left us with a debt pile-up.

We sat down together and came to an agreement. I would work just until our hospital bills were paid, but I would not mention how much we needed the money or try to take credit for being helpful. David would swallow his pride and allow our home to be used for care of other people's children. When the caseworker came to interview us for my child care license, David was very frank with her. She said it was very natural for him to feel as he did because his father had never supported his family and David wanted to be as different as possible.

I enjoyed the care of the children and so did my children who benefited from sharing their mother and possessions. They even seemed to miss their playmates on the weekends. My youngest child would soon be in first grade, however, and I was not sure I wanted to continue to offer foster day care with all my own children in school. The caseworker commented on my ability to relate to children and suggested I complete my education and work with children on a professional level. I was elated at the possibility, but told her David would never consider it.

She dropped by one evening and talked with him for a long time, reminding him of how young we would be when our children were all grown up, how in the event of accident or death I would be in a destitute situation, how many more women were working now than ever before. To my amazement, David consented to my going to college. I am still surprised by the cooperation and encouragement he has given me. Both our mothers are alone now and lonely for their children. Perhaps this has made him realize that a home and a family are not woman's whole life.

David has prospered in the past few years. When I graduate, my working will not be from financial need but because my new career promises great personal satisfaction. David's attitudes about a working wife are deep-rooted. He is sensitive to anything that implies he is not the head of the house. We have gotten this far and are happy, but I don't think he could have tolerated my preparing for a career that was not along traditional woman's lines, namely, child care, or for one that promised greater income than he could expect. I shudder when I look back at some of our troubled years, but I think we are set on an even keel now.

questions for class discussion

1. Why was Marian glad to agree before marriage that she would stay home?
2. Why did David feel threatened by her change of mind when his job could not support the family?
3. Why did Marian choose day care as a way of earning money?
4. Why did David refuse to cooperate in the three months Marian held an outside job?
5. Why is David encouraging her in college study and planning a career?

6. Could any of these developments have been foreseen before the couple married? Could any alternative decisions have been attempted in the years of financial shortage and lack of agreement between the spouses?

7. Do you see any difficulties in the future?

THE FICTION APPROACH

Several of the articles in Appendix III deal specifically with the use of novels, plays, short stories, and other creative literature in family life and sex education. There is increasing reliance upon the insights from fiction to understand the feelings and thoughts of individuals at all stages of the life cycle, and the interrelationships between family and society, as well as among family members. Discussion of the case method shows similarities in the use of cases and fiction.

Many students find recent autobiographies as useful as fiction in expanding their experiential base for many different family patterns and in offering the raw materials of analysis. The language used is often of the streets and may prejudice some students against the characters depicted. But the teacher who understands the appropriateness of the language for the time and place of the events can communicate acceptance by his way of referring to it.

Many students who are at first shocked, not only by the language but also by the nature of the relationships, find they have grown in awareness of the destructive effects of poor environments and the remarkable courage of people seeking to survive in them. A book report written by the student can help him sift through his thinking about the people, the problems, and the solutions. Especially useful for book reports are Pirie Thomas's, *Down These Mean Streets* (Spanish Harlem), Carolina Maria De Jesus's, *Child of the Dark* (São Paulo slums), and Claude Brown's, *Manchild in the Promised Land*. The female counterpart of the latter depiction of the Negro ghetto can be found in Ann Petry's *The Street*. The biographies written about distinguished people are rarely frank about their family lives and do not provide the realistic details that are needed for student analysis of behaviors.

In class discussion of fiction and biography, analysis is facilitated by reducing anxiety concerning trivia and expanding awareness of the many themes in a story. Thus, the students may be helped by an initial brainstorming effort with the teacher or a student writing on the blackboard what the various class members offer in answer to such questions as, "Who are the main characters we shall be discussing? What are the family-relevant themes in the story?" With these two lists on the board, sometimes with a descriptive term next to the character's name, such as "his first wife," "the older daughter," etc., the class can be asked, "Which theme shall we start with?" This allows the student to show interest, assuming that the classroom has an acceptant atmosphere and students do not have to conceal their interest in certain phenomena. A whole class discussion can be focused on the theme selected, with movement to another theme at the teacher's initiative or if a student says, "I hope we'll get to the next topic today." Or a class can be broken into buzz groups, each of which considers one theme. What they bring back to the whole group allows consideration of all themes, with additional comments and insights added to what was initially reported by the small group.

In using a story or biography to test the student's ability to apply to a new case what was learned in the previous ones, the class may be given a form such as the one following this. In some instances, the story will have been distributed at the previous meeting; in others, it will be distributed in the test period. The latter is less desirable since in the tension that usually accompanies any testing situation, the student may be less able to follow the details of the story.

Student's Name _____ Date _____

You have been reading "Peace for Geretiello" and may keep the story in front of you as you answer the following questions.

1. Who are the main characters in the story?
2. What are the main family-related themes in the story?
3. Select two of the above themes and state for each how the instance in the story illustrates or goes counter to a generalization found in your textbook or other readings, class discussion, or other sociopsychological sources.

Possible answers include the following. Answers can be graded according to accuracy of perception.

a. Hostility toward a dominating family member, when the culture or subculture does not permit open expression, may take the form of exaggerating legitimate demands. Thus, Geretiello insisted, because of the norms of the island, on being the sole breadwinner, but he exaggerated this role role and allocated to himself the sole right to mingle with non-kin. His wife and daughters were forced to accept subservience and isolation. They retaliated by exaggerating their demands, asking for more and more material goods, and forcing Geretiello to work harder and harder.

b. The need for approval and acceptance is found in all people. The wealthy people served by Geretiello enhanced their self-concept by maintaining the fiction that Geretiello cared, was devoted to them, that it was not their money that brought his loyalty. In the death scene it is appropriate that the comfort one patron seeks to give the dying man is in using paper money to keep the flies off him.

Substitutes for Question 3 may be:

How did Geretiello manage to dominate the dinner conversation, and why? Why was it important to Geretiello that his daughters have dowries?

TELELEARNING

method

Telelearning is the amplification of an ordinary telephone conversation so that a large group can hear a lecturer or can interact with him through a series of microphones. Details of cost, usually quite modest compared to bringing a lecturer from a distance, can be obtained from the audio-visual department of a school system or directly from the telephone company in the locality, and will depend on how many jacks, microphones, etc., are to be used.

Taping the interchange between the telelecturer and the students requires the lecturer's permission, which is not always given for a number of reasons. It may be played back in part and his remarks be taken out of context. It may be played back several years later when new research does not support his remarks.

preparation

The telelecturer needs information as to class composition, subject matter already covered, and likely questions the class will be asking. The class will need to prepare by a brainstorming session in which students decide what questions to ask the telelecturer.

advantages

Noted resource persons may give consent which they would withhold if it required lengthy travel and an interruption of their own schedules. If the telephone is in their own home, they do not have to dress for the occasion, notes and other materials are easily at hand, and so forth.

There is a good deal of novelty of the experience for both students and telelecturer. The students hear the voice of a person noted in his field, whose writings they may have read. The telelecturer makes contact with an age group not usually accessible to him.

Authoritative information may be obtained, especially when a controversial topic is under discussion. The telelecturer may have completed new research which may take years to appear in professional publications.

Telelecture provides for the possibility of a service to other departments which may want some of their students to participate and report back to their classes. It is also a service to the community if the telelearning is put in press release form and submitted to local media.

disadvantages

Not all telelecturers are comfortable with lack of face-to-face contact. The information may be given in a dull way. Students may lack the stimulation that comes with a live resource person. A photograph of the speaker may be a helpful prop in the classroom, as well as pictures on display that relate to the topic.

Extended correspondence with the telelecturer to invite and prepare him is necessary. The fixed time schedule and need to keep the telephone restricted for this one use may cause inconvenience at both ends. A person-to-person call to the telelecturer may not wholly obviate emergency use of his telephone, and this can upset a class schedule.

Without cues of a visual sort, the speaker may go on too long and the class grow restless at their inability to break through the relentless flow. While questions can be prepared in advance and sent to the speaker, there is no control on how much time he takes for one question or another. The teacher may have to intercede to move the telelecturer on to another question, but this may make for too much teacher control and reduce the spontaneity of telelecturer–student interchange.

conclusion

It is worth trying once or twice a semester.

THE LOG, DIARY, OR AUTOBIOGRAPHICAL MATERIAL

Through these methods, the student tells about and analyzes his own feelings about family, friends, life goals. He may seek ties between previous family experiences and present functioning. Or he may focus at the degree of consistency in present choices.

The confidentiality of the log is of great importance if students are to be willing to share painful moments, gropings, and negative feelings. The teacher may write comments in the margins to suggest aspects the students may wish to think about further. Logs cannot be graded, except perhaps in the degree of seriousness with which the assignment was undertaken.

A series of logs can amount to a personal diary in which thoughts and feelings are freely expressed but with knowledge that they will be read by the teacher and commented upon. While some teachers suggest that the students react in their logs to course readings and discussions, these should be brought in incidentally and not detract from the main focus—the student's own thinking about himself and his past, present, and future family relationships.

Many course designs include an assignment to write a log early in the term's work. It is questionable whether the student can go much beyond platitudes and socially acceptable remarks before he has developed confidence in the teacher. If the teacher has not given him the impression of being (1) shockproof, (2) empathetic, (3) discreet, (4) nonjudgmental, the student may not take the kind of look at his own functioning that is most growth-producing. Some teachers insist, however, that an early log assignment facilitates involvement in course work.

Needless to say, logs should not be left on the teacher's desk for others to glance at. A cover sheet is helpful in this connection.

An anonymous log written by a student now graduated from the school can be on file in the teacher's office for class members to consult in order to ascertain the kind of material that can be included.

In some classrooms, a guidesheet can be helpful, along these lines:

1. Your family background:

   Parents: temperament, occupation, *their* parents, methods of disciplining, marital satisfaction, sexual standards.

Siblings: as above—nature of relationships with self in early years.

Others: kin, lodgers, etc.—their interaction with family members.

Family crises: how are loss of child, divorce, illegitimacy, etc., handled?

Ordinal position and its influence: did parents want child of your sex, etc.?

Sex roles: traditional or equalitarian?

2. Your present functioning:

Relationships to members of family of origin: frequency and kinds of contact.

Friendships: how do these resemble or differ from kinds of relationships with siblings, etc.?

Dating, random, serious, engaged, living together, etc.: present status and degree of satisfaction.

Your feelings about social problems, about the kind of family you are planning or wish to avoid having, about education, occupation, etc.

Thoughts about sex education, your own and what you are likely to offer others.

Feelings about sex role allocations.

Future plans or uncertainties about the future.

WHO AM I?

In many courses the student is asked to write a paper under this heading to help him see more clearly his own interests, needs, values, and puzzlements at this stage of his development. This is usually only for the teacher to read and not the class. In some schools it is done anonymously to encourage openness. How would the following guide sheet used by one high school be adapted for use in another community or by courses at the college level?

1. Indicate the kind of family you grew up in, including size, your ordinal position, home atmosphere, crises met, the family's relationship with other kin, attitudes toward sex, discussions of sex with either parent, with siblings, or others.

2. Your present relationships with your parents and siblings.

3. How you get along with others and the type of relationships you have established and any problems you are working on.

4. Your present standards, values, and philosophy of life, and whether these represent a change from previous views.

5. Your present routines and behaviors: use of time and energies, study habits, etc.

6. Under what circumstances have you recently felt fear, sympathy, joy, anger, hatred, rejection, lowered self-image?

7. Do you like yourself? What would you like to change in yourself?

8. With whom do you have the most empathic relationships at present?

9. What do you see as your dominant personality traits now, and how do you think these will affect your study, work, choice of mate?

10. In what ways do important people in your life (your reference group) help or hinder you in developing self-acceptance?

LEARNING FROM ROCK

Song lyrics in rock and folk music express thoughts and feelings about family relationships, love, sex, and the search for identity. Class reactions to some of these can be elicited by playing a record or a tape, or an excerpt from one. A serious approach to this source of insights may be aided by distribution of a guide sheet containing the words of the lyrics, and some key questions of what to watch for in the song. "What needs in her does he recognize?" "What kinds of models did the parents provide?" "What does the baby mean to her?"

suggested records

Kenny Rankin's "Family" album (Mercury Records)
Buzz Clifford's "You Can See Your Way Clear" (Dot Records)
Delany and Bonnie's "Friends" (Elektra Records)
David Ackles's "Subway to the Country" (Elektra Records)
The Student Body's "When a Woman Has a Baby" (Intrepid Records)
"The Family" in the album "The Frost Music" (Vanguard Records)

background reading

Carl Belz, *The Story of Rock.* New York: Oxford University Press, 1969.
Jonathan Eisen, *The Age of Rock.* New York: Vintage Books, 1969.

student suggestions

The class can be invited to bring in a record that focuses on relationships within the family, including dating, sexual behavior, alienation, and other topics. Since the lyrics carry the main message to be discussed, the words should be written on the blackboard or distributed on ditto sheets.

RECORDS AND TAPES

These classroom resources can promote cognitive and affective growth if used sparingly.

Main uses are:

1. Information source: bring in an expert on a topic.
2. Background for other class experiences, such as role-playing, exhibits, field trips, etc.
3. Discussion stimulus.
4. Allow emotional overtones of statements to be communicated.

Limitations are:

1. One-way communication
2. Easily becomes dated
3. Difficult to maintain listeners' attention unless acoustically of high grade

Sometimes a guide sheet distributed to the class helps focus attention to main points if the tape or record is an information source. Students may be asked to take notes as basis for class discussion following the presentation.

Occasional stopping of the record or the tape to ask, "What do you think he will say next?" Or, "What conclusion can we come to so far?" may offset the boredom of recorded material. A checklist of main points can be given the students if the material is technical or complex.

Records and tapes may be an emotional experience rather than a didactic lesson. Excerpts from interviews, plays, stories bring a diversity of voices and feelings into the classroom. A first listening may be followed by the teacher asking "Should we listen again?" A discussion of a negative chorus of replies may be as useful as the experience itself. Students who opt for a second listening may be encouraged to take notes this time.

STUDENT RESEARCH, TERM PAPERS, AND GISTING

Several class projects have been suggested in Appendix I. By collecting their own data, the students become more involved. Also, the material is current. A study report on a similar topic in a professional journal is usually more rigorous in its methodology and scientifically sound in its conceptualization but may seem remote or out of date. When it is used to compare with the student's own research, it becomes more meaningful. One by-product of student research is greater awareness of the pitfalls of data collection and interpretation, and a more critical approach to reported studies. The student may also become aware of the relative ease of data collection in the classroom as opposed to interviewing or surveying people of other ages, educational levels, or neighborhoods, and the overreliance, therefore, of American sociologists on student populations, especially those in college, for their generalizations about family interaction.

One important component of research, a survey of the studies already completed on the topic at hand, is not likely to be undertaken in student research. However, if term papers are combined with student research, some of the necessary background reading can be acquired by several of the students whose summary reports to the class can help put the class research in perspective. Sometimes the teacher can distribute a ditto or mimeograph "gisting" sheet on which previous research is summarized, issues raised, or provocative quotations cited. Some criticize the gisting sheet as spoon-feeding, offering the students easily digestible facts boiled down from rougher materials. Certainly the gisting sheet is no substitute for student perusal of original research reports. However, time and library limitations may justify occasional use of gisting sheets. For instance, the sheet on in-laws or on values is an illustration of this kind of shortcut in providing a gist or digest or compendium.

VALUES

Values are:

> Our ideas of the good and the desirable
> Learned life experiences
> Operative, actually governing conduct
> Ideals that give direction to choices
> Inferable from behaviors
> Ranked in a hierarchy, with some considered higher than others
> Brought together in a more or less consistent value system
> Changeable as needs and experiences change and knowledge expands
> Often implicit and can be clarified by being brought into view
> Generally accepted across cultures, such as:
>
> Health
> Wisdom
> Life
> Happiness
>
> Different in various cultures, such as
>
> Ambition
> Excitement
> Comfort
> Privacy
>
> Different in various families
> Different in various family members

GISTING AS A DISCUSSION FOCUS

grievances of husbands and wives

What do husbands complain about? Do wives have the same complaints? Do they rank their grievances the same way? A research study several decades ago (Lewis M. Terman, *Psychological Factors in Marital Unhappiness.* New York: McGraw-Hill Book Company, 1938) showed some 800 couples expressing the complaints listed below. This study has not been replicated for current marital pairs. Are these grievances likely to be similar today and ranked more or less in the same order? Will classroom research permit some clues to emerge? (Note that the listing here gives fewer than a third of the grievances mentioned by Terman's couples.) Will a lower-class sample show a different kind of ranking of grievances?

ORDER FOR HUSBANDS	RANK FOR SERIOUSNESS	ORDER FOR WIVES
She		**He**
nags me	1	is selfish and inconsiderate
is not affectionate	2	is unsuccessful in his work
is selfish and inconsiderate	3	is untruthful
complains too much	4	complains too much
interferes with my hobbies	5	does not show his affection
is slovenly in appearance	6	does not talk things over
is quick-tempered	7	is harsh with the children
interferes with my discipline	8	is touchy
is conceited	9	has no interest in the children
is insincere	10	has no interest in the home
is too easily hurt	11	is not affectionate
is too critical of me	12	is rude
is narrow-minded	13	lacks ambition
neglects the children	14	is nervous or impatient
is a poor housekeeper	15	criticizes me
is argumentative	16	manages income poorly
has annoying habits	17	is narrow-minded
is untruthful	18	is not faithful to me

FILMS AND THE CLASSROOM

Two kinds of films can serve as classroom resources. One kind is the film shown in the local theater or on television. The other is the educational film. The first is likely to have greater emotional impact because of its skilled acting, but it is more difficult to plan for due to its length and cost. Watching for reruns of films on television may avoid these difficulties. Class members may be alerted to watch for listings and inform the class when film "classics" such as *Death of a Salesman, Grapes of Wrath,* and *The Dark at the Top of the Stairs* are to be shown on television.

The educational film often has serious disadvantages; it may be too narrow in focus, too centered on pathology, dated by the clothes and the slang. However, if carefully selected, educational films can provide information, point to a dilemma, and involve the students in weighing the consequences of the characters' decision-making.

Having the teacher and/or a student committee preview the film is helpful in determining its relevance for different stages of the course work and in preparing answers for the kinds of questions the film will stimulate. A preview is more easily arranged if the film is distributed by the school system itself or by a local agency, such as a health department. Sometimes films previewed in one semester can be obtained only in the next.

Ideally, a film should not be scheduled until the need for it becomes evident from the way the class is proceeding, but this flexibility is rarely possible. Many audio-visual departments in high schools or colleges require advance booking not only for the films themselves but also for projection equipment and projectionists. The teacher can only guess how relevant a film will be on a certain date. This is particularly difficult in a functional course where student needs and preferences may determine how long the class focuses on one topic. If the class understands these realities, there is likely to be better response to a film unrelated to the current course content. Moreover, the teacher can accept the fact that the discussion will be on a different level or the focus will be on a different subtopic than if the film had arrived at another part of the semester.

The need for flexibility raises some question about the use of film guide sheets —questions about the film to help focus student analysis. The film guide prompts the class to consider topics the teacher considers important in the term's work, but it may turn student attention from what concerns them and force them to focus on what the teacher has decided should concern them. This Appendix offers a guide sheet for the film *Four Families.* Because the film deals with rural families which change more slowly than urban ones, it is still widely shown. Not all the questions will be found meaningful in each class.

film listings

For older films, the *Educational Film Guide* can be used. Some of the films can be adapted for courses on the family by the use of oral or guide sheet questions which direct student attention to the family issues perhaps only obliquely developed in a given film. Some professional journals such as *The Journal of Marriage and the Family* and *The Family Coordinator* list and review new educational film releases from time to time. The National Council on Family Relations has for the past few years selected both long films (over thirty-one minutes) and short ones for prizes and honorable mention. These are usually annotated in one of the quarterly issues of *The Family Coordinator* a few months after the awards have been made. Various curriculum guides and bibliographies list films, such as *Family Life: Literature and Films,* published by the Minnesota Council on Family Relations. Specialized sources appear in such lists as *Sex Education: A Guide to Visual Aids and Programs* by L. Singer and J. Buskin.

Most lists, unfortunately, omit the date the film was made, partly because the information is not easy to obtain from film producers fearful a dated product may not have a large sale or rental market. The preview can reveal whether the bobby socks, bouffant hairdos, and autos of another vintage are likely to distract a class of younger students from the still-present truth depicted in the film. Sometimes a teacher can prepare a class by mentioning these elements of the film ahead of time, but the visual stimulus sometimes undoes the precautions. Films about other cultures are less vulnerable to style erosions.

common hazards in showing films in the classroom

1. A serious atmosphere may be difficult to maintain since films have become associated largely with recreation and relaxation—especially since the advent of TV.

2. Technical problems such as film breakage, balky projector, wrong sound track for the given film may develop. The teacher is free to help the class discuss some aspect of course work if responsibility for repair is in the hands of a student committee or a member of the school's audio-visual department. The problem is not only the loss of valuable class time if it is the teacher who is struggling with inadequate equipment; class impatience with the disappointing showing may quite unreasonably become focused on the teacher-technician. While teacher status is less of an issue in the informality of the functional, dialogue-centered classroom than in traditional settings, it is not to be ignored as a factor in classroom learning.

3. The film may not arrive on the date ordered. It is desirable to have a substitute learning experience prepared for the class, and to fit the film into another class meeting. Limiting the number of films shown in a given semester not only avoids student resistance to this classroom device, but also leaves places in the calendar when the delayed showing can occur. If a series is being shown, student feelings about their value should be encouraged and schedules modified accordingly.

4. As indicated, outdated clothing or speech patterns (especially yesterday's colloquialisms), the background music, the autos in one scene or another, all can create student resistance to the film's positive potential.

5. Expense may limit selection of films only to those obtainable without charge or at nominal fee from health and education departments. The catalogues of these films should be checked before placing orders with commercial distributors. Poor prints are a hazard due to the wide use of free or low-fee films. If several departments in a school system cooperate, they may share the expense of renting or purchasing a film.

6. Students may see the film in several courses, either in the same department in both beginning and advanced courses, or in various departments offering related courses—social studies, health education, home economics. Although the discussion and the emphasis may differ in each showing, there is at least initial student resistance to seeing a film again, especially one lacking in imaginative photographic devices and capable acting more characteristic of the commercial film. This problem is likely to increase since many films are appropriate at several age levels; curriculum expansion may find the same films scheduled in junior high, high school, and college. One solution is careful articulation among the various schools and especially within a given school system. The individual teacher may institute further checks. The film schedule can be read at the first class meeting and a show of hands will indicate what proportion have already seen which films. Cancellation of a much-viewed film or excusing the few students who have seen it are possible alternatives.

7. Some films may be too long to permit adequate discussion time. The fifty-minute class hour is likely to be inadequate for any film beyond twenty or thirty minutes. Fortunately, several lengthy films have distinct episodes which can be shown as a series, or one or another episode can be omitted, with the teacher summarizing the missing part briefly. *Four Families* is a

film that lends itself to this kind of showing. Some classes find the panel of commentators, particularly the highly ethnocentric remarks of the young woman, add little to their understanding. The film can be cut just before each panel begins to comment, and class discussion substituted.

8. Lack of opportunity for previewing films may leave the teacher unprepared for discussion leadership or the assignment of related readings. Cooperation within a school system can allow notices to be sent to interested teachers as to when a class will be viewing a film, so that other teachers may slip in to see it without a special preview arrangement.

9. Study guides for films may not be appropriate. For example, in secular institutions, the films and the guides prepared by the family life education divisions of various churches must be examined for proselytizing intent. Sometimes where the only film available on a given subject does show bias, the teacher may decide to show it but prepare the class in advance and encourage open discussion of what the students perceive as unfair in the presentation.

10. Films may not offer any more effectively what can be found on a poster, chart, graph, or other information-summarizing device. Films may omit important moral and emotional issues and reduce rather than encourage class discussion by their narrow focus. Each viewing should be followed by evaluation. This evaluation would answer both, Was this film necessary? and Did this film make a unique contribution?

11. Films may accentuate ethclass divisions among students by failing to provide characters for identification by boys and girls from different backgrounds. If the only film shown on poor families is one focusing on a black family, for example, it may be desirable for the teacher to have statistical data prepared to remind the class that a majority of poor families are white even though black families are disproportionately represented among the poor.

12. Films may offer a single sociological or psychological framework and fail to provide the students with alternative explanations. Since this limitation may not be perceived by the students it may require more teacher intervention in discussion. For example, *Four Families*, filmed with commentary by Margaret Mead in her most Freudian period, may overemphasize orality and the permanence of the connection between adult character and specific child care techniques (ways of bathing, feeding, etc.). Students may gain more from this film if encouraged to be critical of the commentary by a guide sheet or in brief remarks by the teacher.

13. Films may perpetuate sex role stereotypes as in *Adolescence, Love, and Maturity*.

14. The annotated listings may not alert the teacher adequately to the film's potential. Thus, *All My Babies* is described in one film guide in a way that omits reference to the variety of family patterns depicted among lower income blacks in a southern state. The guide also does not alert the teacher to the fact that the film offers a doctor's eye view of the birth

process. By listing the target audience merely as pregnant women and midwives, the film's usefulness with college students may be overlooked. Similarly, a description of *Phoebe* omits the mother–daughter relationship which some students find as interesting as the issue of premarital pregnancy.

15. Films are often lacking the depth which would illuminate some important relationships, notably the father's role, the stepparent and stepchild, grandparent relationships, death as a universal family experience, and so forth. Sometimes a film shown in another connection contains a brief view of one of the rarely depicted situations. The teacher may need to create his own cross-index file of the multiple purposes that a film may serve. Film guides rarely mention any but the major themes. *Three Grandmothers,* showing elderly widows in Nigeria, Brazil, and Canada, is as useful for a discussion of widowhood in various social settings as for grandmother roles.

ROLE-PLAYING

introduction

Role-playing is an opportunity to assume the role of another person, to feel like, act like, and sound like someone of another sex, age, educational level, and experience. Role-reversal allows a person to try on the shoes of another person in a reciprocal pair. Thus a parent can play the role of his daughter, a wife the husband role, a child the grandparent role, a brother the sister role, and so on.

Role-playing as a classroom tool is to be distinguished from psychodrama used in therapy to help an individual confront his neurotic fears. The purpose of role-playing is to allow the role-player to experience the feelings of other people, and thereby to increase his empathic competence. It allows other class members to analyze human interaction—not in the abstract but as it usually occurs—in an emotional context. This analysis of what the role-players were feeling and saying, and why, also enhances empathic ability, an important component in all human relationships and particularly valuable for teachers, counselors, nurses, and others in the various helping professions.

Role-playing, unlike a skit with a script, has no set outcome. The role-players may move in unexpected directions. If the interaction is too idiosyncratic to be of use to the class, the teacher can suggest that another pair try to cope with the same situation in a different way. Dissatisfaction with role performance is inappropriate because what was offered was just one way of handling a situation. Other pair performances may add other insights.

Role-playing permits students to try new behaviors before they have actually been faced by the specific situation. This "anticipatory socialization" or practice in meeting new expectations can allow the role-player to become aware of his feelings, to see the consequences of a kind of communication (posture, word choice, etc.) on another role-player, and to consider modifying his goals and his behaviors. The student who has never asked for a date may "practice" in a role-playing situation and be helped to confront the problem, "What do I say if he (she) says. . . ." Role-playing can also provide practice in coping with the feelings of others, especially when a player has to impart some unwelcome news to another person, whether parent, sibling, friend. "I've just been cited for speeding" or "I failed the exam" or "Cathy is pregnant" or "I am thinking of getting a divorce" can be the opening line for exploring situations through role-playing.

role-playing procedures

CHOOSING THE MOMENT

A problem, concern, or interest of a group can be delineated either on the spur of the moment or in advance. The former may occur in the course of a class discussion when a student says, "I don't see why he didn't simply tell his father straight out." The teacher or a classmate may say, "Would you like to try it? Who will play his father?" The role-playing may reveal how hard it was to communicate the given news when the student playing the father showed certain feelings, asked certain questions, etc.

Role situations prepared in advance may be basically similar but either there had not been class time available when the matter first came up or the teacher knows from prior teaching experiences that certain issues are likely to arise when a given topic is discussed. The teacher may also consider role-playing a useful device for introducing a topic in which the feeling component is often submerged. He may ask for role-playing volunteers on the subject of death of a family member, telling a child about a contemplated divorce, deciding on an abortion, and so on. It is rare that those recently involved in the given situation will volunteer. The danger of assigning parts to students is that the teacher may not know the home situation of a student and may thereby trigger revelations which the teacher and the class are not prepared to handle.

THE SETTING

To reduce self-consciousness on the part of roleplayers and yet let their dialogue be audible to the rest of the class, it is often helpful to shape the chairs into a "U," with the role-players' chairs placed in the opening of the "U," at an angle that allows the class to see the players at quarter-face or at most in profile. The players do not get a view of their classmates and are not distracted from their interaction. The class should be cautioned to keep utterly quiet so that the players can sustain the illusion of a private conversation. If the classroom has fixed chairs and tables, the two role-players can put their chairs at the teacher's desk, again with their backs more to the audience than their faces. The teacher will want to sit in a position that permits both a view of the role-players and the class for visual feedback on the kind of involvement shown.

TEACHER ROLE

In a spontaneous role-play, the teacher may summarize what the situation is, call for volunteers, and then say, "Mary, Jim has just said to you, 'I've just talked with your father.'" This is the cue to Mary that she will make the first comment in the dialogue. In a prearranged role-play, the teacher will distribute instruction slips, telling one character, "You speak first," and the other, "He speaks first."

The teacher can help a class not used to role-playing by playing one of the characters (speaking first), preferably in a part very different from his usual character, to emphasize for the class that role-playing is pretending to be somebody else.

The teacher can say "Cut!" or "Thank you" to indicate that a role-playing episode is at an end. Each role-play seems to have a natural end, when role-players begin to repeat themselves or sit in silence. Before this wind-down can begin in earnest, the teacher can intercede. If the teacher is not sure whether he has cut it off too soon, he can ask the players whether they felt they were going on to some new interchange and what it was likely to be.

Role-playing is sometimes a challenge to the teacher. It introduces unexpected feelings and needs for information. The teacher who is not flexible and is hesitant to share with the class the fact that he does not have the given data on hand will probably be uncomfortable with this teaching technique. Moreover, sometimes role-playing does not "come off." Role-players may remain too self-conscious or the class may not be absorbed in the interaction. The teacher can mitigate the risk by sharing his hesitations with the class and accepting cheerfully the times when role-playing efforts are not productive. The class may learn much from the teacher's willingness to risk and his acceptance of less than perfect outcomes.

Role-playing, like all teaching/learning methods, may work out well in some classes and not in others. The teacher develops insight into the factors which contribute to maximal returns by efforts to analyze those present on satisfactory days and those missing on less satisfactory ones. The teacher can learn something about himself and his class in both situations.

NUMBER OF CHARACTERS

It is simpler to role-play with two characters, but some situations require a third or a fourth person, the latter sometimes entering after the first two have talked a few moments. For example, a husband and wife are discussing a problem, and a child enters who must be told about it.

IDENTIFICATION

In a one-sex class or in role reversals, the characters may pin on name tags or wear some symbol of gender identity or age level. The boy may put on his handkerchief in granny fashion to show he is a girl; the girl may lower her voice to suggest the father she is playing or pull her eyeglasses low on her nose to suggest a grandmother. There is a danger of reinforcing stereotypes, especially if the grandmother may be a modern woman with contact lenses. It may be more helpful if the pair address each other by the character's name with great frequency to remind class members of gender identity.

THE DE-ROLE PROCESS

Often there is spontaneous applause at the end of a dialogue. This, coupled with the way the teacher addresses the players by their own names and the questions asked them, can facilitate the de-role process. The goal is to dissociate the student from the role played. This frees players to enter into unpleasant and unsympathetic parts without being penalized afterwards by classmates who are unaware they are doing so. Mary, playing a student who refuses to help a needy family member, or a wife who looks coldly at her husband's proposal to bring his aging mother into the home, is helping herself and the class to understand these behaviors, and this contribution should be appreciated. The allegation of some psychologists that the role-playing always reveals something of our own repressed feelings may be useful in therapeutic treatment but serves little purpose in an educational setting.

The student may, to be sure, be surprised to find such great satisfaction in venting hostile thoughts, and may be motivated to examine his own life to see whether there are sources of unresolved anger. But this is a personal quest, not likely to be aided by the probing of classmates. He may wish to share in some later discussion how the experience of role-playing enabled him to respond to family members in ways that showed greater recognition of his own needs.

VARIATIONS

A more complex version of role-playing can invoke the use of the alter ego (a student who stands behind the role-player and supplements what the latter says with an open expression of thoughts and feelings the role-player does not feel free to release). The role-player may also play both parts, pausing after each statement and assuming a stylized stance adding some inner thoughts presumably not audible to his fellow role-player. These methods inhibit to some extent a free flow of dialogue and require a degree of experience with role-playing not likely to be encountered among most students. The device of ego or alter ego speaking inner thoughts can be found in the staging of some of Eugene O'Neill's plays (*Mourning Becomes Electra*); an excerpt from a recording can be played in class for discussion and analysis.

Masks and puppets sometimes free role-players to say things they might be inhibited in expressing if their faces were exposed to view. The change of voice to correspond with the appearance of a puppet held before the face also acts as a means of freeing the role-player to use forbidden language or express unpleasant thoughts. In the style of the paper bag theatrical performers, simple disguises, wrought out of materials on hand, can permit the class to determine whether such variations offer anything beyond the propless dialogue.

summary of role-playing procedures

1. Define the problem.
2. Encourage students to volunteer for parts.

3. Brief the players, according to instructions offered in student-written role-play situations or those planned by the teacher.

4. Role-play the confrontation between two or at most three or four persons.

5. Hear their observations.

6. De-role the players.

7. Encourage class discussion followed by some summarizing and generalizations by class and/or teacher.

8. Allow the class to indicate whether there should be more role-playing or whether they feel this classroom device has been overused in the particular course.

9. Consider why the role-playing was effective or ineffective, and plan to modify procedures accordingly.

EXAMPLE OF A FILM GUIDE SHEET

four families

Your own careful observation of what is happening in this film may be more important than listening to the commentary. While Dr. Mead is a distinguished cultural anthropologist, her emphasis in this film both on the oral stage of child development and the lifetime character implications of modes of infant care is not universally acceptable to psychologists and sociologists.

While the film is most helpful for glimpses of parent–child relations in four cultures, it raises some basic questions about other aspects of family functioning. Does the film permit generalizations concerning all families in India, France, Japan, and Canada? Even among rural families, would there be differences in various regions of a vast country such as India?

You may wish to organize your thoughts as you view the film around the following questions:

1. How is the personal interaction in each of these four families influenced by the values and the material conditions in the given society?

2. In what ways do we see each family relating to other institutions of the society: economic, religious, educational, recreational, etc.?

3. How does the saying, "One man's religion is another man's superstition" pertain to the families' activities in this film?

4. What does the film reveal about each family as (a) a primary group, (b) a transmitter of the culture, and (c) an agency of social control?

5. Can you distinguish between basic biological needs and culturally learned needs in the family members in each of the four societies?

6. What differences might we expect between these families and those in the cities of the given societies?

COMMUNICATION

film: handling marital conflicts

Two couples are shown arguing. Their styles of disagreeing reflect different personalities and different feelings about each other.

discussion

1. The class can form buzz groups or perhaps only two groups, each focusing primarily on one couple. Bringing the groups together for a whole-class discussion can allow the pooling of the conclusions of the various groups concerning their observations of the ways feelings were shown (words, grimaces, gestures, etc.) and the kind of solutions reached.
2. Students may wish to share with the class their own experiences of handling conflict with another family member. Some students may prefer to use the anonymous log method to analyze their efforts at conflict resolution.
3. Students may suggest role-playing situations to be acted out immediately or at the next class meeting which focus on handling marital or other family conflicts.

PROGRESS REPORT

The student who is required to fill out a periodic report on reading and thinking may find this a helpful way of developing awareness of his own growth. It also permits the teacher to share the directions in which students are moving and to determine the kinds of class exercises and assignments that would be useful. The only danger is that the student may not recognize its contribution to independence and may see it merely as a device to check up on him and keep him working. In the latter case, he may fill out the form so perfunctorily as to make it mere busy work. To some extent student handling of the progress report is a morale indicator, perhaps meriting discussion by the whole class. One form that has been found useful is the following, although a monthly rather than a weekly report may be preferable in some classes. The amount of space provided will depend on how detailed an account is sought.

WEEKLY LOG AND PROGRESS REPORT

Last Name   First Name   Week Ending

1. I did the following reading this week. (Be specific in naming books, newspapers, magazines.) Some reactions aroused by this reading were:

2. An experience which was very significant to me this week, and the reason for its significance was:

3. In and out of school this week, here are some issues, attitudes, views, etc., in relation to family life and marriage which came to my attention. (This may include personal problems which have arisen.)

4. Topics, problems, or questions which need more class discussion, more readings are:

5. Class and small group discussions have been more useful or less than usual this week. (This may include problems of over- and underparticipation, kinds of leadership, vagueness of assignment for group discussion, lack of summary to clarify conclusions reached, etc.)

The student may be given some option as to whether to complete the whole form or select two or three questions to answer. A student may read more in one week, and be involved in many personal experiences the next, and so on.

Other ways of obtaining progress reports are (1) book reviews; (2) a reaction sheet which is open-ended and asks one or another of the questions indicated on the above form; and (3) cards or sheets with student notes on readings, together with student questions on one or another point highlighted by indentation, different colored ink, etc.

SELECTED ORGANIZATIONS AND AGENCIES IN FAMILY LIFE AND SEX EDUCATION

Lists of publications, tapes, posters, films, and other classroom resources can be obtained by writing to the following organizations. In each instance an example is given of materials they distribute.

Adult Education Association, 1225 19th Street, N.W., Washington, D.C. 20036. Position statements, bibliographies, journals.

Agricultural Extension Service, your local land-grant college, or county extension office. Bibliographies, popular pamphlets.

American Association for Health, Physical Education and Recreation, 1201 16th Street, N.W., Washington, D.C. 20036. Position statements, journals.

American Home Economics Association, 1600 20th Street, N.W., Washington, D.C. 20009. Tapes, reprints, journal.

American Personnel and Guidance Association, 1605 New Hampshire Avenue, N.W., Washington, D.C. 20009. Proceedings, journal.

American Social Health Association, 1740 Broadway, New York, N.Y. 10019. Pamphlets, reprints, posters ("The Family Life Cycle").

Association Films, 600 Madison Avenue, New York, N.Y. 10022. Films: *You Haven't Changed a Bit*, 15 min. A young couple reconcile after a fight and separation. *The Weekend*, 15½ min. Communication problems of a middle-aged couple.

Atlantis Productions, 1252 La Granda Drive, Thousand Oaks, Ca. 91360. Film: *A Mexican-American Family*, 16 min.

Bailey Film Associates, 11559 Santa Monica Blvd., Los Angeles, Ca. 90025. Film: *Evan's Corner*, 23 min. Evan, one of six children, in a two-room ghetto flat, weighs values of privacy and cooperation.

E. C. Brown Study Center, 1802 Moss Street, Eugene, Oregon 97403. Reprints, newsletter "Focus" available without charge.

Child Study Association of America, 9 E. 89th Street, New York, N.Y. 10028. Reading lists, pamphlets, journal.

Contemporary (McGraw-Hill) Films, 330 W. 42nd Street, New York, N.Y. 10036. Films: *Courtship in Four Cultures*, 60 min. Traditional customs in Sicily, Iran, Canada, and India. *Four Families*, 61 min. The infant in a rural family in four cultures: India, France, Canada, Japan.

Coronet Films, 65 E. South Water Street, Chicago, Ill. 60601. Films: *Anatomy of a Teenage Courtship*, 24½ min. *Anatomy of a Teenage Engagement*, 24½ min. Indecisions and fears of a young couple.

Family Life Publications, Box 6725, College Station, Durham, North Carolina 27708. Educational and counseling instruments such as checklists on roles, personality tests, etc.

Family Service Association, 44 E. 23rd Street, New York, N.Y. 10010. Research reports, Plays for Living.

Guidance Associates, Pleasantville, N.Y. 10570. Films and filmstrips: *Masculinity and Femininity*, 2 filmstrips and 2 records, 21 min. Stereotypes contrasted with realities of changing roles for men and women.

Hogg Foundation for Mental Health, University of Texas, Austin, Texas 78712. Pamphlets, reading lists.

Indiana University, Audio-Visual Center, Bloomington, Indiana 47401. Films: *Maybe Tomorrow*, 19 min. Dating of a black eighth-grade girl and a white high school boy. Written by students and produced in a college film production course. *Modern Woman, The Uneasy Life*, 60 min. Middle class women discuss alternative roles. Their husbands express a variety of views.

Mental Health Materials Center, 104 E. 25th Street, New York, N.Y. 10010. Reprints, pamphlets.

National Congress of Parents and Teachers, 700 N. Rush Street, Chicago, Ill.: 60611. Journal.

National Council of Churches, 475 Riverside Drive, New York, N.Y. 10027. Position statements, pamphlets.

National Council on Family Relations, 1219 University Avenue, S.E., Minneapolis, Minn. 55414. Journals: *Family Life Coordinator, Journal of Marriage and the Family*. Newsletter, proceedings, tapes, reprints, teacher kit.

National Education Association, 1201 16th Street, N.W., Washington, D.C. 20036. Position statements, journal.

Henk Newenhouse, 1825 Willow Road, Northfield, Ill. 60093. Films and tapes.

Planned Parenthood Federation, 515 Madison Avenue, New York, N.Y. 10022. News bulletin, annual reports, pamphlets, films (*The Engagement Ring*, 31 min. Puerto Rican-American couple quarrel over the issue of birth control. English subtitles).

Public Affairs Committee, 381 Park Avenue South, New York, N.Y. 10016. Pamphlets on family, mental health, sex.

Sex Information and Education Council of the United States (SIECUS), 1790 Broadway, New York, N.Y. 10019. Newsletter, study guides, reading lists.

State Department of Health, individual state capital. Film without charge: *All My Babies*, 60 min. Midwife delivers two babies in two very different homes in a rural Georgia community.

Sterling Educational Films, 241 East 34th Street, New York, N.Y. 10016. Film: *Who Cares?* 11 min. Aging widower moves into daughter's home; conflict with teenage grandchildren.

Teachers College Film Library, Columbia University, 525 W. 120th Street, New York, N.Y. 10027. Films without charge: *Childbirth: A Family Experience*, 22 min. Explicit depiction of childbirth with husband present.

United States Government Printing Office, Washington, D.C. 20402. Bibliographies, journals ("Children," monthly; "Publications of U.S. Government Agencies Useful in Parent and Family Life Education").

WCAU-TV, City Line and Monument Avenues, Philadelphia, Pa. 19131. Film: *Hey, Doc*, 59 min. The physician in ghetto schools and her office witnesses the physical and mental stress in lives of poor families.

YWCA, Resource Center on Women, 136 E. 52nd Street, New York, N.Y. 10022. Journal, questionnaires, films.

SELECTING READINGS FOR FAMILY LIFE AND SEX EDUCATION

I. Becoming familiar with what is available.
   A. Look over the library shelves and stacks under the pertinent filing categories determined from the card catalogues.
   B. Scan book reviews in professional journals for recent years such as *The Family Coordinator* and *The Journal of Marriage and the Family*.

C. Note in the references which follow articles in professional journals those books and articles that have appeared recently.
D. Examine the book lists of organizations interested in family life and sex education.
E. Check titles against *Textbooks in Print.*

II. Establishing criteria and measuring books and articles by them.
A. Does the content meet the interests and needs of the given age level?
B. Is the book intended for coeducational classes, or are the male students going to feel excluded, a particular problem in home economics courses?
C. Is the presentation current and does it encourage a functional approach?
D. Is there an awareness of alternative approaches and solutions?
E. Are opportunities provided for learning by students of varied ability?
F. Is the book well printed and illustrated with an interesting style?
G. Are study aids such as bibliographies, film lists, stories, projects offered?
H. Is the book used in ongoing courses and recommended by authorities in the field?

LESSON PLAN: THE STEPCHILD IN A CHANGING WORLD

I. Generalizations
A. Traditional views of the relationships between stepparents and stepchildren may affect current behavior.
B. The stepchild brings special needs into the new environment.
C. The way the stepparent plays his role is influenced by his personality, the expectations of the spouse, and the sex and age of the stepchildren.

II. Objectives
A. To understand that a stepchild may not have the same motive as the stepparent to make the new marriage succeed.
B. To become aware of the positive potentials as well as the difficulties in the relationships of stepchildren and stepparents.
C. To be empathic in all contacts with those trying to work out such relationships.

III. Class Activities
A. Background readings
1. Anne W. Simon, *Stepchild in the Family.* New York: The Odyssey Press, Inc., 1964.
2. Jessie Bernard, *Remarriage: A Study of Marriage.* New York: Dryden, 1956.
3. William Goode, *Women in Divorce.* New York: The Free Press, 1956.
B. Picture exhibit
1. Cinderella story book opened to illustrations.
2. Clippings from mass media.
C. Ditto sheet
1. Distributed by teacher to show statistics on divorce, death, remarriage, underlining fact that one out of ten children in current families is a stepchild.

IV. Choice of student assignments
- A. Interview with women or men who did not remarry, preferably those divorced or bereaved when their children were young, and ascertain to what extent they were reluctant because of anticipated negative effects on the children.
  1. Another group of students may interview those with young children who did remarry, and compare their remarks with those found by Bernard and Goode. Are attitudes toward the stepparent role different today than decades ago? What has changed in the society as a whole that affects the relationships?
- B. What do modern psychologists say about the step relationships? Several students may consult the index of a number of books or read current articles in professional journals.

V. Class exercise
- A. Teacher distributes the following excerpt on a ditto sheet, explaining that those interested in the longer account can find it in *Parents' Magazine,* August 1961, "Is There a Stepfather in the House?" Students are asked to underline statements which indicate emotional needs not satisfied.

  In the bleak, deserted railroad station Jim and his wife, Mary, sat waiting for the 3:40 A.M. train. Fourteen-year-old Mike would be on it according to the wire from Mike's natural father. Mary said nervously, "He'll be here soon." "If he didn't jump the train and run back to his father," Jim said, with his head bowed, cracking his knuckles. "Mary, I'm just about to give up with that boy." Mary pleaded, "He needs you, Jim. Be patient with him." "Patient!" Jim exploded, "I've been patient. Playing hookey and getting into trouble with that gang was bad enough, but now, running away. It's the last straw, I tell you."

- B. Class discussion can focus on the statements the students had underlined. The teacher may ask:
  1. Is the use of the term "natural father" a handicap in the new relationship by implying a stepfather is "unnatural?" What substitute designations for biological and social parenthood may be helpful?
  2. Are Jim's feelings any different from the feelings any boy's father might have in the situation?
  3. How many know some stepparent–stepchild relationships that have worked out well? What were the factors that facilitated this?
  4. In what ways can friends and others outside the nuclear family, such as grandparents, make the stepparent role more difficult? How can they make a positive contribution?
- C. What is the effect of the wicked stepmother story in children's books? How would the following progression of feelings depicted by a psychologist compare with the fairy story?
  1. The child wants his mother. But mother has gone . . . she is dead or divorced . . . and thus has betrayed him. Whom can he trust now?
  2. The child turns to his father. Together, the child thinks, we can accept mother's departure. Father will cherish and protect me.

3. Father deserts the child. He marries another woman and loves *her.* How can he continue to love me too? What is a stepmother?
4. Stepmother is the Enemy. She comes between child and father, child and mother's memory. If she is gentle and wooing, the child thinks he is right in feeling wronged. If she is hostile, he is convinced of it.
5. Stepmother is lovable. The child who no longer contains primitive hatred toward his own (deserting) mother can fit into a place in the family.

Teacher's questions may be directed at ascertaining whether the class recognizes immediate acceptance of a stepparent is unlikely, but that continued kindly effort by the adults around him may allow the child in time to accept loss and restitution.

The variables of class and ethnic background can be discussed, so that the influence of negative living conditions or the insistence on folk myths may be seen to affect the outcomes. The variables of age of the children and their sex can also be seen as influencing the new relationship. Choosing a mate who has children (young or older ones) may be discussed in terms of readiness to play the role of stepparent.

LESSON PLAN: THE NEW BABY

This lesson was prepared for preschool children. How could it be adapted for older children?

  I. Objectives of the lesson. To help the children begin to understand:
  A. What is a family? The difference between biological and social parenthood.
    1. Illustrations
      a. The mother, child family
      b. The father, mother, child
      c. The nuclear plus (grandmother, aunt, distant cousin residing with father, mother, child)
      d. The mother and child in the grandparental home
      e. Mother and child with mother's sister and her children
      f. The adoptive home
      g. The foster parent home
      h. The father, child, and housekeeper
      i. The communal group
  B. Who is in your family? Family-like feelings toward lodgers, servants, men visitors of the mother, etc.
  C. Your place in the family? Your family roles as a sister, brother, daughter, son, grandchild, etc.
  D. The coming of a new baby? The effects on the family.
  II. Main generalizations
  A. Babies need families.
  B. All family members offer something of importance to one another.
  C. We were all babies at one time and we all grew.

    D. There are differences and similarities in families, and when we grow up we have a choice about the kind of family we want.

III. Learning experiences

    A. Mounted pictures shown to the children illustrating families with babies in diverse ethnic and class settings.

    B. Flannelboard story. Suspense and resolution.

    C. Children compose a story about a family with a new baby, and teacher records it as each child contributes a sentence.

IV. Evaluation

    A. Children's increased interest in family relationships, including parental roles, child roles, sibling roles, other roles.

    B. Children's broader concept of the family as demonstrated in art work, comments, puppet play.

    C. Children's ability to express negative feelings in relation to the new baby and other family members as well as positive ones.

    D. Children's awareness of similarities and differences in families as shown in the housekeeping section of the room by flexible role allocations.

FAMILISM CHECKLIST

What are your beliefs concerning the kinds of obligations, loyalties, and dependencies which are desirable among family members? Do you agree with a given statement, disagree with it, or are you undecided? Since your perspective will be affected by your present roles, please indicate the age group in which you fall at the time you answer the following list.

Age: Teens_____ Twenty to thirty_____ Thirty and older_____

nuclear familism

1. Children under ten should always obey their older siblings.
   A.   D.   U.

2. Children under sixteen should give all their earnings to their parents.
   A.   D.   U.

3. Each individual should consider the needs of his family more important than his own.
   A.   D.   U.

4. Each individual should be prepared to sacrifice his life to protect his parents.
   A.   D.   U.

5. Each individual should be prepared to forego his own safety to help any family member being attacked.
   A.   D.   U.

6. The parents should have veto rights in the dating choices of children sixteen years of age and younger.
   A.   D.   U.

7. The individual should feel obliged to help his parents to support his younger siblings.
   A.   D.   U.

8. The family should present a united front to the public and not reveal individual differences in political, religious, and moral beliefs.
   A.   D.   U.

9. As long as children live at home, they should obey all their parents' wishes.
   A.   D.   U.

10. Family members should conceal from the authorities any violations of the laws which one of them has committed.
    A.   D.   U.

extended familism

1. Grown children should contribute to support of indigent parents.
   A.   D.   U.

2. Such support obligation should be contingent on whether the parents had been loving, kind, and generous when the children lived at home.
   A.   D.   U.

3. Such support obligation should be contingent on how the parents had reached their present dependent state, whether by lack of jobs or by squandering their income on drink and other activities disapproved of by their children.
   A.   D.   U.

4. Parents and grown children should visit each other regardless of degree of affection.
   A.   D.   U.

5. Parents should have the right to drop in on their married children without notice.
   A.   D.   U.

6. Married children have no right to deprive parents of grandparent roles, even if they do not approve of the childrearing methods of the older folk.
   A.   D.   U.

7. In planning family size, the married children should take account of the wishes of their parents for grandchildren.
   A.   D.   U.

8. The nuclear family should consult members of the extended kin network before making important decisions that affect the family name, inheritances, and the like.
   A.   D.   U.

9. Sisters and brothers are entitled to each other's help after they are married if any difficulty arises.
   A.   D.   U.

10. Grown children should take the widowed or divorced parent in to live with them if the latter wishes it.

    A.   D.   U.

affinal and other extended familism

1. An individual should be prepared to share his home with his wife's parents if they are in need.

    A.   D.   U.

2. A woman should be prepared to provide custodial care for the infirm parent of her husband.

    A.   D.   U.

3. Husbands and wives should contribute financial and emotional support for all relatives by blood or marriage (all kin on his side or on her side, including aunts, uncles, cousins).

    A.   D.   U.

4. The decision as to whose family to remain closest to, geographically and emotionally, his or hers, must be the result of spousal agreement.

    A.   D.   U.

5. The husband or wife who does not like his or her in-laws should be left out of family get-togethers which involve affinal kin.

    A.   D.   U.

6. A husband should expect his wife's brothers to contribute to their parents' support before he is asked to help.

    A.   D.   U.

7. A wife should have the right to make independent decisions about supporting her parents if she is in gainful employment.

    A.   D.   U.

8. At least one married child and his nuclear family should be expected to live in the parental home and care for aging parents.

    A.   D.   U.

9. Parents who did not approve the mate selection of their children should not expect to be treated in friendly fashion by their child's spouse.

    A.   D.   U.

10. The two sets of parents of the couple should consider themselves relatives and invite one another to share in ceremonial occasions.

    A.   D.   U.

class discussion

1. After students have marked the checklist, a committee can tally the replies, and by use of a projector or the blackboard, report to the class on the results.

2. Some classes would find it more interesting, because the outcomes are im-

mediately evident, to have the teacher ask for a show of hands on each item, and then ask for volunteers to share their thinking with the class. "I said agree because. . . ." "I was undecided because. . . ." Consensus is not likely. Students can begin to see that they subscribe to very different values in most instances even though they are in agreement on some. The implications can be pointed out for mate selection, for childrearing, for expectations in middle and older years. Class atmosphere should be such as to accept all replies. While it is not possible to prove that one choice is better than another, the class could discuss the consequences of one reply as contrasted with another. Each individual student could be thinking of how he arrived at the views he holds and what kinds of considerations will enter into the decision to agree or disagree rather than to continue undecided.

3. Students can be invited to formulate better questions for the checklist, items that come closer to their own thinking. It will become evident that not every contingency can be stated in the checklist and the variables they would introduce must sometimes be left to discussion. However, it will be one of the benefits of using the checklist to see the departure from traditional familism which brooked no contingencies. A brother is a brother is a brother, of former patriarchal emphases, may now be modified to "If he is a brother I like . . ."

4. The teacher may wish to revise the checklist in light of student suggestions and offer the changed checklist for the next class's consideration. The checklist suggested here bears little resemblance to Panos Bardis's "A Familism Scale" which the writer originally used in several classes and gratefully acknowledges. The cutoff point of age eighteen in some of his formulations was considered by the class this past year as hopelessly outdated. Views change too rapidly to permit older instruments to be used in the classroom without modification. A useful student and teacher attitude is that any classroom instrument can be improved, and if not, it should be discarded.

PERSONALITY RATING EXERCISE

1. The traits enumerated below change at various periods in the individual's development, sometimes through conscious effort and sometimes as responses to changing life conditions and opportunities for interaction with significant others who influence self-concept.

2. A checklist can be devised to test the change in the student's own development or to provide experience in rating the personalities of others. The latter might test those who are planning a serious relationship and who may want to apply it to the self as well as to the other. The checklist can thus indicate several points in time (B) or may concentrate instead on degrees to which certain traits are characteristic at a given point in time (A).

A. Do you know somebody well enough to rate him?

Place a small check in the appropriate column on the appropriate line.

TRAIT	DISTINCTLY INFERIOR	RATHER POOR	BELOW AVERAGE	AVERAGE	ABOVE AVERAGE	QUITE GOOD	SUPERIOR
Ability to work with others							
Adaptability							
Common Sense							
Cooperativeness							
Courtesy							
Dependability							
Disposition							
Efficiency							
Initiative							
Interest in study or work							
Punctuality							
Reliability							
Tactfulness							
Trustworthiness							

B. How do you rate yourself now compared to five years ago?

	BETTER NOW	WORSE NOW
Ability to work with others		
Adaptability		
Common Sense		
Cooperativeness		
Courtesy		
Dependability		
Disposition		
Efficiency		
Initiative		
Interest in study or work		
Punctuality		
Reliability		
Tactfulness		
Trustworthiness		

3. Are there any personality traits not in the above list which the students value? What about innovation, courage to maintain an unpopular position, openness to rational discourse, persistence in the face of obstacles?

4. Do the concepts listed mean the same things to all the students? Class discussion can bring out the guidelines each student uses in making a reckoning of another person or of himself.

THE VALUE ASSUMPTIONS IN PERSONALITY TESTS

The Adult Irrational Ideas Inventory states that the most rational choice is "strongly agree" for the following items:

> I think I am getting a fair deal in life.
>
> I prefer to be independent of others in making decisions.
>
> I feel that life has a great deal more happiness than trouble.
>
> My place of employment and/or my neighborhood provide adequate opportunity for me to meet and make friends.
>
> I can walk past a graveyard alone at night without feeling uneasy.
>
> I can face a difficult task without fear.
>
> I like to bear responsibilities alone.
>
> It is better to take risks and to commit possible errors than to seek unnecessary aid of others.

The same inventory states that the most rational choice is "strongly disagree" for the following items:

> Jeers humiliate me even when I know I am right.
>
> I worry about situations where I am being tested.
>
> I worry about eternity.
>
> If a person is ill-tempered and moody, he will probably never change.
>
> I get very upset when I hear of people (not close relatives or close friends) who are very ill.
>
> My family and close friends do not take enough time to become acquainted with my problems.
>
> I frequently feel unhappy with my appearance.
>
> I avoid inviting others to my home because it is not as nice as theirs.
>
> Sometimes I feel that no one loves me.

What does the scoring suggest about the value premises of the psychologists (Fox and Davies, "Test Your Rationality," *Rational Living*, Spring 1971)? With which scoring is there most room for argument?

KNOW YOUR DEFENSE MECHANISMS

Each individual develops characteristic ways of defending his sense of worth and of fending off the anxiety he would feel if he faced up to his behaviors. He fools himself as well as others, by ignoring or misinterpreting various events in daily life. However, others are not always fooled. It is easier to detect the defense mechanisms of others than to recognize them in ourselves. By raising our level of self-awareness, we can reduce the degree to which we invoke defense mechanisms. We are helped by a greater acceptance of ourselves so that anxiety is reduced. This greater acceptance is facilitated by understanding our own and others' sexuality, by recognizing the wide range of feeling we are all capable of and the ambivalence that attaches to family relationships, and by realizing that we do not have to be perfect beings to deserve affection and support. We are also helped by an intellectual alertness to our own functioning, an analysis of our own behaviors in realistic terms to minimize self-deception. We are likely to continue to use defense mechanisms, as our self-acceptance and self-awareness will never be complete, but the goal is to reduce reliance upon them. Among commonly used defense mechanisms are the following.

1. *Displacement:* transferring to somebody else negative feelings roused by somebody we find it difficult to cope with. The emotion produced in one situation is released in another.

   A popular cartoon illustrated this in its chain reaction form. The foreman has a quarrel with his wife and leaves the house with unresolved anger. He releases this anger by overcriticizing the work performance of some worker under him. This worker is angry but dares not show it. When he goes home he releases the anger by blowing up about his wife's cooking. She becomes angry and takes it out on her child for being too noisy. The child vents his anger on the dog for barking too much. The aggrieved dog, who usually lives in a state of peaceful coexistence with the cat, turns on it when it passes his feeding bowl, and so on.

2. *Rationalization:* offering of an explanation for the behavior which could be true, which seems reasonable, but which skirts around the real feelings which motivated the action.

   If in the cartoon mentioned, the child said to the mother, "Why are you so mad at me?" and she replied, "Because you are making so much noise," she would be hiding from herself and from the child her anger at her husband's criticism. Sometimes the bubble of rationalization is rudely pricked, as when the knowing child says, "Aw, I know. You're picking on me because you just had a fight with Dad."

3. *Projection:* attributing to others feelings and motives which one has himself and is ashamed to acknowledge.

   The individual who does not recognize his sexual needs as normal and to be accepted often defines himself as pursued by others with exaggerated sexual motives. The cartoon version of this is the unfulfilled woman who is convinced there is a rapist under her bed or outside the door.

A more common version is the hostile person who demands to know why you are looking at him like that. He does not have to face his own unresolved hostilities toward people if he can see them as the hostile ones.

4. *Compensation:* trying to excel in something in order to hide from our-selves and others certain real or imagined weaknesses. Instead of probing for the reality or accepting the weakness if it is not easily rectified, we may try to draw attention away from it at great emotional cost.

The results of this mechanism are sometimes socially admired but they may have been achieved at the expense of other gains. A boy or girl may plunge into academic or creative activity to make up for lack of friends or dates. The rewards for accomplishments may be consoling, but they do not wholly relieve the loneliness. Frank self-examination may have revealed ways of behaving that repelled peers, and this discovery may permit some modification. Sometimes such self-examination can be facilitated by dis-cussion with an objective outsider such as the school counselor. It may be found that a seeming rationalization—"the kids in this area are all sports-minded and I can't find anybody interested in the things that interest me" —is not a rationalization at all, but reflects objective reality. In this case a change of neighborhood or school may bring new opportunities. The same academic or creative interests may be pursued but with less desperation, less need to serve as compensation for missing other growth-producing experiences.

5. *Reaction Formation:* adopting attitudes or behaviors that deny the original impulse.

If we are fearful of our own sexual needs, we may go overboard in an antisexuality direction. Thus, the man who misinterprets the common homosexual experiences of the pubertal period and fears he may have homo-sexual tendencies may be a strong supporter of stringent laws against homosexuals. Some who oppose sex education may be fearful of open dis-cussion of what they have sought to keep hidden from their own thinking. (It would be a mistake, of course, to assume that all opponents use this defense mechanism.)

6. *Conversion or Hysterical Conversion:* disguising the emotional turmoil by a physical symptom.

The wife who develops a headache rather than face the sexual difficulties between herself and her husband, the child who has a stomach upset the day of the school play, the man with a backache which makes it impossible to attend the wedding of an unloved kinsman are all the everyday variety of this mechanism, familiar to most of us. The doctor will assure you the head aches, the stomach is queasy, the back does not let the man straighten up. These are not imagined. They provide socially acceptable escapes from unpleasant realities and the anxieties that accompany feelings of inadequacy. In more extreme forms, paralysis of limbs, blindness, and speech impairments may be shifting emotional handicaps to physical form.

other defense mechanisms

Other ways of defending ourselves against anxiety are often interwined with mechanisms already defined above. Thus, *denial* is often present in rationalization and in displacement. "Who me, angry?" demands the woman, her face suffused. "Why, I never get angry." We believe our own defense formulations and put off getting to the root of the problem. The student says, "I didn't hear the assignment," and avoids facing up to his need to defy the parental choice of major or occupation.

Overidealization, which differs only in degree from the idealization found as a component in romantic love, is related to projection and to rationalization. The young man (or woman) not confident of his ability to arrange dates may continue going steady with someone who is destructive of his self-image. Instead of condemning the steady as overcritical, he fends off the anxiety aroused by the thought of entering the dating game again and sees the steady as having high standards and functioning as a superior being.

Fantasy is a defense mechanism only when it withdraws the individual from the realities he must face. Daydreaming can be a source of inspiration when the girl fantasizes walking up the platform to receive a high honor, but it is a defense mechanism when her behaviors in real life would make such achievement impossible.

Repression, or the exclusion from consciousness of anxiety-producing thoughts, ties in with overidealization where we repress awareness of the shortcomings of the other person, or with denial where we repress awareness of our own past behaviors when they are too painful to remember. And *regression,* or withdrawal to an earlier state of development to escape the responsibilities of the present moment, can be seen in conversion where we often need the care of parent or spouse for the physical disorder.

handling others' defense mechanisms and our own

While it is helpful to understand the defense mechanisms of others, the most important use of this knowledge is in self-understanding. To confront others directly, to declare bluntly, "I know you have that stomach upset because you are afraid you won't get the promotion, or pass the exam, or get the promised phone call," is none too helpful. To meet the need for empathy, to boost self-confidence, to show unqualified emotional support and acceptance of the individual, whatever his successes or failures, these can reduce the anxiety which calls forth the defense mechanisms. Or to encourage ventilation of the fears, to sift the real from the imagined, can help put the individual closer to his own feelings and in a better cognitive and emotional condition for making decisions.

As to self-understanding, while it may be true as has been said that "the considered life is the only one worth living," there are limits of time and patience to self-analysis. The overzealous search for one's own motivations may inhibit useful activity. The cartoon character who says "Now why did I put my left foot out of bed first this morning?" is hardly a model for self-awareness. It is when we are not achieving a normal degree of satisfaction with our lives that self-examination becomes crucial. When we face making choices which are fairly irreversible it is important to level with ourselves.

RECOGNIZING DEFENSE MECHANISMS

Can you formulate a quiz that will test understanding of defense mechanisms?

One way is a set of questions which ask that the behavior mechanism or mechanisms operative in a given situation be named. One example is: His father insists that when Jim passes through a certain town he look up an old classmate or army buddy about whom Jim has heard his father talk but has never met. Jim travels all day and when he drives into a motel for the night, he realizes that he went through that town and never stopped. He says to himself, "Well, the man would probably not have been home anyhow."

More important than the rote memory work of getting the right name for the given behavior mechanism is recognition of what is at work in Jim's relationship with his father and the way he copes with disagreeable assignments. A quiz based on situations such as the above is more valuable if there is class time allotted for discussion of the answers afterwards.

Another method is a set of questions in which the student is asked to select several behavior mechanisms and illustrate from his own life experiences situations in which they were operative.

Can you think of other classroom exercises which would clarify the concepts or capture the feelings that lie back of the defense mechanisms?

1. What are some role-playing situations to be used in the classroom? Perhaps the teacher will start students thinking along this line by offering a specific instance such as, the girl is angry when her boy friend pulls up to the curb half an hour after the appointed time. The two students who volunteer to play the parts are not instructed as to how to play the roles but are encouraged to let whatever dialogue comes out of the situation flow naturally. The class is alerted to watch for defense mechanisms that can be inferred from their comments. When role-playing stops in a few minutes, the two can be asked how they felt and how typical for their own functioning their playing of the roles was. The boy may tell the class, "I usually hold back and just say 'I'm sorry', but this time I decided to see how it feels to switch to the offensive." Or the girl may say, "I usually hide my anger and get back at him later in the evening, but this time I wanted to see what it was like to let him have it."

2. Students may want to bring into the classroom instances from fiction that illustrate the use of defense mechanisms. The sour grapes of rationalization or the wrong victim of displacement is frequently met in plays and

stories. However, to what extent can stereotyping result from inflexible assumptions? Are all girls who get good grades compensating for lack of romance in their lives or are all girls who seek romance compensating for lack of brains and will power? If A can lead to B, must B always be traceable back to A? The complexity of motivation and the concept of multiple causation must give us pause and make us wary of oversimplification.

3. Students or teacher or both may bring in cartoons or pictures clipped from glossy magazines to be shown on the projector. These may serve as a focus for class discussion of behavior mechanisms. The cartoons may later be posted on the bulletin board. Some pictures do indeed say more than a thousand words. Combing through old magazines in garages or thrift shops may bring forth the one that shows a man stretched out on the sofa and saying to the harassed woman who has paused in vacuuming, "What am *I* doing? I'll tell you what I am doing. I'm planning peace for all mankind, that's what I'm doing."

4. Some students may wish to observe young children in a playground and note the early use of defense mechanisms.

5. Some students who have visited old age homes or nursing homes may have anecdotal material that illustrates defense mechanisms still operating in the later years.

BLACK FAMILIES AND SOCIAL CLASS

Stratification of black families is a little-studied subject. Popular conceptions have all five million black families either in the lower class or all enjoying luxury cars. Among sociologists, too, there are widely differing perceptions. Some claim that in a racist society no black family can be distinguished from another; all are separated by caste barriers from the stratification levels of white families. Others see the stratification of black families coming to resemble that of white families. The following questions may suggest the kind of data required for drawing accurate conclusions.

1. Do black families earn as much as white families? And do as many individual incomes enter into the calculation of family income for white families as for black? After examination of census data, one sociologist concludes that, "Between 1950 and 1962 . . . the median income of Negroes dropped from 61 percent of that of whites to only 55 percent of white income . . . Even at the same educational and occupational levels, Negroes earn less than whites. Semiskilled Negro factory workers earn only 72 percent as much as semiskilled white workers; Negro college graduates earn less on the average than do whites with only an eighth-grade education." [1]

The statistical picture changed by 1970 for certain black families, those living in the North and those with husbands and wives under the age of 35

---

[1] Gerald R. Leslie, *The Family in Social Context* (New York: Oxford University Press, 1967), p. 295.

and both working. Among northern younger black families in which only the husband worked, family income relative to whites showed no gain from 1960 to 1970. Family income among black families at all economic levels is more apt to include the wages of several earners than among white families. In the South there is a much lower rate of wife employment among white professors than among black. In 1970 the family income of the younger (under 35 northern black) family was almost 96 percent of comparable white family income. Sixty-three percent of the wives in the black families worked, compared with 54 percent of white wives, and 52 percent of the employed black wives worked year-round while only 36 percent of the working white wives did so.[2]

2. What is the class structure of black families? Billingsley, a black sociologist, offered the following estimate in the mid-sixties, based on income, occupation, education, and housing. Three out of four black families are urban. (The estimate involves only urban black families.) It also reflects the sociologist's view that the indices of social class used with white ethnic groups must be modified with black groups.[3] For example, the family of a high school principal in a white community may be considered middle class while in a black community the counterpart family would probably be considered upper class.

Billingsley regards 10 percent of urban black families as upper class, 40 percent as middle class, and 50 percent as lower class. Within these categories he finds varied groupings. Thus there is an upper middle, solid middle, and precarious middle, and in the lower class the working nonpoor, the working poor, and the nonworking poor. Unemployment rates in some areas are double for blacks. Billingsley estimates about a quarter of all black lower-class families are the nonworking poor.

Another view of black class structure [4] considers the life style of the upper-class black family to be similar to the life style of the upper-middle-class white family. The student may wish to consider which social constraints make this likely.

Additional data, discussion, and reading references on the variety of black families can be found in the following:

> ROBERT STAPLES, *The Black Family: Essays and Studies.* Belmont, California: Wadsworth Publishing Company, 1971.
>
> ROSE M. SOMERVILLE, "Black Family Patterns," *The Family Co-ordinator,* 19, No. 3 (July 1970), 279–85.
>
> JOHN SCANZONI, *Black Family in Modern Society.* Boston: Allyn and Bacon, Inc., 1971.

---

2 Jack Rosenthal, "Doubt is Cast on Heralded Sign of Negroes' Economic Progress," *The New York Times,* December 20, 1971, p. 40. Summary of a special Census Bureau report released that day.

3 Andrew Billingsley, *Black Families in White America* (Englewood Cliffs, New Jersey: Prentice-Hall, Inc., 1968), p. 122.

4 Milton M. Gordon, *Assimilation in American Life* (Fairlawn, N.J.: Oxford University Press, 1964).

ETHNICITY AND FAMILY LIFE

case materials

1. A newspaper in 1971 reported "vandalism in an outburst of racial animosity." A $53,000 house in a neighborhood that is Irish, Italian, and Jewish was attacked by "thirty men and teenaged boys, with axes and picks." They wrote "Stamp Out Niggers" and "We Hate Niggers" on the walls of the house, as an estimated 200 people stood in front of the house screaming approval, according to investigators from the district attorney's office. One policeman said, "Who do you arrest, a whole block?" What had brought on the vandalism? A rumor had swept the block that a black family was to buy the house, then another rumor that the buyer was a black man married to a white woman, then a further rumor that it was a Filipino married to a white woman. "The truth is it was bought by two Chinese brothers, one of whom is married to a white woman. They say they don't want it any more." (*The New York Times,* June 12, 1971)

2. New York's Commission on Human Rights charged in State Supreme Court that a prospective buyer of a cooperative apartment on East 72nd Street was barred from making the purchase because he is a Jew. The complainant had offered $150,000 for the apartment, plus $4,850 for extra costs. He had letters of reference from various classmates at an ivy league college, one of whom, a son of Governor Rockefeller, wrote "They are a most personable family whom I myself would welcome as my neighbors." However, the representative of the management agents informed the complainant that "because I was Jewish, I would have an extraordinarily difficult problem in purchasing this apartment." (*The New York Times,* May 25, 1971)

3. Mr. Benjamin, a 37-year-old probation officer for Suffolk County and professor of social work at Farmingdale University, is black, along with about 5 percent of New York suburban dwellers. And blackness in the suburbs, as in the total society, makes for some real differences. The father of two children, Paul, eight, and Pamela, six, Mr. Benjamin is vocal in his criticism of the elementary school to which they are bused with some forty other black children from the mostly Negro, new home community.

"Many of the white kids, reflecting the attitudes of their parents, express antiblack feelings in their classroom and play situations and many of the educators and administrators are not able to cope with this problem," he said.

"The black children," Mr. Benjamin went on, "are subject to racial slurs and to rejection in games and classroom activities to the point where black children see the school as hostile. While we sit back and talk about integration, we don't get around to confronting the true problems of the racism inherent in the general society."

Most of Mr. Benjamin's black neighbors are professional men or high-level civil servants. Their ranch or split-level homes generally cost from $30,000 upward. The closest community of white residents, with similar homes, is for the most part made up of working-class families. (*The New York Times,* June 1, 1971)

4. El Museo del Barrio now has quarters of its own in Hispanic Harlem. All day long, people in the community drop in to visit and look. The museum's primary aim is to acquaint schoolchildren with their folk heritage. "I was ashamed of being a Puerto Rican," said the director, Mrs. Martha Vega, "and I want my three kids to be proud of it." (*The New York Times,* July 10, 1971)

5. Schools for teaching children Chinese after the regular school day and on weekends are proliferating. The principal of the New York Chinese School places pride in being Chinese above language training. He said his school sought to teach children "to respect older people, to deal with people peacefully, to help others and public causes, to observe proper manners, to be industrious, and to hold to your self-esteem." There is disagreement as to what Chinese dialect should be taught. Cantonese is considered the practical choice because most Chinese in the United States speak it. It would be easier for children to learn the dialect they speak at home. But those who advocate teaching Mandarin note that it is the official dialect in both Nationalist and Communist China. "If we want our children to communicate with the bulk of Chinese population," one said, "Mandarin is, of course, the logical choice." (*The New York Times,* May 31, 1971)

6. Giuseppe Lupollo arrived in New York from southern Italy in 1905 and began immediately to create a mafia family dedicated equally to crime and to legitimate pursuits. That family, held together with bonds of blood and marriage, has become—in its fourth generation—virtually divorced from crime, according to a three-member anthropologist–sociologist team in their research study. (The real name of the family is disguised.) In 1905 with a capital of $300 or $400, Lupollo set up two businesses, one an illegitimate money-lending operation, the other an entirely legal grocery for sale of imported foods. In succeeding years, he channeled sons, grandsons, and relatives into legitimate and illegitimate businesses, making clear distinctions but always placing more emphasis on the legitimate so that now after four generations, of the twenty-seven males in the family, only four are in businesses which are illegal. "You can trust members of your own family first, relatives second, Sicilians third, Italians fourth, and forget about the rest of them," Lupollo is said to have declared. The sociologist interprets this as "a shared kinship-based moral code; a collective amorality toward authority structures that are outside of the family." (*The New York Times,* May 29, 1971)

HEALTH AND POVERTY [5]

The problems of poverty and ill health tend to be closely linked.

1. There are nearly 40,000 cases of tuberculosis a year, most of them among the poor, the down-and-out.

2. Migrant workers, Indians, and blacks have more than their share of ill

[5] From "Health of the Nation Fails to Reflect the Great Advances of Medical Science," *The New York Times,* July 16, 1971, pp. 1–8.

health. Although not all of the reasons are known, evidence points to poverty as a major factor. Nonwhite American babies die at a rate nearly twice that of white babies. Nonwhite mothers die at a rate four times that for white mothers. On the average, nonwhite Americans can expect to die seven years earlier than whites.

3. Infant death rates in urban slums tend to be markedly higher than in prosperous neighborhoods in the same cities. Yet in Denver Dr. Thomas Sbarbaro said his community's neighborhood health centers had been able to reduce the infant mortality rate among the poor to the level of the

FAMILY INCOME: DATA * AND QUERIES

Population of the United States, 1970:   203,235,298 **

White:	177,612,309
Negro:	22,672,570
Other *** races:	2,880,820

Number of families, 1970:   51.2 million (1965:   48.3 imillion)

White families	46.0 million
Negro and other families ***	5.2 million

Median income of all families ****

	1960	1965	1970
White families	$5,835	$7,251	$10,236
Negro and other families	3,233	3,994	6,516
All families	5,620	6,957	9,867

* Unless otherwise noted, data have been taken from United States Bureau of the Census, Statistical Abstract of the United States: 1971 (92nd Edition), Washington, D.C., 1971.

** Resident population. When members of the armed forces abroad are included, the figure is 204.8 million.

*** In the 1970 census, the population was classified as white, Negro, and other. "Persons of Mexican birth or ancestry are classified as white unless they are definitely of some other racial stock, such as Indian." (p. 2) "Persons of Mexican or Puerto Rican birth or ancestry who did not identify themselves as of a race other than white were classified as white." (p. 3) "The father's race was used for persons of mixed parentage who were in doubt as to their classification." (p. 3)

**** Family income includes the total earnings of all members of a family. The median indicates the point at which half the families earn more and half less.

city's prosperous residential areas. The program appears to have done so simply by providing proper health care for people who never had it before.

4. Even in heart disease, poverty emerges as a health factor. Rheumatic heart disease tends to be more common among the poor.

5. Poverty and illness are intertwined in the whole fabric of life. Poverty begets disease and illness begets poverty.

6. In American society your state of health and chances of getting good medical care depend a lot on who you are, how much money you have, and where you live.

7. Paralytic polio and diphtheria still occur in small outbreaks that seem all the more tragic because they need not have occurred. The chief cause is lack of immunization; and the chief cause of that, again, is poverty.

FAMILIES BY INCOME LEVEL—1970

White families—income under $3,000	7.5%
Negro and other families—income under $3,000	20.1%
White families—income of $10,000 and over	51.6%
Negro and other families—income of $10,000 and over	28.2%

INCIDENCE OF POVERTY (IN MILLIONS)

	1960	1970
Poor persons	39.9	25.5
White	28.3 (17.8%)	17.5 (9.9%)
Negro and other	11.5 (55.9%)	8.0 (32.1%)

DISTRIBUTION OF FAMILIES ACCORDING TO INCOME—1965 †

Family Income	Number of Families (in millions)	Percent of Families
Under $3,000	8.0	17
$3,000 to $5,000	7.7	16
$5,000 to $7,000	9.0	19
$7,000 to $10,000	11.6	24
$10,000 to $15,000	8.5	18
Over $15,000	3.5	7

† Table based on data taken from *Finance Facts,* October 1966 (National Consumer Finance Association).

QUERIES CONCERNING THE DATA

1. Median income of all families rose between 1960 and 1970. Did the cost of living rise in the decade and leave the proportions of low, middle, and upper income families roughly the same?

2. According to the United States Census Bureau, "The term 'family' refers to a group of two or more persons related by blood, marriage, or adoption and residing together in a household." The data show that about a third of American families had incomes of $5,000 or less in 1965, before taxes. Which families, according to the Census Bureau definition, could live more comfortably and which less comfortably on income of $5,000 or less? Could any families of this income manage a middle-class life style?

3. What is an upper-class life style? Could all the 3.5 million families with incomes over $15,000 in 1965 achieve an upper-class life style? One study in 1960 classified upper-middle-class in its sample of families as those incomes of $20,000 minimum and $25,000 average. What does this suggest for the claim that the United States is a middle-class society?

4. A report in 1970 by the United States Census Bureau, based on a sampling of 12,000 families, finds almost three out of ten American families have two or more cars. Among families with incomes over $15,000, 63 percent have more than one car. Among families with incomes under $3,000, a minority have cars; three out of five families are dependent upon friends or public transportation.

Some three out of five families own their homes. Among the over $15,000 families, 85 percent do; among the under $3,000 half do. If, for the United States as a whole, 6.9 percent of housing units were "lacking some or all plumbing facilities" in 1970, 16.9 percent of Negro-occupied housing units were in this situation, particularly in the South where 29 percent of the Negro-occupied units lacked some or all plumbing facilities.[6]

Fewer than one-fourth of American families have a dishwasher and fewer than three out of ten have a freezer. Washing machines, refrigerators, and television sets are in more than nine out of ten families. The condition of the cars, homes, and appliances is not described in the report; analysts note that those used by the poor are often old and in poor condition. However, how do these data reflect on the statement that poverty is relative to the culture?

5. The federal government defines the poverty level by a sliding dollar scale. In 1971 it was set at $3,968 annual income for an urban family of four. This calculation, which permitted the government to claim marked decrease in the incidence of poverty from some 40 million persons in 1960 to fewer than 26 million in 1970, has been criticized by trade unions, social workers, and others who suggest that the poverty line for an urban family of four is closer to $5,000.

6. An announcement in 1971 by the Community Service Society indicated that "instead of continuing to treat the economic and social ills of the indi-

---

6 "General Demographic Trends for Metropolitan Areas, 1960 to 1970," United States Department of Commerce, Bureau of Census, *1970 Census of Population and Housing,* United States Summary, Final Report, October, 1971, p. 4.

vidual family, as it has for 123 years, CSS will take up the lance against the social conditions which create most of the families' problems . . . The community is the client."

A parallel path has been chosen by the Community Medicine Department of Mount Sinai Hospital in New York, in the belief that "the plumber is as basic to health care among the poor as is the physician. The Department is organizing a unit of men who will fan through slum areas fixing toilets, exterminating rats and other vermin, and repairing health-threatening housing conditions."

Are these instances of social engineering? What are the limitations as well as the advantages of this approach to poverty? Will cure of community ills require more power over related institutions than a single social agency can exercise? Is there any justification for the criticism that the battle against poverty has so far consisted of mere skirmishes?

7. In what ways do the middle and upper classes pay for the maintenance of low income strata, deliberately and indirectly? Are middle and upper income families better off in some ways and worse off in others because there are millions of families below the poverty line?

8. In their countries of origin most Jews were in the low income strata. In the United States roughly a third of the almost six million Jews live in families that are in business or professional occupations, similar to the occupational distribution of high status Protestant denominations such as Episcopalians and Presbyterians. In December 1971, it was estimated at a national conference that between half a million and a million Jews were living in poverty. The lower figure was based on a family of four living on less than $4,000 a year. The larger figure allowed for the fact that "most Jews live in cities where the edge of poverty lies closer to $6,000 a year." [7] The lower figure would put Jewish families in the poverty classification in roughly the same percentage as other white families, according to federal government figures on the incidence of poverty in 1970. The larger figure would place the percentage of poor Jewish families midway between white families and all others. In the latter case, the Jewish "success story" may be a less compelling model for black families than those who urge it think. In any case, which considerations make it difficult for one ethnic group to repeat the history of another?

9. The United States Department of Labor in the spring of 1967 calculated three family budgets for a family of four including a boy of thirteen and a girl of eight. The lowest budget was $4,915; the moderate was $8,485, and the higher was $12,549 or $13,319 with renting or owning a home the variable. The study was addressing itself to the question of how much it costs to live. How do these figures relate to definitions of poverty, working class, middle class, and upper class?

10. Some consider poverty "the great leveler." Are there commonalities of poor families that override ethnic differences? Do various levels of poverty make for family differences? Useful sources of information for such comparisons and contrasts include the following:

---

[7] John P. Sousa, "1 Million American Jews Said Living in Poverty," *San Diego Union*, December 26, 1971, p. B–6.

Brown, Claude, *Manchild in the Promised Land*. New York: New American Library, 1965.

Gans, Herbert J., *The Urban Villagers: Group and Class in the Life of Italian-Americans*. New York: The Free Press, 1962.

Lewis, Oscar, *Five Families*. New York: Basic Books, Inc., Publishers, 1959.

Liebow, Elliot, *Tally's Corner*. Boston: Little, Brown and Company, 1967.

Marshall, Catherine, *Christy*. New York: McGraw-Hill Book Company, 1968.

Mayerson, Charlotte L., ed., *Two Blocks Apart: Juan Gonzalez and Peter Quinn*. New York: Holt, Rinehart & Winston, Inc., 1965.

Roth, Henry, *Call It Sleep*. New York: Avon Books, 1964.

Steinbeck, John, *Grapes of Wrath*. New York: The Viking Press, 1939.

Jack E. Weller, *Yesterday's People: Life in Contemporary Appalachia*. Lexington, Kentucky: University of Kentucky Press, 1966.

CLASS TYPOLOGIES IN SEVERAL FAMILY RESEARCH STUDIES

1. A study in Chicago estimated that 12 percent of the population was upper-middle, 29 percent lower-middle, 46 percent upper-lower, and 13 percent lower-lower.[8]

upper-middle

These are "families of professionals, executives, and business proprietors who . . . exercise important authority in their professional and business organizations . . . The incomes of some of the professionals average quite a bit below those of the business executives and proprietors, but they are accorded similar prestige because of the value placed on their advanced training, autonomy, and learned activities . . . They take it for granted that their children (both sons and daughters) will complete college, and that the sons will probably continue into graduate or professional schools."

lower-middle

These are "families of white collar workers who do not exercise managerial or autonomous professional authority and . . . families of skilled workers and foremen who, though engaged in 'blue collar' work, live in a way that conforms to the model set by the white collar portion of the group. Most of these men and women graduated from high school, and quite a few of the men completed college. . . . They are engaged . . . in more routinized occupations, as accountants, engineers, supervisors of clerical workers, etc. Lower-mid-

[8] Lee Rainwater, *Family Design* (Chicago: Aldine Publishing Company, 1965), pp. 22–24.

dle-class families live in good, average neighborhoods in houses or apartments which they strive to maintain in attractive and respectable ways, but they do not place emphasis on sophistication and organized good taste."

upper-lower

These people "generally are in semi-skilled and medium-skilled work; they are in manual occupations or in responsible but not highly regarded service jobs such as policemen, firemen, or bus drivers. They have generally had at least some high school education. Their families live in reasonably comfortable housing, in neighborhoods composed mainly of other manual and lower-level service workers . . . aware that they do not have as much social status or prestige as the middle-class white collar worker or the highly skilled technician and factory foreman."

lower-lower

"They feel at the 'bottom of the heap' . . . They generally work at unskilled jobs, and often they work only intermittently or are chronically unemployed. Few people in this group have graduated from high school, and a great many have gone no further than grammar school. They live in slum and near-slum neighborhoods, and their housing tends to be cramped and deteriorated."

2. A study of male and female college students enrolled in a large university in the years 1946 to 1953 used a sixfold classification of father's occupation: [9]

> Manual laborer other than skilled
> Skilled laborer
> Clerk or salesman
> Farmer or cattleman
> Professional or semiprofessional
> Business owner or manager

The sample was predominantly middle class, however. "Approximately one-half of the males and two-thirds of the females came from families in which the father's occupation was given as business owner or manager, professional, or semiprofessional. Only one-tenth of the fathers of the males and one-twelfth of the females were farmers or cattlemen. Almost one-fifth of the boys and girls came from white collar clerical families. Over twice as high a proportion of young men as young women (approximately one in five as compared to one in eleven) had fathers in the manual laborer classes." Moreover, "since the number in the manual laborer group was small, it was combined with the skilled laborer group to form the 'laborer' group for the statistical analyses."

According to this study, "A surprising fact discovered in the interviews was that in a few instances the individual was more willing to discuss his or her sex behavior than to reveal the identity of the father's occupation when it had a low social prestige value."

---

[9] Winston Ehrmann, *Premarital Dating Behavior* (New York: Holt, Rinehart & Winston, Inc., 1959), pp. 14, 104.

3. A study of the class impact on adolescents used five socioeconomic categories: [10]

class 1

These families are the top of society, both old rich families and newly rich ones. They have influential connections. Their leisure includes travel. The majority attend prestigious colleges. They are members of exclusive clubs, have several automobiles, and servants.

class 2

These are the families of doctors, lawyers, school superintendents, owners of large family-operated farms. Wives are active in country clubs and in civic leadership. They are likely to have a servant. Children are expected to do well in school.

class 3

The lower-middle class comes close to the American stereotype of the average family. They have higher church attendance than any other class. Substantial farmers fit within this class. The husband makes economic decisions; the wife the social ones. About 15 percent of the mothers work.

class 4

The working class family is made up of good, solid people who never get anywhere and are aware of their inferior prestige. They are poor, honest, and hardworking, have few luxuries, and are excluded from the best residential areas. There is no participation in civic activity. Social life is centered mainly around kinfolk. A high percentage of these families are broken by death, separation, and divorce.

class 5

The lower-class family includes semiskilled and unskilled workers, but employment is irregular. The homes are dilapidated. There is a high birth rate. A fatalistic attitude accompanies frequent problems arising from gambling, fights, and drinking. They have mainly elementary school rather than high school education.

4. A study of the father's occupation as a factor in the parent–child relationship mentions five classes in urban America: [11]

Upper class, estimated at 1 or 2 percent. These are families with such occupational roles as major executives and ambassadors.

Upper-Middle, estimated at 10 percent: These families include minor executives and high school teachers.

---

[10] August B. Hollingshead, *Elmtown's Youth* (New York: John Wiley & Sons, Inc., 1949), Chap. 5, "Cultural Characteristics of the Five Classes," pp. 83–120.

[11] Donald McKinley, *Social Class and Family Life* (New York: The Free Press, 1964), p. 19.

Lower-Middle, estimated at 22 percent: These families have such occupations as bookkeeper, photographer, clerk.

Working Class, estimated at 46 percent: These families have such occupations as electricians and bus drivers.

Lower Class, estimated at 20 percent: These families include the erratically employed and the chronically underemployed or unemployed, with the men working as laborers, longshoremen, etc.

5. A study of the effect of social class on the lives of children in a midwestern city of 45,000 population in the 1950s found "so few children of upper class families that they cannot usefully be studied as a group. They associate freely with upper-middle-class children." [12] The study distinguished four social class groups:

class a—upper and upper-middle classes

These families extend from the very top of the prestige structure of the city "almost to the bottom of the professional and managerial groups." The parents have had some college education "and they almost universally expect their children to enter college." They are community leaders in social, business, and professional life.

class b—lower-middle class

These families include minor white collar workers plus a few in highly skilled manual jobs. Their jobs and income are stable. They live in middle residential districts. "Though very few adults of Class B have gone to college, they are increasingly expecting their children to go."

class c—upper-lower class

These families of "respectable, hard-working manual workers and an occasional proprietor of a small business" are the largest group in the city. They have less schooling, with only some parents having graduated from high school, but they want their children to do so. A few children go to college. They do not belong much to associations other than church, lodge, or trade union.

class d—lower-lower class

These families are looked down on by the rest of the community. They include the "very poor, the disreputable, and the demoralized." There is some unemployment even in so-called good times. Few of them have been to high school. The adults are often semiliterate. "There are a considerable number of women in this group who are raising children with little or no help from the fathers," either through welfare funds or by employment as waitresses, cleaning women, or unskilled workers in a local industry.

---

[12] Robert Havighurst et al., *Growing Up in River City* (New York: John Wiley & Sons, Inc., 1962), pp. 10–12.

DATA ON FAMILY STRUCTURE *

Selected characteristics of families, as of March 1970 **: number in thousands

	All Families	Married Couples, Both Spouses Present	Female-Headed Families
Total families	51,237	44,436	5,580
	(100.0%)	(100.0%)	(100.0%)
White families	46,022	40,802	4,185
	(89.8%)	(91.8%)	(75.0%)
Negro and other families	5,215	3,634	1,395
	(10.2%)	(8.2%)	(25.0%)
Negro families	4,774		1,349
	(9.3%)		(24.1%)

Note: While there are three times as many white families headed by a female as Negro and other, such famiiles constitute 9.1 percent of all white families and 28.3 percent of all Negro families. The percentages come closer together in all families with income under $3,000 annually. For a discussion of female-headed families in terms of sex ratio of whites and blacks, see Jacquelyne J. Jackson, "But Where are the Men?" The Black Scholar (December 1971), pp. 30–41.

* Unless otherwise noted, statistics have been taken from United States Bureau of the Census, Statistical Abstract of the United States: 1971 (92nd Edition), Washington, D.C., 1971, p. 39.
** Includes members of the armed forces living off post or with their families on post, but excludes all other members of the armed forces.

ETHNIC DIVERSITY

INTERNATIONAL IMMIGRATION *

Total admitted to the United States (1960-1970): 3.3 million

Selected Years	Thousands of Immigrants
1960	265
1965	297
1968	454
1969	359
1970	373

* An immigrant is defined by the Census Bureau as "an alien . . . admitted for permanent residence." (Statistical Abstract, p. 87). Many more millions of non-immigrants spend temporary periods in the United States, among them foreign officials and their families, travelers, and students.

FOREIGN WHITE STOCK (1960)

Country of Origin	Total	Percent	Foreign Born	Native of Foreign and Mixed Parentage
All countries	33,078	100.0	9,294	23,784
England and Wales	1,955	5.9	550	1,405
Scotland	668	2.0	213	455
Ireland (Eire)	1,771	5.4	338	1,433
Norway	774	2.3	153	621
Sweden	1,046	3.2	214	831
Denmark	399	1.2	85	314
Netherlands	398	1.2	118	280
France	349	1.1	111	238
Germany	4,313	13.0	987	3,326
Poland	2,778	8.4	747	2,031
Czechoslovakia	917	2.8	227	690
Austria	1,098	3.3	304	793
Hungary	701	2.1	245	456
Yugoslavia	448	1.4	166	282
USSR	2,287	6.9	689	1,598
Lithuania	402	1.2	121	281
Greece	378	1.1	159	219
Italy	4,550	13.7	1,256	3,284
Other Europe	1,683	5.1	536	1,146
Asia	483	1.5	201	282
Canada	3,154	9.5	942	2,212
Mexico	1,725	5.2	573	1,152
Other America	389	1.2	229	160
All other and not reported	425	1.3	130	295

Population of races other than white or Negro (1960) in thousands

Indian	523.5
Japanese	464.3
Chinese	237.2
Filipino	176.3
All others	218.0

Spanish-American population (1969) in thousands

	Total	Mexican	Puerto Rican	Cuban	Central or South American	Other Spanish
Total of Spanish Origin	9,230	5,073	1,454	565	556	1,582
Percent foreign born	20.7	17.1	0.5	82.5	63.7	13.8
Spanish mother tongue	6,358	3,658	1,208	536	383	573
Percent of total	68.9	72.1	83.1	94.8	68.9	36.2

OTHER DATA PERTINENT TO FAMILY FUNCTIONING *

DIVORCES IN THE UNITED STATES **

	1960	1965	1970
Number of divorces (thousands)	393	479	715
Rate per 1,000 population	2.2	2.5	3.5

EDUCATION

	1960	1965	1968	1969	1970
School enrollment: higher education (in millions)	3.6	5.7	6.8	7.4	7.4
Years of school completed, all persons 25 years and over Median for whites	10.9				12.2
Median for Negro and other persons	8.2				10.1
Persons completed high school	41.1%				55.2%

* Raw data from United States Bureau of the Census, *Statistical Abstract of the United States: 1971* (92nd Edition), Washington, D.C., 1971.
** Divorce statistics are inadequate. As yet only a minority of states have their local courts forward data on all divorces to a central point for forwarding to the National Vital Statistics Division.

DATA ON THE WORKING WIFE AND MOTHER

FEMALE LABOR FORCE *

	1960 (millions)	1970 (millions)
Total	22.5	31.2
16–19 years		2.9
20–24		4.8
25–34		5.7
35–44		6.0
45–64		10.7
65 and over		1.1
Married, husband present **	54.4%	58.8%
Working mothers, with husband and children present	6.6	10.2
Labor force participation rate	27.6%	40.8%

* United States Bureau of the Census, *Statistical Abstract of the United States: 1971* (92nd Edition), Washington, D.C., 1971, Table XVI.

** "Increasing prevalence of the multi-paycheck home is a major factor in the growth of the upper income bracket. Approximately 55 percent of all households have more than one person in the labor force, but at the $15,000-and-over level the figure exceeds 75 percent. Frequency of multi-earner homes peaks in the $15,000–$25,000 category, drops to about 70 percent in the $25,000–$50,000 bracket, and to 46 percent at $50,000 and above." *Finance Facts*, January 1972, p. 1 (National Consumer Finance Association).

THE EMPLOYED MOTHER: RACIAL AND AGE VARIABLES *

Almost 30 million women in March 1969 were in the job market, either working or actively seeking work. In contrast to 1940 when one out of ten mothers in the United States was in the labor force, almost four out of ten mothers were in early 1969. In absolute figures, the 1.5 million mothers in the labor force in 1940 increased to 4.6 million in 1950, and 11.6 million in March 1969. Their distribution in 1969 according to age of the children was as follows:

	In Millions	Percent of All Mothers with Children of the Given Age
Mothers with children under 18 years of age:	11.6	
a. 6 to 17 (none under 6)	7.4	51
b. 3 to 5 (none under 3)	2.1	37
c. under 3	2.1	26

* Data from "Who are the Working Mothers?" Leaflet 37, October 1970, Women's Bureau, United States Department of Labor.

If in 1940 a tenth of all mothers were in the labor force and in 1950 a fifth, by 1969 two-fifths of all mothers were. Thus the past three decades have seen a dramatic increase both in absolute figures and in percentages.

As the children grow older, there are more mothers in the labor force. More mothers thirty-five to forty-four years of age are in gainful employment than younger mothers twenty-five to thirty-four years of age. Of every ten working mothers, three are in the younger and almost four in the older of these two age groups.

Since most of the working women have several children, there are more children with working mothers than there are working mothers. In 1965 almost eleven million children under twelve years had mothers in the labor force. A larger proportion of black mothers work than white mothers. In early 1969, 62 percent of black mothers with children six to seventeen years and 45 percent of those with children under six were at work; for white mothers the comparable figures were 50 and 28 percent.

Group child care facilities have not kept pace with the increase in working mothers. In 1965 only 6 percent of children under six years of age received group care in child care centers and 1 percent of children six to eleven years of age. The predominant pattern was for the child to be cared for in his own home by a relative or in someone else's home.

The mother at work is typically from a home in which the husband is present. In early 1969, 9.7 million working mothers, or 84 percent, had a husband in the home, compared with 1.9 million women widowed, divorced, or separated from their husbands. The latter are more likely to work when children under six are in the home than women with husband present.

The mother at work is more likely to come from a home in which the husband's income is low. In early 1969, 55 percent of mothers of children six to seventeen years of age were in paid employment when husband's income was less than $3,000; 45 percent when husband's income was $7,000 or more; for mothers of children under six years the figures were 33 and 24 percent.

The proportion of women in full-time work (thirty-five hours or more weekly and fifty weeks a year) increases as children's ages rise. In early 1969, some 40 percent of mothers with children six to seventeen were full-time, year-round workers while 17 percent of mothers with children under three were so employed.

A DATING CHECKLIST

A: Agree   D: Disagree   U: Undecided

1. I am willing to "go Dutch" in steady dating or with somebody I have dated many times, but not on a random dating basis.
   A.   D.   U.

2. I don't consider it a real date if we do things that cost nothing, like walking or picnicking in the park or at the beach, going for a ride, visiting a museum, or dancing at a friend's house.
   A.   D.   U.

3. I don't think parents should have anything to say about the person I date once I am no longer living with them.

   A.   D.   U.

4. If I am older than my sibling and have more dating experience, I should try to guide the dating choices of this younger brother or sister.

   A.   D.   U.

5. I think my parents should supervise the dating of my brothers and sisters still living at home to keep them from disgracing us.

   A.   D.   U.

6. I should respect my parents' preferences about whom I date and what we do as long as I am living at home.

   A.   D.   U.

7. I have different standards about my date's looks, education, religion, race, as well as our sexual intimacy, depending on whether it is a first or second date with the other person or I have been dating that person for a longer period of time.

   A.   D.   U.

8. Nobody in college dates any more. That's for the high school crowd. We live together as a group or as a couple and when we are no longer enjoying each other's company, we make new living arrangements.

   A.   D.   U.

9. I find the sexual part of dating confusing.

   A. Boys try to go as far as they can and then talk about marrying a virgin.

    A.   D.   U.

   B. Girls lead you on and then get insulted if you make a pass.

    A.   D.   U.

10. Girls should be as free as boys to ask for dates and to voice their preferences for the way time and money will be spent.

    A.   D.   U.

11. Boys and girls of whatever age need no supervision on dates.

    A.   D.   U.

12. Boys and girls should be allowed to date whenever they feel ready to do so and not be restrained by arbitrary milestones.

    A.   D.   U.

13. Going steady should be up to the couple; parents should refrain from comment.

    A.   D.   U.

14. The boy and the girl should decide their own time limits and not be limited by parental or community curfews.

    A.   D.   U.

15. It is all right for a boy or a girl to invite the other home when no one is there.

    A.   D.   U.

16. The daters should have flexibility in their activities and not have to keep parents informed as to where they are.

    A.   D.   U.

17. The couple owe each other their complete attention when they are on a date.

    A.   D.   U.

18. There is something wrong with somebody who is not dating.

    A.   D.   U.

19. A girl owes a boy a good-night kiss after a date.

    A.   D.   U.

20. Parents should not force daters to pet in cars. There should be a room at home where a dating couple can have privacy.

    A.   D.   U.

LOVE: MYTH AND REALITY

1. "We fell in love the moment we met."

If love means sexual attraction and friendship, this is not possible, since friendship takes time to develop. Even if they were not in love, they were attracted to each other at once. Perhaps each met the *ideal mate image* to which both had been socialized. Every culture presents people with ideas of what is a desirable mate, in terms of height, weight, facial features, body shape, complexion, and the like. These attributes often have a utilitarian base and relate to the society's values. Thus in an agrarian society the broad-beamed woman is much admired; she will be capable, in the popular view, of bearing many children. Vestiges of what was previously utilitarian may remain, so that the tall, large-muscled man may be the ideal mate image even in an industrial society that does not require outstanding physical strength for survival. By association of ideas, the male who is big is assumed to be more aggressive and therefore more likely to shoulder his way into top jobs and financial success.

Then how do people who do not fit the ideal mate image ever attract anyone? Others may learn to love them through the friendship route. Pleasure in each other's company because of shared interest, confidences, and inspiration may make the extent of departure from the ideal mate image less and less important. Sexual attraction may build on the satisfactions gained in the friendship. Relatives and peers, unduly influenced by externals as defined in the ideal mate image, may wonder, "How can he love her, she is so plain, or so fat, or so ungainly?" or "How can she love him, he is so short or so bald or so frail?"

Some psychologists suggest that peer group relationships are important in early and middle adolescence but in late adolescence and early adulthood they may be dysfunctional. The individual can make a better mate selection on the basis of continued interaction with the other person than is possible under the influence of peers who are likely to express views tied to the ideal mate image.

2. "He doesn't love her. He is only infatuated."

This may be so, but time will tell. Infatuation usually involves a high level of sexual attraction. In time this may lead to a strong friendship as well, and he will love her. However, if the friendship does not develop, and he regards everything but her sexual attractions with repulsion, perhaps hating himself for continuing to relate to her, it is a problem that will not be solved by marrriage. If the infatuation is long-lasting and begins to interfere with his occupational, educational, and marriage goals, he may find counseling useful in coming to understand why he is involving himself in a destructive relationship. If he is enjoying the infatuation, there is no problem, however disappointing it may be to him or provoking to his parents, the girls next door, and others whose expectations are not met.

3. "He chose a girl who looks just like his mother." "He chose a girl who is just the opposite of his mother in looks."

Research indicates that we are more likely to choose someone who resembles a beloved cross-sex parent in personality rather than in appearance, and by the same token, avoid someone who resembles a disliked cross-sex parent in personality. If the ideal mate image is blonde and tall, or dark and short, both generations are likely to make similar choices. In a multinational society such as the United States, there are ideal mate images for many subsocieties as well as the host society. Contact with a variety of appearances is likely, therefore, and the sense of strangeness and emotional distance from the unfamiliar may diminish. The choice of somebody who does not look like the cross-sex parent is not necessarily a rejection of that parent in such circumstances.

Some psychologists tended to make this assumption about black–white and oriental–white intermarriages and for a while seemed to be offering psychological support for antimiscegenation statutes. However, other psychologists have pointed out both the importance of personality in modern marriage and the greater weight that attaches to the individual's emotional history rather than to physical appearance. The son is not apt to have an identical personality with his father; for one thing they have had different fathers! The mate the son chooses for personality fit will rarely be identical to his father's choice of his mother. If there is similarity, it will be because he found his mother pleasant to be with. Friendship with his mother rather than sexual attraction is the likely explanation of his search for a similar personality. The same psychodynamics would be at work in the girl's mate selection and her perception of her father as lovable or hateful.

Insufficiently studied as yet is the influence of siblings in mate selection. Pleasant interaction between brother and sister may motivate them to see as mates those who resemble the other person in personality. Any assumption that similarity in appearance bespeaks similarity in personality may make for great disappointments in mate selection.

4. "I was immediately attracted to him, but he seemed not to know I exist."

Each individual has a different affectional history, with parents especially, but with many significant others as well. The feelings in negative as well as positive interaction often get attached to a particular appearance. The stereotype of the spinster teacher as gaunt, harsh, critical, unloving undoubtedly affected the marriage chances of many women with similar appearances despite very positive personality qualities. Each of us has an aversion for or an indifference to certain physical types, and can in some instances trace these feelings to our affectional experiences. It is no reflection on our attractiveness and worthwhileness, although it may be painful and disappointing, that we trigger off for some people negative feelings by our gestures, appearance, voice tone, etc., while they on the contrary stimulate for us positive feelings tied to a different set of past experiences. While we can sometimes dissipate the first negative associations by continued relationships during which our desirable qualities are given a chance to be observed and the negative responses are more and more extinguished, this is not always possible.

Perhaps at some future stage of societal development, negative experiences will be so reduced in childhood and there will be such a diversity of loving others in the lives of children that we shall be able to accept at first sight a broader array of people than is possible now. Meanwhile there is bound to be a great deal of disappointment that people who attract us are not attracted in turn.

5. "I know he loves me because he is so jealous of other men. It's very flattering."

Some psychologists see jealousy as a symptom of basic insecurity, a fear of not being lovable and therefore not likely to retain the other's affection. Since all of us have some degree of insecurity, there will be manifestations of jealousy. On the other side, some people deliberately provoke jealousy because they are not sure they are loved and think the competitive element will push the other person to greater appreciation or more open declaration.

Deliberate flirtation to arouse jealousy does increase the other's insecurity and cause him to show signs of concern. However, it may also result in such a lack of trust and so impair self-confidence to the point of putting the whole relationship on shaky foundations. While openness of communication can sometimes clear up misunderstandings—"You thought I was putting my arm around her. I was reaching for the album above her head"—it is usually not direct confrontation but continual building up the other's feeling of being lovable and loved that can reduce jealousy. It is difficult to be flattered by jealousy if what it reveals of the person and the relationship is understood.

6. "How can he be in love? He sees her faults so clearly."

This may reveal a confusion in thinking about rational love as opposed to over-idealization. The person in love can care deeply despite the shortcomings perceived in the other, and he knows that he is not perfect either. There is always a judgment involved, implicitly or explicitly stated, that there are more positives than negatives in the relationship, more virtues than flaws in the other person.

However, to dwell on one's inadequacies or those of the other, if they are not remediable, is a sign of immaturity. The individual may take as a clue to his ambivalence the constant references he finds himself making to faults of the other person. He may be trying to unsell himself on the relationship—and this is one way of doing it. If she is very short and he is uncomfortable with this fact, he may have to allow more time to elapse before any final commitment is made. In the extra months he can continue to test his own feelings, his ability to live happily with the facts of her appearance, the state of her health, her way of eating, speaking, and the like. If modifications in each other's behaviors are a necessary condition for maintenance of a love relationship, it should be agreed that they be undertaken, and some progress become evident, before plans for a joint life are made.

7. "They seem too comfortable with each other to be in love."

Nervousness often comes out of the need to impress the other person, to prove something, to present only your "good side." It is analogous to the tension felt by a woman who is convinced that one of her profiles is much better than the other and is always contriving to sit in a way that "puts a better face on things." While the presence of a beloved person is by definition exciting, this should be distinguished from nervousness. Ease comes with knowing you are loved for what you are, that pretense between you is minimal.

8. "Since he fell in love, he is no longer fun to be with."

The perspective of the speaker is all-important. Is she a disappointed friend who had hoped he would fall in love with her? Is it a same-sex friend who is now closed out by the intimacy of the couple relationship? If there is no personal animus, the statement may be true. What are the implications? Perhaps the person in love is more serious and busily trying to cope with problems which stand in the way of marriage: finishing up his school work, accumulating money for the purchase of a home, and the like. He may be more serious also in the effort to weigh the degree of affection he feels, to know whether he feels enough love to want to enter important commitments.

However, the love relationship typically also expands the individual's expressiveness, makes him notice the beauty of nature, the kindness of people, the charm of babies. If the individual in love is tense and cross and his personality deteriorates markedly, making him "no longer fun to be with," there can be some legitimate question raised, preferably by himself, as to whether he is in love.

9. "All the world loves a lover."

There is the possibility that people disappointed in their own love relationships may not cast an encouraging eye at other couples. Discouragement and envy may color their remarks. On the other hand, those who have had positive experiences in a love relationship are reminded by the sight of a couple in love of their own happiness. They are likely to nod approvingly, smile, and respond generously. Perhaps the reality is that "All the lovers of the world love a lover." Even this may be overly sentimental, as many will continue to peer at lovers through the spectacles of social homogamy and respond sourly or sorrowfully when they find traditional rules have been broken.

DATING: TOPICS FOR SMALL GROUP DISCUSSION

Agree or disagree?

1. It's risky to show too much interest in someone you like. Playing "hard to get" rouses and keeps the other person's interest.
2. It doesn't matter what his (her) folks are like. He (she) is an individual in his (her) own right. After all, you are not dating the family.
3. It is up to the girl to say no. A real man goes as far as she lets him.
4. It's more fun to date an older person. People your own age are so boring.
5. If a girl pays her part of the date, it is unfair because she has to spend so much more to look attractive for the evening.
6. Girls shouldn't phone boys and invite them on dates. It's harder for a boy to refuse than a girl.
7. If two couples are out on a date and sharing a car, one couple has no right to spoil the other couple's fun.
8. Girls and boys should not go out on dates unless they are prepared with contraceptives.
9. All boys and girls should go through group dating before they try the experience of one-to-one dating.
10. Boys and girls should not discuss sex on a date, lest they go from the thought to the act.

AM I A GOOD DATE? (A SELF-QUIZ)

Answer with: Yes ☐ No ☐ Not Sure ☐

1. I am a good conversationalist, meaning a good listener as well as able to tell about my own ideas and experiences.

2. I am straightforward in asking for a date or refusing it, but allow the other to save face.

3. I am not a status seeker, demanding that we go only to the prestigious places.

4. I do not embarrass my date by my way of dressing, eating, speaking, or dancing. If I am not comfortable with the norms of the place we are in, I suggest we go elsewhere.

5. I do not force confidences about my date's family members or previous dating relationships.

6. I try to be punctual or if I am not too good at this, I suggest meeting at a place where the other person can wait comfortably.

7. I am conscientious about keeping a date and do not use excuses to get out of it when a better one comes along.

8. If the date proves to be a negative experience, boring, hostile, or degrading, I think through my own conduct and see what I contributed to the unfortunate result rather than blame the other person.

9. I try to be myself most of the time, although I find it fun occasionally to try out a new me, to emphasize some aspect of personality I don't always display, such as frankness, critical ability, independence of thought, or fantasy.

10. I allow my date similar scope and don't begrudge such efforts.

11. I make up my own mind as to whether I liked the date, even though my parents or friends offer negative comments.

12. I don't suggest activities my date or I cannot afford. In a restaurant I watch what the other person is considering and choose in a similar price range.

13. I don't give false clues concerning sexual expectations.

14. I don't use a current date as a stepping stone to another in any obvious way that would hurt the feelings of the one I am with.

15. I try to establish early in the date any time or distance limitations to avoid any wrangle in ending the date.

16. I feel responsible for the other person's safety and do not try to drive when I am not in full control of myself.

17. I respect my dating partner's confidences and do not share them with my friends afterwards.

GOING STEADY

Defined as dating exclusively, going steady may mean very different obligations in various communities and at various age levels. For some it may mean exclusive dating for a few weeks at a time, for others it may mean years. To some it may mean appearing as a couple at dances, parties, picnics, but with no implications for engagement or marriage in the near future or ever. For still others it may be a serious pre-engagement period.

Each person in the couple may perceive the relationship differently. When girls are less career-minded and more anxious for an early marriage, there may be a tendency on their part to assume greater commitment than has ever been articulated. Some young men, especially those in high school who are headed for college, are reluctant, therefore, to enter a steady relationship. Different views of going steady can be seen in the following and can form the basis for class discussion.

1. If Joe and Susan date more than three times in succession, their friends are right in assuming they are going steady.

2. It would be inappropriate for Bill to phone Susan for a date if he knows she has dated Joe three times.

3. Mary is having a party. She would have to invite Joe and Susan as a couple or neither of them.

4. Susan's parents are likely to say just before Joe arrives on the third date, "It's such a relief to know who is taking you out. We never get to see the boys you date only once or twice."

5. Joe's parents are likely to say, "Aren't you seeing too much of that young lady? You have many years of school ahead of you."

6. Susan is likely to think, "What a relief to know I can count on Joe for all the dances and parties coming up in the school year."

7. Joe is apt to think, "I wonder how far I can go. This is the first time I've been out with the same girl more than a couple of dates."

8. The minister may say, "I have nothing against steady dating. Yes, I know I preached a sermon about the dangers a few years ago. Now I'm less concerned about sexual intimacy and more anxious about the danger that couples keep going steady long after their relationship is growth-producing. They're either a habit for each other or they may be fearful of breaking out into the competitive dating world again. Often they feel obligated to keep going steady because their sexual relationship went further than they had intended."

9. Their teachers may say, "Wherever you see Joe you see Susan, not only at the lockers or the lunchroom, but right in the same classes. They might be doing better school work if they looked at the books once in a while rather than at each other."

10. The coach may say, "Joe really had possibilities. It's too bad. If all the boys went steady, we would have no team. They just won't give the hours to practice or keep the curfews."

11. The sociologist may say, "We don't really know the effects of going steady. The subject has not been researched enough. The few studies made show great regional differences, with steady dating starting before the teen years in some places, and almost unknown in others. In fact, a sizable minority of boys and girls do not date until late in the high school years, let alone go steady. It would be valuable to know parental attitudes, but the re-

search would have to be designed to get at real feelings rather than the socially acceptable answers. It would be helpful to know whether marital success, defined as either stability or happiness or perhaps both, correlates with dating history. Are couples better off in their later relationship if they went steady for specified periods of time? In short, is steady dating positive in its effects at several points in time, first when the couple is dating and later in marriage? We all assume more sexual intimacy in the steady dating relationship but could this be because the couple that has had intercourse tends to define the relationship as steady dating in order to make their sexual activity more acceptable to themselves and others? How many studies of sexual behavior have asked those who checked the 'going steady' column how long they had been going steady? It will not be easy to get data now that limitations have been imposed on asking students for sexual histories in some states such as California."

12. The school counselor says, "As soon as they go steady they cut down on their opportunities for education and jobs. I keep hearing, 'No, I want something closer to this town—my girl would be too far away' or 'I'm not sure I want to plan for a career which demands so many years of preparation. I'm already going steady.'"

IN LOVE OR NOT? SOME QUESTIONS TO STIMULATE SELF-UNDERSTANDING

1. Do I only admire the other person's body, or do I find equal pleasure in the conversation, ideas, humor, and nonsexual dimensions of personality? Is petting the only enjoyable part of the relationship on each date?

2. Have my admiration and enjoyment increased or decreased in the last few weeks or months? Am I getting a little bored? Do I contemplate with pleasure or discomfort the thought that increased longevity rates in the United States will make it possible for us to spend almost half a century together?

3. Do I find myself looking forward to group dates so as to hear and be with somebody else of the opposite sex? Am I worried by my interest in a specific third person or by my desire to be with others generally?

4. Am I developing new interests (music, political causes, sports, etc.) only to please the other person and not really feeling pleasure in these activities? Am I counting on giving up skiing or visits to art museums as soon as we get married?

5. Do I find my main pleasure in thinking of myself as a married person, or do I anticipate with delight a close relationship with another person for a long period of time?

6. Do I find myself disappointed that I do not really feel in our relationship the excitement, the intensity of emotion, that people talk about and fiction writers depict? Am I just more sensible than the average, or is there something lacking in our relationship?

7. Do I worry that none of the good qualities I see in the other person seem evident to my friends and relatives even after repeated visits? Why are the humor, the charm, the wit present only in the dyadic encounter?

8. Why do I fear marriage if I love the other person? Can one love and not want to marry? Am I afraid of having my personality submerged and losing my individuality? Must two persons think as one? Will every utterance of my mate be taken as reflecting my views too?

9. Do I like quiet times together, or am I the first to suggest going out and visiting others? Are the silences between us restful and pleasant, or are they uneasy and foreboding of years of lack of anything to say to each other about the world or about ourselves?

10. Do I respond sarcastically more often than I wish? Am I growing critical, even bitter, especially about matters we cannot seem to agree upon?

11. How close to breaking up the relationship have we been, and how many times? Am I always weighing the notion that maybe things have moved too rapidly, that I have been made to feel committed before I was ready, that I would welcome more time?

12. If the other person counts on me to lend support in family feuds, can I remain in love when one part of me is being taught, indeed compelled, to hate? If I find the other person's parents not so bad as depicted, will I be free to create my own emotional history with them or must my feelings follow a predetermined path? Will this create feelings of hypocrisy, pretense at emotions I really do not share? If I truly loved the other person, would all his loves and hates automatically become mine?

13. How much do I care about the other person's welfare? Is his (or her) happiness as important to me as my own?

14. Am I conscious of being loved more than of loving? Is this flattery too gratifying for me to surrender, or am I likely to increase my love in response to the affection lavished on me?

15. Am I unable to love some members of the other person's family because I do not know them well enough as yet or because I already see in them the negative qualities I am dismayed by in my future mate? Can I tolerate them in him, but become anxious when they are magnified through reflection in his kinfolk: boastfulness, too much fondness for drink, stinginess, etc.? Will this require that we see less of his flawed kin? Can my love survive his failure to agree with this solution? Similarly, do I worry about retaining his love when my parents and siblings reflect some of my own less attractive characteristics?

16. Am I disturbed by these questions? Do I need more time to sort out the feelings that came to the surface when I read the fifteen questions? Will class discussion help clarify some of the points? What can I bring up without revealing too much about my family, his family, our relationship? Will the teacher have some suggestions as to how to reconcile my privacy needs and the need for clarification of alternatives?

WHAT I WOULD VALUE MOST IN SELECTING A MATE

Indicate order of preference.

a. Good health
b. Sexually responsive
c. Good housekeeper
d. Imaginative cook
e. Virginity
f. Desire for children
g. Warm and affectionate
h. Good looks
i. Same religion
j. Good education
k. Fair, willing to share unpleasant tasks
l. Ambitious
m. Socially adroit
n. Same race
o. Same nationality background
p. Popular with own sex
q. Popular with opposite sex
r. Liked by my parents
s. Liked by my friends
t. Well-off financially
u. Sports-minded
v. Fond of reading
w. Artistic talents
x. Good sense of humor
y. Good speech
z. other: _____

MARRIAGE READINESS: QUESTIONS AS A BASIS FOR DISCUSSION

1. Has either the man or the woman succeeded in holding a job? For how long?
2. Has either had any experience in taking care of children?
3. Have the two talked freely and observed each other carefully in matters of sexuality, role preferences, relationships with families of origin, church commitments, political activity, friendships?
4. Has either ever had the responsiblity of running a household? For how long?
5. Have the two checked each other's expectations about the kind of wed-

ding, whether there will be a honeymoon, and so on? Are they aware of how their own preferences fit the expectations of both sets of parents? Are they prepared to support each other in their own decisions?

6. Have the two taken practical steps of pricing furniture, apartments, medical protection, and the like?

7. Have the two discussed contraceptives, a premarital medical exam, and been frank about their own medical histories?

8. Is either homesick for the family of origin when off at school or work and unable to see parents and siblings for weeks at a time?

9. Have both had the experience of sharing earnings to help meet the expenses of kin or friends? Has this been on a regular basis or in an emergency only?

10. If both marriage and a new job are both normal critical transitions of everyday life, has the couple planned to have these transitions separated in time so that the strains of adjustment would not be cumulative? If the transitions must coincide (for example, the new job is a considerable distance away and only by marrying can they be together), have they taken into account the special challenges each will face and the extra efforts that must be made to mitigate emotional pile-ups?

11. According to one marriage counselor there are more than a dozen areas a couple should have discussed before marriage: housing, money, education, employment, health, religion, in-laws, children, sexual adjustment, leisure time activities, wedding preparations, interaction including communication and arguing patterns, ability to express real feelings both positive and negative, and habit modifications sought in the other. Can the couple formulate two or three questions for each topic that they have already put to each other? Are there additional questions they have hesitated to formulate?

READINESS FOR INTERFAITH, INTERNATIONAL, AND INTERRACIAL MARRIAGES

Answer with: Yes □   No □   Not Sure □

1. I would be bothered if my parents opposed the marriage.

2. I would be bothered if my siblings opposed the marriage.

3. I would be bothered if the children did not look like my side of the family.

4. I would be bothered if the children were not to be members of my church.

5. I would be bothered if my spouse did not become acculturated, but retained tastes and preferences in food, clothing, sexuality, and role expectations of the other family of origin.

6. I would view the beliefs of my spouse's church as valid as mine.

7. I would consider religion or race or nationality a closed matter to be excluded from further discussion.

8. I would be willing to let the children decide for themselves in their teen

years which church, if any, they would attend. While they are young, church attendance would be on some schedule agreed to before we marry (no attendance, attend each of our two churches on alternate weeks, etc.).

9. I would be willing to observe the feast days, fasts, ceremonies, and birth control methods of my spouse's religion if these are important to him (her).

10. I would insist on all church rites involving our children to be in accordance with my beliefs (baptism, circumcision, bereavement, etc.) and have communicated this expectation to my future spouse.

11. I would accept the idea of supporting my spouse's church financially as well as my own.

12. I would accept the kin of my spouse as worthy as my own of emotional and financial support, despite differences of race, faith, or national origins.

13. I would not be bothered by the criticisms or ostracisms of those friends, business associates, fellow workers, neighbors, and others who do not share my views of the equality of all people.

14. I would want the children named in a way that did not call attention to the faith, nationality, or race to which I do not belong.

15. I would want us to live in a neighborhood in which my own faith, nationality, or race predominates.

THE ENGAGEMENT: THE COUPLE'S FINAL EXAM?

Unlike earlier periods of time in American society when an engagement was a firm commitment to marry, enforceable by law ("breach of promise suit"), engagement today is more of a final testing period of the relationship. It used to be extended in time, but now the pair is apt to know each other fairly well before they make public announcement of their marriage intentions. The short engagement is typically used to arrange wedding details, look for a house or apartment, receive gifts, and so forth.

It would seem desirable, therefore, for many of the discussions advised by marriage counselors to take place well before the engagement. The engagement will inevitably involve a final review, however, of the congruence of the pair's values concerning familism, where to live, religion, roles, money, and family planning. Because these matters are not likely to be limited to talk but are apt to find practical application, unpleasant surprises may occur. They may have thought they agreed about the use of money, but in the selection of the house or apartment or furniture, one of them seems unexpectedly extravagant or overdominant. Suddenly a degree of attachment to family of origin not heretofore suspected even by the individual himself perhaps becomes evident. With a church wedding scheduled, conferences required by some ministers may precipitate different intensities of religious feeling in the pair.

Since sexual intercourse is more tolerated in the engaged couple than all other premarital pairs, they may have entered into a new stage of intimacy which proved disappointing for one or both of them. Agreement on roles in the abstract may have been easily arrived at, but in the concrete when he declares, "We'll sell your car because you won't be needing it after we're married," her response may betray need for further thought and discussion.

It is not unexpected that a sizable minority of engagements, estimated at 15 to 25 percent, are broken. There are inevitably hurt feelings, embarrassments in informing friends, and financial loss in foregoing deposits connected with the wedding, the apartment, etc. On the one hand this may be preferable to discovery of basic differences after the marriage. It suggests also the need for more self and other quizzes before the final exam, more opportunities to observe, probe, think through the relationship before the engagement.

COLLEGE MARRIAGES: QUESTIONS AS A BASIS FOR DISCUSSION

A rare phenomenon in the United States until the 1940s, college undergraduate marriage is now taken for granted on many campuses. Young people and their parents have many viewpoints. Which of these statements by students reflect your own thinking?

1. It brings the couple closer because they are working for the same goal—his future. When he completes his studies and enters his chosen work, they can both be very proud of a joint accomplishment.

2. The romantic aspects of marriage may disappear because the couple faces more problems than in a marriage after graduation. Marriage is a big enough step in and of itself, and I think that being a student takes away from the amount of time one can spend trying to make the marriage succeed.

3. Going to college should serve a twofold purpose—to receive a higher education and to enjoy being responsible only to oneself. Both purposes would be interfered with by marriage. Your mind would not be on your studies enough and you would be accountable to somebody else for the hours you keep, the money you spend, the chores you perform or neglect, and so forth.

4. The college couple can help each other cope with problems of studying, of sexual, emotional, financial, and recreational needs. Somebody is always around who not only cares, but is also in just your spot and able to understand the pressures on you.

5. Marriage is a full-time responsibility. It cannot be shared with a school schedule.

6. There's no solution for the financial problem. If the parents agree to continue to give the same amount of support as before the marriage, they are likely to offer a lot of advice and hassle you about grades even more than before. If you both work part-time and go to school too, you'll be too tired to enjoy each other. If the wife works and he goes to school, he may feel guilty and she exploited. If you take out a student loan you worry about mortgaging your future. What if you decide not to teach or do something on which the loan was based?

7. There's no more financial problem than before marriage. You were both living on something (parent help, summer jobs, scholarships, etc.), so what difference does the marriage make? While two cannot live as cheaply as one, they can live for lots less than when maintaining separate rooms, phones, and so on. As for housekeeping, if you both continue all the tasks you did before, you won't be any worse off and it might be better.

8. It's a great solution. The continual Sadie Hawkins Day Race is over. All the time you spent on dating, phoning, and commuting can be devoted to seeing each other in comfort. The result: more time for study.

9. Parents think you are not a real man if you are not supporting your wife. They think there's a price tag to marriage and you are guilty of shoplifting if you marry before you have a full-time job! Somehow they never told me I was not a real man when they were supporting me in college before I got married. Her parents are even worse than mine. They think she is killing herself going to work while I go to school. She had that job all along, but they didn't start worrying until I moved into the apartment with her. I point out that we are in good shape now, that we don't lose a lot of time traveling to see each other, that we are contented sexually, and that we eat more regularly. We both have gained. But I think they are getting through to her. She looks resentfully at me when I have a late class and she has to get up to go to her job. That alarm clock went off before I moved in.

10. There are lots of things you give up if you marry while at college. Your friends make a fuss over you at first but only the engaged couples or other married ones keep up the relationship. The others seem to think you're a pair of old fogies. The whole social scene is fragmented. Even the couples who are living together and may marry some day seem to see more of one another than they do of the singles or the marrieds. I get the feeling some of them pity us and some of them envy us. Neither is helpful to friendships.

11. Parents cannot seem to separate marriage from babies, even though contraceptives are better now and a crowded world does not need so many new citizens. His parents worry that I'll get pregnant and cause them financial problems and mine worry that I won't get pregnant and will deprive them of grandchildren. It was the other way around before we got married; my parents worried about pregnancy and his worried about never having legitimate grandchildren. Why can't they notice how well we're studying instead of grumbling about college marriages?

TEACH US WHAT WE WANT TO KNOW

Several research studies indicate that boys and girls want to know many things not taught in classrooms today. A report of a survey of 5,000 students in selected schools from kindergarten through twelfth grade in 1967–1968 revealed the following. In response to the question, "What do you wish to know about your body?" children in third and fourth grades, and even more in fifth and sixth, asked to know how babies are made, how they get born, what causes infant abnormalities, and how heredity operates. In seventh grade they asked why grownups keep them from books and movies on sex, and want to know more about menstruation, rape, how pregnancy occurs, birth control, abortion, and venereal disease. In eighth grade these reappear along with questions about prostitution, homosexuality, and Caesarian births. In secondary schools questions are asked about illegitimacy, the positive aspects of sexual experiences, sterility, and physiological differences between male and female.

More interest in human relationships, especially family relationships, than in physiology and anatomy was shown in questions that children in kindergarten through second grade put about divorce. Children of this age also asked about the mother's scolding and her preference for the baby over older children. Children in elementary grades had questions concerning feelings of anger, hatred, resentment toward siblings, fear about death, loneliness, dislike of school, awareness of racial discrimination, anxiety at quarreling and physical assaults, as well as the drinking of parents, the limitations placed on dating and petting, the relationships among friends. By high school questions concerned going steady, conflict with parents, the nature of love, and the lack of places where teenagers could talk about sexual behaviors, marriage, how to be better parents than their own, and how to cope with the many pressures they feel.

The report of a series of discussions in the 1960s with seniors in Oregon high schools showed boys and girls in agreement that parents do not recognize their children's dilemmas. "Adults think we wouldn't ever be in a situation where we are faced with participating in sex, and actually we face it all the time. Who goes to a party these days without also a chance to go to the bedroom?" [13] They suggested that not only do students need a chance to learn about sexuality, ethical choices, new relationships in and out of marriage, and understanding of themselves and the other sex well before high school graduation, but also parents need similar educational opportunities to bring their thinking up to the actualities of the present day.

It is evident from these various reports that young people have to make decisions sooner than their parents had to, and are also less reconciled to inharmonious relationships between the sexes and between generations. Along with biological information they want discussion of feelings, norms, social problems, and alternative solutions as a basis for their own decision-making.

SEXUAL VALUES

How important are congruent attitudes in two people contemplating engagement or marriage? How much agreement is found on these issues among classmates, between parents and their adolescent children, between teachers and parents, between teachers and students?

---

[13] "Adolescent Views on Sex Education," *Journal of Marriage and the Family* (May 1965), p. 293.

Circle all the statements you agree with.

1. The girl who becomes pregnant before marriage should:
   a. Keep the child.
   b. Go to any abortionist available.
   c. Go to a state that allows abortion to be practiced freely by qualified physicians.
   d. Be encouraged to undergo counseling, along with the boy, if the couple had not taken serious contraceptive measures before intercourse.
   e. Be expelled from school or fired from her job.
   f. Be left alone, as she has not done anything that is the business of anybody else.
   g. Be put out of the house if she has been living with her parents.
   h. Be sent to distant relatives so as not to contaminate the younger children in the family.
   i. Be supported by the community because she is contributing a future worker and citizen.

2. Masturbation is a common practice but:
   a. It is sinful and deserves punishment.
   b. It is not sinful but it is shameful and should be stopped.
   c. It is a release of sexual tension and a private matter only.
   d. It is a mark of neurotic disturbance and should be reported by any teacher who observes it in the classroom.
   e. It is a sign in a married person of disturbed marital relations.
   f. It is understandable only in young persons and is a sign of the aging individual's refusal to accept a changed status.
   g. It is disgraceful in a hospitalized patient; the nurse should express disapproval one way or another.
   h. It is a mark of abnormal development in the young child.
   i. It should be discouraged by sermons in churches.
   j. It should be criticized by family life and sex educators in schools.

3. Venereal disease is a problem in American society and those contracting it should be:
   a. Punished either by expulsion from school or job or by fines.
   b. Helped to cure it and encouraged to take measures to prevent recurrence.
   c. Forced to wear an identifying badge to warn off those they may infect.
   d. Ignored; the disease resulted from personal decision-making and if let alone they will sooner learn what the consequences of such decisions are.
   e. Forced to tell family members.
   f. Compelled to surrender custody of children.
   g. Denied adoption rights.
   h. Required to inform a fiancé of this past infection, with failure to do so as grounds for a fraud suit.

4. Premarital or nonmarital sexual intercourse:
   a. Is always wrong, sinful, or shameful, or all three.
   b. Is all right for engaged couples.
   c. Is all right for couples over eighteen who are in love.
   d. Is all right for all couples over sixteen.
   e. Should be discouraged by family life and sex educators in schools.
   f. Should be condemned by the law, the church, and parents.

g. Should be up to the girl and the boy so long as they use contraceptive precautions.

h. Should involve charge of statutory rape only if either partner were prepubertal.

i. Should be a matter for self-determination by boys and girls only after a year-long course in school, church, or social agency by certified teachers in which self-understanding is developed, information about emotions as well as physiology is offered, and a variety of value systems in the United States and abroad is examined.

j. Should be taught in high schools as a skill, with use of sex manuals to ensure full familiarity with all possible coital positions and ways to maximize pleasure.

5. Extramarital sexual intercourse:

a. Is always wrong, sinful, or shameful, and should be punished by job loss, school expulsion, ostracism of neighbors, church penances, and other means of personal and societal disapproval.

b. Is sometimes acceptable, as in cases of illness and long separations.

c. Is acceptable only for the husband in special circumstances; wives can more easily sublimate their sexual needs.

d. Is acceptable for both as a joint activity with other swingers.

e. Is acceptable only if the other spouse is kept unaware and cannot be hurt by knowledge of the infidelity.

f. Is acceptable only if the two spouses confide in each other and have each other's permission.

g. Is acceptable only if the children are kept unaware of the parent's sexual behaviors outside the home.

h. Is acceptable only if there is no expense connected with it and there are no adverse effects on the household economy.

i. Is acceptable only if it is a physical release and does not include emotional involvement with the third person.

j. Is acceptable only if it is an act of love and not a mere physical release.

k. Is acceptable only with a succession of partners to signify lack of emotional involvement with one of them.

l. Is acceptable only if repeated with a single partner and not part of a promiscuity pattern.

m. Is a signal that the marriage is in difficulty and should be examined by the married pair, possibly with professional help, so that alterations in ways of relating and communicating can be effected to create greater satisfaction in the marriage relationship.

n. Is a mechanism for the adjustment of differential sexual need between spouses.

6. Female menstruation is:

a. An inconvenience.

b. A reminder of procreative potential.

c. An unclean phenomenon.

d. A badge of female inferiority.

e. A great privilege, the loss of which at menopause is to be mourned.

f. A matter only women need know about.

7. Homosexual encounters are frequent in the United States and should be:

a. Discouraged in the young lest they result in sexual habits that are hard to break later.

b. Tolerated in the young as part of natural experimentation and awareness of sexual feeling.

c. Explained in high schools so that boys and girls see them as part of a developmental process rather than as proof of abnormal sexual functioning.

d. Seen as a matter for personal decision-making by consenting adults.

e. Seen as a sign in the adult of neurotic fear of the other sex and therefore to be treated as an illness.

f. Seen as a logical outcome of the glandular mix in all men and women.

g. Encouraged in an overpopulated world.

h. Viewed as parental failure, with shame appropriately felt by all family members.

i. Kept secret lest retribution be forthcoming at work, school, or in the home.

j. Viewed as a barrier to work in the helping professions, lest the counselor, teacher, or social worker take advantage of his status and the closeness of the relationship to involve students and clients in such sexual practices.

k. Discouraged by vigilance concerning sleeping arrangements in the homes of kinfolk and friends, as well as boarding schools and summer camps.

l. Further studied in order to reconcile different explanations for the phenomenon offered by various psychologists and psychiatrists.

m. Regarded as a clue to unsatisfactory societal arrangements which produce overdomination, brutality, narrow definitions of sexuality, and impaired self-images in the home.

n. Accepted at all ages, since its early occurrence suggests normalcy and the biological appropriateness of bisexuality.

8. Sexual behaviors short of intercourse are engaged in by most boys and girls in dating situations and should be:

a. Limited for those under sixteen to necking (kissing and hugging, and caressing from the neck up).

b. Limited for those under eighteen to light petting (necking plus caressing the body from the neck down but leaving clothing intact).

c. Unlimited for those over eighteen, with heavy petting at their own discretion.

d. Discussed in homes and school courses so that each young person has a clear idea of the physical and emotional responses likely to be experienced and be able to establish realistic standards on dates.

9. Oral-genital contacts are:

a. Healthy and normal if both partners find pleasure in them.

b. To be discouraged as a regular practice since they represent a regression to a pregenital stage of development.

c. Disgusting and worthy only of animals.

d. More suitable for married couples than for those who have less commitment to each other's well-being.

e. Less suitable for married couples since they need not build up sexual tensions over long periods of time or worry about the consequences of penial penetration.

10. Parents who are regularly seen in the nude by their children:

a. Are likely to have a negative effect on the children as the adult sex organ tends to overimpress young children with parental superiority.

b. Have a healthy attitude toward the body which they are communicating to their children.

c. Are unconsciously seductive and gaining sexual pleasure by the exposure.

d. Are allaying curiosity and making it unnecessary for children to "play doctor," lift skirts or drop pants behind bushes, or peep at the toileting of their peers.

e. Are probably overreacting to emphasis on modesty in their families of origin and offer no better models of acceptance of their sexuality than parents who are more comfortable when seen clothed.

11. Prostitution has existed along with monogamous marriage for thousands of years, and:

a. Is a necessary part of any society.

b. Should be permitted to continue, since it protects the majority population by allowing a special group to cater to the perverted sexual needs of a few.

c. Is a proof that monogamy has never really been tried in the past.

d. Will disappear when male–female relationships are placed on a level of equality, economically, politically, and in family relationships.

e. Proves what happens when people do not take religion seriously.

f. Will continue as long as the church supports a body–soul dichotomy.

g. Differs little from the barter in marriage where material considerations outweigh personal affection.

h. Is a symptom of women's greed and men's lust—both innate characteristics.

i. Should be encouraged now to ensure that the majority of girls will be virgins when they marry.

j. Should be encouraged now to halt the spread of venereal disease.

k. Exploits the economic need of women, forcing them into demeaning sale of their bodies, instead of ensuring self-respecting work at decent pay.

l. Offers young men sexual experience without emotional entanglements, allowing them to undertake long-term educational and career plans.

m. Should be regulated and taxed by the state.

SEXUAL STANDARDS

What are the norms of premarital behavior in your neighborhood, school, or friendship group? How does your experience compare with most of your friends and acquaintances? In discussing in class the results of this anonymous data-gathering form, you may wish to give consideration to the problem of obtaining honest replies to the questions.

Your sex: _____   Your age: under 18 _____
                                                18 to 20 _____
                                                21 to 25 _____
                                                over 25 _____

1. Have you ever engaged in premarital intercourse? If yes:

a. How often in the past six months?

_____ once

_____ less than six times but more than once

_____ often (about once a week)
_____ very often (several times a week)
b. With whom? (Check several if appropriate.)
_____ fiancé
_____ steady
_____ casual date
_____ pickup
_____ other (specify: prostitute, relative or neighbor, etc.)
c. Where? (Check several if appropriate.)
_____ the home of my parents
_____ the home of the other's parents
_____ apartment of a mutual friend
_____ my own apartment
_____ auto
_____ rented cabin, motel room, etc.
_____ outdoors
_____ other (specify: school, dormitory room, etc.)
d. Effects. (Check several if appropriate.)
_____ Felt happy at the time but regretful later.
_____ Felt disgusted.
_____ Felt used.
_____ Felt disappointed in the experience.
_____ Became closer friends after that.
_____ Broke up the relationship.
_____ Felt ambivalent at the time but later glad of the experience.
_____ Other (specify).

2. If answer to number one is no, answer the following:
   a. What was your reason for not engaging in premarital intercourse? (Check several if appropriate.)
   _____ fear of pregnancy
   _____ religious beliefs
   _____ fear of family disapproval
   _____ fear of losing partner's respect
   _____ no opportunity
   _____ fear about sexual competency
   _____ fear about friends finding out
   _____ desire to be virgin at marriage
   b. Which sexual behaviors short of intercourse have you engaged in on a date in the past six months?
   _____ holding hands
   _____ kissing
   _____ necking (from neck up)
   _____ light petting (below neck caressing, clothes intact)
   _____ heavy petting (below neck caressing, some or all clothes removed)

3. Do you approve of premarital intercourse for others?
   a. For men: yes _____   no _____
   b. For women: yes _____   no _____

4. Is age an important consideration in your approval of premarital intercourse for others?
   a. For men: under 18
                 yes _____
                 no _____

b. For women: under 18

        yes _____

        no _____

c. For men: over 18

        yes _____

        no _____

d. For women: over 18

        yes _____

        no _____

5. How many close friends of the same sex have you?
   a. None _____
   b. 1 to 3 _____
   c. 4 to 6 _____
   d. More than 6 (specify) _____

6. How many of these close friends have to your knowledge experienced sexual intercourse in the past six months? _____

7. Are there important questions this listing leaves out, in your view?

CONTRACEPTION: QUESTIONS AS A BASIS FOR CLASS DISCUSSION

1. Which functions are served by the practice of contraception in American society?
   a. The enjoyment of sexual activity without procreation
   b. The control of family size
   c. The spacing of offspring
   d. The improvement of the mother's health
   e. The reduction of venereal diseases
   f. All the above

2. The use of contraception in the United States has increased due to:
   a. The desire to reduce the economic burden of having too many children
   b. The more readily available knowledge about contraception
   c. The introduction of improved methods
   d. The awareness of a world population explosion
   e. The greater acceptability of contraception to religious groups
   f. The desire for sexual satisfaction without fear of pregnancy
   g. All the above

3. Which of the following is not appropriate in a list of principal methods of contraception:
   a. Condom   f. Pill
   b. Diaphragm   g. Coil
   c. Rhythm   h. Coitus interruptus
   d. Jelly   i. Abortion
   e. Douche

4. The wife should be the one to decide on the kind of contraceptives the couple will use.

5. If contraceptive methods are ineffective, the husband should undergo vasectomy.

ENGAGEMENT: ROLE-PLAYING SITUATIONS

1. Joan and Bill are an engaged couple. They have been talking about the children they will want. Joan says, "You should let me handle the discipline of our children. After all, I'm a child development major."

2. Sue and Perry work in the same office. This is their first Christmas as an engaged couple. Perry says, "It was nice of your folks to ask us, but when we're married they'll have to get used to the fact that we'll go to my parents' place every Christmas. You have lots of brothers and sisters. I'm an only child and it's natural for my parents to expect me."

3. Lois and Miles are in a furniture store. Their wedding is only a few weeks off. The salesman has just been called to the phone. Lois says, "I was embarrassed to hear you ask to see a twin bed suite. I always assumed we would have a double bed like my parents. They have certainly been happy together."

4. Peggy and Ramon are leaving a political rally. They first met at a protest meeting and have been active in various community efforts all through the months they have been engaged. Peggy says, "I hope when we're married we can pay more attention to our private lives and not get so wound up in changing the world."

5. Maryann and Joe are in their first jobs. They are not sure just when a wedding date can be set. Joe says, "My folks say they can help us out by fixing up the top floor in their house for us to live in."

BARRIERS TO FREE MATE SELECTION: THE ANTIMISCEGENATION LAWS

Legislation and court decisions on state, and later federal, levels for centuries curtailed the right of the individual to choose a mate across racial lines. Severe penalties, varying in the several jurisdictions, were imposed not only on the couple but on anyone performing the marriage ceremony. Economic gain was the chief motive in the early period. The laws ensured that the offspring of a slave would continue to enrich the owner with unpaid labor. Sexual exploitation of black women could also proceed without marriage commitments by whites. The economic and sexual motives were modified rather than abolished by the Emancipation Proclamation. Resistance to free mate choice continues to the present, as the brief calendar of events below indicates.

1661 Maryland adopted the first antimiscegenation law.
1691 Virginia adopted a similar law.
1705 Massachusetts also forbade marriage between whites and Negroes.
1786 The Massachusetts law was extended to Indians.

1843 Massachusetts repealed its antimiscegenation law.
1863 The Emancipation Proclamation. Of the thirty-eight states prohibiting interracial marriage, nine repealed their laws around the time of the Civil War.
1872 The Alabama Supreme Court declared antimiscegenation unconstitutional, but reversed itself in 1877.
1948 The California Supreme Court declared California's antimiscegenation statute unconstitutional.
1951 Twenty-nine states still forbade intermarriage between whites and Negroes. Of these, thirteen also forbade the marriage of whites with Chinese, Japanese, and Filipinos. The twenty-nine states were:

Alabama	Nebraska
Arizona	Nevada
Arkansas	North Carolina
Colorado	North Dakota
Delaware	Oklahoma
Florida	Oregon
Georgia	South Carolina
Idaho	South Dakota
Indiana	Tennessee
Kentucky	Texas
Louisiana	Utah
Maryland	Virginia
Mississippi	West Virginia
Missouri	Wyoming
Montana	

1954 The United States Supreme Court refused to review an Alabama case challenging the antimiscegenation statute. Fifteen state supreme courts had upheld antimiscegenation laws.
1957 South Dakota and Colorado repealed their statutes.
1959 Nevada repealed its statute.
1962 Arizona repealed its statute.
1963 Utah and Nebraska repealed their statutes.
1964 The United States Supreme Court refused to review Florida's prohibition of interracial marriage, although it did reverse the conviction of a white woman and a sailor from British Honduras who had been found guilty of violating a Florida law which punished extramarital cohabitation if the couple were of different races.
1965 A Gallup Poll showed 48 percent of adult Americans approved of laws which made interracial marriage a crime.
1966 Between 1940 and 1966, a total of ten states had eliminated the barrier to interracial marriage, leaving only nineteen states with antimiscegenation laws on the eve of the landmark decision of the United States Supreme Court.
1967 The United States Supreme Court unanimously declared Virginia's law unconstitutional. A couple married in 1958 in Washington, D.C. were indicted on returning to live in their home state of Virginia because he was white and she black.

Their one-year jail sentences were suspended on condition that they leave the state. They began a court fight which lasted almost a decade to obtain the right to live in any state they chose. The Supreme Court decision presumably invalidated all antimiscegenation statutes, but a number of states continued to try to enforce these laws.

1971 The federal government filed suits to keep Alabama and then Georgia from punishing interracial marriage.

COMMUNICATION: CATEGORIES FOR INTERACTION ANALYSIS BASED ON BALES'S SMALL GROUP RESEARCH [14]

1. Who is doing what?
   a. *Accepting feelings, positive or negative:* Clarifying feelings, relating them to past feelings, or predicting future feelings.
   b. *Praising and encouraging:* Offering support verbally or by gesture and facial expression, nods, body contact, etc. Relieving tension through humor (but not at expense of a group member).
   c. *Building on ideas suggested by others:* Acknowledging stimulation to thought.
   d. *Asking questions:* Seeking clarification of content or procedure.
   e. *Giving facts:* Adding knowledge which is pertinent to task performance.
   f. *Suggesting new modes of tackling task.*
   g. *Criticizing or justifying authority:* Explaining or asking explanation of restraints, proposed rules and procedures, etc.
   h. *Encouraging response by others:* Soliciting replies.
   i. *Initiating and contributing of own accord, without waiting for direct question.*
   j. *Remaining silent but showing interest as opposed to withdrawal or "leaving the field."*

2. Does a particular class member play one or two of these roles fairly consistently, or would a taping of two or more discussion periods show a change of role as mood and subject matter stimulate different behaviors?
   a. If a student notes a consistency in his pattern of functioning in several taped discussions, is he satisfied with his role repertoire or would he like to change in some particulars? Speak less or more? Be more or less supportive?
   b. How does his role in class interaction compare with his behaviors in family discussions, same-sex peer groups, mixed-sex peer groups, work with younger groups?
   c. How does the tape or a diagram of the interaction compare with others' perceptions of his roles? Do they consider his humor as defensive clowning while he sees it as encouraging others through tension release?

---

[14] Adapted from Robert F. Bales and Fred L. Strodtbeck, "Phases in Group Problem Solving," in Dorwin Cartwright and Alvin Zander, *Group Dynamics: Research and Theory* (New York: Harper & Row, Publishers, 1956), p. 387.

COMMUNICATION: QUARRELING WITH
A FAMILY MEMBER

Constructive quarreling is the kind of argument–discussion which makes closer association possible by clearing the atmosphere and resolving points of difference. Guidelines to constructive quarreling include the following cautions:

1. The point of friction should be discussed after anger has somewhat subsided, lest the individual say or do things he will regret.
2. The relief from tension which quarreling permits should be felt by both. It is not enough to say, "Now I feel better." Some regard for the effect on the other person is needed.
3. Related to the above, sadistic seeking out of weak spots or painful areas in the other person cannot have positive effects.
4. Remarks are best confined to the specific area of conflict rather than a total judgment of a negative kind. Thus, the person who lacks a point of information is not stupid or a fool in general, nor does the single act under discussion of, say, lack of consideration make him totally selfish.
5. Other persons are best left out of the quarrel. Comparisons may lead away from the problem at hand and simply raise unrelated issues.
6. Once a problem has been aired and accepted as settled, it is best not reintroduced into a new quarrel.
7. Time is needed for "cooling off," especially for the one who feels most wronged. This is related to number one above, but with the further emphasis that the earlier and the later stages of a quarrel involve different physiological conditions and dominance of different parts of the nervous system.
8. While it is helpful to wait until the first tensions have relaxed somewhat, the frustrations should not be permitted to accumulate and become integrated into larger systems of frustration which ultimately lead to deep-seated hatred.

How are the above rules germane to the following situations?

A. He will not argue with her but walks out, slamming the door hard.
B. She turns on the record player loudly and pretends not to hear anything being said.
C. He says, "If you won't use decent language, I don't want to hear what you have to say."
D. She says, "We must talk this over if it takes all night."
E. She locks the bedroom door and he starts making up the sofa.
F. She rushes to the telephone.
G. He dashes out and gets into the car.
H. She says, "Wait, I hear the children coming up the walk."

I. He says, "If you're going to pick another quarrel, at least I'll fortify myself with a drink."

J. He says, "How dare you make such accusations? I won't listen to another word."

SOME QUESTIONS ABOUT SEX ROLES: MATERIALS FOR A CHECKLIST

The following considerations may be helpful in preparing a checklist.

1. Will there be a separate list for women and another for men, as in the Dunn "Marriage Role Expectation Inventory"? (Family Life Publications, Box 6725, College Station Post Office, Durham, North Carolina.)

2. Will there be a separate list of questions or statements about single women, married women, married women with children?

3. How few questions can be asked to conserve classroom time and maximize discussion, and yet touch on most key issues?

4. How clearly are the statements phrased? Will the checklist be tried out on a sample of students and revised if interviews with these students reveal certain words or phrases were misleading?

5. Is the atmosphere in which the checklist is given and discussed one which encourages frankness but does not punish the student whose responses differ from most of his classmates? Will the feelings aroused by the checklist be discussed as a legitimate subject of inquiry in themselves?

6. How important do the teacher and the students consider the intensity of the reply? Will the checklist have three possible answers—agree, disagree, and undecided—or five—allowing for strongly agree and strongly disagree?

7. Will the checklist statements be couched in general terms, to elicit student attitudes on broad issues, or in specific terms with regard to the spousal expectations of the given student? Example: "It would be proper for a wife and mother to earn the living for the family if the husband agreed to care for the home and children." As opposed to: "In my marriage I expect my wife to work outside the home if she prefers this to staying at home."

The following statements may not be formulated in a way most helpful for the particular class. The teacher and students can modify or reword each statement before including it in a checklist. Possible paths for discussion are indicated in parentheses here but would not appear in the checklist itself.

1. As the main breadwinner, the man should have the final decision as to which occupation he enters and how much of his time to devote to it. (*Discussion:* Among those who agree, what view would they take on the need for occupation to be firmly selected before marriage so that the woman will know he is decided on an army career, a garbage collector, an undertaker, etc., and can decide whether this is compatible with her own needs? Will this require later age for marrying so that occupational decisions have already been made?)

2. As the main breadwinner, the husband need not share with the wife infor-

mation about the family's financial status and business affairs. (*Discussion:* Among those who agree, what implications would this have for open communication between spouses?)

3. The husband and wife should have equal privileges in going out at night, with same-sex friends, or to pursue heterosexual friendships. (*Discussion:* Among those who disagree, what justifications can be found for a double standard?)

4. The husband and wife should decide before they are married who has the right to make decisions about certain matters—style of house furnishings, frequency of family visiting, disciplining of children—and should stick to this schedule come what may. (*Discussion:* Among those who agree, what would be the basis for the division of decision-making and what might be some of the difficulties in keeping to the schedule?)

5. The husband and wife have equal responsibility to support the family and to spend time with the children. (*Discussion:* Among those who disagree, what division of responsibility is preferred and under what circumstances?)

6. The woman should seek a career only if it does not interfere with her duties to her husband, children, and home. (*Discussion:* Among those who disagree, would limits of any kind be set, such as long periods of absence from the home, notoriety that may have unfavorable effects on the husband's career goals, special disabilities of children, etc.?)

7. The woman should enter gainful employment only after her children have reached adolescence. (*Discussion:* Among those who agree, what problems of work discontinuity would this create, what problems of losing pertinent skills, etc.?)

8. The woman needs some time for personal development away from her home and her family. (*Discussion:* Among those who disagree, what threats to family cohesiveness might this create?)

9. The man should earn a good living if he is to expect love and respect from the wife and children. (*Discussion:* Among those who agree, what are the conditions under which the wife and children can expect love and respect?)

10. The wife should take full responsibility for care and rearing of the children so that the man can give his time to earning a living and get the rest and recreation he needs to be at his best at work. (*Discussion:* Among those who disagree, how would this responsibility be affected by the wife's working full-time, part-time, as a volunteer in community affairs, etc.?)

11. It is the wife's duty to be home when her husband gets home from work and when the children get home from school. (*Discussion:* Among those who agree, would any exceptions to this rule be allowed?)

12. The woman should work only in those jobs that do not encourage aggressiveness lest she carry into the home non-nurturing ways of functioning. (*Discussion:* Among those who disagree, are there any positive contributions she can make to the family by not assuming a nurturing role in all instances?)

13. If the woman earns more money than her husband or has a higher status outside the home, she should recognize the threat this may offer to his ego and play down her accomplishments when he is around. (*Discussion:* Among those who agree, what may be the consequences of these efforts?)

14. It is all right for a woman to work to put her husband through school but as soon as he graduates he should not be expected to return the favor. He should

expect to pursue the career for which he prepared even if this takes them away from the place where she can most conveniently finish her schooling. (*Discussion:* Among those who disagree, what are the dangers that may develop in the relationship?)

15. Since a woman's body is her own, she should be the main determiner of how many children to bear, whether to undergo an abortion in the event of an unplanned pregnancy through contraceptive failure, and the spacing of children. (*Discussion:* Among those who agree, what rights does her husband have, if any, in these matters?)

YOUR ATTITUDE TOWARD WIVES IN GAINFUL EMPLOYMENT

A: Agree   *D:* disagree   *U:* undecided

Circle the letter which indicates how you feel about each of the following statements.

1. A wife should work only if there is definite economic need and the couple can agree there is such need.
   A.   D.   U.

2. A wife should work only if there are no children.
   A.   D.   U.

3. A wife should work only if the children are in school.
   A.   D.   U.

4. A wife should work only if she can do so without expecting her husband to take on additional household chores.
   A.   D.   U.

5. A wife should work only if she can have a full-time housekeeper.
   A.   D.   U.

6. A wife should work only if she has special talent or training.
   A.   D.   U.

7. A wife should work only if her job commands a pay check almost as large as her husband's.
   A.   D.   U.

8. A wife should work only if she can earn more than her husband does.
   A.   D.   U.

9. A wife should work only on a part-time basis, even if this means accepting a job below her qualifications.
   A.   D.   U.

10. A wife should work regardless of what her husband feels about it.
    A.   D.   U.

11. A wife should work only if her job brings her enjoyment.
    A.   D.   U.

12. A wife should work regardless of what the norm is in the neighborhood they live in.
    A.   D.   U.

SEX ROLE ALLOCATIONS: BLACKBOARD EXERCISE

1. Teacher writes on one blackboard: DISADVANTAGES OF A WIFE/MOTHER IN GAINFUL EMPLOYMENT, and on another, DISADVANTAGES OF A WIFE/MOTHER NOT IN GAINFUL EMPLOYMENT.

2. Volunteers, preferably one male and one female for each of the blackboards so that each couple may confer before listing the disadvantages, write down their ideas. The couple at one board does not try to see what the other couple is writing.

3. The class is asked to jot down in their notebooks their own listings. These thoughts can be helpful in the class discussion following completion of the lists.

4. Goals of the exercise are to:
   a. Encourage students to see that choice-making is often between alternatives containing negative elements.
   b. Allow a pooling of experience as some students will have experienced only the disadvantages of one situation or the other.
   c. Help students distinguish between personal preferences and social structure, and in the latter instances to suggest what social and legal changes would alleviate the disadvantages.

5. The teacher's role is to suggest disadvantages the student listings may omit. Most common among these may be the sexual component of attitudes and behaviors. The teacher is also to summarize findings and relate them to the need for mate selection in which boys and girls have congruent views of which side of the blackboard is most disadvantageous.

Note: If the class has omitted mention of sexuality, and the teacher points this out, perhaps the class will want to discuss the reasons for the omissions. Or they may want to discuss the facts: Is one of the disadvantages of the homebound woman her sexual overstimulation by the erotic stimuli of T.V., her preoccupation with clothes, figure, hairdo that may result, and consequently an over-expectation of romantic attention from a tired husband returning home from the problems of work and commuting? Or is the homebound woman more apt to be snowed under by chores she finds unfulfilling and in her envy of her husband's more "exciting" life (even if his work is relatively mechanical), may she withhold (unconsciously?) sexual responsiveness as a kind of punishment? Can both disadvantages be found, and is there an ethclass variable in differential behaviors? What modifications on a community or personal level could change the behaviors?

PHT: A BLACKBOARD EXERCISE

1. Teacher writes on the blackboard: WIVES WORKING TO PUT HUSBANDS THROUGH SCHOOL, and under this heading writes on one side ADVANTAGES and on the other DANGERS.

2. Volunteers are asked for, preferably one male and one female for each of the two lists, so that each couple may confer before listing either advantages or dangers. The couple at one board does not try to see what the other couple is writing.

3. The class is asked to jot down in their notebooks their own listings. These thoughts can be helpful in the class discussion following completion of the lists.

4. Goals of the exercise are to:
   a. Allow a pooling of experience since some students will be familiar with some concrete cases and other students with others.
   b. Encourage students to see that there are distinct advantages and at the same time some dangers.
   c. Help students suggest how some of the dangers can be reduced by social and legal changes or by personal efforts.

5. *Adjunct learning experiences:* Before or after this class exercise some students may wish to interview several wives and husbands who have experienced the P(utting) H(usband) T(hrough) situation, either recently or some time ago, and report to the class what satisfactions and challenges the couples had found. Taperecording several of these interviews may allow the emotional dimension to come through (the tone of voice, the hesitations, etc.).

THE WORKING WIFE: A ROLE-PLAYING SITUATION

In the first two years of marriage, Janet learned how to be a good cook and housekeeper. She and John do not want children for a few more years. Janet has been offered her old teaching job, and John agrees that it will fill her time and allow an accumulation of savings for later use.

After a few months Janet is enjoying her work more than she anticipated but is finding the strain of home chores greater. She suggests hiring a maid. John does not want a stranger around the house and resents not only the loss of privacy but the inroads this will make in the savings account in which Janet's check has been deposited each month.

For a month or two Janet tries the solution of reducing her housekeeping by various shortcuts and omissions. John is upset by the change in meals and appearance of the apartment.

Janet is tempted to hire a maid for the hours John is not at home, and pay her out of her own check, putting the balance into the savings account. She knows John will become aware of this sooner or later but thinks he will be reconciled to it because the house will have been cleaned adequately, his wife will have been in good spirits, and his own strong privacy needs will not have been disturbed.

She weighs this against trying once more to convince him, and decides to bring the matter up just as they are finishing dinner. Janet speaks first. "John, wouldn't it be wonderful if I could just put these dishes in a pan and know a woman would be coming in tomorrow to do them while you and I are both out at work?"

CLASS PREPARATION FOR A RESOURCE PERSON

Students can be encouraged to think in advance about what they want to know from a visiting speaker. As a result of this prior class discussion, or by inviting questions to be placed anonymously in a question box, a list of questions can be drawn up. These can be sent the speaker in advance or dittoed and distributed to class members as a kind of checklist or guide sheet for following the speaker's presentation and reminding students of the questions they want to ask.

Questions asked by tenth and eleventh grade girls, in 1968, in preparation for a speaker are listed below. What would a coeducational class of similar age, or of older students, be asking today? How many of the questions listed here are still pertinent now? What does this indicate?

1. How does the young wife's working affect a new marriage?
2. Should a woman always be home when the children return from school?
3. What are some of the effects on children when the mother works?
4. Is it all right for a wife to have better wages than her husband?
5. Should pregnant women work?

CHALLENGE TO PARENTS: A CHILD
DEVELOPMENT QUIZ

Parents love their children in many ways, but not all ways are helpful in meeting children's needs at various growth stages. *Developmental parental love* shows awareness of child psychology and expresses acceptance of the child even when his action or comment is displeasing. *Dutiful parental love* shows the parent carrying out his responsibilities but indicates more awareness of the inconvenience caused by the child than of his needs. *Smothering parental love* shows the parent who needs to feel needed and loves the child as a possession, one that will keep on needing the parent's care. Support is withdrawn abruptly whenever the child makes any moves toward independence.

What would each type of mother or father say in the following situations involving a child of preschool age (from toddler to kindergarten)? Use her or his exact words.

1. Child is eating lunch. He stops and declares, "I don't want the vegetable!"
   a. Developmental Parent:
   b. Dutiful Parent:
   c. Smothering Parent:
2. Child picks up a large, pointed stick and bangs it noisily against the wall and the furniture, as his mother bends over the crib of the new baby.
   a. Developmental Parent:
   b. Dutiful Parent:
   c. Smothering Parent:
3. Child says as his mother tucks him into bed, "Mommy, When I grow up, can I marry you?" Or if his father tucks him into bed, "Daddy, when I grow up,

can I marry Mummy?"
  a. Developmental Parent:
  b. Dutiful Parent:
  c. Smothering Parent:
4. It is dark outside the child stands at the window peering through the curtain at the sliver of moon and says, "I think maybe I won't go next door to visit Jimmy after all."
  a. Developmental Parent:
  b. Dutiful Parent:
  c. Smothering Parent:

discussion suggestions

1. The class may form buzz groups, with each buzz group assigned one of the four situations.
2. The buzz group reports to the whole class, and then other class members are encouraged to comment before the next buzz group is called on.
3. Additional situations can be suggested by class members in which parents show the kind of love they feel. Variables can be introduced in age of child and settings outside the home.

NAMING THE MOTHER-IN-LAW

When I speak to my spouse's mother I shall use:
1. Her first name
2. The name for her my spouse uses—mom, mother, ma, etc.
3. The name I used, or used to use, for my own mother—mama, mom-o, etc.
4. "Oh, mother of my spouse"
5. What she prefers that I call her

discussion suggestions

1. The class may contribute to a blackboard listing of all the names they have heard any person use in speaking to a mother-in-law or to a father-in-law. What are the names used by the students' own parents or married siblings in addressing affinal relatives? Do these names fit preponderantly under one or the other of the above categories?
2. Is age a variable? Are young mothers- and fathers-in-law called by first names more often?
3. Do ethnic subcultures vary in their norms in this regard?
4. Is there a middle-class or a working-class pattern?
5. Do young husbands and wives have strong feelings about the name used for their parents by their spouse?
6. How does naming the mother-in-law differ from or resemble naming the baby?

HOW DO YOU RATE AS MOTHER-IN-LAW?

1. Are you given to dropping in on your married children?
2. Do you disapprove of your son or daughter's choice of spouse?
3. Did you move recently to be closer to your married child?
4. Do you disapprove of the many new shortcuts in housekeeping?
5. Do you believe the modern approach to childrearing leaves much to be desired?
6. Do you have definite ideas on how long a couple should wait before having children?
7. Do you think your child has changed since marriage, and this change is due to the influence of the mate?
8. Have you ever been critical of your spouse's relatives?
9. Have you told your daughter-in-law what your son's favorite dishes are?
10. Have you mentioned the faults of your child's spouse to your friends?
11. Do you think the mother of the bride should handle the wedding details without having to consult the groom's family?
12. Do you think your in-law fails to appreciate some of the things you are trying to do for him (her)?
13. Do you object to the idea of supporting children after marriage to allow them to finish their schooling?
14. Do you encourage your married child to come to you with his (her) problems?
15. When you visit your married child do you tend to "leave out" the young spouse in the conversation?
16. Do you believe that all people have "in-law problems?"
17. Are you angered by the statement, "A mother rocks the cradle but a mother-in-law rocks the boat?"

DEBATE SUGGESTIONS

Resolved: That men and woman should work no more than twenty-five hours a week so that both can be equally involved in child care and community activity and have time to build their personal relationship.

Resolved: That abortion be available on demand by any pregnant female to ensure that all children born are wanted.

Resolved: That men and women should have equal opportunity and receive encouragement to enter occupations now largely filled by one sex or the other (nursery and kindergarten teaching, civil engineering, etc.).

Resolved: That ways of disciplining a child, from corporal punishment to psychological techniques, should be left entirely up to the child's parents.

Resolved: That contraceptive information should be offered in the schools for students twelve years of age and older.

Resolved: That the federal government underwrite the cost of studying alternative family forms as well as alternatives to the family and that the findings of such studies be published as a basis for decision-making by youth.

DIVORCE AND MARRIAGE: DEBATE TOPICS

Resolved: That the state should grant a divorce as a matter of right to any spouse filing a petition.

Background information: Recently a lawyer published the following statement: "A divorce should be available as a matter of right to any spouse upon the filing of a petition. There should be no defenses and no means of delay. With the divorce itself extracted from bargaining, the ancillary matters of alimony, support, custody, visitation, and division of assets could be decided fairly by a court . . . A fair compromise could be expected because the spouse most desiring the divorce would not be at a disadvantage. Making divorce available as a matter of right . . . would prevent the fighting that bargaining engenders . . . By reducing the level of animosity, the post-divorce relations of the spouses would have a better chance of being at least civilized, to the advantage of the children . . . It is pure arrogance for the state to intrude itself into the marriage with the power to decide whether or not it should continue . . . The freedom to make basic personal decisions is becoming an irreducible demand. Marriage will not long be a prison, with the state as jailer. The function of the state with regard to marriage should be and will be only to record its birth and its death."

Resolved: That remarriage not be permitted until the former spouses have had a specified number of visits with a counselor or have taken a course for adults on marriage and the family.

A TYPOLOGY OF MARRIAGE RELATIONSHIPS

JOHN CUBER and PEGGY HARROFF in *The Significant Americans: A Study of Sexual Behavior Among the Affluent* report that the marriages they examined fell into the following five basic types.

1. *Conflict-Habituated.* Much tension and conflict of which family members are aware, although generally the couple is polite and discreet when not drinking.

2. *Devitalized.* Little time is spent together and few interests are shared, in contrast to the earlier years of the marriage. While there is little overt tension, there is an awareness of the disenchantment and lack of zest.

3. *Passive-Congenial.* From the beginning there has been little deep caring and each spouse invests more of his or her own feelings in work, children, etc. Some appreciate the independence from each other provided by a kind of parallel existence.

4. *Vital.* The two are bound together psychologically and each needs the presence of the other to derive maximum satisfaction. When conflict does occur it is in areas that matter, rather than the trivial. They tend to find solutions quickly in order to resume a satisfying relationship.

5. *Total.* More multifaceted than the vital relationship as the points of significant meshing are more numerous, all aspects of life are mutually shared and enthusiastically participated in. Life is experienced with the other and neither has a separate existence.

Checklist on social distance (To be filled in anonymously)

My race (if an intermixture of several, please indicate specifically): _____

My religion (if different now from childhood, please indicate specifically): _____

My national origins (as detailed as possible: parents, grandparents, etc.): _____

	QUAKERS	MORMONS	PROTESTANTS	CATHOLICS	JEWS	BLACKS	MEXICAN-AMERICANS	PUERTO RICANS	FILIPINO-AMERICANS
I would prefer *not* to have as:									
a. a next-door neighbor									
b. a colleague or business partner									
c. a weekend guest in my own home									
d. a weekend guest in my parents' home									
e. a roommate or sharing my apartment									
f. a date									
g. a date to be introduced to my parents									
h. a fiancé(e)									
i. a spouse									
j. parent of my children									
k. in-law, married to my sibling									

Note: a similar chart of social distance can be made up using additional categories —Japanese-Americans; Chinese-Americans; Italian-Americans; Polish-Americans; Irish-Americans; Greek-Americans; German-Americans; etc.

HOLIDAY IMPACT ON FAMILY RELATIONS

You have just returned from an extended vacation (Christmas recess, Easter holidays, etc.). What do your own experiences of the last few weeks indicate concerning the effect on family relationships?

Ways in which family life is strengthened by holidays:

1.

2.

3.

Ways in which family life is weakened by holidays:

1.

2.

3.

Class discussion of the responses: Is there general consensus or does one student indicate as a negative influence what another perceives as positive? Are there any implications for (1) mate selection, (2) women in gainful employment, (3) family reconstruction (alternative forms of the family)?

EVALUATION

If evaluation is a process for determining the effectiveness of progress toward stated educational experiences or goals, which devices measure this progress best and at the same time contribute to the student's awareness of achievement? How can the teacher make evaluation a learning process for the students and for himself?

Evaluation should facilitate learning. This is most likely to occur if the teacher responds to the student's efforts on a quiz or larger exam, either by comments in the margin on various points or by reviewing the quiz or exam afterwards with the whole class. Sometimes allowing a student to read the more adequate responses of his peers will be helpful.

Evaluation should measure each student's progress. The teacher can call attention to improvement in this quiz over a preceding one. Evaluation should motivate a student to do better. If the review of the quiz brings out interesting points, the student will be motivated to go back over prior reading and discussion notes.

Evaluation should serve as a guide for strengthening the curriculum and considering a new course design. Listing all the course experiences to date (mid-semester, final week, etc.), and encouraging the student to respond anonymously in three columns as to whether the experience had been helpful, so-so, or no good, will allow the teacher to discover which films, readings, exercises, and so forth need to be weeded out because student response indicates they are not facilitating the learning process.

Evaluation devices should be varied. They should be sometimes objective questions, sometimes fill-ins, sometimes essays, to tap the differential abilities of the students. Questions need to be clear. Review of an exam will reveal whether students were misled by poor formulations.

EVALUATION OF READINGS

Quiz on "A Daughter of My Own" in Joan Merrill Gerber's Stop Here, My Friend

1. If it was the norm for a mother to join her daughter when a grandchild was about to be born, what were the special social and personality factors that made for difficulties in this instance?

   a.

   b.

   c.

2. In a stream-of-consciousness manner, express the feelings each of the three main characters were experiencing:

   a. Molly

   b. Her husband

   c. Her mother

3. Knowing the personality of each character, to the extent the story reveals this, at what point or points would other ways of behaving have been possible? What are the likely outcomes of the decisions they made?

4. What is the significance of the story's title for changing norms of nuclear-versus extended-family functioning?

EVALUATION OF CLASS EXPERIENCES

Film: The Innocent Party

Student's Name_____ Date_____

1. Was there an innocent party? Justify your answer.

2. Was sexual intercourse the only way the disease could have been transmitted? If there was another way, what are the implications for dating?

3. What attitude on the part of their parents would be most helpful to the young people when the doctor has begun treatment?

4. What is functional and what dysfunctional in the showing of a film like this (1) at the college level, and (2) at the high school level?

5. Had you seen a VD film before? What was your reaction then compared with your feelings about the present film?

6. Other comments?

selected readings in the history, standards, and prospects of family life and sex education

FAMILY LIFE AND SEX EDUCATION: PROPOSED CRITERIA FOR TEACHER EDUCATION *

INTRODUCTORY STATEMENT

The National Council on Family Relations has in the past decade created a number of committees and commissions concerned with the establishment of principles and standards in family life education.[1] Building upon these past efforts as well as attempts by various states, such as Michigan, to clarify the role that schools and universities can play, the members of the Committee on Educational Standards and Certification for Family Life Educators, 1968–1969, formulated the criteria set forth below to serve as guidelines in the preparation of family life educators for junior and senior high school teaching. The criteria were arrived at in joint deliberations with members of the Special Committee on Family Life Education, 1968–1969.

It is recognized that an alternative to the preparation of interdisciplinary specialists would be the establishment of a minimum core of family life courses and out-of-classroom experiences for every undergraduate who plans to teach on the elementary or secondary level so that *all* teachers would have a basic knowledge of family and sexual development.[2] With an entire faculty thus prepared and alert to the "teachable moment," family life education would be woven into the total educational experience of the child through the regular school subjects in every grade, kindergarten through high school. However, this would require such thoroughgoing changes in teacher education curricula as to delay indefinitely the possibility of meeting present student needs for understanding their roles in a changing society.

The Committee, therefore, decided to proceed along the immediate and practical path of recommending the preparation of specialists in family life education. Perhaps such specialists would be needed in any case to help students integrate the learnings from diverse classrooms. It is possible that the two paths of teacher preparation can converge at some time in the future. Indeed, the very existence of a broadened curriculum for preparing family life educators may encourage undergraduates to elect family courses with positive effects upon their role performance as family members and as teachers.

The need for family life education is urgent. It is the Committee's view,

---

* Prepared by the Committee on Educational Standards and Certification for Family Life Educators, 1968–1969, accepted by the Executive Committee of the National Council on Family Relations, October 24, 1969.

[1] Family Life Education Programs, Principles, Plan, Procedures: A Framework for Family Life Education, *The Family Coordinator, 17,* 211–214.

[2] The Committee proceeded on the assumption that sex education is an essential part of family life but only a part of it, and is most usefully taught within a family/society context.

Reprinted from *The Family Coordinator, Journal of Education, Counseling and Services,* Vol. 19, No. 2 (April 1970), with permission of the National Council on Family Relations.

however, that the urgency should not be permitted to dilute standards in teacher preparation. On the contrary, the criteria offered are intended to raise present standards. In this way there can be created the kind of teaching body that will command the confidence of parents, students, and community leaders. This may facilitate the move toward certification of family life educators in the various states.

It will become evident as the criteria are examined that many teachers now offering family life and sex courses are inadequately prepared for the responsibility. The establishment of the NCFR criteria may help promote a wide network of in-service programs to raise the knowledge and skills of such teachers. The Committee recognizes the responsibility of degree-granting institutions to determine for themselves which of the courses they now offer meet the criteria in whole or in part and which new offerings would need to be incorporated into their teacher education programs to meet or exceed the standards set by NCFR.

While the Committee makes itself available as a resource to legislatures and education departments of the various states, aided by the expertise and cooperation of various NCFR members in the several regions of the country, it recognizes that the detailed task of creating certification proposals in each jurisdiction must be left to government agencies and the colleges and universities having teacher education programs in the given states. It is unlikely that colleges will move toward curriculum modification and expansion to meet the criteria of the Committee without some assurances from state authorities and others that their graduates can be employed in the specialty. Therefore, the Committee sees its responsibility as not limited to the formulation of criteria. It will seek to bring together educational administrators and legislators at state and national levels, and will serve as a facilitator of communication among the private and public institutions which hold the fate of a coordinated and systematic educational effort in their hands.

Moreover, while the preparation of family life educators for school systems is the main focus of the Committee's present work, it recognizes the importance of preparing community personnel, both professional and para-professional, for work in adult family life education and in social agencies. Such efforts will be facilitated by the availability of prepared and certified family life educators in the schools, who in many instances will be called upon to add to their responsibilities and, aided by appropriate field experiences and supervision, will be able to serve in programs outside the school setting.

Finally, it will be noted that the criteria are addressed much more to the professional than to the personal qualifications of the family life educator. The Committee assumes that the characteristics that make for a good teacher in any field would apply. However, because teaching about the family including sex may precipitate out for the educator some of his or her feeling connected with past and current life experiences, the criteria offered by the Committee include, it will be noted, a number of opportunities for self-examination and resolution of personal conflict with a view to ensuring objective handling of emotion-laden issues. While each community will set its own standards for its teachers in terms of personal functioning, it is the

Committee's anticipation that as family life education permeates a community, reaching older and younger generation alike, there will be greater acceptance of the individual's capacity to learn and to grow following life crises, with a resultant diminution in the gap between the ideal types sought in educators and the real behaviors of community leaders.

PROPOSED CRITERIA FOR TEACHER EDUCATION IN THE FIELD OF FAMILY LIFE AND SEX EDUCATION

The criteria mention basic areas rather than courses. In some instances a course may include more than one area and in some an area may require more than one course or experiences outside the school setting.

1. The Family: Family patterns in a variety of historical, social, and cultural settings. Comparative family systems as well as ethnic and class subcultures in the United States. The family in transaction with other social institutions.

2. Family Interaction: Dyadic relationships and family alliances at each stage of the family life cycle. The family as a small group: role, status, and power interactions of spouses, siblings, and generations. Crises and adjustments.

3. Marriage Preparation: An opportunity for the student to become aware of his or her own attitudes toward marriage and the family through relevant classroom and out-of-classroom experiences, usually provided in a functional course.

4. Human Development from Birth to Senescence: The individual life cycle and personality theory: findings from the natural and behavioral sciences which clarify the needs and influences at each stage from childhood, adolescence, and middle age through the aging years. Mental health principles. Implication for child-rearing practices and guidance as well as public policy.

5. Biological Sciences: Human nutrition, elementary human physiology, reproduction.

6. Sexuality: Male and female life roles, sexual identity, and the relationship of sexual needs and behaviors to personal and social functioning.

7. Management of Family Resources: The family's transaction with the consumption economy: the impact of handling time, money, and space on personal and family development.

8. Group Processes: Experiences to aid the individual to become more aware of how he functions in a group and his impact on group members. Opportunities for the individual to experience himself in relation to others in a small group setting which is supportive and helpful, encouraging him to clarify his own value positions and to recognize alternative philosophies underlying the behavior of others.

9. Methods and Materials in Family Life Education: Comparative curriculum and history of the field, as well as classroom procedures, instruments, evaluation, textbook critique. Experience with large and small group discussion, films, role-playing, as well as opportunities to appreciate the insights yielded through the humanities. Opportunity to observe and demonstrate a variety of teaching styles and goals. Familiarity with key issues in the field of family life education, including ethics.

10. Practice Teaching in Family Life and Sex Education: At least one term, with supervision participated in by an experienced family life educator.

11. Field Experiences: Direct observation of a variety of family patterns through visits to or supervised field work in the family-serving agencies of the community: courts, clinics, nursery schools, etc. (Where size of community or the lack of cooperation reduces such possibilities, use of films, tapes, etc., for vicarious experience of diversity.)

12. Individual and Family Counseling: Introduction through case study materials, or through field experience as above, to a guidance role including the recognition of behaviors that require referral to professional counselors.

13. Research: Appreciation of the contributions of several disciplines to understanding the family; learning to evaluate new findings in the behavioral sciences.

14. Survey of Basic Laws: Brief and non-technical examination of laws regulating marriage and the family in a given state. Comparison and contrast with selected other states, if possible.

15. Community: Study of community organization with a view to effective work with communities. Knowledge of community resources.

Committee Members

Rose M. Somerville, Chairman
Leland Axelson
Luther Baker
Dorothy Dyer
Theodore Johannis
Richard Kerckhoff
William Marshall
Evelyn Rouner

Consultants

NCFR Special Committee on Family Life Education, 1968–1969:
Blaine Porter, Chairman
Don Carter
Joel Moss
James Walters

NCFR Officers:

Elizabeth Force
Ruth Jewson
Richard Hey

FAMILY LIFE AND SEX EDUCATION
IN THE TURBULENT SIXTIES

ROSE M. SOMERVILLE

The 1960's began on an expansive note. The sixth White House Conference on Children and Youth recommended that:

". . . the school curriculum include education for family life, including sex education," and ". . . family life courses, including preparation for marriage and parenthood, be instituted as an integral and major part of public education from elementary school through high school. . . ."

This positive indication of nationwide interest in and theoretical support of family life and sex education found no consistent reflection, however, in the actual local situations. Nor did the Conference offer specific plans for action in the future on federal, state, or local levels.

Despite some notable accomplishments to be detailed, efforts to expand and enrich community and school programs had consistently met obstacles of various kinds. These obstacles were to loom even larger in the clouded atmosphere of the late 60's. Among such obstacles were the following: (1) difficulty in defining the goals of family life and sex education programs, (2) competition among the disciplines for major responsibility in formulating and implementing programs, (3) low academic status of functional courses, (4) dependence upon volunteer efforts in gaining citizen support and coordinating contributions from laymen and professionals, (5) fear and uncertainty in facing changes, (6) reluctance to modify existing schedules and traditional classroom procedures, (7) lack of professionalization, related to inadequate teacher preparation opportunities and lack of any established standards for family life and sex educators, (8) limited male participation on teaching and student levels.

The list could continue. The fact that some of the difficulties are contradictory, as in the competition among disciplines and the low academic status of the programs, or mutually reenforcing, merely compounds the problem.

In this perspective the emphasis on sex education that was to come with dramatic force in the mid-decade can be seen as a kind of surgical intervention with a somewhat unprepared patient. The professionals in the field (teachers, counselors, administrators) played the role of involved kinfolk and became increasingly polarized over the issue. Some maintained that the sick man of family life and sex education was beginning to grow stronger in the early 60's and needed only time and attention in a quiet atmosphere. Others considered the dormancy akin to death and defended more extreme measures on a now-or-never basis. As in all crises, those affected can learn from the inevitable stocktaking, the assessment of strengths remaining, and mistakes to be avoided. The

Reprinted from *The Journal of Marriage and the Family,* February 1971, with permission of The National Council on Family Relations.

70's can build on a foundation of experience, particularly in facing the forces of organized opposition, that exposed the vital issues in the field.

THE ISSUE OF DEFINITION

The difficulty of defining family life and sex education which marked the earlier decades of the twentieth century continued into the 60's. Some professionals were impatient with this: others saw definitions as essential both in forcing goal clarification and in providing one of the essentials in surveying and evaluating the field.

The lack of precise information as to how much family life and sex education existed or now exists in the United States has frustrated efforts to pinpoint trends or to describe broad historical changes. Contradictory assertions mark the field: "The sex education boom came at about the time of World War I" (Kerckhoff, 1964:883). "Unquestionably, there was little sex education in the schools in the 1920's, 1930's, and even in the 1940's" (Kirkendall and Libby, 1969:8).

On the local scene, community organizations and schools found it difficult to determine how much family life education, if any, they were offering at a given time. "A survey of the offerings of organizations with educational programs relating to family life had been attempted, but the central sponsoring committee was not satisfied with the results and wanted the study repeated," one report recalls (Brown, 1953:37). Much depended on the definition, and consensus on the definition was lacking.

At the college level, confusion was somewhat lessened, but even here there was some question as to whether only functional courses were to be counted as family life education or also those courses considered institutional because they stressed history and family organization. (Some of these latter had been in existence for more than a decade before Ernest Groves pioneered in the 20's in offering Marriage Preparation in Boston University and then at the University of North Carolina.)

There was also some question as to whether child development or marriage counseling courses were to be considered under the family life education rubric. (In secondary schools child development units were a considerable part of family life education.) The two major college-level surveys, by Bowman in the 40's and Landis in the 50's, differed in their definitions, the former excluding child development and institutional family courses (p. 415) the latter broadening the definition and accepting each college's interpretation of "courses in marriage and the family" (p. 21).

The teacher's view of whether family life education was being offered was not always reliable, especially when no operative definition was offered. In the elementary schools of a county project described by Brown (1953:49–50), an effort at precision was made by having a form on which the teacher could record details of one lesson considered to be family life education. When the forty-five lessons were sorted they were found to fall into three categories: those definitely related to family life, some that could have been but were not, and some that definitely were not. It is evident that any nationwide survey based on teacher report without definition or detail would have yielded exaggerated returns.

Nor was the administrator's view of whether family life education was being offered always trustworthy. A survey in 1965 of Minnesota schools found principals reporting courses or units which in sixteen instances proved illusory; the teachers contacted said they were not teaching them (Martinson, 1966:197). Similarly a survey of Indiana public high schools in the late 50's had found principals naming teachers as family life educators "but fully one-third of the present returns (around seven hundred or 71 percent) from these teachers indicate that they do *not* teach family life" (Dager and Harper, 1959:387).

The issue of definition, particularly in delimiting the goals of family life education, relates also to the competition among disciplines that was to mark the 30's, 40's, and 50's, and grow even more tension-filled in the 60's.

At the college level, the majority of courses had been initiated in the two decades prior to the 60's, most typically within sociology departments. The instructor was not inclined to think of himself as a family life educator for several reasons. First, the given course (Marriage and Family, Preparation for Marriage, or Courtship and Marriage, the most common titles) was only part of his teaching load; second, the term family life educator tended to be preempted by home economics departments which had lesser academic status on most campuses; and third, the courses taught had some functional and some institutional dimensions and there was a tendency to associate family life education only with the former. These three considerations continue to operate today.

If sociology departments had a commanding position in the 40's and 50's they began to lose some ground to home economics and health education departments in the 60's. Health education began to rise on the crest of the sex education wave of the late 60's. The Board of Directors of the American Association for Health, Physical Education, and Recreation in March 1966 passed a resolution urging that sex education be offered in the schools as part of health education. While the home economics definition of their responsibility has long included education in child care and family relationships as integral parts of a functional program, it is precisely in these areas that weakness has persisted. At the end of the 60's the response to a questionnaire survey representing about ten percent of the nation's colleges and universities found "the most popular courses in the home economics field were those associated with food and nutrition. Courses in clothing and textiles ranked second as a major field of study for both four-year and two-year institutions." Child development and family relations ranked third (DeNichols, 1970:24–25). While an occasional breakthrough occurred, as at The Pennsylvania State University and the University of Connecticut, college departments largely staffed with clothing-and-textiles and foods-and-nutrition teachers gave sparingly of their resources for expansion in child development and family relations.

Some of this has historical roots. In 1917 the federal government declared homemaking a basic vocation for women (an event worthy of note by feminist historians, coming as it did on the eve of suffrage and the increasing involvement of women in gainful employment) and Congressional funds were voted to teach homemaking throughout the country. With state aid grants, vocational education expanded. If it is recalled (Frank, 1962:208–9) that at that time there were no child guidance or research centers, no nursery schools, no public programs in parent education, it will not be surprising that "for many years . . . work in this educational area tended to focus narrowly on the teaching of specific skills, particularly cooking and sewing" (Brown, 1953:3). This emphasis has persisted despite a series of landmark critiques clearly revealing the inadequacies of home economics programs. In what is termed "one of the important historical documents of homemaking education" (Brown, 1953:12), Dean Stoddard of the University of Iowa found the program concentrating on "technical and traditional offerings for girls" and "relatively deficient in child growth and development, adolescent and pre-marriage guidance, sex education, personality development and adjustment, marriage and family counseling, husband and wife relationships, mental health, economic and social impacts upon the home."

Whatever improvements have been made in the home economics curriculum to increase attention to the behavioral sciences, progress tends to be uneven. In some of the professional journals there seems to be a continued uncritical acceptance of old content under new labels. Thus, as recently as the May/June 1970 issue of *What's New in Home Economics* (Currie, 1970), an article titled, "Elementary School Program Prepares Children for Family Role," makes it evident that cooking and sewing are the mainstay of the program reported, and role definitions are broadened only to allow boys into these activities. Recent pronouncements by some home economists seem to recognize the need for reordering priorities but still do not put the study of family and child development at the head of the list (McConnell, 1970:F-89). Others, however, continue to reveal an insistence on the traditional skills (What's New, 1968:12). Moreover, some journals for home economists were as late as 1970 still including materials for units on self-understanding and personality that would not pass scientific scrutiny (What's New, 1970:34, 36,38). The unevenness finds reflection in out-of-school activities arranged for young girls. While the YWCA through questionnaires and reading lists directs attention to broadened conceptions of women's roles (Southard, 1970, 1971), the elaborate self-evaluation study of Camp Fire Girls in the years 1964–1967 continues to define program activities to stress the "mother-role," with emphasis on "sewing for home" (McCune, 1967).

At the secondary school level, social studies has played a very minor role in family life and sex education. In most schools history and geography are taught without any account of the history of the family or the ecological component in family functioning. It is ordinarily not until college that the student can find these bases for broader understanding in anthropology and sociology of the family. Some improvement can be anticipated in the 70's as a result of efforts by the American Sociological Association in the late 60's to improve social studies in the secondary schools. The year-long high school sociology course, Inquiries in Sociology, which had its national trials in the spring of 1969, found especially positive student reaction to the sections on socialization and social change. New materials for teachers and students will be issued in the 70's (*SRSS Newsletter*, 1970). These developments may reduce the variation among states in the 50's and 60's so far as social science involvement in family life and sex education is concerned. State surveys of secondary schools have indicated that in Indiana sociology had offered nine percent, government, economics, history, and problems five percent, of the schools' 973 units in family life education (Dager and Harper, 1959:386). In the state of Washington social science departments had only three semester courses and 15 units in contrast to 67 and 137 for Home Economics and 25 and 107 for Health Education (Baker, 1969:229) while in Minnesota Social Studies had offered 74 units to 94 by Home Economics and 23 by Health (Martinson, 1966:199).

PROGRAMS, COURSES AND UNITS

At the start of the 60's there were few family life programs in school systems or in communities in the sense of an integrated complex of experiences. A survey of Indiana high schools reported in 1959 there were only 108 courses but 973 units within other courses (Dager and Harper, 1959:386). A survey of Minnesota high schools had found 23 semester courses in 1959 and 93 units whereas in 1965 there were 20 and 117 respectively (Martinson, 1966:197). In Washington, a survey of the state in 1969 found 104 semester courses and 301 units (Baker, 1969:229).

At the college level, a course in marriage and the family might be offered in the sociology department and a similar one in home economics, but with little or no cooperation between them. Also, both psychology and home economics might be offering a course in child development. Few institutions were offering enough courses to constitute a family relations major. At the graduate level, a bare dozen of institutions were preparing men and women for leadership in family life education: Florida State, Michigan State, Pennsylvania State, Utah State, Ohio State, Merrill-Palmer, Cornell University, Purdue, and Universities of Hawaii, Oregon, Minnesota, and Connecticut. The distinguished interdisciplinary program at Teachers College of Columbia University, which had staffed many of these graduate programs throughout the country, was in the process of being phased out soon after the demise of its charismatic leader, Ernest G. Osborne, in whose name an annual teaching award in family life education was established in the mid-60's by the National Council on Family Relations.

Generally, sociology departments had too few courses on the family to encourage masters and doctoral degrees in family sociology to an equal extent with, for example, urban sociology. However, the trend was upward and during the 60's there were clues to considerable growth. While only occasional articles on family sociology continued to appear in *The American Sociological Review,* official journal of the American Sociological Association, the *Journal of Marriage and the Family,* published by the National Council on Family Relations, expanded markedly in the second half of the decade. Its pages became so replete with research studies on the family that a separate journal was established, *The Family Coordinator,* in which family life education, formerly covered in the Teacher Exchange for High Schools and Colleges, a section of the *Journal of Marriage and the Family,* could receive extended coverage. (The new journal was a successor to *The Family Life Coordinator* which had been published since the early 50's by an educational foundation.) The American Sociological Association started a Family Section in the 60's, as a result of which its annual meetings, especially in the latter part of the decade, featured more papers on marriage and the family than ever before.

While there was some expansion in home economics departments, at both graduate and undergraduate levels in the 60's, few of the women who went into the secondary school systems were well prepared to teach the occasional unit on the family assigned them. The several state surveys made in this decade as well as local studies emphasize the lack of teacher education in family life either in home economics or in health education. In Minnesota three of eleven teachers assigned to teach semester courses had no prior family life education and twenty-seven out of forty-nine were unprepared to teach the unit in family life assigned them (Martinson, 1966:200). In the state of Washington, "more than 70 percent of the teachers evaluated their academic preparation to teach family life and sex education as inadequate" (Baker and Darcy, 1970:231).

Because so few high schools offered courses in child development and family relationships, colleges were not preparing teachers in this area in great number. Hence, there were few people available to teach courses when parents and community agencies sought curriculum expansion. Harassed administrators generally sought a solution through in-service education, selecting a few teachers from an assortment of disciplines. The very shallow educational experience tended to ensure a separation of family life from sex education. In none of the states did certification machinery either encourage curriculum expansion at the teacher preparation level or recognize and reward the expanded efforts of a few institutions that took the initiative. Students in the human development program at Pennsylvania State University, for example, who come from departments of psychology and sociology and wish to teach family life and sex education in the secondary schools of that state are not eligible for certification which is limited to home economics education and requires courses they have not had, in textiles and similar subjects. In all states the sociology major who went to teach in high school was certified in social studies and like the home economist had to teach an array of courses in which family relationships were allowed to play only a small part, if any. Despite workshops to upgrade the competencies of high school family life teachers, problems persist of limited behavioral sciences backgrounds as much of the undergraduate program had included cooking and sewing to permit students to be certified as home economists.

THE FEMALE CLASSROOM

For many home economists the level of understanding is limited by the almost exclusively female environment. Careful inquiry usually reveals that only a minority of classes in secondary school or college which are called home economics attract male students and even in these classes the boys are severely outnumbered. A survey of Minnesota high schools showed the situation was worse in full semester courses (456 girls and 68 boys) than in units of courses (1,556 girls and 673 boys) (Martinson, 1966:200–201). In some states the sex imbalance increased after Sputnik when new definitions of "essential subject matter" and "frills" shook the American educational world. In California, for example, a study in 1956 had found 44 percent of family life courses given in social studies classrooms, which were coeducational; replication of this study in 1964 (Landis, 1965) found little offered in social studies owing to the Casey bill. The public image is that of a female-centered discipline. Those addressing teachers of home economics tend to assume their students are girls (Calderone, 1963).

It is increasingly recognized that even if an intellectual understanding of male and female role changes can be achieved in the predominantly or wholly female classroom, it is questionable whether emotional and social preparation for the teaching role can be. It is a curious development that the movement for women's studies sponsored in the late 60's, while critical of traditional home economics classes as limiting female aspirations both in vocational and domestic roles, lays stress on some campuses on the desirability of all-female classes. The unfinished struggle for coeducation thus finds new opponents in the very groups of avant-garde women who in a previous century were its firmest adherents.

On the colleague level, as well as in teacher preparation, home economics teachers tend to live in a one-sex world. Indeed, the effort in the 60's to attract men has raised issues of "sexism." Women who prepared for the family field at interdisciplinary graduate facilities are often not acceptable to sociology departments which question the Ed.D. degree, or there are not enough family courses to warrant hiring a specialist in the area. Now the emphasis on recruiting males in Home Economics departments creates, ironically, problems of unemployment in a field marked by a shortage of doctoral degrees. The value of creating a coeducational world for students by attracting boys to classrooms with male teachers and for teachers by balancing the sexes in the department obviously conflicts with the value of judging teachers on competencies. The dilemma of the 60's is likely to continue into the next decade.

Because of the predominance of women in secondary school teaching of family life, as well as the use of teaching materials which in the years up into the early 60's gave scant coverage to the sexual dimension of various topics, an image had developed of conventionality or indeed of prudery in relation to home economics teachers. Biology teachers were often unprepared and reluctant to teach about human reproduction, and their textbooks often omitted this subject. Health educators were similarly unprepared for the most part, although less reluctant, to tackle the emotional and social dimensions of venereal disease, masturbation, and illegitimacy. In serving as consultant to a number of school systems on the east and west coasts in the 60's, the writer found principals and superintendents somehow more reluctant to consider social studies and home economics teachers for new programs than teachers in the other disciplines.

It should be evident that the difficulty with teacher readiness and teacher images originated in colleges in which the teachers were undergraduates, colleges which offered few courses in the family field. Such preparation for life and for teaching could have had profound effects on teacher and citizen performance. It would have ensured that every teacher in elementary and secondary schools regardless of subject matter would have been prepared to use the "teachable moment" and focus on the relevance of the given phenomenon to personal and family living. With teachers alerted by their own undergraduate and graduate education to the biological, sociological, psychological, and historical dimensions of family functioning, they would be ready and able to use this knowledge in their classrooms. The specialist might still serve a purpose as a coordinator of the many school and community experiences that would be offered, and certification might still be necessary for such specialists or at least the establishment of standards. Undoubtedly this would require wholesale revision of present undergraduate programs and educational philosophy. This may occur in the 70's if student demands of the 60's for relevancy, self-determination, student involvement in classroom decision-making, process-centered experiences, and a general humanizing of the curriculum, grow more persistent.

However, this is only one side of the coin. The other is community readiness, involving adult education and its specialized branch, parent education. The latter has been largely mother education. It was in the 20's and 30's that parent education began to spread beyond the few "relatively well-educated and unusually sophisticated urban families" with whom it had begun (Frank, 1962:225). It must be said, however, that it never reached the proportions that would ensure an informed citizenry in the area of family life education. The turn of the century had seen the beginnings of child care literature which contributed to "faith in the power of new knowledge to guide the rearing of children" (Frank, 1962:209). This literature was to grow dramatically in each decade, but reliance upon traditional beliefs and customary practices was to continue to be as dominant a strain in the American household in the 60's as the scientific approach.

Opportunities for parents to sift through their own feelings about themselves, their children, and society, are present in only small quantity. When controversial issues involving family life and sex education are raised in any community, this very uncertain background of knowledge and value clarification becomes a quicksand in which reason stands a strong chance of floundering. It is a likely hypothesis that the citizen who has been in a family life education program, as a student in school and later as an adult, is less apt to panic than the one who finds sudden challenge to views accepted on faith through succeeding generations. There is need for research to discover whether communities in which parent education programs have been carried on for many years under the federal government's Department of Agriculture, with a Cooperative Extension Service based in land-grant colleges (MacArthur, 1967), did indeed weather the national organized opposition of 1968 and 1969 more successfully than those without this educational opportunity. Brown reported in 1964 concerning Extension Service that "Interest in the study of child development, human relations, and family living has grown so rapidly over the last 25 years that 33 states now employ 41 specialists in these subject matter areas" (Brown, 1964:831). Non-government programs of adult education, including the Child Study Association, the General Federation of Women's Clubs (Home Life Department), the National Congress of Parents and Teachers, the Association for Family Living, may also wish to study themselves or be studied to determine how effective their past efforts have been in preparing parents and other adults to meet the exaggerated criticisms which made the last years of the decade so crisis-filled.

There is considerable room for disagreement to be sure, on the answers to the complex questions facing family life education today. The uncertainty exists in the public at large, among the experts to a lesser degree perhaps, and inevitably affects the way a school system interprets its responsibility. Most administrators have for the past few decades been more influenced by the opposition, real and anticipated, in their communities, than by the demands of those seeking curriculum expansion in family life and sex education.

COMMUNITIES AND SCHOOLS

Much work had been done to bring communities and schools together for joint solving of problems in the family life area. In some communities a number of promising programs were allowed to die out. On the other hand, some older programs lived on and, for their very endurance rather than for any growth demonstrated, were deemed "successful." Irony reached a high point when in the controversy of the late 60's a number of these older programs were cited as models for more advanced communities to follow.

It was difficult to ascertain in the 60's just how much was left of the work which had been carried on for community and school family life education in the three previous decades with federal agency and private support. Two particularly notable efforts had been made, the first beginning in the 30's and the second in the 50's. These have been selected because of their broad coverage. In addition, it should be noted, individual states were engaged in pioneering work. Oregon, in particular, forged ahead under the leadership of educators associated with the University of Oregon, aided by the half-million dollars left for the establishment of the E. C. Brown Trust. Films and courses were developed, and publications issued, all with emphasis on "sex education as part of family life education," which were to be helpful in other parts of the country (Avery *et al.*, 1969:17–26). In 1933 the Home Economics Education Service, along with the Bureau of Vocational Education in which it functioned, was transferred to the United States Office of Education. These were the years of the Great Depression, and a sense of urgency concerning families, which were faltering with the economy, pervaded national agencies. The Works Progress Administration, under Harry Hopkins, had authorized federal funds for nursery schools and parent education programs. The Home Economics Education Service decided to work with one community in each of four different states that shared a belief in family life education, that is a view that "an educational program which aids in making family life function more effectively is of primary importance to society and that every person as a member of a home should have an opportunity for an expanding educational experience dealing with this phase of his life, from early childhood into adulthood and parenthood" (Brown, 1953:16). A county in Utah, another in Tennessee, a city in Ohio and another in Kansas began to participate in the project. The details of organizational efforts will not be of concern here, although they bear reading for the contrasts presented with some of the relatively hurried efforts at community organization for family life and sex education in the 60's.

What is of more significance was a) the failure to achieve official status for family life education in government bodies locally, and b) the tendency for activities to cluster where there was paid leadership to ensure their continuance.

Thus, in the Utah county the central sponsoring committee for the community family life education program sought to become a subcommittee of the county planning board but was unsuccessful. This may not be unrelated to the fact that in 1950 the program came to an end. The improvements in the high school did continue, however. The county in Tennessee focused mainly on health education, with nutrition and tuberculosis central concerns, along with setting up family recreation centers. Evaluations tended to be consistently over-enthusiastic. For example, the judgment that "cooperative, creative problem-solving has become a community habit in the county" as a result of these efforts finds little substantiation in reports that an adult education program was lacking, "Negroes have not yet really been included" (Brown, 1953:89), and efforts to establish a nursery school were unavailing.

The question of how family-life-education-minded a community remains after years of guided effort has implications for policy formation today. The study of communities in which parent education organizations and agencies have long labored should include examination of the degree to which the communities in the project under consideration were able to withstand the organized attacks on family life and sex education in the late 60's.

The account of the Ohio city project reveals the vulnerability of partial programs to exigencies of the moment. "So often progress made in one year or one semester is lost the next because of schedule changes or the resignation of a teacher" (Brown, 1953:121). When few teachers are prepared, replacement becomes difficult or at least a good excuse for reluctant administrators to terminate a program. Nursery schools are important adjuncts to high school courses in child development. The two W.P.A. nursery schools in the Ohio city were discontinued, however, even before the war was over, because "there were no longer enough eligible children in the nighborhood to keep it going" (Brown, 1953:117). The community had evidently not been sufficiently educated to the values of nursery schools to resist definitions of eligibility that ensured their demise. Back of administrative failure often lies the assumption, sometimes correct, of community indifference to family life and sex education.

The city in Kansas was able to build on a parent education program already under way when federal encouragement of family life education began in the late 30's. However, as in any program where Home Economics provides leadership, there is a tendency for lessons in food, clothing, and home decoration to figure more prominently than parent-child relationships. As in the other three communities of the project, cooperation was sought amongst the many agencies on the scene, from the Y's to service clubs, PTA's, and Junior League, which could further the program. An innovation in the city of Kansas was the showing at successive meetings of a series of films prepared by the Commission of Human Relations of the Progressive Education Association. How arid was the soil in which family life education considered as human relations education was being planted is revealed by the commentary on the film program: "In some ways the results of this experiment were disquieting. Children and grown-ups frequently responded in terms of old stereotypes and prejudices" (Brown, 1953:170). While some progress had undoubtedly been made by the 60's, the negative experiences of the earlier decades may also be seen as clues to the depth of cleavages that were to emerge in the late 60's.

The second and larger of the two nationally organized efforts to expand community and school family life education began in 1953 and continued until 1962. It was under the auspices of a private agency, the American Social Health Association, which was aided by private foundation funds amounting to almost three-fourths of a million dollars. ASHA considers its nine-year demonstration in family life education to be "the most comprehensive such program in the history of the movement" (ASHA, 1966:14). Five regional projects involved 23 states and the District of Columbia. Unlike the earlier project, the ASHA plan did not start with assumptions of the superiority of one discipline over another in the family life education responsibility. Perhaps more important than its consequent ability to gain greater cooperation among various disciplines was the ASHA awareness of the focality of teacher preparation and its attempts to involve teacher education institutions in the regional projects.

The ASHA projects concentrated on the *education* in family life education. There was recognition to be sure, that food, clothing, and shelter were essentials in family functioning and that family life education could facilitate and accompany the development of community efforts to solve these problems as well as those of recreation and health care.

ASHA defined family life education as "a body of knowledge and an active process as well—includes what we know, feel, and do as family members. In other words, family life education deals primarily with the behavior of people not merely as individuals but as members of a family and of other groups" (ASHA, 1966:10). It saw as the primary aim of such education "to provide the knowledge and develop the attitudes which will raise the standards of home life and enable people of all ages to live more constructively" (ASHA, 1966:10). Churches, professional health and welfare agencies, youth agencies, and civic groups were viewed as capable of forming their own programs in family life education as well as lending support to program development in the schools (ASHA, 1966:11).

The nine-year-projects were an intensification of efforts that had characterized ASHA soon after its founding in 1914. In the 40's its educational program had included lectures, conferences, and teacher workshops in response to requests from community organizations and school systems. Much of the work was carried on by the affiliates in the various states and localities.

While the nine-year projects sought to build programs in communities with a high degree of readiness, ASHA proceeded on the assumption that "readiness can be created," that a concentrated and sustained effort to encourage leadership among teachers and administrators would have as its consequence increased community appreciation for the role which family life education could play in schools, and outside, to provide children, youth, and the older generations with the perspectives and interpersonal skills that allow more effective personal and family functioning.

The ASHA projects secured the cooperation of key bodies, such as the National Education Association, the American Association of Colleges for Teacher Education, and the National Congress of Parents and Teachers. Project staff members served as consultants to local schools and agencies. Thus, the decade preceding the 60's saw unprecedented activity in the Midwest (Minnesota, Iowa, North and South Dakota), the Central Atlantic (Delaware, Maryland, North

Carolina, Virginia, West Virginia, and the District of Columbia), New England (Massachusetts, Connecticut, Maine, Vermont, New Hampshire, and Rhode Island), the Middle States (Colorado, Kansas, Nebraska, and Missouri), and the Rocky Mountain States (Utah, New Mexico, Arizona, and Nevada).

The reports of the ASHA projects which extended into the 60's are replete with details of concrete accomplishments. In each region materials of high quality were prepared for publication. These served as models in many parts of the country in the 60's. In the Midwest project, a curriculum guide for teacher education institutions, followed by another for teachers in elementary and secondary schools, received distribution in a majority of the states. Workshops begun at teachers colleges became annual events. Television series and library commissions broadened community awareness. In the Central Atlantic project, resource guides were compiled, containing ideas and methods still useful today, and in-service workshops involved thousands of teachers. In New England, public school systems in a number of cities and counties introduced courses and units and various teachers colleges increased their offerings. Similarly in the other projects, there was an expansion of curriculum and teacher workshops, the development of exhibit material (shown at the 1960 White House Conference on Children and Youth as well as at various state conferences), the use of radio and television.

In the Middle States project, a questionnaire survey of the status of family life education in teacher preparation institutions in the four-state area revealed that of the 71 colleges responding (almost three-fourths of those queried), 87 percent offered special courses in family life education and 84 percent gave some attention to it in other courses. Undoubtedly, the expansion in college courses encouraged by ASHA, accounts in part for the quantitative growth reported by Landis (1959).

It should be noted that these projects which extended well into the decade under review here, pioneering and dedicated as they were, rarely affected a majority of schools or communities in the various states. Even where a state board of education approved family life courses, and drew up guidelines for teaching the courses, little was done for years afterwards (Brantley, 1966).

A SPECIAL DECADE

Each part of the decade, the early 60's, the middle 60's, and the late 60's, saw different forces at play, with different consequences for family life and sex education. Almost every issue raised in the latter part of the 60's had already received some consideration in the earlier years. What was to become evident was that there had been little resolution of differences. These issues were as follows:

a. sexual behaviors, especially premarital intercourse

b. sex education apart from family life education

c. privacy

d. home and school roles in family life education

e. teacher preparedness

f. child readiness, especially in K-4

g. moral codes and attitudes towards masturbation, homosexuality, etc.

h. interdisciplinary cooperation

i. value differences between teachers and parents, parents and children, states and communities

j. legislation mandating or prohibiting programs

k. audio-visual materials

If the issues were common to several decades, the social matrix in which they occurred varied greatly. The 60's represent a very special decade in American history so far as the sexualization of society is concerned. In the mass media the use of sex in advertising reached new levels of exposure. New publications appeared, such as *Playboy,* easily available in the supermarket and displayed on newsstands. Films were increasingly imported from countries with less traditional attitudes or produced in this country under relaxed interpretations of the codes. National magazines devoted covers and pages to "Sex in the United States: Mores and Morality" (*Time,* 1964) and "The Morals Revolution on the U.S. Campus" (*Newsweek,* 1964). While viewing with alarm, particularly in adult contemplation of youth's manners or morals is not new, the sheer quantity of attention given sex in periodicals and books was undoubtedly unique. Television and the radio reflected and encouraged a new freedom of discussion by bringing into the home talks about and depictions of childbirth, abortion, V.D., and illegitimacy.

All these nonacademic forces had an impact on parents, teachers, and students alike. Private schools as well as public ones felt these pressures. In 1964 the National Association of Independent Schools, an organization with 750 member schools, held a much publicized conference to discuss what curriculum changes would be appropriate in face of the new pressures. Particularly in New York, where the sexual component was at that time almost wholly omitted from instruction, private schools perceived themselves as having the needed flexibility to innovate changes without excessive delay, and to serve as models for public school programs (Southard, 1967). Schools tended to lag behind more informal socializing agencies in open discussion, however. Textbooks in the early 60's tended to reflect the fears of adults, not necessarily of those who wrote them, but of the administrators who approved them for purchase and the publishers who continued to assume, as they had in prior decades, that open discussion of sexual issues would decrease sales in traditional markets.

On the professional scene, changes were becoming more evident. Professional journals and books as well as national conferences began to discuss the findings of sex research to an even greater degree than when the Kinsey findings first appeared a decade or more earlier. It is noteworthy that in most of these publications, schools were not regarded as contributing significantly to the sexual scene. The special edition of the *Journal of Social Issues* (April 1966), devoted to "The Sexual Renaissance in America," contains barely more than a sentence and a footnote (Reiss, 1966:133) on sex education.

In the 50's and into the early 60's, curriculum guides for home economists, even those with newer emphasis on concept development and readiness to use the contributions of psychology and sociology, rarely included sex in topics where it would have seemed unavoidable (Pieretti, 1963:128). The ASHA, long experienced with sex education programs, had sought to incorporate the sexual dimension into the nine-year projects. Their optimistic assessment of the outcome may overstate the realities. "Although sex education aspects of family life education were viewed with some misgivings by school leaders at first, the content relating to sex soon became a natural part of the whole. Through workshops, administrators and teachers became more competent and confident in handling sex education as part of the family life programs" (ASHA, 1966:16). Because so many family life educators tended to avoid the sexual dimension, the titling of courses and programs began to change in the 60's, to remind teacher and student alike of the interconnection of family life and sex education (Morgan, 1966; Somerville, 1967).

The recommendation in 1948 of the National Conference on Education of Teachers that sex education be part of the curriculum for all teachers had not been implemented. Several studies show sex among the areas receiving least attention in teaching at the secondary level (Martinson, 1966:202). Moreover, the discomfort with which even biologists, doctors, and nurses face discussion of sexual matters suggests the inadequacy either of the total college and professional curricula (Coombs, 1968) or of the system of required and elective subjects which makes it likely that most college graduates have not encountered any frank discussion in their classes.

Partly as a result of the reluctance of family life educators to handle the sexual component, there sprang up a movement for sex education as a separate subject. Warnings against this had been offered in each decade. One early figure in the field had declared, "In my opinion it is a mistake to confine sex teaching to a single course such as health or personal hygiene, since its ramifications in human behavior are so broad" (Beck, 1955). Later, Reiss (1966) was to declare, "In light of the goals of sex education, it may well be better to build broad social science course materials in all grade levels . . . rather than just adding an isolated sex education course at the junior high school level" (p. 134).

A demand in the 60's to start "putting the sex back into sex education" (Scriven, 1968:485) indicated the path that had been taken by the separate sex education programs in the previous decades. Many agreed with the judgment that "Sex education so far has usually been a half-hearted venture into the physiology of reproduction with some vague remarks about dating behavior" (Scriven, 1968:486). The American Association of School Administrators in its Sixtieth Yearbook had declared: "The fairly common practice of inviting a physician to speak to boys or girls may be seriously inadequate. Few physicians (except psychiatrists) by training or practice have studied the essential problems of sex. They have been taught the names, functions, and physical disorders of various sex organs, but that is a minor contribution to the great problems of affection, courtship, and marriage in modern society. Most of the conflicts that keep youth awake in troubled nights are psychological and social problems . . .

persons well trained in psychology and sociology will be able to help much more than any but the very exceptional physicians" (AASA, 1938).

The separate course in sex education offered in some school systems was usually offered under health education or physical education auspices. Few teachers in these fields were prepared to offer sex information, let alone sex education. The shortcomings lay in the education they had received as undergraduates, in the hypocrisy of community leaders who tended to demand of schools and teachers preachments of behavior they were not themselves willing to live by, and in the poor scheduling and in-service practices of the schools. To be sure, some of this was to change in the later 60's when health educators and others began to come to serious grips with the challenge to upgrade their offerings (*Journal of School Health*, 1967).

NEW ORGANIZATIONS

It was against this background of the sexualization of American society on the one hand, and the inadequate attention given in schools, churches, and social agencies to the sexual aspects of man and society, that a new organization was announced in 1965 after months of preparation. The Sex Information and Education Council of the U.S. (SIECUS) created a stir from its beginning, both among professionals and in the public at large.

After five years of SIECUS there are still marked differences among professionals in calculating the outcomes. Most would agree perhaps that until it was attacked in 1968 and 1969, it was "the single most important force in the realm of sex education today" (Powers and Baskin, 1969:13). Space will not permit a detailed examination here of various SIECUS activities. Mention of these can be found in the *SIECUS Newsletter* which together with eleven brief study guides and a handbook comprise almost the totality of SIECUS publications. The spoken word rather than the written, whether in speeches, panels, or consultancies, has been most used.

Discussion here will be limited to the ways in which the founding of SIECUS brought to the surface uncertainties and confusions in the whole field of famly life and sex education as well as new opportunities.

SIECUS defined itself as a health organization and its goal, "To establish man's sexuality as a health entity." To some professionals this seemed to give a clearer mandate to health education than to other disciplines despite SIECUS mention of "a broad interdisciplinary approach" in publications and speeches. The unsettled issue of which disciplines should take primary responsibility came to the fore again.

Related to this was the issue of separate sex education or including the sexual component within the study of individual and family development. SIECUS seemed to speak both of a "sharp and direct" focus on human sexuality and of bringing about "within the framework of family life education" constructive dialogue between youth and adults (*SIECUS Newsletter*, 1965). Kirkendall (1970) reports that "in the first informal meetings at which the formation of SIECUS was discussed, the question arose as to whether the incorporation of such an organization would retard or advance the cause of sex education. Some believed it meant pulling 'sex out of context' and spotlighting sex in an undesirable way." He himself had long been inclined to question the appropriateness of a family life context for all sex education. "How does one teach about sexuality among the permanently unmarried in a family life context'?"

Thus, the establishment and functioning of SIECUS reminded professionals of the unsatisfactory state of terminology in the field. "Family life education" is a name no one is too comfortable with. Some think the individual and society are more certain pivots, and prefer *human relations education* or *human development education*, with sexuality and family relations only aspects of the larger area of study. However, some prefer to use family life education as the umbrella term, maintaining that the individual always carries with him the impact of his family of origin, and therefore even if he does not enter into a family of procreation, his sexual and other relational behaviors can be viewed in the family life framework. However psychologically sound this argument may be, there is an equally astute consideration to counter it, that "because the word 'family' suggests dependency and restraint at a time when they are striving to sever the psychological umbilical cord with their family group," adolescents will react more favorably to study of Human Relations than Family Living (Lindquist, 1968:59). Sex education has connotations of emphasis on the physiological, and *Sexuality Education* has been suggested in its place. A compromise term, family life and sex education, came to be frequently used in the 60's, despite misgivings that "and" suggests divisibility of subject matter.

SIECUS also reminded professionals of their divided state on the issue of special courses versus integration of family life and sex education into all parts of the curriculum. The thrust of the E. C. Brown Trust and its leaders, Avery and Johannis, had been in the direction of integration, and this was to be echoed by Barr (Avery *et al.,* 1962; Barr, 1967). The impact of SIECUS, however, had been in the direction of the separate course or unit on sex, not that this was advocated in any of its publications, but because the public, and educational institutions responding to that public, interpreted it this way and because some departments saw this as a path to speedy enlargement of student enrollments. "SIECUS barnstorming conveys a sense of urgency which coincides with nationwide concern over the sexual morality of the rising generation," one volume comments (Powers and Baskin, 1969:14). Those who listened to the speeches, particularly those on television and radio, by SIECUS representatives did not always read the publications which warned against haste and the need for thorough community study before program formulation. If the mailbags of existing organizations such as NCFR (Jewson, 1967) and ASHA had been heavy in the early 60's as communities and schools demanded help in getting teaching materials for family life and sex education, they were swamped as was SIECUS in the mid-60's when TV appearances of Mary Calderone made sex education a household topic (Somerville, 1967). "One New York school system which recently received nationwide publicity for its program of sex education was inundated with over 3,000 requests for its curriculum guide" (Burleson, 1967:9). The fact that the guide was of questionable quality in the view of some professionals did not stem the flow. Criticisms were not welcomed or taken seriously. There was general awareness that qualified teachers were in short supply but the issue was not raised in all its seriousness until almost the eve of the reaction of 1968 and 1969 (Malfetti and Rubin, 1967). The National Council on Family Relations, aware of the influx of self-designated family life and sex educators into the field in the mid-60's, appointed a number of commissions and committees to look into the establishment of teaching criteria. The writer chaired the Committee on Educational Standards and Certification for Family Life Educators in 1968 and 1969 which formulated a set of Criteria accepted by NCFR at its Washington meeting. These criteria seek to ensure that whatever departments are involved in offering courses and units, the teachers will have multi-faceted professional preparation (Somerville, 1970).

The establishment in 1968, with the aid of the Commonwealth Fund, of the Center for the Study of Sex Education in Medicine, under the leadership of Dr. Harold Lief, Director of the Division of Family Study in The University of Pennsylvania, is an example of the attempt to establish standards within a given profession. It marked the culmination of more than five years of effort to get medical schools to broaden their curriculum to include education about sexuality. NCFR, AAMC, SIECUS, and other organizations cooperated with medical leaders and by 1968 there were 35 medical schools in contrast to three in 1964 with expanded curriculum (Lock, 1964; Mathias, 1966).

THE ISSUE OF TIME

The new programs tended to underestimate even more than the older ones the amount of time needed not only to prepare the teacher but how much time he would need to explore the subject with his classes. Even the often-cited programs, at Anaheim, Evanston (Furlong, 1967), San Diego, Flint (Somerville, 1966), Winnetka (Marland, 1961) gave at most five weeks and in some instances only days in any given year. Often expediency is at work and brings on a tendency to accept what seems possible over what is more defensible but difficult to obtain. For the most part, however, there seems to be a genuine misconception concerning the nature of the task among parents, administrators, and teachers. Thus, an educator offers the view that in the second year of high school "the program need not be lengthy. One class period for imparting information and another for discussion should be sufficient" (Wake, 1966). Perhaps it is not unexpected that he hastens to add, "The teacher is on safe ground if he sticks to the broadly accepted sexual standards."

In teacher education, the 60's brought the establishment of a few graduate and undergraduate programs offering broad pre-service preparation. The main reliance, however, was on the brief workshop. It is likely that haste in teacher education in the 60's was encouraged by precedents in health education of introducing brief V.D. and drug units as well as other "crisis" material into ongoing programs (Kaplan, 1967).

The 60's did not contribute to the resolution of an old dispute in teacher education, whether the workshop should be regarded as a refresher for the experienced professional rather than as the main way of preparing family life and sex educators. The long-established tradition of workshops has to some extent both mitigated the difficulties caused by lack of pre-service teacher education opportunities and increased those difficulties by seeming to offer an adequate solution. In the 60's the number of workshops, especially in the summer months, seemed to increase, with listings appearing in the *NCFR Newsletter*, the *Journal of Home Economics*, the *SIECUS Newsletter*, and other publications. Most of these workshops, having been "developed entirely independently of SIECUS" (SIECUS Newsletter, 1970:3) were not subject to the vicissitudes of that organization when it became the main target of organized opposition in the late 60's. They can be expected in the 70's to be affected by new Criteria adopted by NCFR (Somerville, 1970) and by several state departments of education, as, for example, the Pennsylvania Department of Education's Recommended Standards for Sex Education Teachers. SIECUS called a small working conference in 1970 with a view to developing "a unified curriculum for training teachers." Dissertations in the graduate schools are likely to help focus attention on this issue of teacher preparation in the next decade (Shimmel and Carrera, 1970).

It should be noted that there are differences among workshops not only in quality of teaching personnel but in time. Some run only for a week of two, some six weeks (Luckey, 1968:90). Some have as their students mainly professionals with graduate degrees in related disciplines while some have people for whom the course work is almost entirely new. Workshop outcomes will obviously vary, depending not only on time allotted but on quality of faculty and of students. Time is stressed in this discussion because it has received least attention. Its importance is suggested by the experience of a teacher workshop in Winston-Salem which, with a brilliant roster of resource persons available to them in a "medical school town," nonetheless found the 33 hours inadequate for needed discussion and reflection.

Class size became an increasing problem in the 60's. So few courses are offered in the colleges which are helpful in the preparation of future family life and sex educators that when a class is scheduled, enrollments are apt to rise spectacularly. When there is an entire program rather than a single course, a large class with an inspiring teacher may serve an introductory function, with detailed discussion to be found in other classes. There is the danger, unless Criteria are carefully observed, that the student and the administrator may evaluate this large-class experience for more than it actually offers. The 70's will undoubtedly see the enrollment battle still being fought out. Underlying the issues of time and class size is the assumption of the importance of discussion, the dialog-centered classroom. While this has strong professional support, it is by no means unanimous.

OTHER UNSETTLED ISSUES

While SIECUS was the main organizational target of the highly publicized attack on sex education in 1968 and 1969, family life education came under criticism too. The most obvious reason was the misuse of the latter designation by those who devised programs which omitted the family and social contexts in which sexual behavior occurs. Whatever resistance family life education had met in the earlier decades was mild in comparison with national nervousness over sex education. Newspapers, magazines, radio, and TV devoted an unusual amount of time and space to the attacks. Only occasionally was a fair picture presented by inviting both sides to comment or summarizing the issues on a pro and con basis. Often the pictures that accompanied stories, as in *Life* and *Look* "spoke more than a thousand words" in revealing the nature of the opposition, and are testimony for the need for adult education. In the furor of the late 60's many family life programs were curtailed along with sex education. It may be painful for some life educators to realize that several of the questions concerning sex education can logically be raised about family life education, especially when the latter meets its responsibility of handling the sexual component. These questions which were raised in an atmosphere of hostility in the 60's will need to be answered if the 70's are to proceed on a basis of greater agreement.

home, school, and church

The roles of these three socializing agencies have not been clearly demarcated for many years, particularly where children and youth are concerned. It is a rare textbook or syllabus that does not take an apologetic tone to some degree, either stating or implying that if parents were only better equipped with knowledge and fortitude there would be no need for formal programs in family life and sex education.

All agree that some learnings take place in the home concerning family and sex, if only by the models offered and the emotions developed and suppressed there (Calderone, 1965; Force, 1970). However, an analogy may distinguish this from more formal learnings. Parents are not regarded as historians because they discuss a recent world event at the dinner table or reveal by their tension their disagreement with a TV commentary. Similarly, parents can plant the seeds for an appreciation of art or literature but these disciplines exist and the school offers knowledge and skills the home cannot be expected to supply. It is only in relatively simple societies that the family can fulfill the total educational function.

One of the complaints against family life and sex education most frequently heard in the latter part of the 60's, but certainly not unknown before then, was that family life and sex education usurps the parental prerogative. Some would hold however, that even the best educated parent cannot handle this responsibility alone, for lack of time, knowledge, and teaching skills, and perhaps above all, for lack of the essential component in such education, a group of peers for interaction. Some would hold that the incest taboo and inbuilt role conflict necessitate that others than the parents take on the formal educational task (Mace, 1963). This does not mean that family life and sex education for parents and other adults is not valuable. Indeed, it may be, along with teacher education, a prerequisite for the successful functioning of school programs for youth. It may also be essential if the informal learnings in the home are to make a positive contribution (Kirkendall, 1970; Calderone, 1965).

It is probably the issue of values, however, that dominates the feeling behind the "parental prerogative" argument. This is not lightly dismissed or quickly settled. As Christensen succinctly puts it: "Values are the mental and emotional sets which aid persons in judging the relative worth or importance of things, ideas, or events . . . In decision-making theory, values, simply stated, are the criteria one used for choosing among alternatives" (1964:969). It is claimed that "Probably most leaders in the field today agree that family life education should not consist of foisting one set of values, the teacher's, in place of another set, the pupil's" (Kerckhoff, 1964:898). It would be difficult to make this statement about teachers rather than leaders. With inadequate teacher preparation, it is not unexpected that teachers often show an inability to examine value systems objectively.

One contributing factor may be the ubiquitous use of "wholesome," and "healthy" when attitudes are mentioned in curriculum guides and professional writings. It is not easy to find consensus on such value-laden concepts. According to Rutledge (1961) after a three-day effort, "As we discuss the sexual area of life it becomes increasingly clear that vast chasms exist not only between what is taught and practiced, but between professional viewpoints of what is health or unhealth, healing or destructive." Awareness of difference and of diversity is characteristic of the writings of leaders in the field. As Luckey (1967) puts it, "Most social scientists agree that it would be difficult if not impossible to define the norm of sexual behavior in contemporary American society" and "Just as there is no unified political opinion in this country, nor single religious belief, there is no one ethic." In recognition of this, religious leaders in an Interfaith Statement on Sex Education issued in June 1968 to supplement an affirmation in 1966, urge that "Sex education in the schools must proceed constructively, with understanding, tolerance, and acceptance of differences." Chilman (1969) suggests that "Values about sex which are different from those to which the student has been exposed at home or in his neighborhood can be presented as another way of looking at the subject, not as *the* way, or a *better* way."

Thus, when parents insist that the teacher present all sides of a question rather than propagandize for one view, they are on firm educational ground. However, there is a tendency for parents and other adults (including some teachers) to accept traditional propagandizing and to become critical of the classroom only when material not supportive of their particular value position gets presented. Sometimes this is only inferrable, but in the late 60's many of the more extreme opponents, such as LaHaye (n.d.) frankly condemned those who preferred "education over indoctrination." Moreover, any attempt to get beneath the majority assent to sex education reported in polls, such as the Gallup poll of 1967, is likely to find parents either demanding that the teacher believe in chastity or teach it as an absolute if a course in their school is to be required. Even in the sample from a suburban town with higher economic and educational levels than in the country at large, almost three out of five parents thought the teacher should teach that chastity before marriage is best in order for the sex education program to be required (Libby, 1970). A journalist's account of the situation in Anaheim in 1969 reveals in personal interviews some of the more extreme processes of the organized opposition on the value issue (Breasted, 1970).

In the late 60's the long-smoldering hostility towards secular education because of its emphasis on science spread to family life and sex education. One point of entry was the contrast between the traditional Judaeo-Christian position held by many Christian evangelical as well as orthodox Jewish groups that sex outside of marriage is wrong, and the view of situational ethics supported by many other religious bodies which holds the moral implications of an act to be different at different times and places and circumstances (Duvall, 1965). While the issue of sex, premarital and extramarital, became an important weapon in the arsenal aimed at family life and sex education in the late 60's actually it was, together with masturbation, abortion, homosexuality, illegitimacy, and other related topics, only part of the total argument. The dispute can be seen to center on church-state relationships, the use of science rather than revelation in teaching about the family and sex, and the kind of society sought by conflicting political groups.

With the best of motives but with inadequate appreciation for the complexities and the irreversibilities, many parents wanted the schools to act as a brake on the runaway train of change. Few parents were willing to recognize that they in their own youth and in present marital relationships did not live up to the preachments they were asking family life and sex educators to enunciate in the classroom. In the 60's the Kinsey reports were often cited as though they described the youth of today instead of their parents and grandparents (Somerville, 1968).

It is a principle of religious freedom in the USA that people may indeed live by the dictates of their churches. Many family life and sex education workshops and meetings have been made available within the framework of church educational programs (National Council of Churches et al., 1968). Many church leaders have sought to keep up with the research findings in the family field by membership in NCFR and by attendance at its annual meetings. Special conferences have also taken place in the 60's such as a week-long set of meetings called by the Canadian Council of Churches and the National Council of Churches of Christ in the USA in 1961 where more than 500 Protestant clergymen met with sociologists and psychologists (Duvall, 1961).

Just as the teaching of evolutionary theory in schools has been opposed and still is in some jurisdictions (California State Department of Education, 1969:64) there is fear that the scientific approach in family life and sex education will reduce religious faith. The split among churches on this issue became dramatically evident in the late 60's when the more extreme attacks on family life and sex education programs were tied in with political movements some of which sought to violate the constitutional guaranties of separation of church and state and to prevent the application of pluralistic principles.

Despite the hue and cry in the late 60's (U.S. News and World Report, 1969; Ulman, 1969; Zazzaro, 1969), most of the family life and sex education programs in this decade as in previous decades had been supportive of conventional sex-value systems and only faintly reflective of the franker level of discussion that characterized the arts and the mass media. A national magazine had concluded that "most sex education tries to perpetuate by sweet reasonableness, the same morality that was once enforceable by social or religious canon and parental fiat" (*Time*, 1964). Of the Anaheim program, brought to a close in 1969 with the election of a new school board, it was said: "Though the moralizing is camouflaged, the course relies heavily on case histories which point up the dread consequences of unwanted pregnancies and the danger of contracting venereal diseases" (Powers and Baskin, 1969:22).

the young child

The fears of some parents and teachers that family life and sex education will be "the wrong kind," came to a head in the late 60's on the issue of such education for the very young. This was not immediately discernible. As late as 1967 even a responsible journalist could declare: "In the early grades, sex education, far from being controversial, strikes most people as rather cute" (Goodman, 1967:65). But by 1969 another widely distributed journal was reporting that "The issue is sex education for little children" and "the recent shift of sex education to the elementary grades has stoked anger, fear, and mistrust" (*Life*, 1969).

Kindergarten and elementary schools as logical starting places for family life education, however informal and flexible the actual teaching, had been endorsed and to some extent used in the decades preceding the 60's. Good teacher education in early childhood programs had stressed the teachable moment, the desirability of allaying fears and satisfying curiosity, and helping young children develop acceptance of themselves, their friends, and their families. Some teachers used "organized conversations," puppets, and reading aloud as means for allowing feelings to be expressed and knowledge to be acquired. The 40's and 50's were marked, perhaps, by a tendency to overemphasize happiness in family relationships, to take a somewhat narrow view of "proper" family structure and functioning, and to make short work of sex questions. One guide declared in the 40's: "Questions about sex, if there are any . . . should be answered simply and not elaborated upon" (Stevenson, 1946:51).

In the 60's more specific sex education programs were directed at the primary grades (*Medical World News*, 1965; Minnesota State Department of Education, 1970; *Scholastic Teacher*, 1967).

During the conflict of the late 60's, both sides tended to blame the other for making an issue of sex education for young children. Moreover, many parents were not able to reconcile themselves to having children able to discuss sex with relative ease, since their own educational experiences rarely had given them the same competency. The moral issue was raised, too. The various assurances given that sexual promiscuity was more rooted in a poor self-image and ignorance of consequences, and that early sexual play among children was common in any case, were not accepted by large numbers of anxious parents.

At the adolescent level, similar parental fears but with different curriculum implications intruded into the educational picture of the 60's. Many sought extended sex education as a kind of vaccination against premarital intercourse, abortion, unplanned pregnancy, and venereal disease. The arguments for sex education expansion offered by many community councils of parents, educators, and representative citizens bore little relation in some instances to the more cautious view of the seasoned family life educator expressed in the literature: "While specific social and personal problems dramatize our lack of knowledge, insights and competence, family life education does not focus primarily on promiscuity, delinquency, illegitimacy, incorrigibility, and the like. Its focus is on how individuals as parts and products of family life may become physically healthy, emotionally secure, understanding, disciplined, responsible, tolerant human beings, with the capacities to support themselves and to care about other human beings" (ASHA, 1966:11).

There was widespread anticipation among many professionals of mental health benefits from both reduction of guilt as a basis for decision-making and the support which school family life and sex education programs could offer youth in coping with negative consequences of unwise decisions. However, it became evident in 1968 and 1969 that many parents, in addition to the organized opposition, were not reconciled to guilt reduction, regarding guilt as insurance against evil behavior and as deserved punishment for departures from traditional codes.

In addition to these value gaps which split the population in a number of different segments, there was uneasiness in the communities as it became evident that some parental fears concerning programs and teacher qualifications had a realistic basis. There is little agreement among educators as yet concerning the sequential family life and sex education experiences that should be offered at any stage of the individual life cycle. Careful evaluation of differing programs might suggest the variables involved, but little has yet been done in comparison of programs. As Chilman (1969) puts it, "No research has been done on how information about sex is best imparted, what its content should be, or what the effects of sex education are" (p. 65). Most family life and sex education programs have not been open to outside observation and evaluation, and as a result there has been almost complete dependence on self-report of those involved in the given program. Moreover, with the diversity of course goals, time, quality of faculty, school atmosphere, etc., the measurement of a single program or a group will not permit easy generalization.

A case in point is the issue of separation of the sexes in the classroom. Some hold that the communication barriers between men and women are widespread and there is a need for more rather than fewer opportunities in which boys and girls search together for definitions of roles and clarification of expectations. Community demand for segregated classes sometimes derives from standards of modesty that do not fit well into the out-of-school experiences of young people. Again, there would seem to be a need for the community to permit various kinds of programs to be tried and for the professionals to test their hypotheses and at the least to recognize them as such rather than as proven truths.

who shall teach?

While parental fears about teacher competency have been complicated by issues of values, there has undoubtedly been justifiable concern about level of knowledge in the family life and sex education classes. The issue became particularly acute in the late 60's when it became evident that the rush into sex education of the mid-60's had proceeded without adequate attention to teacher preparation. Manley (1969) sees "the curriculum for prospective teachers of health" as "generally inadequate," with no attempt to deal with sex "as a teaching area in which a future teacher would have to be proficient" (p. 54, 55). Malfetti and Rubin (1967), serving as consultants to a survey undertaken by the Information Center on Population Problems, declared, "There is a shortage of persons equipped to teach even the most rudimentary facts of human reproduction." Few teacher education institutions were found in the 1967 survey to be preparing sex educators in any definition of the term (Information Center on Population Problems, 1967). A survey of school districts involving almost a million students in 1961–1963 showed that in the majority of such districts physical education teachers tended to be "also the health education instructors" (Slipcevich, 1964:27). Colleges were urged to revise their curricula (Johnson, 1967).

The National Council on Family Relations has taken the position that those who teach in family life and sex education programs need to have certain academic and field experiences along with opportunities for self-awareness and supervised practice. The establishment of criteria avoids the fruitless struggle among disciplines for hegemony in the field (Somerville, 1970). However, there may still be some disagreement in colleges and universities as to which disciplines should be involved in offering the core experiences. In one institution it may be the psychology department, in another home economics, in still others health education or sociology, or a combination of these. While certification of teachers has come increasingly under criticism in some fields, it has not been tried in family life and sex education and may be one of the mechanisms whereby the many disciplines involved can be encouraged to meet nationally recognized standards. Clark Vincent (1967) points out that we require certification for language teachers and none for teaching family life and sex education "although marriage and human sexuality are far more complex subjects than any foreign language" (p. 51). The issue of who shall teach will undoubtedly persist well into the 70's. In addition to NCFR criteria, several state departments of education have formulated their own standards. Doctoral dissertations will undoubtedly be increasingly devoted to the issue. It is not difficult to foresee a problem in reconciling the various sets of criteria, and possible confusion for college administrators and public alike.

the issue of privacy

Still unsettled in the aftermath of the turbulent final years of the decade is the issue of privacy. Parents are understandably concerned about revelations children may make in family life and sex education classes involving their own family life. Just as the doctor or social worker is the recipient of much personal data and is expected to maintain high standards of confidentiality, so too the family life and sex educator with better preparation will be less liable to violate professional standards. At the same time parents will have to recognize that schools are not to be blamed for the negative view their children may have of marriage and family life. In a study of thousands of 8th through 12th graders, Duvall (1965) found "less than half of these students wanting their marriage to be like their parents'." In the industrial areas, only four percent of the boys wanted to reproduce their parents' patterns in their own plans for marriage" (p. 97). It is important for the classroom to permit that kind of airing of discontent that permits inconsistent and unrealistic expectations of marriage and family life to come to light and to encourage students to examine causes of behaviors and alternative solutions to problems. Moreover, many teachers have learned to develop classroom safeguards which allow the problem and not the child or his family to become a discussion focus. On the other hand, parent education may help reduce excessive concern with privacy as parents learn to reevaluate their own attitudes and personal behaviors. The 1960's offered little improvement in teacher skills and parent tolerance, and the privacy issue loomed even larger by the end of the decade (Kerckhoff et al., 1970). Crude legislative intrusions did little to solve a delicate problem. Thus, Senate Bill 669 approved by Governor Reagan, July 31, 1968, changed the California Education Code by requiring written notification to parents and written permission from parents before any pupil in K-12 classes can be given a "test, questionnaire, survey, or examination containing any questions about the pupil's personal beliefs or practices in sex, family life, morality, and religion" or any questions about his parents' beliefs and practices in these areas.

FAMILY LIFE AND SEX EDUCATION OVERSEAS

The ferment that marked the American scene in the 60's had its counterparts abroad, although no country had anything similar to the organized opposition to family life and sex education that developed in the United States at the end of the decade. The Groves Conference on Marriage and the Family, meetings of the International Planned Parenthood Federation, and meetings of NCFR, ASHA, and SIECUS all brought attention from 1965 to 1970 to the development of new programs in many parts of the world. Some took paths not widely trod in the USA, as in the reliance upon volunteers, while others watched the American scene closely and used materials and personnel from here. Only brief mention can be made of a few of the highlights.

Canada, the site of the NCFR annual meeting in 1965, had at that time no university offering any course specifically to prepare the teacher of family life or sex education. Some of the local schools had been offering boys and girls separately a brief unit on reproduction within the health or science course or in special evening lectures by doctors or nurses. Some schools called this family life education as "a less disturbing name" than sex education (Guest, 1966). Also, in many schools aspects of family life and sex education had been included within a variety of subjects, Personal Development, Psychology, Sociology, and Home Economics (Alberta Province) as well as in Biology (Saskatchewan and Ontario). It was only after some twenty years of this pattern (Canadian Education Association, 1964) throughout Canada that in the mid-60's an effort was made in Winnepeg to create an interprofessional committee in which representatives from the clergy, the YWCA, health educators, the Child Guidance Clinic, and the Home and School Associations would meet on a regular basis for a year or two to work out the kind of program they would like their community to offer. The founding of the Vanier Institute of the Family in Canada in 1965 resulted in a number of activities. Family Life Education is one of its concerns and it has sponsored a survey which was begun in 1967, and is currently still under way, to discover and classify all programs now offered in churches, schools, social agencies, and other institutions in Canada. Preliminary returns indicate that 1,529 schools among those responding have reported involvement with family life education while almost twice that number, 2,946, reported no involvement. In universities and colleges, 163 of 308 responded and of these 136 were involved and 27 were not (Vanier Institute Annual Report 1969a, 25–27). There would seem to be some basis for the announcement in 1970 that "Family life programs are springing up all over" (*Transition*). Both reflective of this expansion and a spur to it was the National Consultation on Family Life Education sponsored in 1969 at Baniff by the Vanier Institute (1969b) which brought government and organization representatives together from the various provinces to make recommendations concerning family life education. One college in Canada has begun to publish "The Family Life Educator," a newsletter reporting new courses, books, and teaching concerns. With all this activity, there is, however, a degree of reliance upon teacher educators from the USA as staff for Canadian workshops which suggests a lag in development yet to be overcome.

In Great Britain, family life and sex education is at an early stage quantitatively, even more so inside the schools than outside where youth clubs and adult organizations have had various brief series offered them. Health education personnel predominate in the school program of a city like Leeds (Paget, 1965:58) serving as peripatetic teachers in the familiar San Diego pattern, while in Gloucester teachers in the school are given brief training for this responsibility (Paget, 1965:54). The use of volunteers, carefully selected by the National Marriage Guidance Council and given some preparation, became widespread when the counselor movement spread to the family life and sex education field in the 60's. "The education work of the NMGG has grown steadily during the last twelve years," it was reported in 1968, "and today our counsellors, who are all volunteers, are also running discussion groups in schools, colleges, youth clubs and other institutions, in many different parts of Great Britain" (Sanctuary, 1968). In mid-decade only the University of Edinburgh among 23 responding to a researcher's request for information had a university program in family life education. The lack of parent education programs was also seen as a retarding influence.

In Australia in the 60's a pattern developed similar to Britain's in which there is mainly as yet reliance upon Marriage Guidance Organizations to "offer lecture courses or discussion programmes in marriage and family living to help young people prepare for marriage" (Attorney-General, 1966). The organizations approved by the Attorney-General as marriage guidance organizations in the first half of the 60's include welfare agencies and religious institutions as well as regional branches of the national MGC.

In New Zealand where the Justice Department decided early in the decade to enter the field of marriage counseling in order to safeguard standards and, as in Britain, have the national government offer financial aid in selection and preparation of personnel, the work was extended by mid-decade to family life and sex education in secondary schools. As in Britain, lay people were accepted for training as counselors and family life educators. Unlike professionals, their accreditation has to be newly established in each community in which they work. While there had been nothing in the law to stop the introduction of family life courses in primary or secondary schools, the lack of prepared teachers had been a factor in delay. By using the men and women volunteers selected and trained by the MGC, schools could test parent response and if this were negative, withdraw them more easily as the courses would not be a firm part of school curriculum and teacher assignment (Clements, 1970).

The International Planned Parenthood Federation (1970), interested in having population programs in formal educational systems in order to help develop "rational knowledge of sex and reproduction, together with an understanding of the responsibilities involved in interpersonal relationships" brought representatives of fourteen countries together in late 1969 to identify common aims in Responsible Parenthood and Sex Education (REPASE) and to arrive at standards concerning content and teacher selection. Recognition of the need for an informed body of parents and of a receptive public generally led to the conclusion that early efforts in family life and sex education would place reliance upon volunteers and concentrate on innovative programs to establish what can be done.

In Chile, preparation for family life education to be introduced into the school system included visits to the United States and Europe to ascertain what kinds of programs and teacher education were found effective. The team included a psychologist and a sociologist. Their tour in this country was financed by the United States government (*Social Health News* 1969). The demand for such education had been voiced by teenagers in 1967 when a public session on Youth and Sex had been opened to them in Santiago by an international conference (*Planned Parenthood News* 1967).

In the African nations where family patterns are changing rapidly and traditional sources of sex education are less available to the urbanized population, the usefulness of new programs is recognized. Many obstacles exist, including the need to develop a behavioral sciences base, the desirablity of including secular groups in an area dominated by religious pressure, especially since the traditional emphasis is often inappropriate, and the lack of published material pertinent to the local conditions.

Sweden and Denmark attracted the attention of American magazines in the 60's to an extent that makes fact and fiction difficult to separate in the realm of family life and sex education. This served to confuse the public many of whom thought Sweden, for example, had had a model program and that its inadequacies foredoomed American attempts (Moskin, 1966). The professional was aware through the corrective of authoritative books such as Linner's (1967) or reports at conferences such as Wickbom's (1967) that the Scandinavian experience was not offered as a model but modestly recognized its own problem in teacher preparation and parental consensus. Swedish sex education, begun in the 40's and made compulsory in the 50's, was integrated into the national curriculum for all school-age children from first grade on in 1962. "Sex education is given chiefly in the biological lessons but according to recommendations from the National Board of Education it is touched upon also in . . . other subjects in which questions of sex may arise naturally," the headmaster of Katrineholm Secondary School, near Stockholm, reported recently. In the final year of compulsory schooling, the ninth grade when boys or girls are 15 and 16, the amount of time in the school curriculum is increased and for students who continue in school, the teachers' handbook on sex instruction issued by the Royal Board of Education includes additional topics to be covered. Television and radio add to school coverage. However, not all teachers feel adequately prepared and there is some tendency to avoid the responsibility.

In France, schools are not permitted to include sex education in the curriculum. Evening courses are arranged for parents. There has been little study as yet of the kind and extent of children's learnings through the parents, or indeed of the parents' own learnings.

In the countries of Eastern Europe a lack of family life and sex education programs has persisted; the repeated demands for curriculum expansion in this direction may be supported by recently increased research on the family and the publication in educational journals of proposed new courses (Somerville, 1965; Zverev, 1968).

SUMMARY

For four decades family life and sex education has struggled against an array of disciplinary, conceptual, and public relations obstacles to achieve a secure place in community and school programs. Many governmental and private agencies have contributed funds, personnel, and imaginative effort. In the 60's the sudden burgeoning of specialized programs in sex education, although unsupported by a commensurate reckoning of teacher preparedness, brought strong public reaction, at first favorable and often over-eager, but in the final years of the decade questioning and among some groups harshly critical. In some instances, proponents of such programs were vulnerable on the grounds of ill-defined goals or questionable premises. In others, political malice grossly exaggerated shortcomings. The situation threatened to polarize family life educators. The irrationality and the political machinations of fundamentalist and anti-democratic minorities alienated most professionals, however, and both individuals and organizations were stirred to dissociate themselves from the extreme attacks. Position statements were issued by various organizations stating their belief in the validity of family life and sex education. The challenge for family life educators to recognize more fully the sexual dimensions of their subject matter and for sex educators to recognize more fully the psychosocial dimensions has brought a measure of theoretical unity to the whole field.

However, many issues have not been settled. Evaluation studies, experimental programs, agreement on teacher preparation criteria and expansion of teacher education, as well as parent education may have to be high on the priority lists of the 70's if progress is to be made. While undoubtedly more education of the public will be necessary to offset the confusion sown by the organized opposition, a recent survey shows that this confusion, although serious, has not stopped many communities from undertaking or continuing the study of ways of developing programs (Force, 1970). There seems to be little retreat among some of the religious groups. A survey by the United States Catholic Conference, Family Life Division, found one-third of the dioceses offering or preparing to offer programs (Boston, 1969) and it is expected that increasing numbers of the 12,000 Catholic schools with their five million elementary and secondary school students, will follow suit (McHugh, 1968). The variety of the Catholic programs reveal awareness of community differences and cooperation with secular schools systems in workshops for teachers and adaptations of teaching guides (McHugh, 1969).

Undetermined yet is the amount of governmental aid that can be expected in the 70's. Here and there, mention is made of federal funds that have underwritten new programs, such as that at New York University. There is a general impression that the change of political administration curtailed some financial support on the federal level. The Children's Bureau had announced in the 60's that improving family life education was one of its current emphases and it was cooperating toward this goal with several other federal agencies through a Subcommittee on Parent and Family Life Education of the Interdepartmental Committee on Children and Youth. The establishment of the Office of Child Development in 1970 within the Department of Health, Education, and Welfare may have positive effects on the Federal Government's recognition of the need for studying and expanding family life and sex education programs. Major reliance will undoubtedly continue to be on private foundations, university grants, and the donation of time and effort by leaders in the field.

Legislatively the field of family life and sex education continues to be wide open. According to one survey, as late as June 1969, "most states had no law either authorizing or prohibiting the teaching of sex or birth control education in their schools" (Rodick, p. 157). However, this can change abruptly, and the California experience has shown that restrictions on material to be used in the classroom, as in the Schmitz bill, can in only a few months so threaten teacher effectiveness that new legislation must be proposed, such as the Rodda bill, to lessen the negative consequences. Governors' Councils continued to function in the 60's (Somerville, 1969).

The flood of materials that poured over the educational scene in the mid-60's will need careful evaluation to ensure that only the best writings and films are adopted for classroom use. Wholesale condemnation based on connection with the name of SIECUS is irrational. California has outlawed not only the few publications offered by that organization but even the books and films recommended by them. Many of these were high-grade materials reviewed and recommended in various professional journals. Similarly reevaluation will have to be made in the 70's of materials rejected earlier. The TV series, "A Time of Your Life," including its most controversial segment, "A New Life," is currently finding additional uses in teacher and parent education. Even for schools, a national magazine reports that "In California, Hawaii, and New York, the opposition has tended to lose its bite as the programs are actually aired" (Jobin, 1970). Generally, the fate of a local program in the menacing atmosphere of the late 60's should not prejudice the materials issued in connection with it or the books written by those temporarily removed from positions of influence (Schulz and Williams, 1968; Cook, 1969).

The turbulence of the 60's shook up the family life and sex education field and left in its wake the need to take stock and to rebuild along new lines offering greater shelter against unexpected or unreasonable furies.

references

AMERICAN ASSOCIATION OF SCHOOL ADMINISTRATORS, *Sixtieth Yearbook.* Washington, D.C.: American Association of School Administrators, 1938.

AMERICAN SOCIAL HEALTH ASSOCIATION, *Family Life Education—A Cause for Action.* American Social Health Association, 1966.

ATTORNEY-GENERAL'S DEPARTMENT, *Organizations Approved by the Attorney-General as Marriage Guidance Organizations under the Provisions of the Matrimonial Causes Act 1959–1966.* Canberra, Australia: The Attorney-General's Department, 1966.

AVERY, CURTIS E., DAVID S. BRODY, and MARGIE E. LEE, *Sex Education: Concepts and Challenges.* Eugene, Oregon: E. C. Brown Center for Family Studies, 1969.

AYRES, WILLIAM H., and MARILYN MC CURDY, *Time of Your Life: Family Life and Health Education for Intermediate Grades.* Preliminary Teachers Guide, Programs 10–15, KQED Instructional Television Service, n.d.

BAKER, LUTHER, "The Rising Furor over Sex Education," *The Family Coordinator* (July 1969).

BAKER, LUTHER, and JAMES B. DARCY, "Survey of Family Life and Sex Education Programs in Washington Secondary Schools," *The Family Coordinator* (July 1970).

BARR, DONALD, "Sex, Love, and Modern Education," *Columbia College Today* (Fall 1967), pp. 35–39.

BECK, LESTER, as quoted in *The Bulletin of the National Association of Secondary School Principals* (December 1955), p. 16.

BOLTON, BENNET, "Bishops Open Drive for Sex Education," *Daily Californian,* September 26, 1969.

BOWMAN, HENRY, "Marriage Education in the Colleges," *Journal of Social Hygiene* (1949).

BRANTLEY, LIB, "How Far Should Schools Go in Family Life Education?" *Winston-Salem Journal,* 1966.

BREASTED, MARY, *Oh! Sex Education!* New York: Praeger, 1970.

BROWN, MURIEL, *With Focus on Family Living.* Washington, D.C.: U.S. Government Printing Office, 1953.

————, "Organizational Programs to Strengthen the Family," in *Handbook of Marriage and the Family*, ed. HAROLD CHRISTENSEN. Chicago: Rand-McNally, 1964.

BURLESON, DEREK L., "Sex Education: What Are the Issues?" *Scholastic Teacher*, April 21, 1967.

CALDERONE, MARY, "Sexual Energy—Constructive or Destructive?" *Western Journal of Surgery, Obstetrics and Gynecology* (November–December 1963).

————, "Sex and Social Responsibility," *Journal of Home Economics* (September 1965).

CALIFORNIA STATE DEPARTMENT OF EDUCATION, *Guidelines for Moral Instruction in California Schools*. Report Accepted by State Board of Education, May 9, 1969.

CANADIAN EDUCATION ASSOCIATION, *The Present Status of Sex Education in Canadian Schools*. Canadian Education Association, September, 1964.

CARRERA, MICHAEL A., *Guidelines for the Preparation of High School Teachers of Sex Education*. Chapter IV, mimeographed.

CHILMAN, CATHERINE S., "Some Social and Psychological Aspects of Sex Education," in *The Individual, Sex, and Society*, eds., CARLFRED BRODERICK and JESSIE BERNARD. Baltimore: Johns Hopkins Press, 1969.

CHRISTENSEN, HAROLD, "The Intrusion of Values," in *Handbook of Marriage and the Family*, ed., HAROLD CHRISTENSEN. Chicago: Rand-McNally, 1964.

————, "The Impact of Culture and Values," in *The Individual, Sex, and Society*, eds., CARLFRED BRODERICK and JESSIE BERNARD. Baltimore: Johns Hopkins Press.

CLEMENTS, L. C., "Criteria for Selection of Sex Educators: A New Zealand Experience." Paper prepared for 1970 SIECUS Conference.

COOK, PAUL W., *Family Life and Sex Education Program in the Anaheim Union High School District*. Mimeographed, 1969.

COOMBS, ROBERT, "Sex Education for Physicians: Is it Adequate?" *The Family Coordinator* (October 1968).

CURRIE, BETTIE, "Elementary School Program Prepares Child for Family Role," *What's New in Home Economics* (May–June 1970).

DAGER, EDWARD Z., and GLENN HARPER, "Family Life Education in Indiana Public Schools: A Preliminary Report," *Marriage and Family Living* (November 1959).

DE NICHOLS, WILLIAM, "A Marketing Specialist Looks at Home Economics," *Focus* (May 1970).

DUVALL, EVELYN M., "How Effective Are Marriage Courses," *Journal of Marriage and the Family* (May 1965).

DUVALL, EVELYN M., and SYLVANUS M. DUVALL, *Sex Ways—In Fact and Faith*. New York: Association Press, 1961.

Family Life Educator (newsletter), published by Sheridan College of Applied Arts and Technology, Brampton, Ontario.

FORCE, ELIZABETH, "Family Life Education Survey Report: Western Region, February 15–March 3, 1970," American Social Health Association, 1970. Mimeographed.

FRANK, LAWRENCE, "The Beginnings of Child Development and Family Life Education in the Twentieth Century," *Merrill-Palmer Quarterly* (October 1962).

FURLONG, WILLIAM BARRY, "It's a Long Way from the Birds and Bees," *The New York Times Magazine,* June 11, 1967.

GOODMAN, WALTER, "The New Sex Education," *Redbook,* September 1967.

GUEST, H. H., *Interim Report of the Interprofessional Study Committee on Family Life Education to the Winnipeg School Board,* May 3, 1966.

INFORMATION CENTER ON POPULATION PROBLEMS, News Release, 1967.

INTERNATIONAL PLANNED PARENTHOOD FEDERATION, WORKING GROUP, "Proceedings of the 1970 International Planned Parenthood Federation, London." Mimeographed.

JEWSON, RUTH H., "Family Life Education as Viewed from the NCFR Mailbag," typewritten report, 1967.

JOBIN, JUDITH, "The Sex Battle Takes on a New Meaning," *TV Guide,* May 2, 1970.

JOHNSON, WARREN R., "The Sexual Revolution and the Colleges: A Challenge to Higher Education," *The Journal of the American College Health Association* (May 1967).

Journal of School Health, "Growth Patterns and Sex Education: A Suggested Program, Kindergarten Through Grade Twelve" (May 1967).

KAPLAN, MORRIS, "Schools Extend V.D. Instruction," *The New York Times,* May 19, 1967.

KERCKHOFF, RICHARD, "Family Life Education in America," in *Handbook of Marriage and the Family,* ed., HAROLD CHRISTENSEN. Chicago: Rand-McNally, 1964.

KERCKHOFF, RICHARD et al., "Community Experiences with the 1969 Attack on Sex Education," *The Family Coordinator* (January 1970).

KIRKENDALL, LESTER A., *Kirkendall on Sex Education: A Collection of Readings.* Eugene, Oregon: E. C. Brown Center for Family Studies, 1970.

KIRKENDALL, LESTER, and ROGER LIBBY, "Sex and Interpersonal Relationships," in *The Individual, Sex, and Society,* eds., CARLFRED BRODERICK and JESSIE BERNARD. Baltimore: Johns Hopkins Press, 1969.

LA HAYE, T. F., *A Christian View of Radical Sex Education.* San Diego: Scott Memorial Baptist Church, n.d.

LANDIS, JUDSON T., "The Teaching of Marriage and Family Courses in Colleges," *Marriage and Family Living,* 1959.

———, "Family Life Education in California." Paper presented at the Miami Meeting of NCFR, 1965.

LIBBY, ROGER W., "Parental Attitudes Toward High School Sex Education Programs," *The Family Coordinator* (July 1970).

Life, "Facing the 'Facts of Life'," September 19, 1969.

LINDQUIST, RITA, "Teach Sex Education as the Fourth 'R'," *What's New in Home Economics* (February 1968).

LINNER, BRIGITTA, *Society and Sex in Sweden*. New York: Pantheon, 1967.

LOCK, FRANK R., "The Challenge of Change," *Obstetrics and Gynecology* (September 1964).

LUCKEY, ELEANORE B., "Helping Children Grow Up Sexually: How? When? By Whom?" *Children* (July–August 1967).

———, "Sex Education and In-Service Training Program," *The Family Coordinator* (April 1968).

MAC ARTHUR, ARTHUR, "Family Life Education Through Extension Programs," *Journal of Marriage and the Family* (August 1967).

MACE, DAVID, "Should Parents Undertake Sex Education at All?" Paper presented at the Groves Conference on Marriage and the Family, Baltimore, 1963.

MALFETTI, JAMES, and ARLINE RUBIN, "Sex Education: Who Is Teaching the Teachers?" *Teachers College Record* (December 1967).

MANLEY, HELEN, "Starting a Program of Sex Education," in *The Individual, Sex, and Society*, eds. Carlfred Broderick and Jessie Bernard. Baltimore: Johns Hopkins Press, 1969.

MARLAND, S. P. JR., "Placing Sex Education in the Curriculum," *Phi Delta Kappan*, 43 (December 1961), 132–34.

MARTINSON, FLOYD M., *Sexual Knowledge, Values and Behavior Patterns: With Especial Reference to Minnesota Youth*. St. Peter, Minn.: Gustavus Adolphus College, 1966.

MATHIAS, JAMES L., "What Doctors Don't Know About Sex," *Medical Economics* (December 12, 1966).

MC CONNELL, EDIE, "The History of Home Economics Education," *Forecast for Home Economics*, Part 1, September; Part 2, October, 1970.

MC CUNE, SHIRLEY D., and BETTY JONES, "Camp Fire Girls Final Report, Potomac Area Council, December 1967," Washington, D.C., mimeographed, 1967.

MC HUGH, JAMES T., "Sex Education in Catholic Schools: An Overview of Diocesan Programs," *Catholic School Journal* (March 1968).

MC HUGH, JAMES T., ed., *Sex Education: A Guide for Teachers*. Washington, D.C.: Family Life Division, United States Catholic Conference, 1969.

Medical World News, "Biologist Suggests Sex Talks to Toddlers," (December 3, 1965).

Minnesota State Department of Education, *Guidelines for Family Life and Sex Education, Grades K-12*. Curriculum Bulletin No. 32, 1970.

MORGAN, MILDRED, "Family Life and Sex Education in the Schools," *Social Health News* (June 1966).

MOSKIN, J. ROBERT, "Sweden's New Battle over Sex," *Look*, November 15, 1966.

National Council of Churches, Synagogue Council of America,

United States Catholic Conference, *Interfaith Statement on Sex Education,* June 8, 1968.

Newsweek, "The Morals Revolution on the United States Campus," April 16, 1964.

PAGET, NORMAN, *Education for Family Living in the United Kingdom.* Buffalo, N.Y.: DeGrey, 1965.

PIERETTI, GENEVIEVE, "A Guide for Teaching Personal and Family Relationships," *Home Economics Education* (November 1963).

Planned Parenthood News, "Students Turn Out for Sex," May, 1967.

POWERS, G. PAT, and WADE BASKIN, *Sex Education: Issues and Directives.* New York: Philosophical Library, 1969.

REISS, IRA, ed., "The Sexual Renaissance of America," *Journal of Social Issues* (April 1966).

The Royal Board of Education in Sweden, *Handbook on Sex Instruction in Swedish Schools.* Stockholm: The Royal Board of Education, n.d.

RUTLEDGE, AARON L. et al., "Sex Ethics, Sex Acts, and Human Need: A Dialogue," *Pastoral Psychology* (October–November 1961).

SANCTUARY, GERALD, "Family Life Education in Britain," paper presented at the Groves Conference on Marriage and the Family, Boston, 1968.

Scholastic Teacher, "Sex Education in the Elementary Schools," April 21, 1967.

SCHULZ, ESTHER D., and SALLY R. WILLIAMS, *Family Life and Sex Education: Curriculum and Instruction.* New York: Harcourt, Brace and World, 1968.

SCRIVEN, MICHAEL, "Putting the Sex Back into Sex Education," *Phi Delta Kappan* (May 1968).

SHIMMEL, GILBERT M., and MICHAEL A. CARRERA, "Guidelines for Teacher Preparation Programs," *SIECUS Newsletter,* April 1970.

SIECUS, *Newsletter,* 1965 and 1970.

SLIPCEVICH, ELENA, *School Health Education Study: Summary Report of a Nationwide Study of Health Instruction in the Public Schools, 1961–1963.* Washington, D.C., 1964.

Social Health News, 1969.

SOMERVILLE, ROSE M., "The Family in Yugoslavia," *Journal of Marriage and the Family* (August 1965).

————, "Family Life and Sex Education: Proposed Criteria for Teacher Education," *The Family Coordinator* (April 1970).

————, "Governors' Councils and Family Life Programs," *The Family Coordinator* (January 1969).

————, "New Materials for Study of the Family: Study of Sexual Aspects of Family Relationships," *Journal of Marriage and the Family* (August 1966).

————, "The Relationship Between Family Life and Sex Education," *Journal of Marriage and the Family* (May 1967).

————, "The Sexual Revolution?" Keynote address at the Symposium on Sex and Family Life Education, University of California, Irvine, March 1, 1968.

SOUTHARD, HELEN, "The Revolution in Sex Education: What Schools Can Do," *Teaching and Learning* (1967).

————, Communication to the author, November 18, 1970, including questionnaire used in the summer of 1970 with 15 and 16 year-old girls.

————, "Readers' Guide," *YWCA Magazine,* January 1971.

SRSS Newsletter, American Sociological Association, Spring 1970.

STEVENSON, ELIZABETH, *Home and Family Life Education in Elementary Schools.* New York: John Wiley, 1946.

Time, "Sex in the U.S.: Mores and Morality," January 24, 1964.

Transition, Quarterly Newsletter, Vanier Institute of the Family, 1970.

ULMAN, NEIL, "A Delicate Subject: Sex Education Courses are Suddenly Assailed by Many Parent Groups," *The Wall Street Journal,* April 11, 1969.

U.S. News and World Report, "Why the Furor Over Sex Education," August 4, 1969.

Vanier Institute: Annual Report for year ended December 31, 1969. Mimeographed (1969a); a kaleidoscope report of a National Consultation on Family Life Education, Banff, Alberta, September 7–10. Mimeographed (1969b).

VINCENT, CLARK, "The Pregnant Single College Girl," *The Journal of the American College Health Association* (May 1967).

WAKE, F. R., "Are Parents the Best Sex Educators?" *PTA Magazine,* November 1966.

What's New in Home Economics, "Skills Found Lacking" (April–May 1968).

————, "Follow the Signs," (November–December 1970).

White House Conference on Children and Youth, *Recommendations: Composite Report of Forum Findings.* Washington, D.C.: U.S. Government Printing Office, 1960.

THE RELATIONSHIP BETWEEN FAMILY LIFE EDUCATION AND SEX EDUCATION

INTRODUCTION *

The urgency of the need to clarify the relationship between family life education and sex education became manifest in a panel discussion at the 1966 meet-

---

* By Rose M. Somerville, editor of a series of articles on this subject. Reprinted with permission of the National Council on Family Relations from *The Journal of Marriage and the Family,* May 1967.

ing of the National Council on Family Relations, held at Minneapolis in October. While this relationship is an old issue, it has been fanned to new flame by the winds of change blowing in from increased community demand for curriculum expansion,[1] declarations and resolutions of governmental authorities and professional associations,[2] franker programs offered in the mass media,[3] and the establishment of new agencies, commissions, and committees.[4]

---

[1] Those who serve as consultants to boards of education in various communities or as speakers and discussion leaders are finding themselves deluged with requests. The mailbags of professional organizations and service agencies grow ever heavier. Ruth Jewson, Executive Officer of NCFR, drew up a ten-page listing of excerpts from recent letters asking for help in formulating curriculum proposals, in evaluating programs, and in acquiring classroom materials. They pertain to every level of education and diverse disciplines. They concern general populations and very specialized ones, such as the men in a penitentiary or the families of U.S. naval personnel. The mailbags of the American Social Health Association, the National Council of Churches, the Community Service Society, the Sex Information and Educational Council of the U.S., and many others reflect a similar ferment.

[2] Most noteworthy is the statement issued by Harold Howe, Commissioner of Education in the Department of Health, Education, and Welfare, in Washington, August 30, 1966. "Policy on Family Life Education and Sex Education: The United States Office of Education takes the position that each community and educational institution must determine the role it should play in the area of family life education and sex education; that only the community and its agencies and institutions can know what is desirable, what is possible, and what is wise for them in this realm. To assist communities and educational institutions which wish to initiate or improve programs in this area, the Office of Education will support family life education and sex education as an integral part of the curriculum from preschool to college and adult levels; it will support training for teachers and health and guidance personnel at all levels of instruction; it will give aid programs designed to help parents carry out their roles in family life education and sex education; and it will support research and development in all aspects of family life education and sex education. The Office will work closely with other agencies, both federal and state, to insure the most effective use of our resources in the implementation of this policy."

Among recent resolutions is that adopted by the American Association for Health, Physical Education, and Recreation, a department of the National Education Association, at its annual convention in March, 1966: That the AAHPER urge colleges and universities to include family living instruction, including sex education in the general education of all students."

[3] Not only are classroom bulletin boards covered with articles taken from *Look, Redbood, McCall's*, and other periodicals with mass distribution, but television has offered programs dealing with once-taboo subjects, such as abortion, illegitimacy, etc. Ira L. Reiss reminds us of "thirty years ago when the Surgeon General of the U.S. was not allowed to use the word syphilis on the radio." *The Sexual Renaissance in America*, special issue of *The Journal of Social Issues*, April, 1966, p. 2.

[4] Governors in various states have established advisory commissions on the family, on youth, on women; offices of education in various states have set up special committees for study of curriculum expansion; NCFR has created a family life education commission and is considering the publication of a new journal; SIECUS was established in 1965 "to help bring about, *within* the framework of family life education, constructive dialogue between youth and adults on the pros and cons of the various sexual patterns that can be identified in American life." Wallace Fulton, *SIECUS Newsletter*, February, 1965, p. 1. The Canadian Education Association has conducted a survey of ten provincial departments of education as well as 55 urban school systems to determine how much sex education was given either as a separate program or as part of regular subjects. *The Present States of Sex Education in Canadian Schools*, Research and Information Division, CEA, Report No. 2, September, 1964, 22 pp.

TEACHER EXCHANGE [5] within weeks of the Minneapolis meeting, had extended an invitation to some 40 NCFR members to contribute brief articles on this problem. They were selected from various regions of the United States and Canada and included those whose work in teacher education institutions and community agencies represented not only diverse disciplines but familiarity with ongoing programs in schools and churches, in private and public agencies. It was expected that on such short notice, to meet a February deadline, and at a busy holiday season, there would be response from only a few. However, more articles were forthcoming than can be published in a single issue. It is the hope of TEACHER EXCHANGE that by publishing a few of these manuscripts, in whole or in part, the groundwork can be laid for the extended discussion which the subject merits in the many workshops on the family which will be offered in the summer months ahead as well as the regular courses in the new school year.

Since several of the articles refer to the definitions and the questions in the original invitation to submit manuscripts, our readers will doubtless wish to be acquainted with these. It was recognized that yeoman work had already been performed by leaders in the family field in defining the subject matter and the goals of family life education,[6] but it was felt that some brief operative definitions were necessary to serve as a point of takeoff for the contributors to this particular project, although each was encouraged to "offer your own definitions if preferred." The following "definitions for purposes of discussion" were offered:

> Family life education is the study of the behavior of people as family members. It is based on the findings of the social sciences, psychology, and a number of other disciplines. While historical and cross-cultural perspective is sought, the emphasis is largely on contemporary attitudes and activities in the United States. This is to broaden the student's understanding of the alternatives from which he can choose in his functioning as a family member in a changing society which brings new responsibilities and opportunities in spousal, parental, filial, sibling, and grandparental roles.
>
> Sex education is the study of the biological and culturally-learned sexual needs of men and women, and how these can find fulfillment in ways that are consistent with stable family life. Knowledge of physiology serves as the basis for a view of individual sexuality as a part of total personality, with sexual behavior the result of self-understanding, value priorities, and changing community norms.

After the definitions there was a listing of "possible questions for clarification," as follows. (A footnote invited the formulation of better questions and a freedom to "concentrate on a single issue which appears to you to be central in any discussion of the relationship between family life education and sex education.")

---

[5] A section of *The Journal of Marriage and the Family* edited by Dr. Rose M. Somerville.

[6] Curtis E. Avery, Lester Kirkendall, and Margie R. Lee, aided by the E. C. Brown Trust in Oregon, labored long and well in this regard. Their articles appear in the *Family Life Coordinator.* In addition to those cited in the following pages, the reader may wish to consider Curtis E. Avery, "Sex Education through Rose Colored Glasses," *Family Life Coordinator,* Vol. XIII (November 4, 1964), pp. 83–90. Reprints are available at 25 cents from E. C. Brown Trust Foundation, 3170 S.W. 87th Avenue, Portland, Oregon 97225.

1. If family life courses and sex courses are offered separately in a given school, is there educational validity to such separation, or is it an historical accident which should be changed if possible?

2. If family life courses are designed so as to include the sexual dimension of each topic studied (dating, mate selection, spousal relationships, family disorganization, aging, etc.), is there a need for sex education courses? Is any family life course justified in omitting the sexual dimension?

3. If sex courses are designed to include the family relationships dimension of each topic studied (menstruation, pre-marital sexual behaviors, reproduction, etc.), is there a need for family life courses? Is any sex education course justified in omitting the family relationships dimension?

4. Are there problems of staffing that are greater in 2 above than in 3, or vice versa? Where visiting teachers are used, rather than pemanent members of the school's faculty, what kinds of problems arise?

5. Is there a minimum duration necessary for any course, whether family life or sex education, to achieve its goals? What is the place of one-shot sessions, short series, or brief units, or indeed school club hours, rather than semester or year-long courses?

6. Taking cognizance of the size of today's classes in K-12 grades, particularly in the public schools, which teaching methods are possible and how can a climate be provided in which facts and attitudes are examined and discussed?

7. How can articulation be achieved both in grade levels and in topics when responsibility for coverage is divided among various departments, when for example, health educators teach sex courses (or units within health courses) and home economics and social studies educators teach family development?

8. How can the special competencies of the guidance counselor, the school nurse, the literature teacher, the biology teacher, etc., be utilized in family life or sex courses?

9. Is a widescale program of teacher education necessary for curriculum expansion and is this to be undertaken simultaneously with teaching such courses (in-service) or as a prerequisite? Which courses are basic in the preparation of teachers to meet the needs of their diverse student populations who represent a broad spectrum of socioeconomic and ethnic backgrounds? Which procedures can best ensure teacher readiness (certification, etc.)?

10. Should family life or sex courses be elective or required?

11. At what intervals (in which grades) should courses be offered during the K–12 years?

12. What kinds of parent education programs should accompany the introduction or expansion of curriculum offerings? How can schools, churches, extension services, and social agencies work together *towards lifelong study of family relationships?*

It will be evident that the articles that follow helped clarify some of these matters. Perhaps most noteworthy is the general agreement that family life education is broader than sex education and can include the latter in most educational programs.[7]

It will also be evident that the articles raise a number of other important questions. Perhaps the most basic one is whether by devoting our time to such discussions we are "chasing mice." It is a sobering question, but it may reduce itself to a value issue and perhaps challenge each of us to distinguish between the mice and the elephants in our value systems. There are also some objective, empirical elements involved. Will the willingness to proceed with a limited sex education program in the hopes that it is a "stepping-stone" allow the teachable moment to vanish? It may well be argued that the present favorable climate for curriculum expansion permits the formulation of the most educationally defensible offerings. Moreover, there is some question concerning the educator's responsibility in bandwagon movements or a new kind of conformity. If sex education is "in," perhaps this derives from our own failure to clarify to our communities both the difference between reproduction education and sex education and between social ills that can be mitigated by education and those that require more extensive social action.

Or to use the figure of another of our contributors, if there has been a "forced birth of sex education," do we now assume the role of complacent godparents or do we frankly recognize the weaknesses and insist on the special nurturing that prematurities require? [8]

While in a few happy instances the doubts raised by one contributor are answered by another, as for example when it was shown that the middle-class nurse or teacher could go beyond "hearing about" to "knowing" the relationships in lower-income families, in many other instances the doubts must linger. For example, are curriculum guides and course outlines accurate indicators of the degree to which sexual aspects of topics are actually explored in the classroom? Even where sex education is required in a school system, as in Sweden, the reluctant teacher can manage to omit the areas with which he is uncomfortable. And contrariwise, the least promising guides and outlines can be interpreted by an experienced teacher in a way that is consonant with the fullest

---

[7] This agreement seems to go beyond national boundaries. A report of the UNESCO Institute for Education declares: "Sex education is also a part of family life, and rather than teaching it separately, it should be taught within the framework of learning to create a happy family life." *Health Education, Sex Education, and Education for Home and Family: Report on an Expert Meeting, February 17–22, 1964,* Hamburg, 1965, p. 5. Preface by Gustaf Ogren. Cf. also, H. H. Guest, "Interim Report on the Interprofessional Study Committee on Family Life Education to the Winnipeg School Board," May 3, 1966, p. 1: "The committee decided at the outset to refer to its study as 'family life education' because this term put relationships between the sexes in a meaningful context."

[8] Naming the baby may be more than a detail. Some names have resulted in the exclusion of boys from courses they need; others create false expectations or arouse unnecessary opposition. The awkward titling of new courses, workshops, and institutes may be inevitable consequences of negative connotations built up in connection with previous designations. One course to be offered in the summer of 1967 is "Family Life Education with an Emphasis on Sex."

exploration of every topic. Moreover, administrators have begun to cooperate in this.[9] However, it would be instructive for present and future educators in the family field to examine the degree of distrust of the teacher built into some of the syllabi. Will this distrust diminish as the more extended programs of adult education (parents, administrators, teachers) proposed in these articles get under way? Will it diminish also as teacher education moves from brief in-service experiences to long-term professional education? Will it diminish even more markedly as teaching conditions are improved so that every class is small enough for the discussions that are an essential part of the family life teaching process? Some of the summer workshops show awareness of the size factor and either control registration or increase the staff, or both. One workshop scheduled for teacher education in the summer of 1967 will have five regular faculty members and a dozen guest speakers for a student body limited to 60. Will this serve as a model "when winter comes" in that institution or the others to which the workshop members return?

And, finally, it will be evident that to some of our questions the contributors did not address themselves at all, for lack of time or of interest. Perhaps only a series of programs frankly labeled pilot or experimental will suppply the answers.

CREATIVE LITERATURE FOR STUDY
OF THE FAMILY *

There is increasing interest among educators in broadening still further the interdisciplinary field of family study by inclusion of the humanities. It has long been recognized that imaginative writings in all their diverse forms—novels, plays, short stories, poems—depict family interaction perceptively and constitute a rich resource for classroom use. This recognition has not been matched by reported research on the kinds of fiction which would offer most to each academic level or the ways in which a given play or story could be best assigned and discussed. Fortunately, in the last decade the beginnings of such efforts to provide teaching aids have become evident. Appropriately the main organizations of family study specialists have encouraged the presentation of papers and the publication of articles by those of their members who have tested in their classrooms various forms of creative literature; university presses have begun to cooperate in making

---

[9] Cf., *Family Life Education—A Cause for Action*, Documentation of the Family Life Education Project Conducted by the American Social Health Association, 1953–1962, New York: ASHA, 1966, p. 16.

* Introduction by Rose M. Somerville, editor of a series of articles. Published by the *Journal of Marriage and the Family*, May 1966; reprinted with permission of the National Council on Family Relations.

such findings available in convenient form.[1] The most recent of these efforts took place at the 1965 Annual Meeting of the National Council on Family Relations, held in Toronto, where an entire session of the Education Section was devoted to "Creative Literature in Family Life Education." Articles based on both the papers and the audience discussion are offered in our present issue and will continue to be published in future issues if our readers find them helpful.

It will be evident that the efforts are exploratory and the conclusions only tentative. Moreover, most of the work to date has gone on in college and graduate level classes, as well as in adult education. The younger students have been relatively neglected. It can only be conjectured that this may be because family relationships courses and units are newer in the elementary and high schools, and the experimentation that comes with a surer curriculum footing is necessarily delayed. Another possibility is that the family is studied in a narrower range of departments than in higher education and can count on less cross-disciplinary cooperation. Whatever the reasons, the present lag [2] in classroom testing of imaginative literature for family insights constitutes a challenge to K-12 teachers as well as to the master's and doctoral programs of family study centers. The "intelligent guesses" made by the symposiasts in Toronto as to which of the readings used in colleges could also serve the younger student can be verified only by the classroom teachers themselves. They may be able to count on the cooperation of the literature teachers of their schools who have increasingly been exposed to the human relations dimension of fiction.[3] However, this cooperation should proceed on a basis of equality, with the teacher of family relationships offering special awareness of family significances in fiction and the literature teacher offering special awareness of student readiness for various forms of literature. The pages of Teacher Exchange welcome reports on such efforts as well as response to the articles in this issue. The summer months ahead offer the family educator many hours for pleasurable reading in anticipation of the next academic year, when imaginative literature willl be introduced or expanded as a source of family insights in many courses.

---

[1] Cf. Rose M. Somerville, *Family Insights Through the Short Story: A Guide for Teachers and Workshop Leaders.* (New York: Teachers College Press, 1964). The 1966 meeting of the American Home Economics Association, in San Francisco, included a session on the literature approach to family study in which Dr. Somerville was invited to demonstrate the use of fiction for classroom teaching.

[2] The lag may be greater in the reporting of efforts than in actual action research, if the college experience is a clue to other levels.

[3] Various issues of *Elementary English* and *English Journal* have for several decades offered articles which urge that the teaching focus not be limited to the esthetic dimensions of literature.

THE LITERATURE APPROACH TO
TEACHING FAMILY COURSES *

ROSE M. SOMERVILLE

Even farther back than Aristotle, as the parables show, it was known that a well-told tale both evokes feelings and suggests ideas. In using imaginative literature for family insights the educator is faced by a choice as to how much of the one or the other should be emphasized. This choice raises the issue of teaching goals in the family course or unit. There is broad consensus on the following: "To assist the student in developing an understanding of the relationships in modern marriage, and to help him understand himself in relation to the other members of his family." [1] Possibly the sociologist would tend to concentrate on the first of these goals, and the psychologist and home economist on the second; but the increase in functional courses, on the one hand, and the demand for academic excellence, on the other, have tended to spread both goals to many classrooms. Nonetheless, there are shadings of emphasis on scientific knowledge of the family and immediate applications of self-other understanding which distinguish one classroom from another. Does the literature approach lend itself more to the one or the other, or is it equally applicable to all family courses and units?

The answer lies in the fact that fiction with its vast potential for both emotional and rational growth can fit in with whatever emphasis already exists in the classroom. In this sense there might be said to be three literature approaches to teaching family courses. In the first the stories, plays, and novels are examined for what they reveal about a particular cultural setting in which family interaction takes place. Historical and cross-cultural perspective is sought, or the impact of social change on a given society, or the retention of a single stereotype in a culture.[2] Since the goal is learning about objective life conditions and societal

---

* Reprinted from *The Journal of Marriage and the Family*, May 1966, with permission of the National Council on Family Relations.

1 This was the most frequently chosen of the 15 possible goals listed by G. A. Christensen and distributed among 475 school and college family life teachers. G. A. Christensen, "An Analysis of Selected Issues in Family Life Education, 1958," unpublished doctoral dissertation, Michigan State University, 1958.

2 Rose M. Somerville, "Family Images Projected in the Modern Short Story," paper given at the Fifteenth Annual Meeting of the Society for the Study of Social Problems, Chicago, 1965. D. Y. Deegan, *The Stereotype of the Single Woman in American Novels*, New York: King's Crown Press, Columbia University, 1951. The broad implications of reading the fiction of another society in translation are suggested by the following comment by a Moscow student in a senior high school: "I could not conceive until then [until having read Salinger's novel *Catcher in the Rye*] of a young American who could love Burns. I thought that they all loved baseball, that in the evenings they sat in bars and paid very little attention to the fact that poetry and young children exist in the world." L. S. Aiserman, "Contemporary Literature Through the Eyes of Upper-Grade Pupils," *Soviet Education*, January 1965, p. 4.

goals and values—although this may include the subjective reactions of men, women, and children to family role expectations—what is sought is reenforcement of learnings derived from textbooks and reference works. The teacher relies on the emotional strength of the fiction to motivate the student in reading the work and thinking about it, but does not inquire into the emotions roused. Depending on age and ability of students in the given classroom, the whole gamut of literary works can add to cognitive growth. The dramas of ancient Greece, the novels of rural Russia, the short stories of an American metropolis all lend themselves both to the institutional family course or to the one with more academic than functional emphasis.

The very same literature can serve a different approach, although it is not likely that without special help the average student can identify with those characters who do not speak in the contemporary idiom. In this framework of emphasis upon the emotional, the teacher is likely to select modern fiction to facilitate the goal of extending the student's feeling repertoire in relation to family situations. Through this vicarious emotional experience, the student is enabled to live through family challenges that may await him in the future and to penetrate the narrow feeling confines of ordinary daily existence. But just as the first approach to literature emphasizes the rational but does not denigrate the emotional, this second approach rarely relies solely on feelings alone. The teacher either lectures or assigns readings that will provide cognitive underpinnings for the emotional experience. He does, however, tend to give explicit recognition to the feelings roused by the literature.

The third approach seeks to relate the emotional returns from reading fiction to the goal of intellectual growth and in a sense keeps a footing in both the feeling and cognitive worlds of family interaction. This approach resembles, but also differs from the case method of teaching, already long established in professional schools of law, business, medicine, and more recently in psychology, social work, and guidance. The case method has as a typical goal the development of competence in analysis, so that as new problems present themselves the student can utilize already developed skills to cope with them. What teachers of the case method have to say about developing skills of interpretation is highly pertinent to the use of fiction in the family course. Their view of insight as comprising an ability to understand relationships, synthesize disparate facts, and apply abstract concepts lends itself to the goal of cognitive growth through story analysis. The following steps in interpretation are regarded as basic: [3]

---

[3] E. Jackson Baur, "A Student Guide for Interpreting Case Material," *Improving College and University Teaching*, 8 (Summer 1960), pp. 104–108. See also, Hunt and Pearson, "The Case Method of Instruction," *Harvard Educational Review*, Summer 1951; Marston M. McCluggage, "Teaching Sociology by the Case Method," *Midwest Sociologist*, Winter, 1955; K. P. Andrews, ed., *The Case Method of Teaching Human Relations and Administration*, Cambridge, Mass.: Harvard University Press, 1953. An extended illustration of step number one can be found in the interpretive chapters written by Gordon Allport, *Letters from Jenny*, New York: Harcourt, Brace and World, 1965, pp. 148–223, in which he tries out various theoretical frameworks for analyzing the case material offered in Jenny's correspondence. It may be worth exploring how the case and literature approaches lend themselves to the classification of educational goals in the cognitive

1. choosing an appropriate frame of reference, and if more than one conceptual model is employed, making clear which one is being used at a given time;

2. identifying and classifying the parts of the case, whether persons, groups or values;

3. relating these parts to one another by standing back and seeing the case in its entirety, noting which changes in one part are connected with changes in another;

4. explaining these connections, causally if possible, by applying abstract principles or theories and showing that this is a specific instance of a general class of events;

5. applying this knowledge of causes to the realm of prediction or of change, explicitly stating, in connection with any course of action recommended, the objectives and the values involved.

Not every teacher will wish to utilize this rigorous framework. Some may insist that following these steps will inhibit the student's free flow of ideas or that time will not permit these steps to be clearly spelled out with each story. But consciousness of these steps is an undeniable prerequisite for the development of maximum skill in the analysis of a case or a story. It also helps teacher preparation for a given literature experience. Step 4, for example, calls for a background of knowledge concerning psychology and sociology on the part of the student which can be offered through lectures or text and reference readings. Realizing this, the teacher will be aware in assigning fiction that prior or coordinate learning experiences will be called for, and will plan for them in relation to the discussion themes of a particular story or play. There will not always be a precise fit between the student's knowledge of behavioral science and the assigned fiction. This lack of congruence can have a positive value when it alerts the student to additional reading he needs to do or to the gaps that exist in present research in family relationships.

Where fiction and cases part company as teaching resources is not on the level of the cognitive, but of the emotional. If the case is well-written, it may arouse some feelings in the student. However, this is generally considered incidental and rarely put to pedagogical use. Creative literature, on the other hand, is assigned precisely because it is emotion-rousing and offers the student opportunity for identification and empathy. The teacher can count on the heightened emotional involvement of the student to affect positively his sensitivity to the family interaction and thereby his ability to complete step 3 of the interpretation process. Moreover, in courses which stress self-understanding, the stories are valued for facilitating recall, offering reassurance as to normality, and lessen-

---

and affective domains devised by Bloom and his colleagues. Cf., Benjamin Bloom, *et al.,* *Taxonomy of Educational Objectives, Handbook I: Cognitive Domain,* New York: David McKay, 1956, and David R. Krathwohl, *et al., Handbook II: Affective Domain,* New York: David McKay, 1954.

ing defenses against self-exposure. This adds a conscious element of self-examination to the emotional emphasis of the second approach described above, although in an educational setting it stops short of the direct confrontation on which therapy relies.

It should be noted that the fifth of the interpretive steps permits the case or the story to provide a point of departure that will vary with the goals of the course. The "helping professions" orientation will encourage the student to offer a course of action to achieve some goal, "to help individual families from their sorrows." [4] For the future sociologist, more value will be derived from teasing out hypotheses through suggesting changes in some of the variables found in the story, departing from the "givens" of the story, and broadening the examination to include many dimensions not within the creative writer's purview. In this sense, the play or story serves most fully by "getting lost," by turning the attention of the class to wider considerations.

All three approaches, with their many variants or shadings, require decisions as to the amount of time to be given to creative literature and the kinds of written and oral responses to literature that will be expected by the teacher. As to time, while it is possible for a whole course in family relationships or a family unit in a social studies course to be based solely or mainly on creative literature,[5] the more usual use of fiction will be on an occasional basis. Because family-related stories, plays, and novels are numerous and easily available for the most part, as the lists offered in this issue indicate, the decision to use fiction will have to depend on class needs and teacher willingness to allocate time to garnering student reactions to the literature experience. Term papers, book reviews, examination questions permit the student to write down his learnings. Panels, debates, symposia, and group discussions permit a sharing of student learnings.[6] The oral methods pose problems in large classes, but offer so many advantages that teachers may be motivated to adapt small group devices to their increasing enrollments. Where class time is too limited for extended probing

---

[4] Donald A. Hansen and Reuben Hill, "Families Under Stress," *Handbook of Marriage and the Family* ed. by H. T. Christensen, New York: Rand McNally, pp. 782–783.

[5] "Family Interaction: Insights through the Short Story" has been taught for some years by Rose M. Somerville at the New York School for Social Research; Val Clear tells elsewhere . . . of the social problems course he has taught at Anderson College using the novel and biography. Other courses which also rely mainly on drama, novel, and story are occasionally included among summer offerings in a number of institutions but have yet to find acceptance in the regular sessions.

[6] A book review of unusual perceptiveness written by a college junior reveals both the values to be gained by written response to the literature experience and the problems of permitting others to share in the student's insights. Dixie Merrell's review of *Black Like Me,* omitted from publication for lack of space, is available to readers upon request. Professor J. Joel Moss, in whose class (HDFR 361—Family Relationships) at Brigham Young University Miss Merrell was a student . . . comments as follows: "As teachers, we often focus heavily on knowledge found in textbooks or drawn from research for the learning experiences of our students. Such action is sound. Yet we know that learning is also an emotional experience. There should be some consideration of this when planning our lessons. In a beginning course in family relationships, I had

into a story, play, or novel, some of the benefits of student interaction to stretch each one's cognitive and emotional range can be derived from small leaderless groups. Following through on these can take the form of requiring individual written reports or asking a member of the group to bring to the larger class points of ageement or difference. In classes for younger children or for poor readers, not only the discussing but the reading of the fiction may require oral presentation. Tapes and records may be useful in such classrooms.

While further research is needed as to the "teachable moment," the timing of class discussion in relation to the reading of the story, experience in a number of classrooms suggests that the following assumptions can be made:

1) A "cooling off" period is needed so that emotions are not at their height when the story is discussed. Students tend to be less articulate and more defensive when they are in the first throes of reaction to the story. Wordsworth's concept of recollections in tranquillity is perhaps more relevant to the creative writer than to the reader, for as soon as class discussion begins, many of the original feelings are recaptured. However, even though the "tranquillity" tends to disappear, there is a diminution in the level of intensity, and problems of immobilization or over-assertion are less in evidence. It is possible that interviews with students will indicate that immediately upon reading the story, they are busy with the process of recall and bound up by chains of association with events in their own lives. Only some lapse of time permits the degree of objectivity that is essential if the steps of interpretation outlined above are to be taken. (In bibliotherapy, in contradistinction to educational purposes, immediate use of recall might prove most effective.)

2) A second reading of the story adds to cognitive growth. A single reading offers an emotional experience and will need supplementation if the student is to go beyond this level. It is not known how much separation in time between the two readings will maximize ability to analyze the story. This may differ for various students. They can be encouraged to try different time spans and discover for themselves which relates positively to the ability to contribute to class discussion.

General instructions not to read the story the day of the class and to allow enough time for two or more readings will be helpful to the students.

Much remains to be worked out through greater theoretical refinement as well as action research in the classroom, concerning the literature approach to teach-

---

been offering students many facts about social class, rural-urban groups, etc., in relation to family life. But I felt that many students were learning facts without putting them in a personally meaningful context. Hence, following the session in the 1965 NCFR meetings on the use of the short story, novels, and other creative literature in class sessions, I decided to assign my students the reading of a novel or biography concerned with how an individual experiences family life in another segment of our social structure. The book review by Dixie Merrell indicates that she had an emotional experience which gave her a basis from which many of our usual facts about family life in various socioeconomic levels of society could become more meaningful."

ing about the family. But some groundwork has been laid to test the claims made through the centuries that the imaginative writer through his understanding of man's motives has "power to influence his thinking, to move his heart, and even to alter his behavior." [7]

THE SHORT STORY AND FAMILY INSIGHTS IN SECONDARY SCHOOLS *

ROSE M. SOMERVILLE

It would seem highly appropriate for the interdisciplinary field of family study to add the human relations aspects of imaginative literature to the findings culled from sociology, psychology, biology, anthropology, home economics, religion, law, and philosophy. The neat fit between the use of fiction and the outcomes sought in family life education has already been described.[1] Also, for the college and adult education levels, there is already a guide to the selection of stories that illuminates the main topics of family courses.[2] What is lacking is aid to teachers of younger students. While the attempt to offer some suggestions here must rest on an extrapolation from college and adult education experience, there is some basis for thinking that sufficient similarities in goals, content, and methods exist in family study at all levels to make this feasible.

The weights attached to knowledge, attitudes, and skills differ from classroom to classroom, but high schools and colleges do not divide up evenly on one or the other side of the functional institutional line. A narrow concept of the functional is likely to be discarded at all levels of education, as even a practical emphasis must reckon with neighborhoods, nations, and the world in which families exist. Among the major topics in family courses, as reflected in the textbooks they adopt, are changing sex roles, dating and mate selection, and intergenerational relationships. Family disorganization figures more markedly in the college textbook, but several textbooks on the secondary school level now

---

[7] Caroline Shrodes, "The Dynamics of Reading," *ETC.: A Review of General Semantics*, April 1961, p. x. The literature approach in no way conflicts with the use of brief case histories, films, role-playing, and other methods of teaching family courses. Brief case histories can be found in a number of textbooks on the family; a convenient collection is offered in Jessie Bernard, Helen E. Buchanan, and William M. Smith, Jr., *Dating, Mating, and Marriage Today: A Documentary-Case Approach*. New York, Arco Publishing Company, 1959.

* Based on a paper given at the annual meeting of the National Council on Family Relations, Toronto, October 1965. Reprinted with permission of The National Council on Family Relations from the *Journal of Marriage and the Family*, May 1966.

[1] Rose M. Somerville, "Imaginative Literature in Family Life Education," *Journal of Home Economics*, June 1963, pp. 409–412.

[2] See "Master List of Stories" and "Index of Problem Areas Covered," in Rose M. Somerville, *Family Insights through the Short Story*, New York: Teachers College Press, 1964, paperback.

include the broken home [3] and working wives.[4] Adoption and in-laws [5] as well as the family's relation to the community [6] are topics moving the high school course away from some of the shallow concerns for which it has been criticized.[7] The gap between high school and college is probably widest in the treatment of spousal interaction and sex standards before, during, and after marriage.[8] Creative literature may be able to bridge some of the distance in these regards.

As for teaching methods, both high school and college courses on the family seek to replace traditional lecturing with a wide array of group discussion techniques, audiovisual materials, resource persons, and field trips. If there is often discrepancy between course-outline promises and classroom actualities, it is not necessarily more characteristic of high school than of college. Indeed, there is danger that the latter is more menaced by the trend toward larger enrollments without commensurate increase in faculty.[9]

While these commonalities allow us to suppose that the positive experiences in the use of creative literature with older students can serve as a model for younger ones, there are some special considerations in selecting and using fiction in high schools which need examination. These involve student and community readiness.

SOCIOECONOMIC LEVEL

There are more students from disadvantaged homes in high schools than in colleges. This is markedly evident in urban areas. If on a nationwide basis poor people are estimated to constitute at least a fifth of the total population, in the large cities the proportion is greater.[10] This presents elementary and high school

---

3 Elizabeth Force, *Your Family Today and Tomorrow*, Boston: Harcourt, Brace, 1955.

4 Evelyn Duvall, *Family Living*, New York: Macmillan, Rev. Ed., 1961.

5 Judson and Mary Landis, *Personal Adjustment, Marriage, and Family Living*, Englewood Cliffs, N.J.: Prentice-Hall, 1960.

6 M. and R. Smart, *Living in Families*, Boston: Houghton, Mifflin, 1958.

7 Hyman Rodman, "The Textbook World of Family Sociology," *Social Problems*, Spring, 1965, p. 449. It is possible that the deletions of the publishers which reduce the high school textbook's usefulness do not deter various teachers from exploring a wider range of material through other sources. Cf., for example, Curtis E. Avery, "Inside Family Life Education," *The Family Life Coordinator*, April 1962, pp. 35–36.

8 Even in these areas, high schools do not uniformly exclude consideration. In some teaching guides, the topics of steady dating, petting, and the sex relation of married couples are listed, together with relevant films and readings. Cf., *A Guide for Teaching Personal and Family Relationships*, prepared by Genevieve Pieretti, Office of Public Instruction, Carson City, Nevada, p. 97. To be sure, there are teaching guides which suggest that if petting is included as a topic the class "discuss the dangers," and marital interaction is perceived in so restricted a way that sex is omitted from among the "reasons for conflict" listed. "Discussion of sex adjustment during marriage has no place in the high school classroom," states one curriculum bulletin. Cf., *Family Living for High School Seniors*, Kansas City, Missouri. As new editions of course outlines and guides are issued, however, there continue to be modifications in the direction of expanded subject matter.

9 Joan Gadel, "The Large-Lecture: A Menace to the Undergraduate and his Teacher," and Thomas Colwell, "Class Size and Quality Education," speeches at a conference in educational ecology, *Action*, May 1965.

classrooms with a dramatic challenge—to develop teaching approaches and use reading materials which take account of "domains of concern far beyond what is normally thought to be the domain of childhood." [11]

It cannot be said that the family educator has pioneered in recognizing and meeting this need. In the first of the books that focused on the lower-class child, that of Riessman, the classroom cited for successful innovations were not those where family life was studied. There is reason to believe that creative literature can facilitate a breakthrough. But a teacher who has worked successfully with the lower half of the lower-class, the children from the slums, warns that it cannot be through the use of "prosaic good-boy stories" in which good conduct is always being crowned with success. When students include, as his did, girls who in a "fifth grade class had as much sexual experience as do many married women" [12] and who jump rope to such revealing chants as "Policeman, policeman, don't arrest me; arrest that Negro behind that tree. He steals money, I steal none. Put him in the jailhouse just for fun," the stories, plays, and novels assigned must make some contact with the realities that are part of these students' lives.

The children who come from families at the bottom of the socioeconomic scale are likely to "witness parental drunkenness, battles, and sexual activities and experience parental neglect and abuse. Alcoholism, violence, promiscuity, and prostitution are not abstract concepts . . . Threatened desertion, homelessness, and police action continually hang over their heads." [13] Even for children from families somewhat higher in the income ladder, if because of racial barriers to housing choice they are kept within ghetto confines, familiarity with social deviancy comes early. "Stable and unstable groups—fragments of families, footloose bachelors of both sexes, transients and the stable family units—live in the same building." [14] Thus it is that "every adolescent in Harlem knows something about narcotics addiction and has been exposed to it either directly

[10] Riessman accepts the estimate that in 1960 one child in three was "culturally, deprived" in the fourteen largest cities of the United States where almost one-sixth of Americans live. This designation, which he uses interchangeably with "underprivileged," "lower-class," etc., is not a precise one for at least two reasons. Not only can there be said to be a culture of the poor, but not all those of low income are deprived of access to the cultural resources of the larger society, since customs and values differ among various ethnic subgroups. Harrington's reminder is also relevant here that poverty is relative to the culture and century in which it occurs: "The American poor are not poor in Hong Kong or in the sixteenth century; they are poor here and now, in the United States. They are dispossessed in terms of what the rest of the nation enjoys, in terms of what the society could provide if it had the will." Cf., Frank Riessman, *The Culturally Deprived Child*, New York: Harper, 1962; and Michael Harrington, *The Other America: Poverty in the United States*, New York: Penguin, 1963, pp. 173–174.

[11] Christopher Spaeth, "Black Magic in Philadelphia," *Teachers College Record*, December 1964, p. 230.

[12] *Ibid.*, pp. 229, 231.

[13] Charles A. Malone, "Saftey First: Comments on the Influence of External Danger in the Lives of Children of Disorganized Families," *American Journal of Orthopsychiatry*, January 1966, p. 7.

[14] Suzanne Keller, *The American Lower Class Family*, p. 27, a report prepared for the New York State Division for Youth, 1965.

or indirectly; therefore, he finds it strange if everyone else does not understand how common it is to his everyday experience." [15]

If learning theory as applied to deprived children suggests that they have a special need "to have the abstract constantly and intimately pinned to the immediate . . . the topical," [16] the short story is likely to be helpful in many urban classrooms. The story is a specific instance; through it the student can be led toward broader generalizations and abstract formulations. Moreover, stories can be assigned in a sequence that leads from the simpler to the more complex, building up skills and motivation on the way. In one attempt to evoke interest in and understanding of Shakespeare's plays among children from the slums, one of the factors that contributed to its success, in addition to the teacher's own empathy for his students and his enjoyment of the challenge, was the preparation of students through carefully planned earlier experiences. The year began with Mother Goose and not with Shakespeare. As Riessman puts it, the youngsters may ultimately be ready for plays by Shaw or Tolstoy, but the start must be made with their existing interests.

Where are stories to be found that can help the slum child, that will have meaning for him, and that will contribute to his liberal education by freeing him to feel and to reason? One educator, properly critical of the fiction assigned children whose values, developed in an effort to cope with a threatening environment, focus on masculinity, strength, endurance, and search for excitement, suggests adventure stories, science fiction, and simple biographies for the very young. For the older ones she suggests "books that deal frankly with the facts of life." [17] Unfortunately, no suggestions are offered of specific writings that would meet this latter criterion. Perhaps the chronological age of the child should be given less weight than his social maturity; the nature of his life experiences may indicate that for the high school student from the impoverished home, the stories read by the college student would have more meaning than "what is normally thought to be the domain of childhood." There is a story about a fifteen-year-old boy who lives with his tired, bitter, nagging, hard-working mother after his father's desertion and who longs for a motorcycle to bring him both a sense of mastery and escape.[18] There is a story that tells how a

---

15 Maurice V. Russell, "A Community Mental Health Program in a Municipal Hospital," *Social Casework*, November 1965, p. 557.

16 Riessman, *op. cit.*, p. 68. The beneficial effects of meeting this need extend far beyond the classroom. "It is clear that self-control and self-direction vary directly with cognitive maturity, and especially with the ability to manipulate situations symbolically, to anticipate consequences, to weigh, to judge, and to decide between alternatives. . . . The educator's charge is clear. Everything that he can do, every technique that he can use, to enhance 'cognitive maturity,' to encourage symbolic thinking of all sorts, will help." Joseph L. Church, *Language and the Discovery of Reality*, New York: Random House, 1961, quoted in J. O. Baker and N. N. Wagner, "Social Class and Mental Illness in Children," *Teachers College Record*, March 1965, p. 535.

17 Patricia Sexton, *Education and Income*, New York: Viking, 1961, p. 259, quoted in Riessman, *op. cit.*, p. 35.

18 "The Bronco-Buster," (9). Bibliographical data for each story for which a number is indicated can be found in the "Master List of Stories" in *Family Insights through the Short Story*, see footnote 2 above.

child feels when a long-absent father returns to take up the mother's time and attention and when a new baby arrives to divide the parents.[19] There is a story that shows a father who bosses his daughters and beats them for trying to date the local boys.[20] It is significant that two of the three stories are written by Europeans and that stories like these which would have direct relation to the life experiences of slum youngsters are not too common among American writers. Fortunately, many stories with a middle-class setting will permit identifications too, if the issues presented are not petty ones and the feelings are masterfully conveyed. This would generally indicate making selections not from stories specifically written for a "teen-age market," but stories that are primarily a contribution to modern creative writing in which the sensitivity of the artist has alerted him and, therefore, his reader to the motivations and the social pressures in the lives of family members. The short stories selected for the college student are of this kind and can serve as a resource for testing in high schools.

This may raise a problem of reading skills, since these are often poorly developed in children who attend overcrowded schools and whose parents have neither time, skill, nor motivation to supplement the teacher's efforts. It may be necessary, particularly among junior high school students, to motivate reading by telling the story and introducing role-playing and other visual aids that facilitate movement toward a higher verbal and conceptual level. The experience of one teacher with younger students from disadvantaged homes may be instructive for the family course or unit that uses fiction. "Announce a lesson in 'literature'—especially one in poetry—and you will receive an assortment of groans. Announce that you will tell the class a story and you will receive respectful but reserved expectancy. State further that this is the story of two sets of parents who, because of their unwillingness to adapt to the present time, contributed to the destruction of their own children, and you will have your audience in the palm of your hand . . . you have motivated the class to the study of Shakespeare's *Romeo and Juliet*." [21]

The barriers of socioeconomic class that keep the middle-class teacher from functioning effectively with lower-class students can be reduced by the teacher's own growth through the use of fiction. Empathic capacity can increase as the stories offer the teacher vicarious experience with the difficult life conditions of the children and an understanding of the roots for unfamiliar mores. The student needs acceptance rather than pity, help in classroom achievement rather than charity. One factor in the creation of social distance between teacher and slum child is the latter's use of four-letter words and the tendency of the former to over-react to these. When teachers make their peace with the fact of the existence of such words and their customary status in the slums, they will be better able to serve as adult role models of a different kind from the family

---

19 "My Oedipus Complex," (57).
20 "Peace for Geretiello," (69).
21 Personal communication to Riessman, *op. cit.,* pp. 69–70.

members who share the children's monotonous and limited vocabulary.[22] The teacher may not be able to add variety to the slum child's vocabulary and move him toward cognitive maturity until his own symbolic thinking has been enlarged. Fiction can aid teachers to face themselves.

STORIES FOR MAJOR CONTENT AREAS IN FAMILY COURSES OR UNITS

The majority of students in secondary schools are not from ethnic subgroups or within a poverty classification. There is a wide range among them of socio-economic background, and recent studies suggest that the parents' level of education itself constitutes a significant variable within a single economic class.[23] But all high school students share a need to gain perspective on the opportunities and difficulties that lie before them as future family-founders in a rapidly changing society. Their families of origin typically cannot offer this perspective. While some studies suggest that there is a penetration into all families of findings from the behavioral sciences, with increasing flexibility of role concepts and increasing acceptance of developmental rather than traditional modes of child-rearing, others remind us that in the upper lower-class (Hollingshead, Class IV; Warner, Class V), in which semi-skilled and skilled occupations predominate, families are largely isolated from the "intellectual mainstreams" of the industrial society in which they live and are therefore "slow . . . to modify their conceptions of marriage in ways which would prove more conducive to happiness under changing conditions." [24]

Nor are middle-class parents without need of the school's assistance in providing perspective on modern marriage. Their own socialization as adolescents took place several decades before their children's, and they often find their own experiences irrelevant to current needs and alternatives. The high school student may find in the family course or unit offered in social studies, health education, home economics, or other departments the only opportunity to explore emotion-laden issues in an objective setting. The coeducational class not only adds a realistic dimension to the search for congruence of expectations but offers

---

22 Riessman urges that the deprived child has a "spontaneous language" which is called forth in response to role-playing rather than to words alone. However, this is only relative, for economic impoverishment has its corollary on the verbal level. Even granting some inventive word power on the part of the deprived child, although several instances cited by Riessman may derive from an intellectual elite, such as the beatnik, there can be no doubt that the repetitive use of the colorful slang term adds little to his store of words for the "public language" needed in the classroom and eventually in the job world. Riessman, *op. cit.*, p. 75.

23 Mirra Komarovsky, *Blue-Collar Marriage*, New York: Random House, p. 21.

24 *Ibid.*, p. 46. "Regional parochialism also characterizes some of our classrooms. For example, the relative lack of exposure to family customs other than those inherent in the Iowa scene should encourage consideration of national and international family living conditions and their problems within every area of the home economics curriculum." F. E. Whitehead, *et al.*, "Selected Characteristics of Majors in Home Economics, Sociology, Language, and Art," *Journal of Home Economics*, November 1965, p. 710.

practice in discussion between the sexes. This is particularly needed by students from lower lower-class families, where "relations between the sexes are characterized by suspicion and hostility" [25] and by students from upper lower-class families where communication between husbands and wives may be inadequate owing to norms of sex segregation or failure to "recognize the therapeutic value of talk." [26]

DATING AND SEX

For most high school students dating and sex are topics of immediate interest. Relatedly, the problems of mate selection and sex role allocations attract adolescent attention long before actual choices must be made. Stories can permit exploration of such issues as "free choice" of dating partners and mates, sexual behavior on dates, the right as opposed to the necessity of women's working after marriage, and the relationship of dating to other adolescent tasks. Social homogamy can be examined through a story like "The Apple Tree" and the high school student may, like college students among whom the story is a favorite, be motivated to examine research studies of socioeconomic factors in date and mate selection.[27] Among the middle-class students who predominate in college,[28] there is a tendency to use the fact that the story is set in England as a "can't-happen-here" escape from the discomfort of facing realities. The high school setting may bring forth other kinds of resistances. The lyrical style and the sensitive appreciation of nature place this story high on the adoption list of literature teachers, and cooperative planning for its assignment should not be difficult. Similarly useful in clarifying mate selection considerations is "The Magic Barrel," [29] but the students may have to be helped to see the analogues between the values of the given ethnic group and the host culture.

Many other stories are suggested in chapters on "The Changing Roles of Men and Women," "Adolescents and Young Adults," "Dating and Mate Selection," and "Sex Standards," in *Family Insights through the Short Story* [30] that have potentialities for the high school. If the slum child needs realistic fiction that makes contact with his concerns and the middle-class child needs to broaden

---

[25] Suzanne Keller, *op. cit.*, p. 33.

[26] Mirra Komarovsky, *op. cit.*, p. 17.

[27] "The Apple Tree," (1). The level of the discussion may depend on the teacher's answer to searching questions recently posed—"Do we take the fact that there are few interracial marriages and few full-time career women to indicate that these matters are somehow against human nature and therefore best to avoid? Or do we take these as indicative of cultural obstacles that should be removed?" Hyman Rodman, *op. cit.*, p. 448.

[28] A changing situation as college enrollments increase is suggested in the following description of a public college: "They come to us by and large uncultivated, often barely literate, and in many instances devoid of intellectual interests. Their mode of thought is uncritical, unsophisticated, and their sense of human dignity is 'underdeveloped,' stunted by the institutions and patterns of life of a technocratic mass society." Joan Gadel, *op. cit.*

[29] "The Magic Barrel," (47).

[30] Somerville, *op. cit.*

his experience of the many family forms that exist, why cannot all the stories offered at the college level be freely assigned to the younger student? It must be acknowledged that problems of censorship arise for secondary schools which are more dependent on local influences. A student body that might benefit most from a frankly stated story may be located in a community which has a parent body, a librarian, or a local organization which is threatened by any open expression of hidden relationships. Whatever the basis for this resistance—prurience, overprotectiveness, or guilt feelings concerning their own fantasies or acts—it is a factor to be reckoned with. Since one of the values of using fiction in the high schools is to open channels of communication between students and family members, the story cannot be too markedly beyond the comprehension and tolerance of the community. However, the teacher must be wary of exaggerating the form or the continuation of resistance. Many teachers of family courses are familiar with the progression from the beginning of the semester, when a student may report, "My mother is amazed that we have such discussions in class," to the end when the comment becomes, "My mother wishes she had had a course like this herself."

Moreover, problems of censorship can sometimes be avoided by early cooperation with literature teachers, the principal, and the P.T.A. Some explanatory work may have to be undertaken, as even at the college level the short story has still to find its full place in literature departments.[31] However, high schools are revising their reading assignments with the encouragement of the National Council of the Teachers of English. Classes for gifted students have begun to include, even in the ninth grade, the stories of Sherwood Anderson, Carson McCullers, Katherine Anne Porter, J.D. Salinger, Willa Cather, John Steinbeck, and other realistic modern writers. The use of writers such as these in the family course may allow all boys and girls to possess a lifelong resource, an ability to read fiction for its human relations insights and thereby achieve the continuing education which is required through the whole life cycle in a complex and changing civilization.[32]

Many stories do not raise any censorship issue but do require a judgment as to student readiness. Fortunately, stories about over-attachment between parent

---

[31] "Most undergraduates have not even discovered, let alone read, the abler young American writers, despite their availability in paperbacks," it is reported of an informal poll at a distinguished college. "An astonishing majority had never heard of Jean Stafford . . . Swados, Flannery O'Conner . . . or Herbert Gold." Cf., "On Campus, It's the Generation of the Mixed Book Bag," *Book Review of The New York Times*, January 14, 1962, p. 3.

[32] That the high schools are a crucial factor is suggested by the following: "Educators have known for a long time that children . . . from the ninth grade onward . . . diminish their interest in reading. This downward trend continues through high school and into college until most students read practically nothing that is not assigned and leave school or college with a distaste for reading." Herman Ward, "'Don Camillo' Instead of 'Silas Marner,'" *New York Times Magazine*, April 1, 1962. Professor Ward urges that distinctions be made between "fossilized classics" and others, and that "lively books" be chosen which make the student eager to comment on the "problems that face us all."

and child, usually mother and son, permit discussion on a surface level of independence-training as well as examination on a deeper level of unconscious wooing or of rejection. Moreover, stories on the over-attachment theme, such as "Bridgeport Bus," "Family Scene," "It's an Old Story," and "Main Currents in American Thought," [33] which are particularly illuminating as to failure to marry, also offer important subthemes, such as sibling relationships, care of aging parents, and role changes with illness, which would justify their assignment. High school teachers who use these stories may themselves be helped to avoid judgmental attitudes on the one hand or the sentimentality which views all mother-child interaction as positive in its consequences.

There are stories which have fewer problems of censorship or of student readiness, and these usually have a young child as a major character. Perhaps because high school students have experience with younger brothers and sisters or "sit" with the children of neighbors, stories about children seem to evoke immediate interest. However, if they follow the pattern of many college students, they will be inclined to identify with the children and indulge in harsh judgmental pronouncements about the parents; or they will fail to see the children's behaviors in a developmental framework. Two stories that offer much to the educational process are "The Downward Path to Wisdom" and "Uncle Wiggily in Connecticut." [34] Both indicate that biological motherhood does not always ensure psychological readiness to play a nurturing role; they help to develop an awareness in students of the demands of the parental role which can be pertinent to their own decisions concerning early marriage. "My Oedipus Complex" [35] offers a more cheerful tale in which a significant concept is introduced: but its very charm creates a need for skillful discussion leadership if students are to get below the surface and examine "parenthood as crisis" and changing roles.

Many of the stories listed in the chapters on family disorganization, aging and the aged, and bereavement would have to be examined carefully for high school assignment. "Tell Me a Riddle" and "What the Cystoscope Said," in

---

[33] (8), (28), (37), (48).

[34] (19), (94).

[35] (57). The optimistic tone of this story is exceptional among effective family-related fiction. Teachers who seek "short stories for youngsters which present a picture of healthy, growing family life," a common quest, may have to rely on the analysis of family problems to offer positive paths as most stories stress negative influences in kin relationships. Novels and biographies with a cheerful outlook and with a more consistent stress on positive elements in family relationships can be found, curiously enough, in hospital book guides. Cf., "Selection of Recent Books About Handicapped Persons: A Checklist of Popular Fiction and Biography," revised July 1964, 16 pp.; "Books to Help Children Adjust to a Hospital Situation," February 1956, Supplements 1958, 1960, 1962. Brief annotations, subject index, and age categories (K-12; adult) facilitate selection. Single copies of these bibliographies are obtainable on request from the National Society for Crippled Children and Adults, 2023 W. Ogden Avenue, Chicago 12, Illinois. The Society's journal, *Rehabilitation Literature,* offers reviews of new fiction pertinent to bibliotherapy but useful also in educational settings. The pages of Teacher Exchange are open to reports on efforts to use these resources in family study.

which illness and death are central, make special demands of cognitive as well as empathic competence. The first story requires some background to understand the problems of immigrants and the depths of poverty in which they were caught. It may be difficult for the more protected boy or girl to understand how the exhaustion—physical and emotional—of childbearing and childrearing in harsh circumstances results in an inability to play a conventional grandmother role. The latter story, for all its usefulness in a discussion of the emotions surrounding terminal illness and cremation, depicts sex being used punitively and may require more knowledge of psychology than the average high school class can command. However, "The Long Winter" and "Neighbor Rosicky," perhaps because of their rural settings, do permit illness and death to be explored without too much challenge. The former offers an additional advantage for the younger student, by posing in the relationship of an adolescent boy and his recently widowed father, the value issue of rugged individualism versus humanistic interdependence. Similarly, "The Heyday of the Blood" and "The Leader of the People" offer simplicity of language and a protected framework of presentation that permit illness and aging to be discussed in a wide range of classrooms.[36]

The high rates of separation, divorce, and remarriage make it likely that a significant minority in all classrooms have been exposed to this experience in their immediate families or among friends and relatives. Many know of these phenomena through the mass media. The classroom use of fiction offers an opportunity to sift out myth from reality, to examine painful phenomena objectively. "Love and Like" details movingly the effects of family dissolution on the principals and the very young children. However, even at the college level, students often have difficulty in understanding the instance it offers of infidelity deriving from feelings of inadequacy rather than from strong sex drives and of marital disharmony despite sexual satisfaction in the relationship. Similarly, "Faces of Hatred and of Love" may be of limited use in most high school classes, with its effective but involved interweaving of factors of desertion, illness, pregnancy, and impaired self-image. However, some of the same issues are more simply presented in "My First Two Women" and "We're All Guests,"[37] with the latter particularly illuminating in respect to the variables of sex and age in children's reactions to a mother's remarriage.

---

[36] Stories in the order in which they are mentioned in this paragraph, excluding "The Long Winter": (87), (98), (59), (31), (42). A series widely used in high schools may offer the teacher immediate access to a number of stories without the need of special ordering. *Adventures in Reading*, Volume 1, intended for the ninth grade but appropriate also for later grades, includes "The Long Winter" by Walter Havighurst. *Adventures in Appreciation*, Volume 1, intended for the tenth grade but also appropriate later, includes "The Duke's Children." *Stories*, intended for the final high school years, includes "My First Two Women," by Nadine Gordimer and "Molly Morgan" by John Steinbeck. *Great Short Stories*, similarly intended for juniors and seniors, includes "Neighbor Rosicky" by Willa Cather, "The Leader of the People," by John Steinbeck, and "The Jilting of Granny Weatherall," by Katherine Anne Porter. Harcourt, Brace, and World is the publisher of the series.

[37] Cf., footnote above for "My First Two Women"; "We're All Guests," (97).

QUALITY FICTION OR SECOND-BEST?

It is evident that story selection is more difficult at the high school level than in college courses on the family. There will, therefore, be a greater temptation to use lesser fiction. The latter can be found in magazines that are part of the Establishment and are read by the more conforming segment of high school students. Such titles as *Seventeen, Charm, Glamour,* and *Co-Ed* come to mind in this connection. Their most obvious disadvantage is that the stories in them are directed to girl readers rather than to both sexes; and even when some identifications are possible, boys are not apt to read a magazine obviously designed for the other sex. There is also a more subtle disadvantage. While the themes are often important ones—peer group influence on the decision to go steady, sibling rivalry, the working mother, early marriage, stepmother relations—they are presented on a shallow feeling level and bear an obvious message, such as, "Don't go steady"; "Be satisfied with your home town and stop dreaming of distant horizons," "Don't marry early," etc. Moreover, they tend to bypass life's complexities in order to assure happy endings.

Similarly, the special paperback compilations for high school youth rarely offer high level creative writing, in part because they tend to cull their stories from the youth magazines just mentioned. *First Love* [38] is an instance of this. *Family* is somewhat more broadly selective and includes a few stories that may be worth assigning.[39] *Ten Modern American Short Stories* also offers a few possibilities.[40]

The high school teacher of family courses and units will find the pursuit of quality fiction [41] brings greater returns in the long run in terms of such con-

---

[38] Gay Head, ed., New York: Scholastic Book Services, 1963, 187 pp., paperback.

[39] Murray Rockowitz, ed., New York: Scholastic Book Services, 1961, 184 pp., paperback.

[40] D. A. Sohn, ed., New York: Bantam, 1965, 154 pp.

[41] Stories that first appear in obscure literary journals are often sifted through by anthologists who bring them together in annual and periodic collections, such as *The Best American Short Stories, New World Writing,* and *Prize Stories: The O. Henry Awards.* Many of these go out of print quickly, sometimes within a year of publication, but some of the stories turn up in new collections, such as *Stories to Remember,* sel. by Thomas B. Costain and John Beecroft, New York: Popular Library, 3 volumes, 1956, 1957, 1958, paperbacks; *Short Story Masterpieces,* ed. by Robert Penn Warren and Albert Erskine, New York: Dell, 1954; and *Fiction of the Fifties,* ed. by Herbert Gold, New York: Doubleday (Dolphin), 1959. Help in locating a later anthology in which an out-of-print story may appear is provided by *Short Story Index,* New York: Wilson, 1953, with its Supplements, 1956, 1960. Other bibliographic aid can be found in *Reading Ladders for Human Relations,* Margaret Heaton and Helen B. Lewis, Washington, D.C.: American Council on Education, 1955. Permission for mimeographing a story for classroom use may be sought from the copyright holder. For such duplicating purposes, hardcover editions of some collections can be found in libraries. Current book reviews can alert the teacher to new family-related stories; colleagues, relatives, and students can be enlisted in the search. Special literary competencies are not required; two simple yardsticks will serve. Was the story told movingly? Did it illuminate some aspect of family relationships?

siderations as student involvement, raising of the cultural level, relations with other departments and with administration, and action research which can benefit the whole family field. In this latter connection there is opportunity for experimentation in the grouping of stories, devising examination questions that help students relate textbook reading and field work experiences to the specific instance of the story, coordinating film showings and role-playing to reinforce learnings, and utilizing panels, buzz groups, and logs for garnering student reactions, with a view to guidance that is both personal and academic. Valuable · teacher exchanges can be anticipated that will maximize interaction among school districts and states as well as among various educational levels.

IMAGINATIVE LITERATURE IN FAMILY LIFE EDUCATION *

ROSE M. SOMERVILLE

As the functional emphasis becomes predominant in marriage and family courses on the college level (*1*), the search for deeply-involving classroom materials takes on increasing importance.

This search for new teaching materials relates itself closely, of course, to goals and methodology. To the extent that a marriage and family course is functional, it seeks to maximize the student's self-understanding and his ability to understand others in family relationships. Such a course proceeds on some or all of the following premises:

1. INTERRELATIONSHIP BETWEEN SELF-UNDERSTANDING AND THE UNDERSTANDING OF OTHERS

Through an awareness of his own feelings, behaviors, ideals, and attitudes as a family member, the student is enabled to grow in sensitivity to others' needs and goals.

Support for classroom procedures developed on this basis can be found in a growing body of research in empathy. In the view of Dymond and others, "It seems very likely that the ability to take the role of another (empathy) is positively related to the ability to understand ourselves (insight)." (*2*)

Empathic competence can be increased by practice in inferring the affect and the intent of other persons in family interaction.

2. STUDENT ACTIVITY IN THE CLASSROOM

The self-understanding of the student can grow as the classroom provides him with a place in which he can clarify his ideas, recognize his own emotions, try

---

* Reprinted from the *Journal of Home Economics,* Vol. 55, No. 6 (June 1963), with permission of the American Home Economics Association.

out new ways of communicating, and learn from the efforts of his fellow students as they similarly seek new knowledge and perceptive skill. Positive results have been found to accrue to "a high degree of interaction among . . . students" and "warm, friendly personal relations in the classroom." (3)

3. THE EMOTIONAL AND THE RATIONAL

Ideas may remain inert unless the student perceives them as personally meaningful.

Classroom encouragement of both the emotional and the rational is based upon ancient insights and current classroom experimentation. Aristotle had perceived a two-fold satisfaction in literature: catharsis, or the ventilation of feelings previously repressed, and learning, or "gathering the meaning of things." (4)

The goal is "the kind of objectivity that comes not from a rejection of the emotional aspects of human life but from an acceptance of them and an attempt to deal with them within a realistic framework" (5). The subjective is not regarded as a substitute for objective analysis but as a motivating force in this regard.

4. LIFE TASKS

A functional emphasis in a marriage and family course requires tailoring the course design to fit the needs of the students.

Course scheduling, however, does not always permit the neat formation of sections in which all those with similar task urgencies are enrolled. The two or three married students in a college class may be impatient with the group's lingering on what for them seems outdated problems. They may even be threatened by any discussion of areas in which they have already made fairly irreversible decisions. Nevertheless, recognition of the divergencies of needs within a class permits the family life educator to make special provisions for individual students or for groups through counseling interviews, modified reading assignments, committee work, and the like. (6)

5. VALUES

Recent studies examine the obligation of the college "to reveal choices" and to "foster a greater concern in each student with forming his own values" (7). The nature of the subject matter in a family course facilitates the raising of value issues. It becomes evident to the student that "our life problems . . . such as choosing a mate, a job, a home, a way of living, impose a choice between alternatives" (8). The discussion group may serve as a "cultural island" (9), permitting the student a freedom of self-exploration he may not enjoy in more inhibiting social settings.

THE USE OF IMAGINATIVE LITERATURE

All these five basic elements in the aims and procedures of a functional family course can find their match in imaginative literature. To be sure, markedly different elements characteristic of other ways of teaching and other subject matter could similarly find support. What is important for the family life educator is that a human relations approach to literature fits in neatly and richly with the underlying bases of functional teaching.

Many forms of fiction share in the advantages offered by imaginative literature as a teaching aid. Short stories, however, are particularly well adapted to the needs of both teacher and student in a family course. Their brevity permits flexibility of assignment and ease of focus in classroom discussion. Major contributions which stories can make toward achieving the outcomes sought in family life education include:

1. *Stories offer psychological insights* into family relationships on a personal level. By providing idiosyncratic instances of the generalizations found in text and reference readings, they both reinforce learning and alert the student to the problems of relating the concrete to the abstract.

2. *Stories provide vicarious experience* in settings and situations which students may not know at firsthand, either because as adolescents they still have a lot of living to do or, even if they are older, because the subculture characteristic of our society set limits to experience across religious, racial, and socioeconomic lines.

3. *Stories provide opportunities for identification and empathy.* The student is drawn into playing the role of imaginary participant in the dramatic events and feels momentarily that what is happening to a character is happening to him (*10*). This emotional involvement with one of the characters affects his sensitivity to the feelings and the motivations of others in the story. Self-understanding can increase as the student becomes aware of the identifications he has made. Empathic ability can grow as the analysis of the behaviors of the story characters provides inference-making practice, and group discussion offers opportunity for validation.

4. *Story characters offer a cloak* for the student's discussion of his own concerns and for his questions about human relationships. Objectification of the problem frees the student from fear of exposure and lessens his defenses against entering areas fraught with feelings of shame and fear.

5. *Stories facilitate recall,* particularly of childhood experiences, and permit the student to relate his present attitudes and feelings to early primary group interaction. For students in their middle and later years the recall of adolescence can be helpful not only in understanding their own development but in knowing the needs of present-day adolescents, whether their own children or those with whom they are in a professional relationship. "Literary people have always understood the vivid emotional experiences of childhood" (*11*). Recent literary productions concerned with adoles-

cence highlight the crucial nature of the whole period before adulthood. *(12)*

6. *Stories offer reassurance* and reduce feelings of anxiety and guilt. During
   his college years, the student continues to be deeply concerned with the
   self, the "conception of who and what he is" *(13)*, and with group mores.
   He tends to evaluate his own impulses severely. "Literary experience may
   liberate him from too narrow a concept of normality" *(14)*. He may learn
   with relief that his needs and his practices are widely shared—a mental
   health factor of some importance.

7. *Stories help the educator fulfill his guidance role.* The student's response
   to the stories reveals his level of knowledge and the range of his interests.
   With such cues, it is possible to assign additional work, whether reading
   or field experiences, on an individual basis. It has been found possible to
   design a student's academic program on the basis of interests and needs
   revealed in a literature course. *(15)*

8. *Stories aid in value formation* both in the introduction of the value dimension into marriage and family courses and in a widening of the experiential basis for the value choices to be made by the student *(16)*. As the
   stories reveal many alternatives and present dramatically the consequences
   which follow upon this choice or that, the student gains a more realistic
   view of decision-making.

9. *Stories provide a means to continued study* throughout adult life. By
   giving the student the opportunity to approach fiction personally, to let
   it mean something to him actively in the way of self-other understanding,
   there may be developed a stimulus to the use of imaginative literature
   for further intellectual and emotional growth long after college years are
   over.

   The family life educator himself may find value in the literature experience, as teachers generally resemble their students in the tendency to
   lay fiction aside. "A discouraging preponderance of the teachers in a
   number of samples report the annual reading of no more than one book
   of even current fiction beyond whatever professional reading they do." *(17)*

10. *Stories are enjoyable* whether for either or both of the reasons Aristotle
    gives *(4)*. By heightening the student's pleasure in the marriage and family
    course, stories affect study motivations positively.

With imaginative literature offering these many advantages, why has it not
been more widely used as a teaching resource by family life educators? It has
been much less discussed in the professional literature and in conferences than
films, role-playing, panels, and other related foci of class discussion and means
of student involvement.[1] In marked contrast, psychology teachers as well as

---

[1] General endorsement of the idea of using imaginative literature in family life education was given by several leading figures at the International Conference on the
Family held in New York in 1960. The paucity of detailed reports on classroom experience, however, has given an impression of lack of interest in a literature resource for
courses in the family.

literature specialists themselves report with some frequency their experience in using stories for human relations insights. *(18, 19)*

Psychotherapists working with the emotionally disturbed are increasingly using fiction as a resource *(20)*. This new field of bibliotherapy, while still lacking in experimental research, assesses hopefully the possibilities that imaginative literature has in clinical settings: "The library will one day be a major weapon of reeducation and rehabilitation" *(21)*. Any advance in this area will undoubtedly have positive effects upon the scientific status of all efforts to use fiction with mental health objectives.

Family life educators may have been deterred from an equal interest in using imaginative literature by several factors in their own education and professional functioning. They may have experienced in their own undergraduate days only one of the possible approaches, the esthetic; they may have been aware of a negative view taken by some literature teachers both to encroachment across departmental lines and to departure from an esthetic emphasis; and it may have seemed to some teachers of family courses that the use of imaginative literature would tend to dilute their claims to "respect for academic scholarship" *(22)*. Imaginative literature makes a good course better; but it should not be expected to overcome handicaps of poorly prepared teachers, overloaded classrooms, inadequate libraries. Moreover, the use of short stories may be said to be educationally valid only if the course into which they are integrated has a defensible educational philosophy, a clearcut idea of content, and an appreciation for the ways in which family study has developed and can continue to grow.

Possibly exceeding other deterrents to the use of fiction by family life educators has been the enormous volume of literary productions. Few teachers have time to survey the whole field, and specific aid in the selection of stories has been lacking. Reading lists in family and mental health textbooks, have, if they have included any imaginative literature at all, mentioned mainly novels. The short story has, despite its easy availability in inexpensive format and its marked preoccupation with family themes, been largely overlooked. It was to make this resource better known that the writer undertook to survey the short-story field and to create a handbook for college teachers of marriage and family courses. *(23)*

THE SHORT STORY IN FAMILY LIFE EDUCATION

Criteria of selection derive from the objectives of the family course. The abundance of short stories permits careful selection to ensure that three basic criteria are met:

1. If the student is to make identifications with fictional characters, he should be helped rather than hindered by the *writing style*. The language of the story should minimize barriers to close involvement. A modern writing style facilitates communication; the turn of the century may be taken as the cut-off point for story selection.

2. The criterion of *socio-psychological insight* rules out most of the stories in the mass circulation magazines. Fortunately, the many obscure magazines which print stories of sufficient literary merit and social sensitivity to war-

rant inclusion in a college course are more or less regularly combed through by anthologists. *Short Story Index,* the single most useful bibliographical aid in this field, has almost one hundred themes that are obviously family-related as well as many more that would justify some checking.

3. Another criterion has to do with *diversity,* whether of story locale, socioeconomic class, or cultural subgroup. It is often necessary to turn to good translations of stories written abroad to obtain a broader socioeconomic canvas against which family interaction can be seen in all its diversity. The resultant sociological insights do not diminish the psychological rewards. Hollingsworth's theory of redintegration has been offered as an explanation why fiction may concern "a different era, a strange nationality" and yet "start chains of association from the reader's own life along with their respective emotions." *(21,* p. 61)

Stories selected on the basis of these three criteria are potential material. The individual family life educator knows the students he is working with and what is likely to "get across" to them. However, he must be prepared to let actual experience in using the story in the classroom confirm or refute his initial judgment.

It will take widespread use of stories in family courses and the devising of new ways of measuring classroom effectiveness before anything approaching exactness in evaluating the different methods of using imaginative literature can be attained. The writer's exploratory efforts sufficiently support the hypothesis that the short-story experience will increase understanding of family relationships to warrant detailed research by family life specialists.

references

1. LANDIS, J., "The Teaching of Marriage and Family Courses in Colleges," *Marriage & Family Living, 21* (Feb. 1959), pp. 36–40.

2. DYMOND, R., "A Scale for the Measurement of Empathic Ability," *J. Consulting Psychol., 13* (May, 1949), pp. 127–133.

LUCHENS, A. S., "A Variational Approach to Empathy," *J. Soc. Psychol., 45* (Feb. 1957), pp. 11–18.

STOCK, D.. "An Investigation into the Interrelations Between Self-concept and Feelings Directed Toward Other Persons and Groups," *J. Consulting Psychol., 13* (June 1949), pp. 176–180.

FLAPAN, M., "The Cultivation of Empathic Abilities Project," 1960, 24 pp., typewritten manuscript on file at Teachers College, Columbia University.

3. WINGO, G. M., "Methods of Teaching" in *Encyclopedia of Educational Research.* Third edition. New York: Macmillan, 1960, p. 848.

BIRNEY, R., and MC KEACHIE, W. J., "The Teaching of Psychology: A Survey of Research Since 1942, *Psychol. Bull., 52* (1955), pp. 51–68.

CANTOR, N., *The Dynamics of Learning.* Buffalo. N.Y.: Henry Stewart, 1956.

EGLASH, A., "A Group Discussion Method of Teaching Psychology." *J. Educ. Psychol.*, 45 (May 1954), pp. 257–267.

HARE, A. P., "Interaction and Consensus in Different Sized Groups" in *Group Dynamics: Research and Theory,* DORWIN CARTWRIGHT and ALVIN ZANDER, Editors, Evanston, Ill.: Row, Peterson, 1956, pp. 507–518.

ROGERS, C., *Client-Centered Therapy: Its Current Practice, Implications, and Theory.* Cambridge, Mass.: Houghton Mifflin, 1951.

4. MC KEON, R., Editor, *The Basic Works of Aristotle.* New York: Random House, 1941, pp. 1, 547.

5. GIBSON, H., "The Case Method in Human Relations" in *Accent on Teaching,* SIDNEY J. FRENCH, Editor. New York: Harper and Brothers, Publishers, 1954, p. 215.

6. Cf. WOMBLE, D. L., "Functional Marriage Course for the Already Married," *Marriage & Family Living,* 23 (Aug. 1961), pp. 278–283.

7. BARTON, A. H., "Studying the Effects of College Education: A Methodological Examination of *Changing Values in College.*" New Haven, Conn.: Edward W. Hazen Foundation, 1959, p. 22. Cf. pp. 94–96 for a bibliography of recent studies on value.

8. MURPHY, G., "Social Motivation" in *Handbook of Social Psychology,* GARDNER LINDZEY, Editor, Vol. II. Cambridge, Mass.: Addison-Wesley, 1954, p. 618.

9. TROW, W., *et al.,* "The Class as a Group: Conclusions from Research in Group Dynamics," *J. Educ. Psychol., 41* (1950), pp. 338.

10. KAGAN, J., "The Concept of Identification," *Psychol. Rev.,* 65 (1958), pp. 296–305.

MACCOBY, E., and WILSON, W. C., "Identification and Observational Learning from Films," *J. Abnormal & Soc. Psychol., 55* (1957), pp. 76–87.

11. PRESCOTT, D., *Emotion and the Educative Process.* Washington, D.C.: American Council on Education, 1938, p. 2.

12. KIELL, N., *The Adolescent through Fiction.* New York: International Universities Press, 1959, p. 13.

13. JERSILD, A. T., "Self-understanding in Childhood and Adolescence," *Am. Psychol., 6* (1951), p. 123.

14. ROSENBLATT, L., *Literature as Exploration.* New York: D. Appleton-Century, 1938, p. 80.

15. Cf. RAUSHENBUSH, E., *Literature for Individual Education.* New York: Columbia University Press, 1942.

16. WOODRING, P., "The Ford Foundation and Teacher Education," *Teachers Coll. Record, 62* (Dec. 1960), p. 227.

17. NEWLAND, T. E., "Programs for the Superior," *Teachers Coll. Record, 65* (April 1961), p. 521.

18. GRIFFITHS, D. E., and HOBDAY, A. F., "A New Kind of Case Study," *Educ. Research Bull., 31* (1952), p. 20.

19. HERTZMAN, M., "Psychology, Literature, and the Life Situation," *Psychoanalysis, 3* (Winter 1955), p. 52.

20. MC DANIEL, W. B., 2D., "Bibliotherapy—Some Historical and Contemporary Aspects," *Am. Library Assoc. Bull, 50* (Oct. 1956), pp. 584–589.

21. FLOCH, M., "The Use of Fiction or Drama in Psychotherapy and Social Education," *Hospital & Inst. Book Guide, 1* (Dec. 1958), p. 64.

22. BUTTS, R. F., "Tension in Teacher Education," *Educ. Forum, 25* (Nov. 1960), p. 11.

23. SOMERVILLE, R. M., "The Short Story in Family Life Education," Two volumes. Doctor of Education Project Report. New York: Teachers College, Columbia University, 1961, typewritten.

DEATH EDUCATION AS PART OF FAMILY LIFE EDUCATION: USING IMAGINATIVE LITERATURE FOR INSIGHTS INTO FAMILY CRISES *

ROSE M. SOMERVILLE

The study of child development and family relationships through novels, plays, and stories has received some attention in the past decade in professional journals, in the design of new courses, and in teacher education workshops. (Somerville, 1966) At three recent annual meetings of the National Council on Family Relations, papers have been presented on the various ways in which fiction can serve as a classroom resource: in Toronto, 1965; in New Orleans, 1968; and in Chicago, 1970. As a consequence, it is rare to find family life and sex educators at any academic level who are unaware of the many aspects of man-woman, parent-child, and family-society interactions which find reflection in creative literature. Even in kindergarten and primary school where stories have long been a mainstay, their potential for organizing discussion about personal development and family relationships has begun to be recognized.

However, there is one area where fiction could be of particular use that has been neglected in high schools and colleges as well as with younger children. Death is a significant and universal family experience. Two American families are bereaved every minute in peacetime. In war years the rate rises. Lieberman estimates, for example, that 50,000 men killed in Viet Nam have left 18,000 widows, 12,000 orphans, 80,000 bereaved parents, and 60,000 grandparents, as

---

* Adapted from a paper given at the Annual Meeting of the National Council on Family Relations, Chicago, October 1970. Reprinted from *The Family Coordinator,* July 1971, with permission of The National Council on Family Relations.

well as numerous bereaved siblings and fiances. (1970) Yet this is not a subject which receives much attention in family textbooks. This makes the fictional resource all the more important.

A recent edition of a study guide on marriage and the family (Kirkendall, 1970) lists nine textbooks which include death and bereavement among personal and family crises. However, examination of the given textbooks will find most of them treating these topics with extraordinary brevity. In many family textbooks, bereavement, crisis, death, widowhood, and the like cannot be found in the index. In one study of ten junior high and senior high textbooks, death was included in only three and was allocated at most 23 lines. (Rodman, 1970) There is a curious contrast between the recognition given to the importance of crisis preparation in the abstract and the lack of adequate discussion in the concrete. It is stated firmly that "knowing about a critical event and preparing for it in advance mitigates the hardship and improves chances of recovery." (Martinson, 1970, 354) Also, "There is general agreement that the ability of a marriage or a family to meet the inevitable crises that will affect it depends on such factors as . . . the preparation the family had made in advance for meeting just such emergencies." (Klemer, 1970, 307)

It may be claimed that the textbook omissions reflect the lack of data. It is indeed true, as one textbook writer puts it, that

> Bereavement has not been well studied. Much of this lack can be attributed to the inertia, taboos, and inherent methodological difficulties that surround studies of this nature. Society, in general, is against investigating this most universal of crises. (Womble, 1966, 491)

However, the state of research is not quite as dismal as textbook omissions would suggest. A recent bibliography (Irish, 1970) included more than 250 articles and books on death and bereavement. Another bibliography (Fulton) is even more inclusive and its compiler comments in a subsequent article (Fulton, 1970) on the dramatic increase in studies of death and bereavement that has marked the past decade.

Little of this material has been incorporated in the family textbook. In textbooks for the younger reader there may be only a single sentence: "A serious illness, loss of job, death of a close relative, or a bad fire all create unexpected problems to be tackled together." (Hoeflin, 1960, 247) Not only does this suggest that death of a close relative brings "unexpected" difficulty, but it ignores completely the task of helping students face their feelings in each of these crises. Some textbooks make the latter more difficult by their easy generalizations. "An overwhelming loneliness is nearly always felt by the surviving partner following the death of the husband or wife." (Landis, 1954, 325) This may ill prepare the survivor for feelings of relief, even euphoria, depending on circumstances or the nature of the spousal relationship.

The textbook situation has its curriculum guide counterpart. There is recognition in the abstract that "the challenges, interests, needs, and problems of life, both individual and social are the foci around which learning experiences are developed" (Georgia, 1962, 3) but the pages on child care and development or on personal, social, and family relationships or even those on home nursing, offer no clue to death and bereavement as "challenges" and "problems of life" for which learning experiences are needed. One guide for teaching the high school senior suggests that the class concern itself with the problem, "How may children and/or the family be helped to adjust to a divorce, illness, or death?" However, it offers no guidance for exploration of death and bereavement. (California, 1967) A guide for the eighth through twelfth grades does examine concepts of social maturity, defense mechanisms, and crises, but does not attempt any interrelation of these concepts. Instead, the following exercise reminiscent of Rodman's (1970, 19) criticism of easy solutions offered in textbooks, is suggested: "Select some typical crisis common to families and using the steps for meeting family crises as given in *When You Marry* by Duvall, work out solutions for the problem." (Nevada, 1963, 139) When a curriculum guide mentions widowhood only in connection with the "empty nest" period and retirement, (Missouri, 1965) there would seem to be no recognition that after the thirteenth wedding anniversary, death is more likely than divorce to terminate the marriage. (Jacobson, 1959, 145) Not only is the student thus given little preparation for the loss of a parent rather than a grandparent, but the death of a friend, of a sibling, of a boy friend, seems to be ignored as a possibility.

There are several possible explanations for textbook and curriculum guide inadequaces in the area of death and bereavement. One has to do with the functional nature of many courses and units offered in high school and college, which leads to concentration on dating, marriage, and early years of the parental role. If it is pointed out that even these topics allow for some anticipatory socialization since marriage and parenthood may still be some years away when discussed in high school or even the first year of college, it may be necessary to turn to a second explanation. This is a marked reluctance to explore topics which bring feelings of sadness and discouragement into the classroom, realistic as these feelings may be. This may derive from inadequate teacher education in the humanities for family life and sex educators. As a colleague put it, "In teaching literature I am always involved in death. All great writing implicitly or explicitly handles the theme of death. It is inevitably part of all thinking about the self and about others." In contrast, state surveys of family life education show a tendency to omit divorce, death, bereavement, aging, broken homes, abortion and illegitimacy, and other topics which may challenge traditional ways of thinking about the self and about others.

In a survey of Minnesota high schools in 1965, "broken homes" appeared almost at the bottom of the list in number of hours spent on twelve different major sections of family life education. (Martinson, 1970) Moreover, the category of "broken homes" does not always include those broken by the death of a spouse or a parent. A survey of Indiana high schools in 1959 made a list of 47 subtopics in eleven broad content areas in the field of family life education. One such area was "broken homes" but the only two subtopics were separation and divorce. (Dager, 1966) Perhaps the omission of death and bereavement is not unexpected since with the present level of teacher preparation many are influenced by textbook emphases and omissions and the most commonly used basic textbook in family life courses in Indiana high schools did not include crisis, death, bereavement, or widowhood in its index. A recent survey in the state of Washington does not include bereavement in its listing of topics covered by 40 percent or more of teachers in that state. (Baker and Darcy, 1970)

If generalization to the country as a whole is possible from the few state surveys available, it is necessary to conclude that death education is not part of family life education at present in American high schools. The situation in the colleges would seem to be little different.

TEACHER EDUCATION

The college situation undoubtedly affects the high schools. The teacher-to-be who has not in college years had an opportunity to work through feelings about death and bereavement is not likely to feel comfortable with the thought of offering this challenging subject matter in the elementary or high school classroom.

It has been said that death and sex are the two subjects parents find most difficult to talk about with their children. Some of the same difficulty shadows teacher-student and student-student dialogue. Moreover, the parental reluctance in the case of both death and sex may influence school willingness to broaden curricula. Fiction is not a magic wand that will transform influential social forces, such as the emphasis on youth and happiness and a tendency to merge the two, or the aversion to planning ahead on personal and societal levels, but it can serve to increase teacher competency and thereby both meet student needs now and create a better prepared parent body in the future. There is no doubt that death, bereavement, and aging are topics requiring a range of teacher competencies that are not adequately developed with present programs. If the new criteria accepted for teacher preparation by the National Council on Family Relations (Somerville, 1970) become the standard in the various states, this situation will undoubtedly change. Opportunities for the teacher to have examined his own feelings about death will assure the broad perspective and the acceptance of emotion in the classroom which can facilitate classroom discussion. Creative literature reveals the wide range of feelings, from guilt to relief, that may accompany the death of kin, and depicts the various changes in roles and intimacy structure which allow families to survive the loss of a member.

One challenge to the teacher is the fact that his own readiness does not always find a match in student readiness. In many instances the student will be more comfortable in discussing "happy problems," such as who pays for the date or personality fit in mate selection. If given a checklist of preferred topics at the beginning of the semester, he is least likely to select aging or death. Fiction makes it possible to meet present felt needs and yet offer some degree of anticipatory socialization in an area in which denial and withdrawal are common. Many plays, stories, and novels, as well as some recent autobiographies which come close to fiction in the intensity of feelings communicated, do not make death and bereavement central issues and yet they include them as among the events which affect the characters. Thus death becomes through fiction *one* of the topics of classroom concern and may thereby meet less student resistance than when introduced in sharply-focused didactic materials. Once interest has been aroused and gaps of knowledge revealed, it is possible to send the student to various readings. Steinbeck's *Grapes of Wrath,* Salinger's *A Catcher in the Rye,* and Smith's *A Tree Grows in Brooklyn,* can serve in this regard as can fiction already assigned in literature classes, from Greek classics to Shakespeare to nineteenth century novels. The catharsis provided by a powerfully told story is as helpful to the adolescent who in a sense acquires practice in weeping for events not yet experienced, as for the adult who is helped by fiction to complete his grief work. Moreover, the adolescent who has already experienced a death in the family can be helped by the reading and the class discussion to gain new perspective on the alternatives that were open to him as well as on present functioning, whether in relation to other siblings, to a widowed parent, or to a surviving grandparent.

The effort to include death education as part of family life education will undoubtedly be facilitated by the establishment of Thanatological Institutes as part of sociology departments, as at the University of Minnesota, or of Thanatology Foundations, as at Columbia University's College of Physicians and Surgeons. These are dedicated to the study of dying, including both medical and psychological effects on family members, and will improve nationwide efforts to help families and individuals face death realistically. (Hicks, 1970)

Parent education is an essential part of this new effort. As the adult population is helped to face its ambivalences toward death and bereavement, it will begin to see the school as an ally in preparing individuals and family members for crises. In the transition period, however, it can be anticipated that the objectivity of the teacher and the secular nature of the public schools will be found threatening to some parents who may demand, as in sex education, that death education not be offered in the younger grades—"Let children be children . . ."—or that a particular approach to death be propagandized rather than a broad educational consideration of historical and cross-cultural factors, ethical dilemmas, and conflicting individual and societal needs.

It should be noted that the exceptional teacher has in the past managed on occasion to get past the hurdles of textbook and syllabus omissions and introduce a unit on death. Avery reports a class of eleventh grade girls who were encouraged to suggest life cycle units in a health program and who included death among the areas in which they felt a lack of knowledge. Discussion, aided by use of resource persons, included "individual attitudes toward death, how to accept death . . . of a family member, and what to do for a bereaved friend." (Avery, 1962, 36) More recently on the college level teacher initiative met exceptional student response, with 200 at Harvard enrolling in a course on death instead of the anticipated 20. (Schneidman, 1970)

SELECTING FICTION

Fiction can illuminate many aspects of death and bereavement. Only a few will be suggested here, but it is hoped that the suggestions offered will encourage the teacher to seek out for himself additional aspects in other novels, stories, plays, and biographies. Through fiction the following questions can be explored:

1. What is the range of possible human response to death of a family member? How does society or a given subculture sanction some reactions and determine the limits within which a family or a family member may express feelings?

2. What are the newer norms concerning the duration of mourning and its outward expression?

3. Does grief for loss of a role or of a relationship manifest itself differently than grief for loss of the given person?

4. Do all varieties of burial rites have the same effects on the feelings of the bereaved? On what basis can decisions be made concerning the open coffin, cremation, ceremonial services, and the like? *Whose* body is it: what weight is to be given to the dying person's wishes if they conflict with those of other family members or with community standards? Why are there such conflicting feelings about the body of the deceased?

5. Is the bittersweet quality of the gathering of kin at a funeral typical or exceptional?

6. In what ways does bereavement precipitate out the confrontation with one's own mortality, with what possible consequences for the individual and the family?

7. What is the relationship between the duration and kind of dying (accident versus prolonged illness) and the mourning process?

8. What is the range of normality in the feelings of guilt and self-accusation, in the expression of aggressive feelings, etc.?

9. What kinds of support can relatives, friends, neighbors, professionals (medical, religious, educational) provide that will facilitate facing reality, completion of grief work, and reallocation of roles?

10. What is the relation of death and bereavement to the life philosophy, value system (individual, family, society), and coping mechanisms of each family member?

Not all of these questions are raised by a particular work of fiction. However, discussion tends to eddy out from one issue to another, and often the particular instance of the story is forgotten as the whole realm of the sociopsychological comes into view. This does not happen with every story, novel, or play. The goals of family life education, increasing awareness by the student of his own feelings and increasing sensitivity to others' needs as influenced by social pressures, can also be served by limiting the focus to the particular work of fiction. By examining the factors that led to a particular outcome and suggesting analogous and contrasting situations, problem-solving abilities can increase. (Somerville, 1966, a,b,c) Empathic competence can grow in a classroom that encourages articulation of ideas and expression of feelings without penalizing frankness. Ordinarily a work of fiction is needed in its entirety for clues to behavior. However, where classroom time will not permit this, excerpts from plays or stories can be taped, or a commercial recording played in part, to highlight one brief interaction, with class discussion focusing on inferences as to the kinds of relationships that led to the incident and the likely consequences of the recorded encounter.

Knowledge of fiction that has a death or bereavement dimension can be gained by reading current book reviews or by consulting catalogues with topical listings. A new volume of *Short Story Index* appeared in 1965 and includes those published from 1959 to 1963. A more recent supplement includes stories published from 1964 to 1968. It is noteworthy that death is an increasingly popular theme with short story writers. Fewer than 50 stories are listed under Death in the 1965 volume while over 200 can be found in the later supplement. Similarly the *Play Index* and the *Fiction Catalog* provide lists which are easy to consult. In high schools and colleges, students will often bring titles that have come to their attention. Colleagues in literature departments are valuable resource persons. But it will be the family life educator himself who will come to some judgment concerning the quality of the fiction and its usefulness for his particular students, sometimes only after trial and error. The classroom as a center of teaching and learning permits the needed flexibility in fiction selection.

TOPICS RELATED TO DEATH AND BEREAVEMENT

death by suicide

The majority of all deaths in the United States now occur in the hospital or the nursing home. Family members must cope not only with their own feelings and those of the dying patient but with members of the institutional staff. As a recent study puts it,

> The American attitide that suicidal persons do not deserve respect or extensive care is rather starkly expressed on emergency services in our hospitals. If the suicide arrives already dead, staff members display little sympathy for him. If he is alive, they will try to save him, but with traces of contempt and disgust. (Glaser, 1965, 83)

In contrast, "the staff takes a relatively charitable attitude toward suicidal acts if the patient has suffered a great deal." If death and bereavement are missing in the index of many functional textbooks, suicide is even more likely to be omitted. (Peterson, 1964; Blood, 1962; Lantz, 1962) In institutional textbooks suicide is more likely to be mentioned but usually in connection with the family pattern of another society or in brief mention of the differential suicide rates between men and women. In the United States the divorced male or the widower is more likely to commit suicide than the divorced female or the widow. Research and speculation both seem to be lacking in most textbooks as to the causes of this higher male suicide rate. If it should turn out that one factor were the lack of permission in the dominant culture for the male to express grief and to manifest dependency needs, the use of fiction could be salutary in drawing student attention to the arbitrariness of this limitation in light of changing definitions of masculinity and femininity. The teacher who is alert to this possibility can use any story or scene which depicts the behavior of surviving kin or close friends, and raise the pertinent questions even when the author seems to be giving approval to the stiff upper lip tradition. Even a story that does not deal with death and bereavement but suggests some cultural limitations to male expression of feelings can become the takeoff point for discussion about latitude for the male in expressing sorrow. Thus a broad range of stories can be tied in with death education.

Stories that romanticize suicide, as in Galsworthy's "The Apple Tree," in which the jilted country girl ends her life, require skillful discussion leadership if students are to examine the consequences of such a decision. The crossroads burial, even if mentioned only briefly in the story, can allow discussion of both punitive attitudes still held toward death by suicide, including problems of euthanasia, and the effects on family members of different kinds of burial.

"The Death of a Salesman" by Arthur Miller ends with a suicide. Even though the play is more than two decades old and developments in recent years, such as old age payments under Social Security, affect several problems presented in the play, it still has tremendous vitality. In 1966, some seventeen million television viewers reacted so favorably as to encourage the presentation of other great dramas. Miller himself claimed that the play's success in revival "proved the existence of a large audience for the gutsy drama dealing with harrowing human problems." (Frank, 1966, 5) It is worth noting, however, that in some classrooms where students present written reports and there is no joint discussion, many of the students tend to ignore the suicide or to take it as a "fitting ending" and "deserved demise." Students seem to need encouragement, often available only through class discussion, to probe their feelings about self-destruction. Miller's play is less challenging than some others because it is dealing with an aging family member but discussion can broaden this to include younger persons as well, and to consider the variables of terminal illness, disfigurement of accident and war victims, and other crisis-related phenomena.

hospitals and grief

Classroom discussion of fiction can encourage understanding of how the hospital death makes the direct expression of grief more difficult. Medical personnel have their own problems in working with dying patients and their familes and tend to protect themselves from the emotional burden of coping with the despair of both by either setting difficult standards of "proper dying" and "dignity" or keeping family members physically at a distance from patient and nurse. This unhappy triangle of nurse or doctor, patient, and family members develops in a setting complicated by institutional standards. "Patients are not allowed to manage their own dying when it interferes with the social-organization of the hospital. Thus dying patients may be given narcotics if their pain disturbs other patients and interferes with hospital routines." (Glaser, 1965, 212) In some instances medical personnel do not distinguish between "high grief" and "low grief" deaths (Fulton, 1970) and may distribute their limited time inappropriately. In other instances they may substitute themselves for family members instead of seeking to maintain family involvement in the patient.

Nor are family members permitted to manage their own reactions to their loss. The hospital tends to be less concerned about the mental health outcomes for family members and more concerned about having them "able to decide upon and attend to such matters as autopsy, disposal of the body, dispersing the patient's personal effects and meeting his obligations to the hospital." (Glaser, 1965, 150) Sometimes the hostility directed at physician or nurse by family members or by the patient is undeserved and is a displacement for guilt and anger, two common emotions in a situation of bereavement, normally felt toward the self or toward another family member. A story that permits discussion of this on the college and adult level is "What the Cystoscope Said," by Anatole Broyard. The son who has not gotten along well with his father is at the dying man's bedside in a hospital. He directs his anger at a beautiful nurse whose radiant health seems an affront to him. He punishes her by seduction. Depending on the student level, the class could also discuss this in terms of the need for some life-affirming act in the often desperate moment of realization of death's finality. Donorship of body parts can also be discussed in this context.

The diversity of student views on many of these issues can help them understand the failure of kin to agree on many decisions that must be made in connection with death and bereavement, and to anticipate the strain which is almost unavoidable in the presence of diverse value systems. The act of the mother of the dying child where she agrees to the hospital request for organ donorship can be seen either as "heartless," the view perhaps of some of her kinfolk as well as some members of the class, or as an effort to ensure that her child's death perpetuates life. Once the class is reassured that consensus is not the aim of class discussion but a sharing of diverse feelings and interpretations, a broad range of decisions in a given crisis can be explored.

Death education within the medical profession itself admittedly needs improvement and it may help family members to know in advance that nurses and physicians may not have much to offer in the way of emotional support. "What can you say to a mother whose child is dying?" asks the nurse in a recent popular article. (*Look*, 1969) It is possible that the sensitivity sessions mentioned in that article may help her and other staff members to cope with their own feelings and eventually be able to communicate better, verbally and non-verbally. Role-playing in the classroom is a useful supplement to fiction in encouraging emotional expression.

A story by Gerber, "The Cost Depends on What You Reckon It In," suggests that in some instances guilt feelings, however inappropriate, such as those associated with the use of a rest home for an aging parent, can act as a barrier to permitting autopsy or similar acts that could contribute to the advance of science and the relief of human suffering.

aging and death

Updike's *Of the Farm*, a brief novel, permits discussion of ways ill and aging family members may seek to gain acquiescence, to exert the control, they could not fully achieve through the years. And on the part of those who will survive there is the temptation to make promises and yield in response to knowledge of a family member's imminent demise, particularly if there has been some feeling of guilt and inadequacy. Class discussion can focus on the issue of a "just peace" among family members and the difficulties in the path of achieving this peace in the weeks or months of a lingering death. Students can be encouraged to examine the value issues and the psychological consequences attendant upon a choice between bland relationships and unreconciled ones. Joey's mother begins to make biting comments about his new wife, Peggy, and he finds himself agreeing. "Perhaps it was merely that, feeling my mother's fright at her coming death, I needed a great grief of my own as an answer, a mirror, an exchange." Capitulation to maternal domination, or as in *I Never Sang for My Father* to paternal domination, may seem to many students a large price to pay.

The issue is similar in Flannery O'Connor's "Everything that Rises Must Converge." The adult son quarrels endlessly and unproductively with his mother. He does not give the impression of caring deeply about combatting the racial prejudice which she expresses by word and deed. It is largely a peg on which he can hang his other grievances against his mother. When she dies unexpectedly of a stroke after a brief physical encounter provoked by her attempt to patronize a militant black woman, her son is devastated. He is left not with a cause worth fighting for but merely memories of the misery through which they had put each other. The story can serve as a springboard for discussion of what death solves and what it cannot solve in family relationships.

The love-hate which characterizes not only some parent-child but some spousal relationships seems to take on particular poignancy in later life when death is in the offing. Indeed the prospect of death sometimes frees family members to voice the anger they have long withheld. The distress of their kin must be weighed against the long-suppressed need to express hostility. In "Tell Me a Riddle," the adult children look on in anguish as their aging parents reveal the deep cleavage between them. A terminal illness brings the aging wife to no forgiveness but the surviving husband is able in the long months prior to her death to regain feelings of tenderness and to lessen the feelings of guilt that might otherwise overwhelm him. It is the warmth and compassion of a grandchild who serves as nurse that facilitates this process. Students can discuss the alternatives kinfolk have in situations of terminal illness and death to exacerbate the guilt feelings of immediate family members or offer support and aid.

Aging is generally associated with death, perhaps so much so that the shunning of the elderly which is more characteristic of the dominant American culture than of more traditional subcultures finds some explanation in this fact. Aging is also associated with chronic illness. One report indicates that 77 percent of persons over 65 suffer from heart disease, cancer, arthritis, diabetes, and other serious ailments. (Cavan, 1969) With approximately a tenth of the population in the U.S.A. aged 65 and over, bereavement can be expected in tens of thousands of families each year not suddenly but as a natural consequence of lengthy illness. However, the mechanism of denial frequently continues to operate for the older person, as shown in the reluctance to draw up a will, as well as for other family members who rarely acquaint themselves with the decisions they will have to make concerning final arrangements, including disposal of the body.

With only a minority of aging parents living jointly with their grown children, a crisis can be created in the several families of these children when confronted with prolonged illness of parents or parents-in-law, the need to keep several households going, and the determination of sibling responsibility for economic and emotional support of the ill parent as well as the surviving one. At the turn of the century, a son or daughter was still living at home when a parent died, since the first spouse to die usually did so a few years before the last child left home. There was, therefore, some assurance of availability of aid for the dying parent, and especially for the surviving parent. At present, the empty nest comes earlier and longevity rates ensure childless households for the majority of elderly parents.

The most common experience for all Americans is loss of the father and coping with the mother's needs at time of bereavement. There are almost four times the number of widows as widowers in the population. Fiction can remind the students that not all surviving family members are equally able to face the ordeal of the dying and the funeral. A common escape is through psychosomatic illness. Paul in "What the Cystoscope Said," explains "It was too much for my mother. One morning she couldn't get out of bed to go to the hospital. The doctor came and diagnosed her illness as one that would last a little longer than my father." She did indeed remain bedridden until after the cremation had taken place. The story suggests that this dropping out and leaving the death scene to one family member is not always unwelcome to him. The bedside deception, to keep the dying person from knowing his situation is hopeless, can be quite prolonged, and is somewhat harder to play out with fellow actors present. There is some criticism of this deception by sociologists and anthropologists. (Glaser, 1965; Gorer, 1965) The arguments pro and con are worth airing in the classroom as it is a point of family policy which will find diverse viewpoints even within a given family. The story suggests, however, that decision-making as to ways of disposing of the body, kinds of funeral, and so on, may be simplified sometimes by the withdrawal of most of the relatives. It also suggests that for the dying some degree of contentment or dissatisfaction with the kind of life he has lived is derived from the presence or absence of caring kin at the bedside.

the young widow; the young orphan

Loss of a parent or of a sibling is less common for the young child today in comparison with the situation at the turn of the century. However, about a fifth of new widows each year are under 45, and two out of three widows in their twenties were found to have children under five years of age in the 1960 Census. Fiction suggests the diverse problems of grief management for adult family members when death education for young children is also required. While more is written about children of divorce, children of bereavement are almost as commonly encountered. In mid-1955, 2.7 million children eighteen years and younger had been orphaned by the death of at least one parent, while 3.3 million children of that age group had divorced parents. (Bell, 1963)

Fiction reveals a number of problems in death education for children not only when they lose a parent, a grandparent, or a sibling, but when they experience an even more remote loss. There is a tendency for stories and plays to emphasize the ordeal aspect rather than the positive sociopsychological function of the funeral. The issue of viewing the dead person or being forced to touch or to kiss him is central in a number of stories. The popular film, "Rachel, Rachel," draws attention to the child's eye view of death and the problem of growing up in an undertaker's family. Cassill's "The Covenant" offers a contrast in Miriam, at least on the surface. Perhaps her very casualness at funerals is a clue to use of the denial mechanism. In any case the author is concerned mainly with two other children who are attending the funeral of an uncle, their mother's brother, Luke. Harlan is thirteen when Uncle Luke is killed in a highway crash. Chris, his little brother, is five. Their mother utilizes the church service as an opportunity to pay off old scores with her fashionable niece. Fiction reminds one that the awesomeness of death does not cause suspension of old rivalries and resentments in many families, a point made equally strongly in "We Know Your Hearts Are Heavy" by Joan Merrill Gerber.

Harlan, in "The Covenant," feels faint when, seated near the coffin, he looks "down through the white tent of gauze peaked above his uncle's face to keep the flies away," and is glad his little brother, seated on the mother's lap "couldn't see the unacceptable changes on Luke's face." But suddenly his mother gets up, carries Chris to the coffin, puts aside the gauze, and insists that Chris place a rose in Luke's dead hands. "Put it in his hand," she told her youngest. "There, now, there. In his hand, like that." Her straining hands bent the fingers of the dead man and forced the living ones to leave their gift. "Now kiss him," she said. (In Sean O'Casey's *I Knock at the Door*, the mother allows her frightened child to lay a finger on the coffin in lieu of kissing the corpse.)

At the cemetery Chris refuses to accompany his parents to the grave and Harlan is asked to stay with him at the outskirts, near the hearse and near Miriam who has come along for the ride into the country. Harlan can glimpse the ceremonies at the grave but Chris is too small to be able to see down there. Burial of Luke does not become a reality for the younger boy and the effects on him in the ensuing months take up most of the story.

When grief is mild—Harlan had not been close to his uncle—the need for working through the sorrow is likely to be at a minimum. Hence as he and Miriam chat near the hearse about getting a trumpet and joining the school band, Harlan is able to benefit from her casualness. "What she had taught him in the few minutes they stood together was that life doesn't pause at all for death."

The students may wish to discuss whether this fact, the inexorable flow of events which takes no cognizance of the death of a loved one, is a comforting truth or an existential challenge to those deeply grief-stricken. Some may gain perspective on their own impatience with traffic snarled by a funeral procession or by a body which has just hurtled from a skyscraper or with a favorite shop closed for the day and a black-rimmed card in the window. The commercial interest in furtive removal of the body to avoid a pall on holiday spirits is suggested in Bunin's "A Gentleman from San Francisco."

For older family members, especially those whose early socialization occurred in rural communities, the frenetic pace and emotional detachment are in sore contrast with the broad participation in village funerals or with the doffing of the hat and solemn silence with which the passing cortege was recognized in small towns. The classroom can encourage discussion of the relationship between human indifference, and prepare the students either for the acceptance of recent norms of funerary behavior or for social action which may decrease alienation. For young people who have never experienced anything other than current urban norms in the U.S.A., it may be instructive to read excerpts from the tome, *Funeral Customs the World Over,* which comes to a definition of man as "a being that buries his dead with ceremony." (Habenstein and Lamers, 1963, 787) The diversity of customs presented will provide a basis for weighing those which are helpful to the survivors and those which are in need of what Sumner urged as rational revision of the folkways. Students may have to be alerted, however, to the bias in the volume which is perhaps not unconnected with sponsorship of the study by the National Funeral Directors Association. Another useful work of non-fiction in exploring cultural variations in funerary behavior is Oscar Lewis' *A Death in the Sanchez Family.*

The guilt felt in going on living while a loved one is dying, and the envy of the living felt by the dying member, can be examined through Thomas Mann's *The Magic Mountain.* While the tuberculosis sanatorium is less common an institution today than earlier in the century, it is reminiscent of any hospital today, with different personalities revealing themselves in the great confrontation.

The shame that attaches to loss of beauty in a woman or loss of strength in a man as they lie dying can be discussed in terms of such culturally induced complications in the family's handling of death. In Sean O'Casey's *I Knock at the Door,* the dying father keeps his children at a distance. He wastes away behind a closed door, not wishing the young ones to see the pale wraith he is becoming. The youngest child, particularly, cannot be expected to understand the motivation that lies back of what looks to him like hostility and rejection. Once Johnny tried to peek in at him; the suffering man cried, "Go away, go away, you, and shut the door at once—this is no place for little boys."

Relatedly, the cosmetic efforts of undertakers are subject to conflicting valuations, on personal and national levels. Contrasts can be found in even two very similar cultures, the British and the American. Gorer reports that "beautifying and rejuvenating of the corpse," as well as embalming, seems to be "a very uncommon practice" in Britain. (Gorer, 1965, x) On a theoretical level there are wide disagreements. Some argue that to look at death is to face its full reality, that the momentary suffering caused by a clear view of the deceased is offset by the mental health benefits of fixing the image clearly in mind. (Jackson, 1963) Others argue that one's own body image, and feelings tied up with that image, are so closely connected with what is done to the body of a family member that cosmetic efforts may permit not reality but falsity to come through. Many stories emphasize the latter. In "The Sojourner" by Carson McCullers, John Ferris is thinking of his father's death. "He saw again the outstretched body on the quilted silk within the coffin. The corpse flesh was bizarrely rouged." (1954, 341) Classroom discussion can bring out the difficulty of achieving the goal of affirming "the reality of death without over-emphasizing the gruesomeness of it." (Jackson, 1963, 60) This will probably lead into consideration of the conflicting principles of individualism and fam-ilism in the sphere of death. Is it true and if so, in what sense, that "The body of the person who dies is probably more the concern of his next of kin than of himself" and that "the funeral is not for the dead but for the living." (Jackson, 68, 69) And to what extent does the undertaker intrude into the final decision-making?

Preliminary analysis by the author of 185 student responses to a question-naire, You and Death, (Schneidman, 1970) administered in a state college in the southwestern part of the U.S.A. in February, 1971, indicates a wide range of views among upperclassmen. Asked how they felt about an open casket at their own funeral, most disapproved, some strongly, but the number who "don't care one way or the other" or who approve, while a minority, suggests the differences in individual feelings that may make family decision-making diffi-cult. Similarly, student preference was fairly evenly divided between having a small funeral with only relatives and close friends present, or accepting any kind of funeral the survivors wanted, but a minority wanted no funeral at all. Classroom questionnaires, particularly if they can be completed at home or in dormitories, can serve as a stimulus to thinking and discussion with kin and friends, and usefully supplement experiences through fiction.

Just as medical personnel are favorite targets for the hostility of the be-reaved, the undertaker tends to be an object of suspicion and dislike, dating back to the stoning of the Egyptian embalmers. Despite some of the apologia, (Jackson, 1963) the danger of kinfolk being mulcted by death salesmen who stand to profit by decisions made in moments of greatest guilt and grief would seem to be real. Novels, plays, and stories have been singularly silent on this theme, despite its traumatic potentials, and death education may have to rely more on didactic materials for this aspect of death and bereavement problems. (Bowman, 1964; Mitford, 1963)

The class may wish to explore that analog of the mother-in-law joke, the undertaker joke, as an expression of both hostility and anxiety. The tension connected with knowledge of the inevitability of one's own demise and the reminder of it that comes with each funeral finds some release through humor. But not when the loss is still fresh. It may be appropriate, therefore, for the class to become aware of recent bereavements among its members and to con-duct the discussion in empathic awareness of this fact.

The comfort that can be offered to the young widow by her kinfolk is sug-gested in James Agee's A Death in the Family, which is also known in play form as "All the Way Home" by Ted Mosel. Set in a different time period, just before the First World War, the story permits students to see the rituals which involve various friends and relatives and which by reminding the be-reaved woman of her obligation to remain part of the social group, serves to offset tendencies to withdraw into depression and apathy. Waller's emphasis (1938) on the social usefulness of mourning can be examined in various geo-graphical contexts, with recognition of the greater problems introduced by urbanization, physical dispersal of family members, and the norms in commercial funeral parlors which tend, like the hospital, to protect the staff and other clients rather than encourage the expression of strong feeling. Rufus, the young son who is six, becomes aware of mourning as a socially approved method of gaining attention and ego gratification. His feelings are mixed, for there was not only deprivation but also increased status: "something had happened to him that had not happened to any other boy in town." (204) The class can discuss the kinds of satisfaction derived through the cemetery syndrome, the perpetuation of the status of mourner entitled to special exemptions and privileges, and what family members can do to provide substitute satisfactions.

For the older child, the experience of death and funerals can be a push toward maturity and new perceptions of family roles. The limited size of modern families, the awareness of how few relatives each has, may be borne in on kinfolk when they gather at a funeral, as in Updike's "My Uncle's Death." With a sixteen-year-old boy's perspective, the story can be useful in high school as well as in college and adult classes. "The Manatees are not a family of breeders, and the number of relatives was small: walking up the aisle to the front pew with my parents, and my aunt, and my two cousins, I felt tall and prominent." He takes pleasure in the looks on the faces of others in the church:

> An odd, motionless, intent look, almost an odor, of sympathy and curiosity and reverence for grief. The look, no doubt, was primarily directed at my aunt, the widow, who, on the arm of my father, led our ragged, rustling procession. But we all—all the relatives—shared in it and were for the moment heroes of bereavement: a surviving band, a clan. I carried my role proudly, though doubting that I had enough sorrow to earn it. I was just sixteen, still an inch or two short of my eventual height, but walking down that aisle I entered, through that strange odor of respect, pity, and wonder, the company of adulthood. (1965, 200)

The older child may be aware of the imminent demise of a close relative and get much of the grief work over before the actual death. Relatives who are unaware of this may create resentment as in Sherburne's "From Mother . . . With Love," in which a high school girl has been told by her father that her mother had a terminal illness.

"She tried not to hate the people who urged her to cry. 'You'll feel better, dear', her Aunt Grace had insisted and then had lifted her handkerchief to her eyes and walked away when Minta had only stared at her with chilling indifference." (Sherburne, 1955, 43) The high school class for whom identifications would be easiest because of Minta's age, or the adult class which could identify with the father, could discuss the need Aunt Grace had to see her niece weep, to feel her sister had been loved and was mourned. This story, although limited by its middle-class setting, can serve with teacher encouragement to stimulate discussion of the details of bereavement, the need to give away the clothes of the deceased, the decision to occupy her favorite chair, and similar seemingly commonplace decisions which are fraught with feeling and will be differentially perceived by various family members.

death, ritual, and pluralism

The precision of ritual associated with death, burial, and mourning, stressed by Waller three decades ago as a functional contribution to family reintegration into the larger social structure (Waller, 1938) may not be the same kind of support today. The secularization of society can influence individual family members in a variety of ways, resulting in less inclination on the part of some toward conformity with established rituals. Some of this departure from tradition is undoubtedly salutary, as in the instance of lesser adherence to set periods of mourning which often do not coincide with the feeling level of all the family members. Moreover, higher rates of marriage across religious and nationality lines make for different perceptions of proper rituals. Even in Agee's story, Jay who had never been baptized was not given the complete funeral service. Family members need to be prepared both for the degree of conformity exacted by churches, funeral parlors, and burial places, and the lack of consensus they are likely to find in members of their kin network.

The self-determination possible in an earlier period of society, when a child could be prepared for burial by the family and placed under a favorite tree on the family farm must be contrasted with the rigid controls established by health agencies in most communities today. A family life educator tells of relatives in rural Ohio who "always buried their own dead without consulting authorities of any kind." (LeMaster, 1970, 57) Also, the right to have a spouse buried in a given cemetery may depend on religious conversion prior to death. Sometimes newspaper clippings can usefully supplement fiction in revealing modifications of ritual in a changing society and the new alternatives which offer the boon of flexibility or the burden of uncertainty.

"The Rose Tattoo," a play by Tennessee Williams, permits discussion of Serafina's decision to cremate her husband's body despite the priest's view. The play is also useful in discussing set mourning periods—hers was three years—and the dangers of extended mourning periods preventing recovery from grief. Discussion of cremation could include the scene from "What the Cystoscope Said," which serves as a reminder of the importance of preparing family members, already vulnerable from the hospital experience, the fatigue, and the grief, for what they are to see. Paul describes the velvet drapes which parted to reveal his father's coffin moving along a track. "I was as close as I'll ever come to screaming when my father disappeared into the flames." Discussion could focus on cultural contrasts, the public cremation in India, for example, witnessed by young children amid the support of kin and ritual, and the degree to which velvet curtains stifle genuine feeling.

death and life philosophy

Many stories serve to remind one of the relationship between the death of a family member and the increased consciousness of our own mortality or that of other loved ones. This raises questions concerning our sense of accomplishment and fulfillment, or the lack of it. "What is the meaning of your life?"

may be raised only tangentially in the story, and students may have to be reminded of it. Thus in "The Sojourner," the journalist who had returned to this country to attend his father's funeral is made aware of the passage of time, if only because all the relatives at the funeral look older. He notes his own receding hair, the spareness of his body. But above all, the fact that he is childless and has not remarried, while his former wife now has two children by her new husband, confronts him almost for the first time as a result of experiencing the funeral. He seems ready to say with Aegeus, "When death comes, Medea, it is, for a childless man, utter despair, darkness, extinction. One's children are the life after death." (Euripides, 1952, 405)

That bereavement can sharpen the time sense and result in a decision to use one's remaining years in a life style quite different from an earlier one is suggested by Brecht's "The Shameless Old Lady." A dutiful wife and mother for fifty years, the widow proceeds to break every rule on aging and widowhood among the French bourgeoisie to which her sons now belong. She refuses to accept the traditional role of helpless burden and boring visitor to her sons' homes and begins exploring a life she had never experienced, going to movies, acquiring a set of young, somewhat disreputable friends, buying a car, and going off on vacation with the friends. Her family looks at her conduct as shameless. One son's bewilderment has a tinge of financial interest; he sees his mother's small estate squandered instead of coming to him. The play (and film) suggests that the stereotypical widow's role is emotionally a burden but that efforts to break away from it can be threatening to other family members. The shameless old lady does inspire her grandson Pierre to be similarly independent and not let the family over-influence individual decisions. A similar inspiration is offered in "The Heyday of the Blood" where the great-grandfather by his example teaches a little boy the joy of risk by driving off to a fair in a nearby town. Some students may salute this "last fling" while others may argue that the aged family member with his own demise so close can afford to risk in a way other family members cannot. In any event, both works of fiction allow conflicting value positions to come out clearly.

"The Tree of Life" by Harvey Swados suggests that the final years may be spent in altruistic efforts, as when an aging uncle seeks out a nephew who is "slowly being overwhelmed by the terror of growing old to no purpose" and by his own acceptance of life and of death, inspires a similar ability to cope with existential realities.

SUMMARY

Death and bereavement as universal family experiences have been largely ignored in family life education, even when other family crises find some inclusion in textbooks, teaching guides, and checklists of student interests. The diversity of norms in a rapidly changing, highly stratified, and multi-ethnic society add to the confusion, alienation, and guilt felt by family members who have not been exposed to prior consideration of the kinds of decision-making they will face when death comes.

Fiction permits the classroom, for young and adults alike, to serve the educational task of crisis preparation, and does so by offering vivid pictures of the emotional climate that can prevail and by providing specific instances of the diversity of motivations, feelings, and choices which are possible in intra-family and family-society interactions. Specific novels, plays, and stories are suggested for high school, college, and adult education classrooms as examples of the insights teachers and students can derive from a wide variety of creative literature, whether specifically focused on issues of death and bereavement or only briefly revealing psychological causes and effects in this area.

Using student initiative and colleague cooperation in acquiring titles of plays, novels, and stories, as well as biography, is suggested, along with efforts to eliminate those works of fiction that do not meet standards of literary richness and behavioral science accuracy.

Unlike other subject matter for which textbook materials can serve as background for fiction reading, death and bereavement have to be studied, at least for the next few years until textbooks fill in their omissions, through selected articles from professional journals in several disciplines (sociology, psychology, social work, etc.) and the specialized books written in this area. It is suggested that fiction can arouse the interest which will send students to these non-textbook sources. It is urged that whatever values accrue through individual book reports, classroom discussion can add the necessary dimension of student awareness of diverse attitudes, needs, and expectations which can prepare them for the difficulty of achieving family consensus in matters of death and bereavement. It is also suggested that fears and hesitations which may mark initial efforts to explore this subject matter tend to diminish as opportunity to share these feelings bring a kind of relief emotionally and a kind of excitement cognitively. Creative literature for insights into death and bereavement can meet contemporary demands for educational relevance and affective-cognitive growth.

selected fiction for discussion of death and bereavement

AGEE, JAMES, *A Death in the Family*. New York: Avon, 1959.

ANDERSON, ROBERT, *I Never Sang for My Father*. New York: Random House, 1968.

BRECHT, BERTHOLD, *The Shameless Old Lady* (film). Based on Berthold Brecht, Die Unwerdige Griesin, *Kalendar Geschichten,* Frankfort-am-Main, Suhrkampverlag, 1948.

BROYARD, ANATOLE, "What the Cystoscope Said," in H. Gold, (Ed.) *Fiction of the Fifties.* New York: Doubleday, 1959.

BUNIN, IVAN, "A Gentleman from San Francisco," in *A Gentleman from San Francisco and Other Stories.* New York: Vintage, 1962.

CASSILL, R. V., "The Covenant," in *The Happy Marriage and Other Stories.* Purdue University Studies, 1966.

GALSWORTHY, JOHN, "The Apple Tree," in *Great Modern Short Stories*. New York: Random House, 1942.

GERBER, JOAN MERRILL, "The Cost Depends on What You Reckon It In," in *Stop Here, My Friend*. Boston: Houghton Mifflin, 1965.

GERBER, JOAN MERRILL, "We Know Your Hearts Are Heavy," in *Stop Here, My Friend*. Boston: Houghton Mifflin, 1965.

MANN, THOMAS, *The Magic Mountain*. New York: Knopf, 1929.

MC CULLERS, CARSON, "The Sojourner," in R. P. Warren and A. Erskine, *Short Story Masterpieces*. New York: Dell, 1954.

MILLER, ARTHUR, *Death of a Salesman*. New York: Viking, 1949.

MOSEL, TED, *All the Way Home*. New York: Samuel French, 1961.

O'CASEY, SEAN, *I Knock at the Door*. New York: Macmillan, 1960.

O'CONNOR, FLANNERY, "Everything that Rises Must Converge," in M. Foley and D. Burnett (Eds.), *The Best American Short Stories 1962*. New York: Ballantine, 1962.

OLSEN, TILLIE, "Tell Me a Riddle," in M. FOLEY and D. BURNETT (Eds.), *The Best American Short Stories 1962*. New York: Ballantine, 1962.

SALINGER, J. D., *A Catcher in the Rye*. Boston: Little, Brown, 1951.

SHERBURNE, ZOA, "From Mother . . . With Love," in BRYNA IVENS (Ed.), *Stories from Seventeen*. New York: Lippincott, 1955.

SMITH, BETTY, *A Tree Grows in Brooklyn*. New York: Harper, 1947.

STEINBECK, JOHN, *Grapes of Wrath*. New York: Viking, 1958.

SWADOS, HARVEY, "The Tree of Life," *McCall's*, June 1965, *92*, 84–85.

UPDIKE, JOHN, *Of the Farm*. Greenwich, Connecticut: Fawcett, 1967.

UPDIKE, JOHN, "My Uncle's Death," in *Assorted Prose*. New York: Knopf, 1965.

WILLIAMS, TENNESSEE, *The Rose Tattoo*, in *Three Plays*. New York: New Directions, 1964.

references:

AVERY, CURTIS, "Inside Family Life Education," *Family Life Coordinator*, 1962, *11*, 36.

BAKER, LUTHER, and J. B. DARCY, "Survey of Family Life and Sex Education Programs in Washington Secondary Schools," *The Family Coordinator*, 1970, *3*, 228.

BELL, ROBERT, *Marriage and Family Interaction*. Homewood, Illinois: Dorsey Press, 1963.

BLOOD, ROBERT, *Marriage*. Glencoe, Illinois: Free Press, 1962.

BOWMAN, LEROY, *The American Funeral: A Way of Death*. New York: Paperback Library, 1964.

CALIFORNIA, HAYWARD, *A Teacher's Guide for Sociology 1, Family Living Instruction*, Grade 12, 1967.

CAVAN, RUTH, *The American Family*, Fourth edition. New York: Crowell, 1969.

DAGER, EDWARD et al., "Family Life Education in Public High Schools of Indiana," *Family Life Coordinator*, 1966, 5, 131.

Euripides. Medea. JOHN GASSNER (Ed.), *Best American Plays.* New York: Crown Publishing Company, 1952.

FIDELL, ESTELLE, *Fiction Catalog 1961–1965. Supplements*, 1966, 1967, 1968, 1969. New York: H. W. Wilson.

FRANK, STANLEY, "T.V., A Force in Family Life," *T.V. Guide*, October 8, 1966.

FULTON, ROBERT, *Death, Grief, and Bereavement: A Chronological Bibliography*, 1843–1970. University of Minnesota: Center for Death Education and Research, no date.

FULTON, ROBERT, "Death, Grief, and Social Recuperation," *Omega*, 1970, *1*, 23–28.

GEORGIA, UNIVERSITY OF, *Curriculum Guide for Homemaking Education*, July 1962.

GLASSER, B., and A. STRAUSS, *Awareness of Dying*. Chicago: Aldine Publishing Company, 1965.

GORER, GEOFFREY, *Death, Grief, and Mourning*. Garden City: Doubleday, 1965.

HABENSTEIN, ROBERT, and WILLIAM LAMERS, *Funeral Customs the World Over*. Milwaukee: Bulfin, 1963.

HICKS, NANCY, "Neglect of Dying Patients' Emotional Needs Linked to Cultural Inability to Face Death," *The New York Times*, August 26, 1970, 13.

HOEFLIN, RUTH, *Essentials of Living*. New York: John Wiley and Sons, 1960.

IRISH, DONALD, "Death Education: Preparation for Living," bibliography, mimeographed. Paper presented at Annual Meeting of National Council on Family Relations, Chicago, October 1970.

JACKSON, EDGAR, *For the Living*. Des Moines: Channel, 1963.

JACOBSON, PAUL, *American Marriage and Divorce*. New York: Holt, Rinehart, 1959.

KIRKENDALL, LESTER, *A Reading and Study Guide for Students in Marriage and Family Relations*, Fifth edition. Dubuque: William C. Brown, 1970.

KLEMER, RICHARD, *Marriage and Family Relationships*. New York: Harper, 1970.

KUBLER-ROSS, ELIZABETH, *On Death and Dying*. New York: Macmillan, 1969.

LANDIS, PAUL, *Your Marriage and Family Living*. New York: McGraw-Hill, 1954.

LANTZ, HERMAN, and E. SNYDER, *Marriage*. New York: John Wiley and Sons, 1962.

LE MASTERS, E. E., *Parents in Modern America*. Homewood, Illinois: Dorsey, 1970.

LEWIS, OSCAR, *A Death in the Sanchez Family*. New York: Random House, 1969.

LIEBERMAN, E. JAMES, "War and the Family." Paper given at Annual Meeting of National Council on Family Relations, Chicago, October 1970.

LINDERMANN, E., "Symptomatology and Management of Acute Grief," *American Journal of Psychology*, 1944, *101*, 141.

Look, "A Love Story: Ward Four West," November 4, 1969, 33.

MARTINSON, FLOYD, *Family in Society*. New York: Dodd, Mead, 1970.

MARTINSON, FLOYD, *Sexual Knowledge, Values, and Behavior Patterns: With Especial Reference to Minnesota Youth*. St. Peter, Minnesota: Gustavus Adolphus College, 1966.

MISSOURI, KANSAS CITY, *Family Relations for High School Seniors. Curriculum Guide for Grade* 12, 1965.

MITFORD, NANCY, *The American Way of Death*. New York: Simon and Schuster, 1963.

MITCHELL, MARJORIE, *The Child's Attitude to Death*. New York: Schocken, 1967.

NEVADA, STATE OF, *A Guide for Teaching Personal and Family Relationships*. Carson City, July 1963.

PETERSON, JAMES, *Education for Marriage*. Second edition. New York: Scribner's, 1964.

Play Index 1961–1967. New York: H. W. Wilson, 1968.

Psychology Today, "You and Death," 1970, *4*, 37, 67–72.

RODMAN, HYMAN, *Teaching About Families*. Cambridge: Doyle, 1970.

SCHNEIDMAN, EDWIN S., "The Enemy," *Psychology Today*, 1970, *4*, 37.

Short Story Index, 1959–1963. New York: H. W. Wilson, 1965.

SOMERVILLE, ROSE M., "Family Life and Sex Education: Proposed Criteria for Teacher Education," *The Family Coordinator*, 1970, *2*, 183.

SOMERVILLE, ROSE M., (a) "Creative Literature for Study of the Family"; (b) "The Literature Approach to Teaching Family Courses"; (c) "The Short Story and Family Insights in Secondary Schools," *Journal of Marriage and the Family*, 1966, *28*, 213, 214, 223.

SOMERVILLE, ROSE M., *Family Insights through the Short Story*. New York: Teachers College Press, 1964.

SOMERVILLE, ROSE M., "Imaginative Literature in Family Life Education," *Journal of Home Economics*, 1963, *55*, 409–412.

WALLER, WILLARD, *The Family*. New York: Dryden, 1938.

WOMBLE, DALE, *Foundations for Marriage and Family Relations*. New York: Macmillan, 1966.

ZIM, HERBERT, and SONIA BLEEKER, *Life and Death*. New York: William Morrow, 1970.

THE FUTURE OF FAMILY RELATIONSHIPS IN THE MIDDLE AND OLDER YEARS: AN APPROACH THROUGH FICTION *

ROSE M. SOMERVILLE

The decade of the 1970s has begun with a notable degree of interest in the future of marriage and the family. On both popular and professional levels there have been books, articles, conferences which reflect increasing discontent with present family relationships and a more determined searching for alternatives. Classroom discussions show "the ambivalence of students toward the institution of marriage and the family as they had experienced and observed it" (Wiseman, Preface) and more frequent favoring of "no marriage, group marriage, no children."

This questioning of "the conventional mystique of family life" (Skolnick, Preface) is sharper at the student level than among the middle-aged and elderly, and reveals a negative evaluation of the marriages of parents, older siblings, and friends. However, older people have offered their own self-criticism. Otto reports that in "more than sixty conversations with members of the helping professions concerning their marriages and divorces," it became evident that "even those professionals who considered themselves happily married were increasingly inclined to question the contemporary institutions of marriage and the family." Fiction writers too, always sensitive to failures in human relationships, have depicted some attempts by the middle-aged to move away from traditional modes of functioning. Occasionally a writer, like Rimmer, will use the novel as a way of proselytizing for some specific solution to marriage failure. The large readerships enjoyed by such novels suggest the storyteller is touching some major discontents.

The college student, the fiction writer, and the helping professions come mainly from the advantaged segments of the community. Their criticisms reflect on middle-class marriage, long upheld as a model for the lower class. Perhaps the middle-class backgrounds of those most articulate in their demand for new family forms account for the lack of emphasis on need for economic changes. Few perceive marriage and the family as dependent variables, with the nature of the economy pivotal in determining the range of possibilities for the work and family lives of men and women. Nor does fiction broaden this perspective. Most writers tend to take the present economic structure as a given and insist that new family wine can be poured into the old bottles of economic relationships.

---

* An expanded version of a paper presented at the Groves Conference on Marriage and the Family, San Juan, Puerto Rico, May 1971. Reprinted from *The Family Coordinator*, October 1972, with permission of The National Council on Family Relations.

The following pages will fit into this limited framework, and will discuss recent studies and the further research needed on a short-term basis. Consideration will also be given to added services that may be necessary if somewhat more varied and flexible definitions of spousal, parental, filial, and sibling relationships are to be achieved without major changes in the economy. It is recognized, however, that the pressure of demands for work opportunities from many now denied them in desired quantity and quality—blacks, Chicanos, and other ethnic minorities, women, youth, and the elderly—may radically upset any short-run calculations. Relatedly the technological potential may have its own historical timetable little affected by, but greatly affecting, the trends to be depicted here as they emerge from present developments in kin relationships.

Despite the widely reported reluctance of students to discuss the middle and aging years, this article is largely directed to their attention. In the first place, they themselves will be middle-aged in a remarkably short time. Secondly, the test of their proposals for change in family relationships has an important time dimension. What are the implications of these alternatives for the second half of the individual's life span? And thirdly, as middle-aged and elderly kinfolk begin to adopt the changes proposed, can the lives of youth be unaffected?

MIDDLE AND OLDER YEARS:
CHRONOLOGY AND FEELING

Who is middle-aged? How old is the elderly couple? What is the future of these shaky concepts? It is commonly recognized among professionals in the family field that psychological, physiological, and social measures of aging would be more precise than chronological age. In addition to objective variables of health and physical condition, account would be taken of the subjective dimension, e.g., how old the individual feels and how he perceives his own potentials. However, such measures are not yet available, and the poor second-best of chronology must guide the discussion here. Studies of the middle-aged are not numerous and the few that exist do not use comparable cutoff points. Studies of the elderly more consistently use sixty-five as a starting place, although sixty is frequently used as well. It can be argued that consistency does not settle the problem: the researcher's acceptance of sixty-five may represent a lag in updating the heritage of longevity rates, energy and disease levels, and population ratios more characteristic several generations ago.

The connotations of middle-age in contemporary American culture are not positive ones. The term suggests decreasing opportunity (occupationally, romantically) and decreasing status (outside the home and in relation to the younger generation inside the home). Class discussion shows students using the term with very different age groups in mind. The younger students say their parents in the late thirties would resent being called middle-aged. Graduate students nervously take issue with classmates who would make thirty or thirty-five a dividing line. Several important fellowships and grants, even postdoctoral ones, do not take applications from those over thirty-five. Just as the phrase "affluent society" tended to direct attention away from the bulging pockets of poverty in the 1950s, so too the phrase "the Command Generation," used by a popular magazine for those in their forties and fifties who are at the peak of power, can direct attention away from the vast majority of Americans in the lower and the lower-middle classes for whom those years represent a decrease in income as well as in decision-making opportunities. Cuber's research suggested that work accomplishment was a consoling force for upper-middle and lower-upper "significant Americans" in the face of passive-congenial and devitalized marriages but offered no support for the welcoming of middle age.

Stratification studies may offer a useful model for solving some of the problems of defining middle-aged and older populations. Just as the simple scheme of upper, middle, and lower class was found inadequate to distinguish effects of income, education, and occupation levels on family functioning and it was found helpful to distinguish between the upper and lower levels of each class, so too it may be useful to distinguish at least two stages of middle-age and two stages of later years. Using chronological age for lack of a better indicator at present, the categories could be early middle age, advanced middle age, early old age, and advanced old age.

While the difficulty of creating cutoff points cannot be avoided, the problem may be eased with the increase of categories. One suggested typology could be early middle age, thirty to forty-five, advanced middle age, forty-five to sixty-five, early old age, sixty-five to seventy-five, and advanced old age, seventy-five and beyond. Research on housing patterns and on self-perception supports this split between the first older decade and the second, as custodial care and definition of the self as "old" have been found more likely at present to occur at seventy-five than at sixty-five. An alternative typology in case it is felt that thirty is an inappropriate start for middle-age would be early middle-age, thirty-five to fifty, advanced middle age, fifty to sixty-five, early old age, sixty-five to seventy-five, and advanced old age, seventy-five and beyond. Either typology would allow for increasing longevity which is likely in the decade or two ahead. At present half of those over sixty-five are over seventy-two and almost 1 in 5 is over eighty. (U.S., April 1970, 10)

Research to date has not been helpful in relating the family life cycle to the individual life cycle. Is the family middle-aged when its founders are? It would not appear so from the categories used by Duvall and also by Rodgers. Both define the middle years of a marriage as those with all children "launched" or having left the family of origin, and continuing on until retirement. (Rodgers, 65; Duvall, 15, 18) In Duvall's charts the mother is in her early forties when the first child marries and in her late forties when the last child marries, with the father about two years older at each of these launchings. Thus the couple reaches the empty nest period, or Duvall's stage of "Families in the Middle Years," when their own ages put them at the beginning of advanced middle-age or at the end of early middle-age, depending on which of the typologies suggested above is used.

While Duvall recognized that not all families will follow the cycle she depicts, as some couples will not have children at all, will marry late in life, and so on, and as Rodgers indicates, the number of children and the spacing will add further variables to those considered by Duvall, nonetheless the basic conceptual scheme offered by both is one in which the middle years of marriage do not match the age of their participants. The middle-age crisis which "seems to mark the passage between early maturity and middle age" is estimated by some (Fried, 2) to occur for women between the ages of thirty-six and forty and for men about five years later. This estimate would have the middle-age crisis occurring almost a decade before the marriage entered its middle years in Duvall and also in Rodgers. Future research will undoubtedly have to cope with this problem of congruence in the categories. This article will use the age of the individuals rather than the marriage stage. More serial monogamy and more remarriage in middle and older years, both likely in the next decade or two, will provide further challenge to the family life cycle concept, not only in the timing of progressions from one stage to another, but in definitions of developmental tasks.

THE MIDDLE YEARS

Recent criticisms of marriage and discussions of the future of the family seem to assume problems of monotony in spousal relationship while the couple is still in their thirties. In Rimmer's novel, *Proposition 31,* David and Nancy had been married fifteen years and Horace and Tanya twelve when they joined their two families in "corporate marriage," a design espoused by the novelist for Future Families of America. The story tells of an attempt to introduce group marriage through the California ballot after the foursome had first tried it out and found advantages in it over conventional marriage forms. While it can be dismissed as a fantasy world of material plenty and sexual competency, it might be shortsighted to do so. For the millions of young men and women who followed Rimmer from *The Harrad Experiment* into this more total commitment of several couples, the significance of the novel may lie not in its suggested shallow solutions to large societal problems, but in its confirmation of their fears that interaction, both conversationally and sexually, between husbands and wives tends to deteriorate when monogamous marriages last for more than a decade, and its confirmation of their hopes for simple solutions, that by putting two or three bored couples together a magical new combination will result. Ellis's judgment that "It is quite difficult to find a group of four or more adults of both sexes who can truly live harmoniously with one another," (92) finds no reflection in the story.

Perhaps more important, since the story is offered at more or less a single point of time, it provides no insights as to what happens as the couples move into advanced middle-age or early old age. Even when the couples are in early middle-age, the time period of the story, how does either couple relate to their families of origin? What problems do the parents of the couples have, or the brothers and sisters of the couples in relating to grandchildren or nieces and nephews brought up with new norms of nudity, multiple sexual partners, and cross-spouse conceptions. While in a sense these adjustments represent perhaps only a difference in degree rather than in kind from the culture shock experienced by some middle-aged and elderly relatives today in their relationships with youth, each degree would seem to warrant some anticipatory socialization to change not revealed by the novel.

Some suggestion of negative outcomes in the maintenance of kin relationships between middle-aged unconventional children and parents in early old age is offered in another work of fiction. Joe and Ruth Allston, when we meet them in Stegner's novel, have already lost their only son, drowned at thirty-seven, but flashbacks permit us to see the troubled intergenerational contacts as the son's choices in education, occupation, and mate selection disappoint his conventional parents. The parental self-righteousness of the Allston's contrasts with still another fictional situation, in which parental self-castigation marks the relationship with a son of early middle-age whose life style is not only different from that of his immigrant parents but from the majority in the host culture. Confusion and self-blame may be common among the 38 percent of the elderly who are foreign-born or who have at least one parent who is foreign-born. (U.S., April 1970, 10) The short story shows how an elderly couple blame themselves for the rarity of visits paid them by their son, Paul, and how desperately they try on these occasions to impress him with their efforts to meet his behavior standards. (Broyard)

Adams' careful study of intergenerational relationships in a North Carolina city would not have pulled the counterparts of the Allston's or of Paul's parents or indeed of any communal families into his sampling net of "married" and "only once." (9) More research is needed on minority family patterns, cutting across both class and ethnic lines, and focusing on the increasing numbers of men and women whose relationships as couples and with families of origin represent a departure from both traditional and transitional patterns. Little research has been done on the interaction between divorced parents and their grown children or divorced middle-aged men and women and their elderly parents. Sussman's parental aid model would permit examination of these increasing phenomena (1965, 403), but researchers may find data collection and interpretation even more difficult than Adams indicates for his still-married children of living-together parents.

The likelihood of more divorces in the future as men and women reach middle and older years after socialization to increased acceptance of this solution to cessation of affection may be offset by a trend to delay in marriage and remarriage. Consensual union, less valued than formalized marriages in most societies, is widely accepted nonetheless. Although its origins may lie in economic difficulty and the poorer bargaining position of women where gainful employment is not an alternative available to them, the institution may be adapted to emotional and ideological considerations.

The complexity and cost of divorce procedures may motivate cohabitation until the couple achieves greater certainty as to their feelings for each other. This may be particularly applicable to those divorced men and women who are considering remarriage, but it may enter into the thinking of the never-married also. Reiss mentions "a trend toward quicker remarriage" in comparing the four or five years it took about half the men and women in the 1950s to remarry after a divorce, with the two years for men and three for women the same proportion took in the 1960s. (302) However, new research may uncover a modification of this trend in the 1970s. Some clue to change is offered in extension courses on divorce or on the stepparent which attract a high enrollment of divorced people. Middle-aged women mention with some indignation and disappointment the experience of dating men who are ready for consensual but not legalized unions. Most of these women are middle-class and were socialized some decades ago when consensual union for that socioeconomic level was a rarity. However, the next decade or two may show the effects of women's liberation movements, some of which stress in their consciousness-raising rap groups the desirability of careers and of living arrangements which maximize personal options and flexibility. Some of these women will reject legal marriages or remarriages. In any case the echoes of their discussions will reverberate in the thinking of many middle-class men and women, and may influence their behaviors.

Thus several trends are likely to develop simultaneously to satisfy a diversity of needs and attitudes. Among the middle-aged and the elderly there can be anticipated an increase in nonmarital sexual relations, in consensual unions, and in remarriages. Not only is the culture likely to continue to be highly eroticized, offering stimuli to sexual expression, but there may be increasing recognition of sexual needs in the second half of life. The stereotype of lost sexuality for the postmenopausal woman and the male in early old age has been in the past both a self-fulfilling prophecy for many and a deterrent to empathic interaction with them on the part of both kinfolk and the helping professions.

Family life and sex educators have not sufficiently brought into the classroom the research findings of Masters and Johnson (249ff.) nor has the professional training of nurses prepared them sufficiently concerning sexuality in older men and women. New realism in the curriculum in high schools, colleges, and professional schools may mark the coming decade (Somerville, February 1971) and if so will undoubtedly affect the level of understanding of professionals and family members in regard to middle-aged and elderly patients, students, clients, and relatives.

THE OLDER YEARS

Remarriage for the middle-aged has met less resistance than for people sixty-five years and older. Nonetheless by the 1960s some 35,000 marriages a year involved people in early and advanced old age. (Rubin, 21) The coming decades are likely to see some marked increases as family and community pressures against such marriages lessen. Marriage would seem to be one of the main solutions for the lack of companionship felt by the elderly who are either divorced or bereaved. While several studies stress the amount of contact maintained between grown children and their parents, this tends to be reduced when there is a lone parent involved except for mothers and daughters.

A study of a North Carolina city found "not a single young male in our sample reports keeping in close touch with a divorcee-father." (Adams, 84) And "the relation of a son to a widower father is strictly one of non-involvement." (*ibid.*) Moreover, "The patterned receipt of help, the sharing of social activity, and ritual interaction are considerably less widespread between the male and a widowed mother than with a pair of living parents." (Adams, 86) The popular conception of widow domination of a son would not, according to the Adams data, be upheld once he married. In contrast, the young married female increases the help and social activity engaged in with her mother when her father is not alive. Adams' study did not include any men and women married more than twenty years. Other studies will have to answer the question of whether the female intensified interaction, described at a time when the widowed mother was likely still to be middle-aged, would continue into the later years. Also needed are data on mother–daughter interaction with a divorced mother. If the mother–daughter relationship remains close, there may be less motivation for remarriage of the elderly mother and this would reduce the disproportion between men and women seeking partners.

Will the intergenerational contacts which have in the recent past relied heavily on female initiative, from "Mum" in the East London slum to married daughters in the Adams and Komarovsky studies, continue in the future? Sweetser has seen in the change from agriculture to industry the explanation for more mother–daughter closeness. As patriarchal family organization declined, the overvaluation of the son lessened. Moreover, within the industrial setting, "role convergence," the joint playing by female of housekeeping and mother roles, has been seen as a binding element in the relationship. What will be the impact in the decade ahead of women's liberation movements, Population Zero, emphasis on spousal closeness? Friendships may increasingly rival kin closeness, as the element of choice gains valence, or the effort to build spousal intimacy may define both friend and kin, in some instances at least, as extraneous. (Otto, 111ff.)

The story, "A Daughter of My Own," suggests that the traditional assistance of the young woman's mother in the first weeks after a baby is born, or in some instances of her mother-in-law, may not always be welcomed by a young couple eager to make the new experience theirs alone. Not only the son-in-law but the daughter herself may view the older woman's aid as interference. The story suggests what may be an area of future research, that the "keeping in touch" dimension of family contact between generations, with writing and telephone calls substitutes for face-to-face interaction, exacts a toll in intimacy and level of identification among kin. Continued geographic mobility in the coming decade may intensify the emotional distance even if frequency of contact on a more superficial level continues or magnifies.

Moreover, "role congruence" may be reduced as the trends become more marked: first, decreased valuation of the mother role; and second, increased participation by men in marketing, child care, cooking, and other activities traditionally allocated to females. "To Room Nineteen" tells a story of lack of satisfaction in conventional women's roles. While the failure to build either a spousal relationship or a career that might reduce the frustrations felt by an educated middle-class woman in contemporary London suggests an extreme level of alienation, Susan's inability to solve her problem, or the problem that domestic arrangements today are seen to create for men and for women, is likely to find sympathetic echoes among American women. The story is widely assigned in Women's Studies courses in the United States. The feeling expressed in the story may well affect the part in the coming decade or two that women will play in maintaining the kin network. "Children? But children can't be a center of life and a reason for being. They can be a thousand things that are delightful, interesting, satisfying, but they can't be a wellspring to live from." (Lessing, 263)

More open recognition of negative effects of childrearing roles on spousal ones may act in the future as a preventive to overinvolvement in the parental role. Research on disenchantment among middle-aged couples combined with counseling insights from contacts with them indicates that estrangement begins in the early years of marriage when the woman's interests may be tied too exclusively to the children. (Blood and Wolfe, 156; Pineo, 7; Peterson, 38) Moreover, it has been found that overvaluation of the parental role can cause difficulties in the menopausal period. "Many women fear that they now have lost their main purpose in life and are no longer desired by their husbands and families. They feel that they are no longer needed and become seriously depressed. With the depression comes loss of sexual interest and activity." (Roundtable, 69) This has a negative effect on the husband's sexual performance which is already under some strain. "The incidence of sexual inadequacy in the human male takes a sharp upturn after 50 years of age." (Masters and Johnson, 263) While this is reversible, it requires a favorable psychological environment.

This environment may be contributed to by women's liberation ideology. The 1970s are likely to see emphasis on the development of woman as a person, with her own needs and interests, in which children play an important but secondary role. One outcome may be more spousal interaction in the early years of the marriage and another may be a welcoming rather than a depressed attitude toward the menopause. While this might augur further breaches in the relationships of middle-aged and elderly people and their grown children, it is possible that an increase in leisure time will mitigate the rivalry otherwise generated between spousal intimacy and interest in extended kin. Kibbutz experience also suggests that parent–child intimacy and devotion need not be impaired by diminution of parentally performed services (or filially-performed ones) or by the increased attention of parents to their work roles and to each other as romantic dyads.

Relatedly, the desire of American women for meaningful work outside the home is likely to increase as women become aware of their unrealized potentialities. The availability of middle-aged and older women to care for their grandchildren, even where their services are welcome, which is not uniformly evident, or of younger and middle-aged women to provide care for ailing elderly parents to a degree that would allow both generations to maintain their own separate residences, will undoubtedly be affected when more women enter gainful employment, particularly if more of the 31 million women now on the labor rolls become full-time workers.

One outcome may be the professionalization of some services for the elderly in the coming decade as a substitute for help in health care and household management now being provided by a daughter or other female relative living in close proximity. Services by the elderly may also be professionalized. In lower income groups the realization that public child care services may threaten their own usefulness to their married children and decrease interaction with their grandchildren has created some grandmother opposition to new preschool and after-school programs. It was a step forward for some of these programs to involve mothers; the coming decade may see the effort extended to grandmothers. The paraprofessional status may create a non-kin basis for services by and for the elderly. Men and women in early old age have already demonstrated their ability to supplement the work of nurses in institutions for mentally and physically handicapped children. Even where child care is not an issue, but understanding and relatedness need encouragement, as in cases of adoption, it is possible that in the coming decade the middle-aged and the elderly will receive briefing in preparation for a new role comparable to that given the adoptive parents.

The present generation of youth is apt to constitute quite a different set of grandparents a few decades hence. Their role definitions and their educational level may necessitate the establishment of a whole set of institutions to provide services now available through the kin network. In the immediate decade, however, it is not likely that the full impact of working lives for women will come into play. Moreover, the government's failure to plan a peace-time economy which could have continued and expanded women's work roles at the same time that hundreds of thousands of men returned from war may have the same effect in the coming decade that caused Betty Friedan's initial protest.

The tensions between the middle-aged and the elderly are not likely to decrease in the coming decade so far as decisions are concerned about nursing homes, joint domicile, and even funerals. (Somerville, July 1971). Those sixty-five years of age and older were socialized in a period when familism tended to outweigh individual goals and feelings. A strong sense of obligation was deliberately inculcated to ensure that married children took responsibility for their aging parents. The present middle-aged generation is caught between norm shifts. Many observed their own parents performing filial duties but face a different set of realities, such as limited urban apartment size, higher spousal expectations, increased educational support for youth, geographical mobility, increased longevity. Even when they act in light of the realities and the newly developing norms, it is often with a strong sense of guilt and regret.

This is in part intensified by the limited alternatives in kinds of nursing homes and institutions for the aged. It is not only a problem of the gross neglect and the low standards of these facilities, documented before Congressional committees in the past decade, but the lack of creativity in connection with them. It has been said that architects and city planners make their designs and calculations for old age institutions on the assumption that they themselves will not be part of the population living in them. Perhaps family life and sex education programs in the coming decade can alert future builders, planners, economists, and above all voters of bond issues to the bleak institutional alternatives that await them.

Some changes require more imagination than money. Just as a decade ago the sex-segregated college dormitory was ubiquitous and has now yielded increasingly to the coed dorm, so too it is possible that heterosexual rooming will take the place of sex-segregated wings in nursing and old age institutions. One outcome may be more meaningful interpersonal relationships within these institutions, including in some instances a sexual component. Relatedly, conjugal visits for the hospitalized aged may catch up with at least the present flicker of awareness of sex needs in the lives of prison inmates. Different individuals have varying needs for privacy and closeness in their later years; awareness of individual differences will require more sensitive nursing and administration than is presently available.

At present the guilt and regret of middle-aged men and women with parents in nursing homes and homes for the aged manifest themselves in diverse ways. The range is from overvisiting to total absence and rejection. It should be noted that institutionalization of the elderly has not risen rapidly: 4 percent in 1960 contrasted with about 2.5 percent in 1940. The great majority are in advanced old age, beyond seventy-five. (Riley, 167) The modal pattern in the contemporary United States is for the elderly to maintain their own homes as long as possible. Among couples with living children, more than twice as many live alone as live in a joint household. The elderly parent without a partner, more likely to be the mother not only because of higher survival rates (four widows to one widower in 1970), but because bereaved and divorced men remarry more quickly than do women, lives alone almost as often as she lives with children. Greater poverty among the black elderly and the lack of nursing homes open to them force more shared households. (National Urban League, 20) There has been little research to date to show the consequences for the various generations. It can be hypothesized that the black elderly suffer less of a sense of rejection. It may also be hypothesized that the middle-aged and the younger generations are hampered in mobility aspirations and take little satisfaction in the enforced interaction.

As middle-aged children become less available to offer custodial care, the nursing home may become a more common resource rather than relied upon mainly as at present when the condition of the elderly person worsens. The aged mother in "The Cost Depends on What You Reckon It In," bedridden with paralysis, had lived with her married daughter's family until lifting her required another person. She is sent to a nearby rest home. The daughter visits three times a day. The timing of these visits so as not to alert her husband and children suggests that disapproval rather than commendation would be forthcoming. Nor do the people at the rest home approve her conduct. The director warned her: "The others get jealous. They don't like your mother already, you visit her too much. Them, their children never visit. Only once in a while." The daughter's frantic efforts to mitigate the guilt she feels, knowing her mother would prefer to be back with the family, take the form of food offerings. "Soup. What do I need soup for? To make me live longer?" "What kind of talk is that," I said severely. "Don't you want to live?" My mother stared at me, her blue eyes blazing, and then put the question to me: "This is living?"

The decade of the 70s is likely to see the issue of euthanasia come more sharply to the fore. At the very least the desperate efforts to prolong life for the terminally ill may be reexamined in light of their own preferences as well as the implications for kinfolk on emotional and economic levels.

Robert Anderson's *I Never Sang for My Father* suggests that the old-age-home solution, even when family finances permit large expenditures, is not welcomed by an older generation with little anticipatory socialization for group life and with traditional definitions of kin as more essential for emotional sustenance than non-kin. Guilt and recrimination permeate the intergenerational relationships when the need of the old father to stay in his familiar surroundings after his wife dies begins to clash with the need of the middle-aged son to establish his family in a different region of the country. Even if a geographic change were not involved, the play suggests the problems that can develop with nobody around to play the housewife role. The son, a widower, is planning to marry a doctor who would hardly be prepared to provide companionship for a lonely old man while his son is at work.

Will communes provide a solution in the coming decades? Three-generation living seems even rarer in communes than in traditional families. Among the latter only about 8 percent in 1960 had three generations living together. (Riley, 170) Communes are varied and future research will have to distinguish among the many types. (Sussman, May 1971) These emerging experimental structures vary from the single household usually found in urban areas to the several households that often make up the rural commune. In each of them there are variations in the degree of commitment to monogamy, some resembling the *kibbutz* with couples all sharing work and resources but not their sexual lives, while in others there are rapidly changing heterosexual alliances and joint commitment to all the children. Still others link biological and social parenthood in groupings of a polygynous or polyandrous kind. What they have in common is group living beyond the nuclear family. The number of communes in existence at the present time can only be guessed at. One estimate is 3,000 urban communes. (Otto, 1971, 17) However, this may include only those that designate themselves as such. Rural communes are more difficult to count.

Whatever the present number, if the communal experience persists and attracts greater numbers of men and women in the coming decade, it may be one of the forces providing anticipatory socialization for the enforced intimacy with non-kin characteristic of institutional arrangements for the aged. On the other hand, the emphasis on "doing your own thing" may make for greater irritation with the conformity that may continue to characterize hospitals as well as old age and nursing homes. Fiction suggests the hardships endured when nursing care is not sensitive to the differences among elderly folk, both in their family histories and their present personalities.

In the English novel, *Memento Mori,* a ward of aged females in a nursing home is described. "A year ago, when Miss Taylor had been admitted to the ward, she had suffered misery when addressed as Granny Taylor, and she thought

she would rather die in a ditch than be kept alive under such conditions . . .
The lacerating familiarity of the nurses' treatment merged in with her arthritis,
and she bore them both as long as she could without complaint." (Spark, 17)
The senile cases in the ward were less distressing to the maiden Miss Taylor
than to her occasional visitors. When the latter cited the antics of the senile as
reasons for her to transfer to a more select establishment, she observes, "That is
our *memento mori*." (172) This ability to perceive the whole of the life cycle
without undue sense of threat may be more widespread in the population in the
coming decade.

One observer declares "There are a rapidly growing number of communes
composed of persons in their mid-twenties to upper thirties." (Otto, April
1971) Research could establish whether the relationship of these communal
groups to their families of origin differs from the more numerous younger
communal groups, where the preponderance of members are in their late teens
or early twenties. Among the latter there seems to be more reliance on members of the commune than on parents, although gifts from the latter as well
as regular checks seem to be an important survival resource. However, affectional and ceremonial linkages may not include parents and grandparents. In
some communes, the birth of a baby is witnessed amidst celebration by all
members of the parafamily. Parents and siblings of the new parents seem to be
noticeably absent on such occasions. (Skolnick, 530)

Where middle-aged people are present in communes, it is more likely to be
the urban household in which women with demanding professional careers
find the sharing of a large house with several other couples as well as some
singles reduces problems of child care and household chores. Income levels are
typically high in this group and permit more privacy and material comforts
than in student communes or in rural communes where heavy physical labor
marks daily living. In the latter the occasional middle-aged member is apt to
be the original owner of the land and may be tolerated rather than welcomed.
A self-deprecating tone permeates interviews with them in the few anecdotal
materials so far available. "We have lots of ideas and very little energy," a
woman in her mid-forties says of herself and the few others of her peers in
one commune. (Otto) Research will establish whether in the "intentional community" the middle-aged and the elderly are intentionally excluded or intentionally exclude themselves. The tendency noted in some communes for mother
and father figures to emerge may create a reluctance on the part of the young
to encourage older people to join them. And if the younger people wish to
avoid the authority structure typical of the traditional and even the transitional family, the older ones may have a corresponding wish to avoid the responsibilities associated with previous family structures.

This latter possibility is suggested by the deliberate age-segregation that has
marked housing among the advanced middle-aged and the elderly in the
past decade. This all-adult grouping has taken a number of different forms.
One is the relatively rare establishment of a household by a group of elderly
men and women. This may increase in the coming decade, however. What the
sexual component is in these arrangements is not clear. Perhaps informally
and consensually they have moved toward the famous suggestion of "Polygyny

After Sixty" (Kassel). Or they may be establishing group marriages which come close to the practical and relatively unromantic motivations found in some marriages of the elderly. (McKain) Student reports on life styles of elderly grandparents, usually bereaved but often divorced, offer clues to greater toleration of these groupings on the part of grandchildren than on the part of the parents who are the children of the innovative elderly. When these grandchildren are middle-aged, they may be more supportive of their own parents' attempts to solve the problem of companionship and care. If so, the trend to group marriage or consensual union among elderly men and women will become more pronounced. This may be congruent also with changed working lives for women in which peer group attachment may outweigh kin contacts.

A more frequently encountered trend toward age-segregation is found in the retirement villages, apartment houses, and trailer courts which, with the encouragement of commercial interests, federal funds, and churches, have created concentrations of older men and women. This began in earnest in the 1950s. Little research is available as to the effects on the various generations and their interrelationships. Gerontologists disagree concerning the motivation of those who choose age-segregation and the consequences. Some see the older folk as making a logical choice of peers as substitutes for the younger kinfolk who are less available to them. Others stress the push given the elderly in this direction by the middle-aged whose own obligations are thereby reduced or who find visiting in a recreational atmosphere an aid in muting value differences. Some criticize the escapism, the fun morality, that magnifies self-indulgence in the more affluent of such communities and discourages citizenship activity. The loss is feared of "an unprecedented opportunity to grow up as they grow older." (Simon, 141) Others point to a "natural clustering" of the elderly either in a defensive alliance against hostile and menacing younger generations, or a confirmation of the "disengagement" theory, much in dispute (Shanas, 1966, 5–6) which considers it normal for the elderly to reduce their involvements and withdraw from social commitments. Still others deny that age-segregation is withdrawal, pointing to lectures, travel, and other activities common in middle-class retirement groups.

A further point of dispute, of significance for the coming decades, revolves about the age of admission to such communities. In places where admission is after sixty-five there is a question of social isolation. In places where admission starts at forty or fifty, the question is raised whether the middle-aged are being brainwashed into early retirement and are being doomed along with the elderly to sterile, self-centered pleasure-seeking as an end in itself rather than as an accompaniment to creative activity and social involvement. Research in the coming decade may show whether the middle-aged move more rapidly toward old age as a result of this daily contact with the elderly or whether they gain from anticipatory socialization to the problems and opportunities of their final decades. These final decades may look less threatening through familiarity. As a character says in *Memento Mori,* "How nerve-wracking it is to be getting old; how much better to be old." (37)

Research may also indicate whether the elderly in joint residence with the middle-aged suffer less from the depression that often accompanies age-segregation with its more frequent funerals and constant narrowing of the circle of friends and kin. The same fictional character says, "Being over seventy is like being engaged in a war. All our friends are going or gone and we survive amongst the dead and dying as on a battlefield." *(Memento Mori,* 37) The presence of those in advanced middle-age may ensure more continuity of friendships for the elderly. However, the effects on the middle-aged may also have to be examined. One variable will undoubtedly be the degree of geographic isolation of the retirement village, the trailer court, or the multiple dwelling. The solution tried in other countries may be adapted here to reduce the degree of segregation: separate quarters for the elderly are either walking distance from or in sight of other age groups, particularly young children, on the assumption that in order to grasp the fullness of existence, older people find comfort in seeing symbols of a life that goes on after they are gone.

Only some of the many areas in which research is needed concerning middle-age and the older years have been suggested here. The special problems where income is low, and this concerns at least a third and possibly a half of all the elderly, and where discrimination of racist and sexist kinds take further toll, are particularly in need of investigation. The small percentage of federal funds allocated to study of the aging since the 1961 White House Conference on Aging brought forth thousands of recommendations (Kent, 4) does not suggest the likelihood of any major breakthrough as a result of the second conference for the fall of 1971. The considerable and increasing number of the elderly, with those sixty-five and older constituting one out of every ten in the population in 1970, could constitute a political force of some dimensions. However, there is little indication that older people can unite across class, sex, and ethnic lines to solve common problems. The future of marriage and the family for the middle-aged and the elderly in the next decade is more likely to be determined by the trends indicated in the foregoing than by any deliberate efforts in their own behalf.

references

ADAMS, BERT N., *Kinship in an Urban Setting.* Chicago: Markham Publishing Company, 1968.

ANDERSON, ROBERT, *I Never Sang for My Father.* New York: Random House, Inc., 1968.

BROYARD, ANATOLE, "Sunday Dinner in Brooklyn," in *Avon Book of Modern Writing, No. 2,* eds., William Phillips and Philip Rahv. New York: Avon Books, 1954.

BLOOD, ROBERT O., and DONALD M WOLFE, *Husbands and Wives: The Dynamics of Married Living.* New York: The Macmillan Company, Publishers, 1960.

CUBER, JOHN P., and PEGGY B. HARROFF, *The Significant Americans.* New York: Appleton-Century, 1965.

DUVALL, EVELYN MILLIS, *Family Development.* New York: J. B. Lippincott Co., 1962.

ELLIS, ALBERT, "Group Marriage: A Possible Alternative?" in *The Family in Search of a Future,* ed., Herbert Otto. New York: Appleton-Century-Crofts, 1970.

FARSON, RICHARD E., et al., *The Future of the Family.* New York: Family Service Association of America, 1969.

FRIED, BARBARA, *The Middle-Age Crisis.* New York: Harper & Row, Publishers, 1967.

GERBER, JOAN MERRILL, *Stop Here, My Friend.* Boston: Houghton Mifflin Company, 1965.

HOFFMAN, ADELINE M., *The Daily Needs and Interests of Older People.* Springfield, Illinois: Charles C. Thomas, Publisher, 1970.

JACKSON, JACQUELYNE J., "Social Gerontology and the Negro: A Review," *Gerontologist, 7,* No. 1 (September 1967), 168–73.

HAVIGHURST, ROBERT J., "Successful Aging," *Gerontologist, 1,* No. 1 (March 1961).

KASSEL, VICTOR, "Polygyny after Sixty," Geriatrics, 21 (April 1966). Reprinted in *The Family in Search of a Future,* ed., Otto Herbert, pp. 133–43.

KENT, DONALD P., "The White House Conference in Retrospect," *Gerontologist, 1,* No. 1 (March 1961).

KOMAROVSKY, MIRRA, *Blue Collar Marriage.* New York: Random House, Inc., 1964.

LESSING, DORIS, "To Room Nineteen," in *A Man and Two Women.* New York: Simon & Schuster, Inc., 1963.

MASTERS, WILLIAM H., and VIRGINIA E. JOHNSON, *Human Sexual Response.* Boston: Little, Brown and Company, 1966.

MC KAIN, WALTER C., *Retirement Marriage.* Storrs, Conn.: Storrs Agricultural Experiment Station, The University of Connecticut, January 1969.

MC KINNEY, JOHN C., and FRANK T. DE VYVER, eds., *Aging and Social Policy.* New York: Appleton-Century-Crofts, 1966.

MOORE, BARRINGTON, "Thoughts on the Future of the Family," in *The Family and Change,* ed., John N. Edwards. New York: Alfred A. Knopf, Inc., 1969.

National Urban League, *Double Jeopardy—The Older Negro in America Today.* New York: National Urban League, 1964.

NEUGARTEN, BERNICE L., ed., *Middle Age and Aging.* Chicago: University of Chicago Press, 1968.

OTTO, HERBERT A., "Communes: The Alternative Life-Style," *Saturday Review,* April 24, 1971, pp. 16–21.

———, ed., *The Family in Search of a Future.* New York: Appleton-Century-Crofts, 1970.

PETERSON, JAMES A., *Married Love in the Middle Years.* New York: Association Press, 1968.

PINEO, PETER C., "Disenchantment in the Later Years of Marriage," *Marriage and Family Living, 23,* (1961), 3–11.

RILEY, MATILDA WHITE, and ANNE FORNER, *Aging and Society.* Vol.

I: *An Inventory of Research Findings.* New York: Russell Sage Foundation, 1968.

REISS, IRA L., *The Family System in America.* New York: Holt, Rinehart & Winston, Inc., 1971.

RIMMER, ROBERT H., *Proposition 31.* New York: New American Library, 1968.

RODGERS, ROY H., "Improvements in the Construction and Analysis of Family Life Cycle Categories," doctoral thesis, Western Michigan University, 1962.

"Roundtable: Sex and the Menopause," *Medical Aspects of Human Sexuality* (November 1970).

RUBIN, ISADORE, *Sexual Life After Sixty.* New York: New American Library, 1965.

ROLLINS, BOYD C., and HAROLD FELDMAN, "Marital Satisfaction Over the Family Life Cycle," *Journal of Marriage and the Family, 32* (1970), 20–27.

SHANAS, ETHEL, et al., *Old People in Three Industrial Societies.* New York: Atherton Press, 1968.

SIMPSON, IDA HARPER, and JOHN C. MC KINNEY, eds., *Social Aspects of Aging.* Durham, N.C.: Duke University Press, 1966.

SKOLNICK, ARLENE S., and JEROME H. SKOLNICK, eds., *Family in Transition: Rethinking Marriage, Sexuality, Child Rearing and Family Organization.* Boston: Little, Brown and Company, 1971.

SOMERVILLE, ROSE M., "Death Education as Part of Family Life Education: Using Imaginative Literature for Insights into Family Crises," *The Family Coordinator,* 20 (July 1971), 3.

————, "Family Life and Sex Education in the Turbulent Sixties," *Journal of Marriage and the Family* (February 1971).

————, *Family Insights through the Short Story.* New York: Teachers College Press, 1964. See Chapter 9, "Aging and the Aged," and Chapter 10, "Bereavement."

SPARK, MURIEL, *Memento Mori.* New York: J. B. Lippincott Co., 1959.

STEGNER, WALLACE, *All the Little Live Things.* New York: The Viking Press, 1969.

STINNET, NICK, et al., "Marital Need Satisfaction of Older Husbands and Wives," *Journal of Marriage and the Family* (19–).

STREIB, GORDON F., "Intergenerational Relations: Perspectives of the Two Generations on the Older Parent," *Journal of Marriage and the Family, 27* (1965), 469–70.

SUSSMAN, MARVIN B., "Relationships of Adult Children with Their Parents in the United States," in *Social Structure and the Family: Generational Relations,* eds., ETHEL SHANAS and GORDON STREIB. Englewood Cliffs, N.J.: Prentice-Hall, Inc., 1965.

————, "The Experimental Creation of Family Environments: Typology of Family Structures," paper given at the Groves Conference on Marriage and the Family, San Juan, Puerto Rico, May, 1971.

———, "An Analytic Model for the Sociological Study of the Retirement Process," in *Retirement: Frameworks for Research,* ed., FRANCES CARP. New York: Behavioral Publications, 1971.

Time, "The American Family: Future Uncertain," December 28, 1970, pp. 34–39.

THOMPSON, WAYNE, and GORDON F. STREIB, "Meaningful Activity in a Family Context," in *Social and Psychological Aspects of Aging.* New York: Columbia University Press, 1962.

UNITED STATES DEPARTMENT OF HEALTH, EDUCATION, AND WELFARE, *Working with Older People: A Guide to Practice.* Vol. II: *Biological, Psychological, and Sociological Aspects of Aging,* April 1970.

WISEMAN, JACQUELINE P., *People as Partners: Individual and Family Relationships in Today's World.* San Francisco: Canfield Press (Div. of Harper & Row), 1971.

index